OUR MEN IN
BRAZIL

Robert Hesketh as a young man

OUR MEN IN BRAZIL

The Hesketh Brothers Abroad

by
Ian Sargen

SCOTFORTH

For Hilary,
whose family this is.

Copyright © Ian Sargen 2009
First published in 2009 on behalf of the author by
Scotforth Books, Carnegie House,
Chatsworth Road, Lancaster LA1 4SL.

ISBN 13: 978-1-904244-53-0

Printed in the UK by Short Run Press, Exeter

CONTENTS

FOREWORD

This book tells the story of the lives of three Liverpool brothers who in the early nineteenth century became British Consuls in Brazil.

Whilst the great events of early nineteenth-century history play some part in the story, this account is based on the day-to-day experiences of the three brothers. Normally, it might be difficult to know much about the daily concerns of people who lived two hundred years ago, unless they left evidence in poems, novels, letters or diaries. In this case, however, the three brothers left very detailed information about their daily lives in South America in a range of dispatches sent home to the Foreign Office, and now preserved in the National Archives in London. The leather-bound volumes, several hundred in number, supplemented by a large collection of cardboard boxes crammed with despatches, also contain the Foreign Office replies, written or dictated by the Foreign Office Secretaries of the day: Castlereagh, Canning, Wellington, Palmerston, or Aberdeen.

The volumes and the boxes yield a wealth of fascinating detail about the work and lives of these largely forgotten officials, and their very considerable contribution to the making of the modern world. They did not live long enough to see the full development of British commerce throughout the world, or the emergence of the British Empire in the later nineteenth century, or the development of the fifth largest country in the world – Brazil, or the total abolition of the slave trade in the western world, but they played a part in laying the foundations for all these developments.

Books about the daily lives of diplomats and consuls are rare. So too are books about Brazil. The European media tend to concentrate only on a limited range of well-rehearsed Brazilian topics – the Carnival in Rio, Brazilian football, or the loss of the Amazonian rainforest. Rarely is there any wider understanding of the extraordinary history of Brazil, of its ambiguous role in the struggle to abolish slavery, or of its volatile relationship with Great Britain.

"Our Men in Brazil" began as a modest attempt to get to the bottom of a persistent belief in my wife's family that an ancestor had been a British Consul in South America in the nineteenth century. A Consular Commission was at one time in the family, but had been lost, and an aunt quoted a story which blamed a family called Campbell for her ancestor's financial losses. It was also intriguing that my wife's father, a clergyman, who rarely touched alcohol away from the communion table, made an occasional exception of a glass of port. Little otherwise was known.

Only a little research, however, quickly showed not one consul, but three, and the existence of those Foreign Office records. More research produced contemporary accounts of life in Brazil which made reference to the brothers – one even included an account of a dinner party given by one of them to a naval officer visiting the Amazon in 1828. When we visited Brazil, we came across some forgotten letters from the brothers, and heard of modern descendants of the family playing a significant part in Brazilian life. Before long, there was a large amount of information on our files, and it seemed possible to write an account of what it was like to represent the British crown nearly two hundred years ago in a far-flung part of the earth, where hazards were commonplace, and where it took weeks or even months to get a message to or from Great Britain.

The last serious study of the work of the British consul was published in 1971 – D.M. Platt's "The Cinderella Service". Perhaps it is now time to look again at the role of that invaluable servant of the British people, cut off from family and friends, doing the bidding of the British government of the day, and sometimes suffering personally as a result. This account shows that noble policies, like the abolition of the Slave Trade, were not implemented in Downing Street or the House of Commons, but in distant places, where consuls and their like got on quietly with the day-to-day business of putting the politicians' fine words into practice, and thus shaping the modern world.

The American H.M. Brackenridge said in 1820 that "The study of South American affaris ...has not yet become fashionable". Perhaps this account may go a little way, not only raising the profile of the consular service of the time, but also casting a little light on the early history of one of the great nations of the modern world.

I.S., October, 2009

A FEW EXPLANATIONS

Place-Names – Brazilian place-names, not to mention street-names, have sometimes changed significantly since the 1800s. Rio de Janeiro, Belém, and São Luis have remained the same, but Pernambuco has become Recife, and Bahia is now known as Salvador. The British, whether in Brazil or in the Foreign Office, referred to Maranhão by its nearest British pronunciation – Maranham. I have kept this spelling when quoting from the original, but used the modern Brazilian form elsewhere. Pará was often used as the name of the city now called Belém, but was more properly the name of the vast province encompassing much of the Amazon basin.

Money – there are many references within these pages to money. It is always risky to try to give modern equivalents for the currency of almost two hundred years ago, so I have not tried. The reader will soon get used to thinking of £20 sterling as a great deal of money in 1820. The Brazilian Empire used the *real* (plural *reis* – pronounced "ray-al" and "ray-eece") and *milreis* – a thousand *reis*, whose value rose and dipped alarmingly at every turn of events in the new Empire of the Brazils. I have tried to make sense of it by averaging its value over the period, and so have taken the *milreis* as worth about 2s.6d. of British money of the time, or 12½p. in modern terms. But the reader ought to bear in mind that it was sometimes worth much more, and often much less.

Spelling, and Foreign words. English spelling has not remained static in the two centuries since the events in this book. I have kept the original spellings (and mis-spellings) when quoting from original sources, along with the sometimes eccentric use of capital letters. I have placed Portuguese words and other foreign words in italics, and tried to give a translation of them in the text.

Notes. The small numbers in the text refer to notes included in the section towards the end of the book.

ACKNOWLEDGEMENTS

A book of this nature relies upon research in many and varied locations, and my wife and I have had good service from a wide range of archivists and librarians, both in Great Britain and abroad. The National Archives have supplied us with the bulk of our primary sources, and we acknowledge their ready help. Other major sources of assistance have been the staff of the Liverpool City Record Office and of the Lancashire Record Office in Preston. The Cambridge University Library has given access to many of the contemporary texts quoted, and I had a useful visit to the Ancell Library at the Foreign Office in London. Abroad, we have had considerable help from Senhor Jorge Barreira at the Ferreira Archive in Porto, Portugal, as well as the Arquivo Distrito and the Arquivo Municipal in that city. In Brazil, Senhor G.M. Coelho, Director of the Pará Archives in Belém, has been most helpful.

We were extraordinarily lucky to be in touch with Mr. J.J. Heath-Caldwell. He is not only a descendant of Robert Hesketh's daughter, Eliza Jane, but is an assiduous collector of family memorabilia. He could not have been more helpful in generously sharing both his considerable information and his materials, which include the Hesketh family bibles. It is with his permission that we include the portraits of Robert Hesketh and his wife, and of Louisa Ann Hesketh, née Beete. Equally kind was Senhor Acy Marcos dos Santos, H.M. Honorary British Consul in Belém, who welcomed us to his busy office with open arms, and conveyed us in some style around the city.

We were also helped, when we discovered original documents about the "Hibernia" and the "India", by the research that the late Bruce Biggar had done in Australia on the background to the "India". We have tried to contact Mrs. Biggar to ask for her permission to use this material in our own research, but have failed to do so; we are very happy to acknowledge our debt here.

Nearer home, members of our family have helped with advice about the text, with medical queries, with translation, and with general encouragement. My wife's sisters, also descendants of John Hesketh, have taken a considerable interest.

We are also grateful to Anna Goddard and her colleague Lucy Frontani of Carnegie Book Production, who have processed the book with cheerful professionalism.

To all these folk, I offer grateful thanks, but my chief debt is to my wife, who has shared with me the whole process of research, writing, and revising at every step. The book would not exist without her, but, of course, its deficiencies remain my responsibility.

ILLUSTRATIONS

SECTION I

PEOPLE

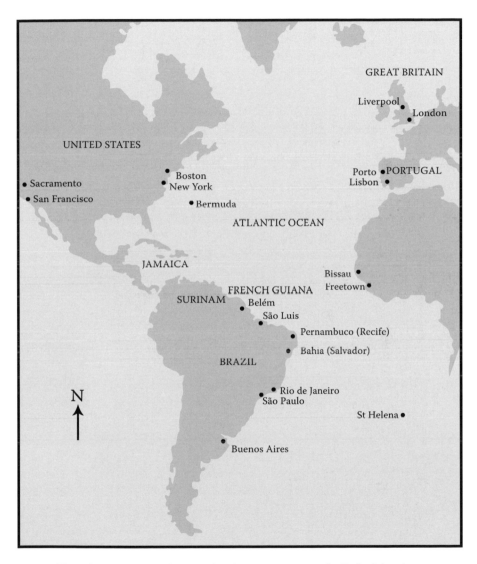

The Atlantic Ocean, indicating the places important to the Hesketh brothers

1

ORIGINS

"...There are few families that can boast a more ancient or more honourable descent than the Heskeths of Rufford..." (Croston Family Histories)

This story, which spends most of its time in nineteenth-century Brazil, begins in Lancashire not far north of Liverpool.

The Hesketh family had long been resident in Lancashire, as well as in other parts of the north-west of England. The majority of those called Hesketh still live there. The first Heskeths owed their name to the Vikings' love of horse-racing, and doubtless lived on or near a race-course – a "hesta-skeith" – set up by the Norsemen in west Lancashire or Cumbria.

By the thirteenth century, one successful branch of the family had acquired considerable amounts of property in west Lancashire: in the Fylde, around Blackburn, and in the vast tract of marshland around Martin's Mere, close to the sandy coast of the Irish Sea, between the estuaries of the Rivers Mersey and Ribble.

By the sixteenth century, the Heskeths were set fair to be one of the leading families of England. Sir Robert Hesketh, who died in 1539 or 1541, was knighted by Henry VIII for valour in France. His son, Sir Thomas, obtained the favour of Queen Elizabeth I as a result of his bravery at the Siege of Leith, when he was severely wounded and had his ensign torn from his hand before recovering it. Many of his family retained their loyalty to the Roman Catholic faith throughout Queen Elizabeth's reign and beyond, but she did not seem to think less of Sir Thomas for that. The Heskeths had other powerful friends, being close to the Stanleys, who lived nearby in central Lancashire, and who were to become Earls of Derby. Sir Thomas kept a troupe of actors at his home at Rufford Old Hall, and a recent writer makes out a good case for William Shakespeare's living and working there as a sixteen year-old.[1]

Sir Thomas Hesketh had six legitimate children by his wife Alice Holcroft, one of whom was the physician and botanist, Thomas Hesketh, a close friend of John Gerard of "Gerard's Herball". Sir Thomas's eldest legitimate son, Robert, married Mary Stanley, and began the line of Heskeths who inherited Rufford Old Hall in West Lancashire. But Sir Thomas, when young, had had two sons out of wedlock: another Thomas, and Hugh, who was born in about 1550. Hugh married Alice Kitchen, who had inherited North Meols Hall in what is now Southport, and began his own dynasty there. Two of their great grandsons, Bartholomew and Barnaby, seem to have been less than virtuous. They were involved in the smuggling of brandy and tobacco from the Continent, and were accused at Ormskirk Assizes in 1688 of mocking and assaulting William Blake, a Customs and Excise man, and then knocking him off his horse as he rode to inspect their ship, the "Mary", which was moored in Fairclough's Lake off North Meols. The influence of their friends, however, seems to have secured their acquittal, in spite of Blake's compelling evidence.

Their elder brother, Roger Hesketh of North Meols married Mary Gelibrand of Warrington in 1678, and had no less than fourteen children. Most of them were born at North Meols, and provided the line which still owns the Hall. Two of Roger and Mary's children were, however, born in their mother's home town of Warrington: Lydia, who married into another well-known local family, the Halliwells, and their second son, John, born in 1690. John married Margaret Singleton in May, 1715, in the Wren church of St. Andrew by the Wardrobe in what is now London's Queen Victoria Street. John's birth in Warrington and his marriage in London have meant that he is missed out of the published Hesketh family trees, but he certainly existed, for he features significantly in his father's will.[2]

John made his living by commerce. He built up a considerable fortune as a merchant in the prospering Lancashire town of Warrington, and had twelve children. One of them, Robert, who was born in 1719, married Catherine Holding at the church of Our Lady and St. Nicholas on the Liverpool waterfront in 1746.[3] Robert had inherited his father's commercial interests, and was a wine merchant in Moore Street, also by the Mersey, but with his house and wine vaults in St. James's Street nearby. We know that he flourished financially, for he imported and sold a great deal of wine from Portugal, at a time when the English passion for Douro wine knew no bounds. He was a Councillor of the City of Liverpool, and for many years served as a Commissioner of "Watches, Lamps, and Scavengers", and of "The Regulation of Pilots", important matters in a port that was admired for its prosperity and for its fine buildings. His younger brother, William, who was also a merchant, was Lord Mayor of Liverpool in 1783–4, and then an Alderman. He too had his public duties, and spent some years as first Treasurer and then Auditor of the Liverpool Bluecoat Hospital. The links with Warrington obviously persisted, for at his death

William was buried in the large churchyard of St. Elphin's Parish Church, where his cast-iron tomb still stands.[4]

But it was Robert's importation of wine that sets this story in motion, for he sent his eldest son, John, who was born in Liverpool in 1750, to Porto in northern Portugal to be his agent on the River Douro. When John arrived in Portugal about 1770, it was only a hundred years since the Abbot of the Monastery of Santa Cruz in nearby Lamego had added brandy to red Douro wine and created "port" wine, which became eighteenth century Britain's favourite drink. Soon after his arrival, and while he was still in his early twenties, John was exporting nearly a hundred thousand gallons of wine each year, a good deal of it to his father in Liverpool, but also to an extensive list of customers all over the British Isles. He became part of the firm of Offley, Campion, Hesketh, & Co. in 1786, and its records, which still exist in the Ferreira Archives in Porto[5] , show him as a vigorous and knowledgeable member of the firm, making the hazardous journey on horseback up the Douro very regularly, and bringing a great number of orders to the firm through his personal contacts. In 1792, the merchants of Porto exported to the British Isles a total of 50,000 pipes or casks of wine. With 115 gallons to the pipe, that added up to a staggering total of 34½ million bottles. John Hesketh's contribution to this total was considerable – his firm was exporting to forty ports throughout the length and breadth of the British Isles, some of them large and well-known, like London, Hull, Bristol, Liver-

Modern view of Porto, Portugal

Louisa Ann Hesketh, née Beete, mother of Robert, John, and William Hesketh

pool, Kings Lynn, and Dublin, but others small, like Portsoy in northern Scotland and Southwold in Suffolk.

By 1786, John was comfortably off, and decided the time had come to get married. His bride was Louisa Ann Beete, who seems to have come to Portugal a few years earlier with her sister, Caroline. Unfortunately, Caroline died in Porto in 1785, but Louisa stayed on to marry John, and to bear nine children. The last, Thomas, was born at the end of 1798, but Louisa Ann died three months later in 1799, and was only the ninth person to be buried in the new English Cemetery in Porto.[6] John stayed on in Porto with his young family until the French invaded Portugal in 1807 and forced out the sizeable English community of merchants. John came back to his father's home-town of Liverpool, and lived in a series of substantial houses in Russell Street near the modern-day university. He set up his unmarried daughters nearby, and lived until 11th. February, 1815, four months before the Battle of Waterloo, when he was almost 65. He was buried by the Rector of Liverpool, Mr. Roughsedge, on Saint Valentine's Day, 1815, and described in the parish register as "a gentleman".[7]

John's commercial success in Porto had enabled him to buy a substantial house in Rua São Miguel at the top of the town above the river. The house had a view across to his firm's wine-lodges over the Douro in Vila Nova da Gaia, still today the home of port. A record exists of a dispute he had with the nuns of the nearby convent in 1786.[8] He was also one of the three signatories of the will of John Whitehead, who served as British Consul in Porto for fifty years, and who designed the splendid Factory House which still stands near the quay. John was one of many signatories to the minutes of the meeting held in 1802 immediately after Whitehead's death, to select a new Consul.[9] So we may safely assume he was one of the English merchants whose hospitality so delighted Captain Costigan during his visit to Porto in the Christmas season of 1778: "the Christmas pies, the fat turkies [sic], the fine sirloins, the jellies and creams of all kinds, and every other delicacy are to be met with in abundance... The Foreign Merchants, especially the English, who are by far the most numerous, not only live in affluence themselves, and much better than the same person would do in London, but the natives follow their example..."[10]

It was in this atmosphere that John and Louisa's children were brought up. We know little of their education in Porto, but the usual approach at the time, particularly abroad, was to rely on the chaplain or some other leisured parson to act as tutor to the local children, perhaps the Rev. John Bell, M.A., or his successor, the Rev. Stratford Conway. The children's education was obviously perfectly adequate, for Robert Hesketh, the eldest son, wrote fluently and fulsomely in later life, and was only in his early twenties when he was appointed a British Consul in Brazil. His younger brothers, John and William, also wrote well, although perhaps less adventurously, but with an efficient enough style.

In later years, some long-standing members of the British community in Porto acquired a reputation for stubbornly refusing to learn Portuguese, but it seems likely that John's children learnt the language at an early age. The brothers who went to Brazil later on seem to have had no difficulty in using Portuguese in their commercial and consular work, and translating it accurately and confidently for the benefit of the Foreign Office.

The family kept up their links with Liverpool. The children's paternal grandfather, Robert Hesketh, lived there until his death in 1793, and the family was linked by marriage to many of the leading Liverpool merchant families of the time, such as the Bolds and the Crosbies. Indeed, John's son Robert named some of his children after them half a century after their deaths – his second son was named William Crosbie. Liverpool ships were also frequent visitors to the Douro, waiting to be loaded with wine and other Portuguese exports.The "Brothers", the "Rochdale", the "Hope", and the "Olive" frequently made the dangerous crossing of the Bay of Biscay loaded with large pipes of port destined for the Mersey, and on one occasion at least off-loaded a few pipes a few miles short of Liverpool at Hoylake on the Wirral.

So John's young family would have been used to living in a lively foreign city, and would have been used to the different customs, religion, and culture of Portugal. They would also be used to the company of other Britons, and would have kept up their close links with their father's city of birth. In later life, whenever they were back in England, Liverpool was always on the itinerary, even if it was only the starting or the ending point for their voyages to and from South America. In recent years, it has not been easy to recapture the buoyant mood of eighteenth century Liverpool, when she rivalled London for the quantity of her trade. As the eighteenth century advanced, the Mersey was full of ships, the docks were bustling, and her merchants were growing rich. Some of her eighteenth century buildings, like the Town Hall, were quite outstanding by any standard. Of course, a substantial proportion of the city's prosperity was based on the "Africa Trade", which involved the transport and sale of slaves, but by no means all Liverpool money was made on this alone. A contemporary source says that a quarter of Liverpool ships were engaged in the Africa trade. The rest busied themselves in the import of such goods as sugar, cotton, and, as we have seen, wine, and the export of an increasing quantity of manufactured goods. Trade was good, merchants prosperous, and the port and city of Liverpool growing. The dramatic rise in the population of Liverpool in the mid-nineteenth century is well-documented, but there was an equally dramatic rise in the city's population a hundred years earlier; with the population rising from under six thousand in 1700 to sixty thousand in 1793. There was also a long tradition of sending Liverpool sons out to foreign countries to represent family firms, and to encourage trade.

In John Hesketh's case, the French invasion of Portugal of 1807 put an end to his very profitable involvement in the port wine business. John cannot have hesitated for very long before deciding to return with his family to his birthplace. He was of an age, 57, to think of retirement, he had an ample fortune, and he had a supportive family back in Liverpool. Some of the British community in Porto went back to Portugal after the Napoleonic Wars, but John must have felt he had no need. His family were all with him, and his will, which is written on a vast parchment sheet, shows his concern for his family, especially for his daughters.[11] After his death, they could afford to live in Mount Pleasant, which was then a fashionable address.

Nearby was smart Rodney Street, which was the birthplace of Gladstone in 1809. In spite of the fact that John's children became scattered on both sides of the Atlantic, they remained a close family, using their family ties for profit. Fifty years later, they were still close: when Robert's younger sister, Mary Ann, became ill in the early 1850s, she left Liverpool and joined him down in Southampton in the house to which he had retired in 1852. Earlier, Louisa and Mary Ann had taken on the very considerable task of bringing up three of their brother John's younger orphaned children.

In 1808, therefore, John Hesketh's family was back in Liverpool, living off the fruits of their father's expertise and hard work in Portugal. While the girls, especially if they did not marry, could look forward to a very comfortable time living on their father's money, the boys were expected to take a rather more positive approach to earning a living. With their father's successful background in commerce, and with their own experience of living abroad, a similar career must have seemed appropriate. The Brazils, with their close links with Portugal, and with their enormous potential for trade with Great Britain, looked very promising, particularly as the Portuguese Regent, Don João, had opened up the Brazilian ports to international trade upon his arrival in Brazil in 1808. From now on, the future of at least three of the Hesketh sons lay across the Atlantic in Brazil.

FROM MERSEY TO MARANHAM

"South America ... as she increases in civilization, opens new channels to this branch of our commerce [cotton]. That continent ... contains 3,260,418 square miles, adequate to support an increase of population." ("The Commerce, Statistics, and Institutions of Liverpool ...", Smithers, 1825).

Sitting in his large house in Russell Street[12], part of an imposing brick terrace on the hill overlooking Liverpool, in or around 1808, John and his boys must have given much thought to their next move. John still owned a house in Porto, and had an ample fortune for his own and his daughters' maintenance, but it was not large enough to keep his sons as well. It was important that they began to earn their own living.

Across the turbulent river Mersey was the Wirral and the growing town of Birkenhead, but in the river itself a large fleet of merchant ships swung at anchor in the rough swell, or was busy discharging or loading cargo at the quays or the Old Dock. Some were entering the river from the vast expanse of Liverpool Bay, and others nosing out into the current at the start of their voyages. Smaller vessels were weaving their way through the anchorage, some going upstream to Runcorn or Weaverham, others ceaselessly crossing "over the water" to the Wirral. But it must have been the brigs and the schooners bound for foreign parts which particularly caught their eye.

In some ways, the political situation made their position very unfortunate – the family's flight from Portugal in the wake of the French invasion was only part of the cataclysm that was affecting almost the whole of Europe. It was two or three years since Nelson's victory at Cape Trafalgar, but on land the British war against Napoleon was going far less well. The disaster of Walcheren in the Low Countries lay ahead in 1809, when the British tried to attack the French fleet in Antwerp. At the turn of the new year of 1810, Sir John Moore led a pell-mell retreat to Corunna through the snows of Galicia, harried by the French army. The more successful campaigns of the Peninsula and Napoleon's disastrous retreat from Moscow were still two or three years ahead, and the war had another eight years to run before the temporary peace of 1814, Napoleon's return from Elba, and his final narrow defeat

Shipping in the River Mersey in 1810

at Waterloo. The war with Napoleon had drawn in most of the nations of Europe, and Napoleon's Continental system put out of reach any commercial opportunities in the ports of Northern Europe or the Mediterranean.

Nor was England at peace with itself. The war with Napoleon had seriously weakened the economy, and there was sporadic rioting in many of the cities of the north as the price of grain and therefore of bread rose. The manufacturing districts of Lancashire and Yorkshire were beginning to be convulsed with the social consequences of mechanisation and the spread of the steam-engine. Simmering resentment would shortly give way to the Luddite attacks on mills and mill-owners, and radicals like Hunt and Burdett were attacking the establishment, backed by outbreaks of popular rioting in London and elsewhere. The government itself was far from secure, and only a year or so later, Castlereagh and Canning, colleagues in the same cabinet, went so far as to fight a duel over the Walcheren adventure. It was only four years before the British Prime Minister, Spencer Percival, was assassinated, by, as it happened, a mentally disturbed merchant from Liverpool.

Nevertheless, the Hesketh family had escaped from Portugal unscathed, and there was still a part of the world which was as yet unaffected by the

European .conflict. At the same time as the Heskeths had escaped from Porto, the whole Portuguese court had fled from Napoleon's clutches by sailing in the nick of time from Lisbon for the Portuguese dominions of the Brazils. Supported by four British ships of the line, they had made landfall at Bahia, and then in March, 1808, at Rio de Janeiro. Great effects were to come from this: a crowned European head (or at least her Regent) setting up Court in the Americas was certainly unprecedented, and injected a great boost of confidence into the colonial Brazilians. Rio saw a rush of new houses, new roads, and new trade over the next ten years, and the far-flung regions of the Brazils began to grow in confidence. The ports north of Rio, Bahia and Pernambuco, had already had regular contact with Europe, but now Rio itself, and the northern ports of Maranhão, Ceará, and Pará began to benefit from the increased economic activity.

However, the support the Portuguese Royal Family received from the British came at a price. British manufacturers needed their outlets, and with much of Europe closed to British trade, South America offered a promising alternative. The Treaty of 1810 between Brazil and Great Britain set down the friendship and the support Great Britain proposed to offer the displaced regime, but it also laid down the price – special conditions for British trade, and the abolition of the mainstay of the Brazilian economy – the slave trade.

Nevertheless, the 1810 Treaty offered some years of peace to both Brazil and Great Britain. It enabled the Brazilians to move fairly peacefully from colony to independent nation, and gave Great Britain an unrivalled opportunity to sell its products within a protected market. Coffee and sugar were already well-established as exports from Brazil, and now it seemed as if cotton might also play a large part in the country's export economy. It was only twenty-five years or so since the first arrival of cotton in Liverpool. John's uncle William, Lord Mayor of Liverpool in 1783/4, was one of the first to receive a batch of Brazilian cotton, sent by his nephew in Porto to his premises in Chapel Street, Liverpool. The Manchester cotton mills were growing fast, and Lancashire would soon have 400,000 workers ready to process raw cotton. Each day, twenty pack-horses travelled from Liverpool the thirty-five miles to Manchester, loaded with cotton bales. Soon, the number of daily pack-horses grew to seventy. Cotton imports came either from the United States or from Northern Brazil, but the touchy and competitive relationship with the newly-born United States made them uncertain commercial partners, and Brazil appeared to offer more stable trading conditions, as well as cotton of high quality.

With all this in mind, the family decided to transfer their expertise from port wine to cotton, and from Porto to Maranhão on the northern coast of Brazil. Maranhão produced several other exports, such as rice, but the most important and the most promising was cotton. Robert, the eldest son, decided to go to the port of São Luis, and set up there as a merchant. He was certainly there by 1812, when he was no more than twenty-two, and it is even possible that he may have been in Brazil a year or so before that. Not long afterwards, his brother William joined him, and remained there for the rest of his life. William was eighteen in 1812, so, assuming he too left England at the age of 20, was probably there from about 1814. Their youngest brother, Thomas, who was only thirteen or fourteen in 1812, eventually set himself up as a cotton merchant in Liverpool. He acted as the receiving agent for his brothers' cotton, ensuring its onward passage to Manchester, and sending back to Brazil the manufactured goods that the developing nation of Brazil needed and craved. He had various business addresses during the 1820s and 1830s, but all were within the imposing Cotton Exchange buildings in Liverpool.

John, the second oldest son, who was twenty-one in 1812, seems to have initially run his own business in Liverpool. Gore's Directory of Liverpool, which produced a yearly list of businesses and leading citizens, has him in

The Liverpool Cotton Exchange, from which Thomas Hesketh ran his cotton agent's business

1818 with his own counting-house in Molyneux Place off Water Street on the Liverpool waterfront, with a house in Gloucester Place up the hill from the present-day Lime Street Station. In his earlier 1814 and 1816 editions, Gore had listed a John Hesketh as a Book-keeper, with a different address. They may be one and the same. In about 1819, however, John took the step of joining Robert and William in Brazil, and set up business in the city of Santa Maria de Belém in the Province of Pará. Pará was the gateway to the Amazon, which was beginning to produce a bewildering variety of nuts, wood, medical drugs, and foodstuffs. His life in Belém is a major theme of this book.

Another brother, Henry, born in 1796, took a different direction – west. He went to California, which in 1846 became part of the United States. He seems to have had a mercantile business in either Sacramento, which became the new state capital after 1846, or in San Francisco. Unfortunately, most nineteenth century records of the area disappeared in the disastrous 1906 San Francisco earthquake and fire. He was not a consul, as far as we know, and the only information about him is that he was very well-established in California in the 1850s, when his nephew Henry, one of John's sons, went to see him with his new wife, Sophia, from Liverpool. Unfortunately, Uncle Henry died while they were in California, and Henry and Sophia came home with their new-born son, who was also named Henry after both his uncle and his father.

So by 1820, the Hesketh family had transferred itself from the Old World to the New, and again began to make money. We know that Robert in São Luis prospered hugely, so much so that in 1829 he was able to lend his brother £4000 with only moderate pain, as well as settling outstanding debts of a further £1000. Even though Robert did not operate as a merchant after 1826, he retired to Southampton in 1852 with enough money to buy a substantial mansion, and then to move to a prestigious house in an expensive area of the city. The accounts of Hesketh & Co. and Hesketh Bros. & Wilson, have, as far as we know, disappeared, but Robert was never without considerable resources. William too seemed to have lived comfortably, and until 1829 at least, John also prospered.

So, as they sat in Russell Street in 1808, the future must have looked promising. It became even more promising at the end of 1811 or the beginning of 1812, when Robert, establishing himself as a merchant in São Luis, was invited to serve as His Britannic Majesty's Consul in Maranhão, Pará, and Ceará. The welfare of the whole of British trade and of British ships along the whole coast of Northern Brazil was to become his responsibility.

3

JOINING THE
CONSULAR SERVICE

[Consuls were] "Martha to the Marys of the Chancelleries ..." (Geoffrey Moorhouse, 1977).

We know that Robert Hesketh became a Consul in 1812, for his Commission is dated in that year, and he refers later to a preparatory meeting he had in February, 1812, with William Hamilton, the Under-Secretary at the Foreign Office This means that he was approached by the Foreign Office during 1811. There is little evidence to help us determine whether his commercial career was already under way, or whether it predated his consular appointment.

Whatever the timing, the British merchants in São Luis de Maranhão, his destination in Northern Brazil, will have welcomed him, for they had not had a consul of their own before. Robert's appointment was a recognition by George III's ministers of the growing importance of the Lancashire cotton industry. The Lancashire mills needed a regular and reliable supply of "cotton wool", and that meant that the small merchant ships which brought it across the turbulent Atlantic from São Luis to Liverpool needed the support of a British Consul in Northern Brazil, to sort out their problems, and to negotiate with the sometimes prickly local junta. And given that most of those ships were based in Liverpool, the Foreign Office would have thought it appropriate to appoint a young Liverpool merchant to the new consulship in Northern Brazil. This appointment would doubtless have pleased the Liverpool Brazilian Association, which was becoming influential, for, whenever it made representations to the Foreign Office, it was listened to with respect. The Foreign Office had strong links with Liverpool for much of the early nineteenth century, with George Canning, Foreign Secretary in the 1820s, serving as its M.P., and John Backhouse, the long-serving Under-Secretary at the Foreign Office, growing up there, the son of another Liverpool merchant.

Robert Hesketh was a good candidate for the job. He was young, energetic, and as well as coming from a well-known Liverpool merchant background, had been brought up in Portugal, and spoke fluent Portuguese, the language of Brazil. As we have seen, his father, John Hesketh, had not only been a successful merchant in Portugal, but had also been a close friend and associate of the long-serving Consul in Porto, John Whitehead, and Robert would have learnt a great deal from him.

Robert was also the route through which his two brothers joined the Consular Service. William's periods as Acting British Consul in São Luis were entirely at Robert's behest and in Robert's place, and John was appointed as Vice-Consul in Pará directly by Robert, with, of course, the approval of the Foreign Secretary.

So what did Robert Hesketh expect his role as Consul to be?

What he had observed of John Whitehead in Porto would certainly have shown him that the role was demanding, especially in times of political disturbance. Whitehead had to look after the interests of his fellow-merchants throughout the middle years of the eighteenth century when the Marquis of Pombal fundamentally reformed the Douro wine-trade. Later on, Whitehead also had to deal with a great deal of religious pressure. He was a man of wide interests, with an excellent library of theology as well as of science, and some of his scientific experiments – investigating lightning, for example – made him very unpopular with the local Roman Catholic hierarchy, which regarded all scientific exploration with profound suspicion. He was investigated, but escaped further action.

Whitehead was also an amateur architect of some skill, and his *Feitoria Ingleze* – the Factory House – is still in excellent condition today, and one of the most distinguished buildings in Porto. The construction of the Factory House must have involved a great deal of consultation as well as money-raising amongst the British community in Porto, and Whitehead was a very skilled manager of his fellow-Britons. Robert and his brothers must have learnt a great deal from him. His career in Porto lasted for fifty years, and his seniority and experience must have made his relationships with both the local government and with his superiors a hundred and twenty miles away in Lisbon easier than most. Nevertheless, even Whitehead was a member of a professional sub-class.

British Consuls were never, at least until 1943, regarded by their Government as the professional equals of those in the Diplomatic Service. D.C.M. Platt, in the "The Cinderella Service", documented the numerous ways in which this manifested itself in the nineteenth and early twentieth centuries. The lower professional status of the consuls, their lower pay, their poorer conditions, and their lack of pension rights, were largely due to their lower social status.[13] Diplomats and consuls were both responsible to the Foreign

Office, but their roles were strikingly different, at least in theory. Diplomats were regarded as a direct link with the foreign government, and were expected to report on the most significant developments of policy. Their lives were often filled with glittering social events, and they did not usually descend to the level of dealing with the ordinary British citizen abroad. They were quite often close relatives of Government ministers. Consuls, on the other had to concern themselves with trade, encouraging it, regulating it, and looking after the agents of that trade – British merchants and British seamen of all kinds. Consuls often came from merchant families, and very rarely from the ranks of the aristocracy. However, we shall see that the distinction between the duties of diplomats and consuls was sometimes not as clear-cut in Brazil as it was elsewhere.

When Robert was appointed in 1812, the Consular Instructions of Castlereagh in 1815 and the Canning Reforms to the Consular Service in 1825 were in the future. Though Great Britain had had consuls abroad, particularly in Europe, for many centuries, the role had never been clearly defined. Up to the seventeenth century, consuls were not state officials, but rather the representative of British merchants abroad, appointed not only to represent them but also to keep them in order. The seventeenth century saw the Crown claim them as its own, but it did not offer a job description more extensive than its Commission (its document of appointment) and its assumptions of loyalty. As late as 1809, it was possible to say, as Cockburn did in 1809, that appointing a consul was "like sending a lost sheep into the wilderness"[14] Joseph Chitty in 1820 said: "Great Britain certainly appears to have paid less attention to the office of consul ... than some others of the states of Europe."[15] There was no training, no instruction manual, and only general expectations. The French did things differently, with a much tighter system of appointments, and an official being appointed to a consulship only after three years' experience as a vice-consul. The English attitude was summed up much later by Viscount Palmerston, who "always maintained that the duties of consuls... required no particular previous education and could be carried out by any man of good sense."[16] Palmerston preferred to carry out the preparation of his consuls reactively, giving them very little in the way of previous training, or even clear instructions, but coming down on them from a considerable height if their behaviour, ideas, and language required it. Palmerston's predecessors, Castlereagh and Canning, had offered little more than this, apart from precise instructions about the sending of despatches. It is a particularly English approach to trust to a general and liberal education as a basis for acquiring administrative and technical skills. The tradition dies hard, even today.

Not that British Consuls were alone in being untrained. The United States, in spite of its desire to reject the institution of monarchy and all its works, had adopted the British tradition where the training of consuls was concerned. Charles S. Kennedy, writing about American consuls, describes them as "untrained men ... acting on their own with minimal guidance, responding to local events, each according to common sense and instinct."[17] It is no surprise to find that American consuls and vice-consuls consorted happily with their British counterparts in Brazil, however fractious might be the relationships between their governments – they were like-minded men whose governments expected much the same of them.

So Robert was lucky to get a meeting at the Foreign Office with the Under-Secretary before he took up his post – that would be all the training that he would receive. Nor had he much, if anything, to offer in the way of experience. Some of the earlier wisdom about consuls had stressed the long experience required to act as consul in a trading port. Bandinell describes a consul as "the Head, acknowledged by their Government, of the merchants of their country resident in their Consulate."[18] Robert, however successful he was later, can only have begun by being inexperienced, and working hard to achieve the *gravitas* his role demanded.

So Robert was to spend his time in São Luis working hard as a merchant, but also carrying out the duties of the British Consul. The Foreign Office was at the very least a month's sailing time away, and his nearest colleagues in Pernambuco and Bahia a long and slow voyage distant. To send a message to his immediate boss, the Consul-General in Rio de Janeiro, might take as long as sending one to London.

But in the port of São Luis de Maranhão, ships arrived at all hours of the day and night, bringing a multitude of problems with them, and the political stability of the Province of Maranhão, where São Luis was situated, was never to be counted on. Consuls' duties were supposed to be practical everyday ones, largely concerned with maritime matters, but the isolation of his port meant that Robert would have to act as diplomat as well as Consul, representing the British Crown to a sometimes hostile provincial president and government.

São Luis, which slumbers now in the warmth and comparative comfort of its status as a World Heritage Site, with money for refurbishing its beautiful old buildings, was at that time the busiest port on the northern coast of Brazil, and the fourth busiest in Brazil. Later on, it was to be eclipsed by Belém further west, which grew fast in the rubber boom of the second half of the nineteenth century, and also eventually by Fortaleza further east, whose port facilities were built by the British. But in 1812, São Luis was a busy mercantile community on the edge of a largely undiscovered continent. A mile or two inland from the island city, the tropical countryside began, and, though some merchants had estates or country houses, few of them lived very far away from the city. The foreign merchants must have been a small and close-knit community, reliant on their own resources and with no quick way of summoning assistance. The Royal Navy paid occasional visits, but often only in the shape of a small schooner, and though the prestige of the British navy was great, it was its reputation rather than its immediate fire-power which tended to impress the locals.

So, alone and unadvised, except by his brother, his friends and his colleagues, Robert had to look after British interests, which comprised both property and persons, had to encourage British trade, had to serve the needs of British ships and seamen, and had to convey suitably helpful trading information back to London.

But why appoint a man who already had a job to an important role representing government? One of the few contemporary attempts to deal analytically with the role of consuls during the early nineteenth century was that of David Warden[19]. He set his heart resolutely against what were called "mercantile consuls". "I am decidedly of opinion, that a Consul... ought to have no interest in trade", and "A Consul must have no commercial engagements. Services of this kind cannot be proffered by him, whose kind is absorbed in the pursuit of gain." The French, as we have seen, trusted to a professional cadre of men. British policy was not always so consistent, with some men appointed because of their social or political connections rather than their proven local skills and knowledge. However, the philosophy of Britain's being represented by a man who lived and worked locally, and who could speak on an equal footing with other British residents, was maintained. In the 1820s, "The Times" expressed the common view that merchants were the best choice as consuls by listing with disgust recent appointments – "military men, court retainers, or other persons quite ignorant of commercial affairs"[20]. Given that a merchant could be expected to have a comfortable income from his commerce, it was possible to pay a consul slightly under rather than over the odds, always an attractive proposition to the penny-pinching demagogues in the House of Commons. But again, there was little consistency here, for, as we shall see, Robert went from a comfortable official salary at Maranhão, which buttressed his substantial mercantile earnings, to a pittance at Rio de Janeiro, where it was quite impracticable for him to operate as a merchant.

There were obvious difficulties in the dual role, one of which was the suspicion that a consul could take advantage of his official position to forward his commercial interests. It was by no means unknown for South American consuls to be accused of feathering their own nests at the expense of their colleagues and competitors. There was a particular case in Bahia in the 1830s. A second difficulty was also an obvious one – the need to balance time and energy in fulfilling both roles. Again, we shall see later the dire consequences of getting that balance wrong.

The early nineteenth century saw at least two *volte-faces* in British policy over the appointment of merchant consuls, both of which affected the Heskeths. Canning in 1825, in line with Warden's view a decade earlier, decided to reform the service to eradicate merchant consuls Unfortunately, he was not able to guarantee a sufficiently permanent scale of remuneration, and his reforms lasted only a few years, before economies demanded a return to the old ways. Robert, in particular, suffered from this inconsistency, giving up his mercantile business in 1829, only to find in 1832, when he was translated to Rio, that he was expected to resume his merchant career in a totally new environment and with a thousand other things to do at the busiest port in South America.

Naturally enough, the other British residents of the South American ports, as well as the British seamen, and the distressed British subjects stranded there, could not be expected to understand the various conflicting pressures that consuls were subjected to. In Bindoff's words, the consul was "the sole resort of British subjects and foreigners alike for advice and assurance".[21] Some problems of a non-maritime nature seemed often to be quite time-consuming. In Rio de Janeiro, for example, the role and the person of the Anglican Chaplain seemed often to occupy a great deal of time and trouble. Compared with that, the consul's responsibility for intestacy, for example, must have seemed manageable

The lack of a systematic approach to consular appointments, together with a lack of consistent criteria for appointing them, has led not only to a neglect of their contribution by historians, but a sometimes dismissive attitude to them. Temperley, who chronicled the life of Canning, calls them "a miscellaneous and undesirable set"[22] – though why the first epithet should lead automatically to the second is not clear. C.R. Middleton says "There was little glamour in being a consul, but there was also little work at any but the most important ports".[23] "Consular affairs," he intones, " have too often been entrusted to whoever [sic] could be found to manage them." We shall find that there is an element of truth in this last comment, but the reality in Brazil was that consuls generally worked closely with their diplomatic colleagues, and had plenty to do as trade and commerce grew between Europe and the new Brazilian Empire. Platt says of them: "The range of functions expected of the Latin American consuls ... was far larger; ... consuls acted as agents for the expansion of British trade."[24] In the words of a modern consul quoted by Geoffrey Moorhouse: "With the exception of the administration of the Sacrament of baptism and exercising the business of executions, it would be difficult to say what duties I cannot be called on to perform."[25] Moorhouse, having met a great number of modern-day consuls, says: "Listening to the reminiscences of Consuls can restore a lot of faith in human nature and diplomacy." I suspect that the Hesketh brothers might also have demonstrated that faith. They certainly had plenty of personal experience to base it on.

4

THE SPIDER OF
DOWNING STREET

"... The complete knowledge and control of the Foreign Minister over all the details of his work..." (C.K. Webster on Lord Palmerston)

London was always the hub around which the whole of the Foreign Service revolved. Ever since 1782, when the Foreign Office had been set up, every diplomat and consular official in the service reported directly to the Foreign Office. The Foreign Office headquarters building in Downing Street, not to be replaced until the 1860s, creaked and groaned with age. A whole range of services and operations was based there, and its denizens included not only the Foreign Secretary and his immediate staff, but clerks and translators, Mr. Hertslet (the librarian and archivist), the Royal Messengers who reported to Mr. Hertslet, and, after the mid-1820s, the Slave Trade Department and the Consular Department. Up in the attic was "The Nursery" – the living quarters of the young clerks, who lived over the shop, and who were expected to be available at all hours of the day, and sometimes of the night. When Lord Palmerston arrived one Sunday morning accompanied by Lady Palmerston, he was irritated to discover that many of the clerks were absent. Lady Palmerston had to remind him that some people attended church on Sunday morning, unlike her husband, who was not an assiduous churchgoer.

In an age before the telegraph, the typewriter, and the computer, all communication had to be by hand-written despatch. Every despatch sent from abroad had already been checked and copied, and then reproduced in fair copy at its origin. Upon its arrival at the Foreign Office, it had to be opened, read, copied again, and filed. Later on in the process, each despatch, even the most formal acknowledgement of the receipt of a circular from the Foreign Office, was bound together in leather-backed volumes. For much of the period, copies of despatches were shared with the Monarch, and copies, or at the very least, abstracts, were sent to the rest of the Cabinet daily. When a reply was deemed necessary, each reply had to be drafted, copied, checked, and dispatched. Lord Palmerston got into considerable hot water

The old Foreign Office headquarters in Downing Street, London

with Queen Victoria when he streamlined the process with the young Queen. He found it particularly helpful to let her have copies of his despatches *after* he had sent them rather than before. In this way, his business was not held up in waiting for Her Majesty's responses, or, more likely, those of Prince Albert, who took a particular interest in foreign affairs. It also avoided any danger of royal objections to his sometimes trenchant remarks or to his unilateral statements of Foreign Office policy. The Queen could be particularly touchy where her European relatives were involved, and she saw Palmerston's "forgetfulness" as a challenge to her rather fragile authority.

But it all meant that the Foreign Office was a vast copying-shop. The early nineteenth century saw the amount of copying expand enormously, simply because the number of despatches in and despatches out grew so considerably in number. In 1829, for example, a total of six thousand despatches arrived in Downing Street; in 1849, twenty years later, the number had grown fivefold to thirty thousand, an average of over eighty a day, many of them of a substantial nature. It was Lord Palmerston's proud boast that he read every one: one might almost sympathise with him when he complained of diplomatic or consular prolixity or poor handwriting. But Palmerston was not responsible for the basic rules of despatch-writing – those had been set by Viscount Castlereagh in 1815, and reinforced by Canning, his successor as Foreign Secretary. The Castlereagh rules required a despatch from every British outpost every week; Canning insisted that each should be written on large folio paper in a round hand, be numbered consecutively, and be limited to one subject. Palmerston's particular contribution was to ensure that these rules were observed scrupulously. Philip Guedella, in his biography of Palmerston, talks of "an increasing passion for plain sentences and blacker ink". Palmerston's irritation with poor handwriting sometimes produced a shaft of exasperated wit. His comment on sloping handwriting is typical: "Iron railings leaning out of the perpendicular, & backward-sloping like the masts of an American schooner."

So in 1831, Parkinson, the Consul in Pernambuco, was rebuked for using the wrong size of paper. Others were frequently in trouble for their handwriting and even their ink. Ink was not always a very stable chemical in tropical climes, and though most of the documents were and are still legible, others faded before arriving in London: Palmerston complained of "invisible ink despatches". One of the Hesketh brothers, John, had to endure criticism of his handwriting. Palmerston found it neat, but difficult to read, and John Bidwell, the Head of the Consular Department, was enjoined to "desire him to write a larger and rounder Hand, and point out that the word "transpired" is used by him in a sense which does not belong to it; he means "happened"."[26] Bidwell, with rather more sensitivity and personal knowledge of John's circumstances than his boss, neglected to tell John of the second criticism. When this missive arrived in Brazil, John was fleeing with his family from the horrors of the Cabanagem Rebellion, and it says much for his forbearance as well as his obedience that he accepted the criticism, and promised to do better. His reply was a model of humility and restraint:

> "I notice Viscount Palmerston's desire that my Despatches be transcribed in a more distinct and rounder hand, & which I shall for the future endeavour strictly to comply with & have to apologise to His Lordship for my past deviation from the forms to be observed in Official Correspondence..."[27]

John Hesketh was not the only Consul in Pará to be rebuked in this way.
Robert Ryan, who was Consul in the 1840s, had his despatches returned to
him, "which should not have been forwarded to this Office in their present
state... you will send to this Office amended Despatches properly Docketed
and correctly spelt, and written in black ink on the proper sized Despatch
paper, and you will be careful not to mix up different subjects in one
Despatch."[28]

Palmerston was equally forthright with his more senior diplomats. W.G.
Ouseley, who led the Rio de Janeiro mission without complaint all through
the long furlough of Hamilton Hamilton, the Envoy Extraordinary, received
the following note from John Backhouse, the Permanent Under-secretary at
the Foreign Office:

> "I am directed by Vsct. Palmerston to point out to you that the verb
> "to resume" does not mean "to sum up" or to "recapitulate", which is
> the sense in which you have used it, but that it means "to take back
> again".[29]

High rank was of little significance to Palmerston, and Hamilton Hamilton himself was undoubtedly in mind when Palmerston delivered a more general side-swipe: "I should like to give some of our Diplomatists a Hint also to write their Despatches to this office in English, and not to slide into such Gallicisms as "Reclamation" for Complaint or Remonstrance."[30] On another occasion, he addressed Hamilton Hamilton personally:

"If Mr. Hamilton would let his substantives and adjectives go single instead of always sending them forth by Twos and Threes at a time, his Despatches would be clearer & easier to read."

All this writing and copying added up to a vastly increasing burden on everyone involved as the century progressed. It was in vain that Watts, another consul in Brazil, pleaded that he had not had the time to write and transmit one of his regular reports. It was only when the electric telegraph made its appearance in 1861 that everyone began to be freed from the tyranny of the hand-written despatch.

The despatches having been read, copied, circulated, and filed, it was not Castlereagh's, Canning's, or Palmerston's style, or indeed Aberdeen's, to delegate much if at all of the consequent decisions. The three long-serving Under-Secretaries – William Hamilton, who interviewed Robert Hesketh in 1812, Joseph Planta, the Under-Secretary during the latter part of Castlereagh's tenure and during all of Canning's, and John Backhouse, were allowed on occasions to make administrative decisions, but it was much more normal for them to be writing on the Foreign Secretary's behalf, and often in his precise words. Planta was highly regarded in government circles, and travelled to the Congress of Vienna in 1815 with Lord Castlereagh. He was greatly trusted by Canning after Castlereagh's suicide, transferring to the Prime Minister's Office with Canning in 1827, but even he had a subsidiary role. John Backhouse served for many years in the Foreign Office, but he confessed privately that he was very scared of Lord Palmerston. Fear, or at the very least great respect, was expected to be the proper and normal attitude of all in the Foreign Service to the Foreign Secretary. Even the most self-opinionated consul, such as W. Augustus Cowper, briefly Consul at Pará before moving to Pernambuco, minded his p's and q's when writing to the Foreign Secretary, and all made sure that they headed and ended their letters in an appropriately respectful style, sparing not the ink in addressing His Lordship in the fullest possible manner. In a formal acknowledgement, the curlicued courtesies could take up half a page Here is John Hesketh ending one of his routine letters to the Foreign Secretary, shortly after he was promoted from Vice-Consul to Consul in Pará:

"I have the Honour to be,
Your Lordship's most obedient and very humble Servant,
John Hesketh,
Her Majesty's Consul."

There were two Under-Secretaries at a time employed at the Foreign Office throughout most of the early nineteenth century. After 1830, one of them became permanent, and therefore pre-eminent. The Permanent Under-Secretary for most of the period that the Hesketh brothers served in Brazil was John Backhouse, who knew the Heskeths personally, doubtless because he too came from Liverpool. Canning introduced him to the Foreign Office. He was the son of a merchant, and had come to London to represent the Liverpool merchant body in the capital, but was quickly spirited to the Foreign Office by Canning. He was given considerable responsibility, and eventually became the Permanent Under-Secretary when changes to the system were made in 1830. He was a senior member of staff for many years, until his retirement in 1842 on the grounds of ill-health. But far from enjoying his seniority, he found his later years were stressful, because of his daily fear of Palmerston and his sharp tongue. Lord Aberdeen, however, thought very highly of him, and gave him a generous eulogy when he retired. A'Court, who also worked with him, said of him that he was "a valuable man, clear-headed, steady and industrious, and of very pleasing and unas-suming address and manner".

Also long-serving was John Bidwell, who was put in charge of the new Consular Department in 1825 by Canning. He was often the mouthpiece of the Foreign Secretary in writing to consuls, and it is not hard to distinguish in his letters the contrast between the harsher voice of authority and Bidwell's gentler and more tactful approach. The setting-up of the Consular Department was an attempt to get a grip on the escalating business created by a host of new consular appointments, especially in South America. It was meant to ensure that communications with them were efficiently handled, and that their interests and contributions were valued. In fact, it had the unlooked-for result of allowing the rest of the service to dismiss the consuls as unimportant, and to pigeon-hole them at a lower level of prestige and importance than their diplomatic colleagues. It took over a hundred years before the British Foreign Office grasped this fact, and integrated the two parts of the service in 1943. In the nineteenth century, for example, consuls were not allowed to aspire to belong to the same clubs as the diplomats in London, and even in Istanbul.

The Foreign Secretaries were only too aware of the strengths and weak-nesses of both diplomatic and consular staff, though much of the information about them came through only two routes: their letters, and complaints about them received from British residents abroad. There was no hint at this period of a systematic attempt to assess the quality of their work, and judgement on their competence was left to the individual view, not to say prejudice, of the Foreign Secretary. This could sometimes lead to unfairness, but could also on occasion lead more happily to letters of approbation, which arrived occasionally for the Heskeths as well as for other diplomats and consuls. The tone of these letters seems condescending to the modern ear, and though they were doubtless welcome, they served to reinforce the gap that existed between master and servants. A goodly number of the Foreign Secretaries' confidential notes about their correspondents still exist – Palmerston's, often with a pungent comment, were written on distinctive little square pieces of paper, bearing a few words and the ominous "P" with the date. Castlereagh, Palmerston, and Aberdeen had no personal experience of diplomatic or consular roles, and Canning was the only Foreign Secretary of the period who had had served in the diplomatic service. When his career stalled in 1816, he had accepted the post of Envoy in Lisbon, and stayed there for a short period until he resumed his career and his enemies in London. Canning's boss at that time, Castlereagh, was a keen traveller, especially to the post-Napoleonic European conferences of the Holy Alliance. Canning and later Palmerston were less keen both on travel and on European conferences, being suspicious of what they saw as the very mixed motives of the French and the Tsar, but both Foreign Secretaries were astute and well-informed, even when closeted for much of the time in the Foreign Office. Canning even lived there, and Palmerston spent so much of his time there that he did not apparently visit Broadlands, his country house in Hampshire, for three years. Castlereagh, Canning, and Palmerston could not be faulted for their commitment to their role, and they each brought considerable gifts to it. Castlereagh was much admired on the continent for his open attitude, Canning undoubtedly applied his considerable intellect to the problems of his day, and Palmerston, though not a visionary, became very popular at home for his defence of British people abroad. His later reputation for defending the rights of British subjects, for instance in the Don Pacifico case, when he defended a Gibraltarian with a British passport against the Greek Government, has rather obscured the many occasions earlier on when he showed considerable respect for the proper rights of foreign governments. Aberdeen, though inclined to be more sensitive and sympathetic, was not always regarded as strong, and it is ironic that it was he rather than Palmerston who incurred the enormous wrath of the Brazilians in 1845 for his unilateral imposition of stringent "stop and search" rules on Brazilian ships.

The Foreign Secretary, in short, was like a large spider sitting in the Foreign Office building in Downing Street at the centre of a global web, in touch with the farthest corners of the world, and guiding and manipulating not only all those in foreign parts, but his own staff as well. There was no one else at this period who was allowed to have the complete overview which the Foreign Secretary had. Even his senior under-secretaries were but minions, subject to constant supervision and daily interference. Delegation had not yet been invented in the Foreign Office.

The virtue of the system was obvious – direct, daily supervision of every aspect of foreign policy, but its corresponding weakness was that even a very able man could not work more than twenty-four hours a day. Philip Guedella quotes Palmerston as commenting:

"The life I lead is like that of a man, who on getting out of bed every morning, should be caught up by the end of a windmill and whirled round and round till he was again deposited at night to rest."

The system reposed enormous power and influence in one man's hands, which gave the possibility of decisive action but also of mistakes proceeding from prejudice or haste. It was particularly easy for other politicians or the self-important to bend the ear of the Foreign Secretary, perhaps suggesting he appoint an impecunious or unemployed relative to the diplomatic or consular service. He could make inspired appointments at times, but also diabolically inappropriate ones. He could react with irritation to one possible candidate, as Palmerston did when William Hesketh was trying to negotiate what he considered a proper level of salary in Maranhão, and appointed a man unknown to all, almost as a sort of punishment. When John Moon, who became Consul in Maranhão after Robert Hesketh left in 1832, died in Lisbon in 1842, he was succeeded not by William Hesketh or William Wilson, both of whom had considerable experience of the role in Maranhão, but by R. Falconer Corbett, a friend and associate of the opprobrious Henry Dickenson in Pará. But perhaps the prize for making one of the Foreign Office's most unsuitable appointments must go to the man who appointed W.D. Christie, the former M.P. for Weymouth, as Envoy Extraordinary to Rio de Janeiro in the 1860s. Christie seems to have been one of the most undiplomatic men ever to be employed as a diplomat, and he derailed British-Brazilian relationships for a considerable time, coming close to causing open warfare between the two former allies.

The Crown often took a lively interest in the appointments being made by the Foreign Secretary. King William IV was always on the *qui vive* for any appointee tainted with radicalism. Queen Victoria and Prince Albert took a personal interest in appointments, both for diplomatic and consular posts.

Royal interest perhaps added to the impression that the Diplomatic Service at least was specifically designed for the financial comfort of the ruling class. Even Palmerston, who was never seen as any man's but his own, nevertheless saw himself as beholden to promote the sons and nephews of his political friends and colleagues, at least in the early stages of their careers. The radicals, aware of royal disapproval of their candidates, saw this as insider dealing, and Bright said famously of the Diplomatic Service that it was "nothing more or less than a gigantic system of outdoor relief for the aristocracy."[31]

Where the diplomatic service was concerned, that first step on the diplomatic ladder was all-important, but had often to be financed by the new recruit or his family. A common first post was that of an unpaid *chargé d'affaires* in a large embassy, where the newcomer was expected to live in the household of the envoy, pay his own bills, and prove his competence before receiving his first paid appointment. After that, no regular system of promotion was offered. Some men prospered in the sunshine of the Foreign Secretary's approval, whilst others were either left to stagnate, or sent to unpopular locations, which were usually those most distant from London. Those sent to China could often say goodbye to Great Britain permanently. South America had a similar reputation, although the career of Henry Stephen Fox showed how useful influential relatives were. He was a nephew of Charles James Fox, the influential Whig politician. H.S. Fox, after a spell as unpaid *attaché*, took only six years to be appointed as Envoy Extraordinary to Rio de Janeiro, and his three years there, during which he got on warmly with Robert Hesketh, were followed by his rapid promotion to one of the pearls of the diplomatic service, the Embassy in Washington, as important then as it is today.

If diplomats could rarely count on access to something like a career ladder, consuls had even less opportunity to do so. They all assumed that their virtues and their loyal service were being noted in the Foreign Office, but it was rare for the Foreign Office to reward them directly with a promotion. Robert Hesketh's letter to Palmerston in 1831 pleading his case for a new job was rewarded with the offer of the Consulship at Rio, but that was only because Palmerston had decided to abolish Consuls-General, and had therefore created an unexpected vacancy in the Brazilian capital. The swingeing cut in Robert's salary following his move to Rio must, in any case, have indicated to him that it was at best a transfer rather than a promotion.

The position of the Foreign Secretary was thus hugely influential. It was, it was said, the second most interesting job any politician could aspire to. The responsibility was supposed to be shared with the Prime Minister, but it would have been only natural for the P.M. to leave the detail, and eventually the direction, to the Secretary for Foreign Affairs, as Lord Grey, Prime Minister for four years from 1830, often did.

The expectation of all governments of the period was that its expenditure on the Foreign Service would benefit British commerce. For all Foreign Secretaries, therefore, the touchstone of all diplomatic and consular activity was trade. Great Britain had not yet reached the point at which the acquisition of territory was an end in itself. Indeed, all three great Foreign Secretaries of our period had forsworn the acquisition of territory as a proper end of British foreign policy. Canning developed a strong belief that Great Britain should not interfere in any way with the internal politics of other nations. Trade was another matter, and all Foreign Secretaries believed that this was the chief route to prosperity and influence for the island nation. The Navy and sometimes the Army had therefore to be kept in reserve to defend legitimate trade, but their use to acquire territory and extend the borders of the British Empire was a later nineteenth century invention.

That was not to say that Great Britain's Foreign Secretaries were easy in their minds if *others* attempted the seizure of land. The first half of the nineteenth century saw an almost obsessional concern that France would act *ultra vires.* In South America, the anxiety centred on parts of Northern Brazil, or on lands adjacent to the Rio Plata. As we shall see, John Hesketh in Pará was deeply concerned when his careful report of French advances along the Oyapock River, which divided Brazil from French Guiana, was apparently ignored, and mortified when Palmerston by implication accused him of not letting him know about the supposed French advances.

Equally excitable was the relationship with the United States. Great Britain had been at war with her as recently as 1812, and official hostility between governments was often the mode of diplomatic interaction. The Monroe Doctrine, formulated by the American President in 1823, attempted to warn off the European powers from involvement or interference in the affairs of the Americas, largely because the Holy Alliance was threatening to restore to Spain her South American colonies, and re-establish the role of monarchy in the continent. Canning, Britain's Foreign Secretary at the time, did not share the Holy Alliance's enthusiasm, and was noticeably supportive of the new republics, but the United States tended to think that Europe had no business to be concerning itself with South American politics in any shape or form. This led to suspicion and hostility between the two powers at government level. On the more local level, co-operation and friendship between diplomatic and consular officials of the two countries was common. In Belém, the American Consul, Mr. Charles Smith, and John Hesketh, the

British Consul, were close friends, and dined together regularly. When trouble came to Pará, they worked closely together. Later, in Rio de Janeiro, Robert Hesketh went so far as to marry into the family of the American Vice-Consul. This closeness was helped by the fact that it was not unheard-of for British citizens to act as consular agents for the United States.

Although trade was the paramount issue, the Foreign Secretary was never averse to a little useful political intelligence. In Brazil, the diplomats spent hours writing verbosely about every twist and turn of Imperial politics. Independence, the subsequent making of the constitution, and the Regency period from 1831 to 1841, offered ample opportunities for a blow-by-blow account of goings-on in the Senate, as well as the negotiations which preceded every change of government. But perhaps even more useful, and certainly more interesting, were the snippets of intelligence from consuls in more remote places. There was nothing new about this – back in northern Portugal fifty years before, His Majesty's Vice-Consul in Viana do Castelo, Mr. Allen, gave very full and regular updates on the progress of the French Army as Napoleon tried to consolidate his hold on the whole of the Iberian Peninsula.[32] In Brazil, the doings of the French were always of interest, and the consuls, unlike the diplomats, had daily and intimate contact with the British sea-captains who exchanged information in foreign ports, or who met others on the high seas.

In addition to this consular intelligence, the Foreign Office also ran a secret service, whose accounts were known to no-one outside the Downing Street building. Regular and considerable sums were disbursed by the diplomats and consuls, without letting slip the slightest information about the nature of the intelligence or the identity of the operatives involved. The formula that was followed was always the same: – a sum of money (£52, £98, perhaps or £138.13s.4d.) was drawn on J.B. Bergne of the Foreign Office for Her Majesty's Secret Service. There is a specific cluster of claims around 1839 and 1841, when the Brazilian Regency was particularly fragile, and when the British Navy was being targeted by the slave-traders of Brazil. In Brazil, however, it was the Envoy Extraordinary who was given direct contact with "Her Majesty's Secret Service", and there is no trace in the Foreign Office records of consuls being required to note their expenditure. Consuls indeed were normally excluded from any knowledge of their activities.

Apart from trade, there was one issue which united all the Foreign Secretaries in the early nineteenth century: the abolition of the Slave Trade. The British Government's prohibition of British involvement in the trade in 1807 was followed by continual attempts to use treaties to persuade other countries to disengage from the Slave Trade. Brazil and Portugal were particular targets, and Castlereagh, Canning, Palmerston, and Aberdeen all took a strong personal interest in British efforts to end the transatlantic trade in Africans. Canning set up the Slave Trade Department in the Foreign Office in 1824, with James Bandinell at its head, and Palmerston became unpopular with the Navy as a result of his strong insistence that it provide suitable ships in adequate numbers for the Brazilian and West African Squadrons. Perhaps all four Foreign Secretaries have not been given sufficient credit for their consistency and their leadership over this issue.

Whatever the matter in hand, however, there can have been little doubt in the mind of any diplomat or consul, wherever in the world he was situated, that he represented the government of Great Britain, and that the policy of that government was mediated to him through only one man – the Foreign Secretary. All lines could be traced back to the spider in Downing Street, and all official instructions arrived, however long the sea-journey, from him.

THE APPOINTMENT

"We appoint a Consul ... to take care of the affairs of Our subjects..."
(Queen Victoria)

Powerful as the Foreign Secretaries of the time were, they did not always use their authority to ensure that Foreign Office policies were consistent. The Hesketh brothers' service as consuls and vice-consuls covered a period of extremely inconsistent official policy. In 1815, Castlereagh tried to impose some form and discipline upon the British Government's functionaries abroad. In 1825, Canning's major ideas for reform were embodied in the Consular Act of that year, and, if they had been carried out for more than a year or two, might have produced a systematic and organised consular service. But as the Heskeths' experiences show, greater forces were at work in the Foreign Office and in Parliament, and the opportunity to produce system and logic was soon lost. By the date of Robert's retirement in 1852, the consular service was creaking at the seams, and not in a state suitable to support the rapid growth of the British Empire in the second half of the nineteenth century. All three brothers suffered, both in their careers and in their pockets, from the failure to produce a proper system. In John's case, the strains put upon him may well have contributed to his early death.

Nevertheless, for all this inconsistency at the top, to be a consul was still regarded as a highly desirable role in life. When Robert was faced, after Canning's 1826 Reforms, with either giving up his business or his consular role, he seems not to have hesitated to remain as consul. His import and export business in São Luis had been highly lucrative, and he had been able to take advantage of the powerful demand for cotton back in home in Lancashire and the Pennines. The growing Brazilian economy was demanding more and more of Great Britain's manufactured goods, and Robert's firm seems to have found it easy to fill the holds of its ships on both the outward and inward journeys. After 1826, however, in spite of the prospect of making even more money, Robert readily acceded to Canning's new principle of appointing salaried consuls, and gave up all his business interests within a relatively short period of time. Even though Sir Roger Casement was later to complain dismissively: "In a place like the Congo, Delagoa Bay, or Para I have to get anyone I can", there never seemed to be a shortage of candidates in the relevant ports.[33] To wish to serve the British Crown in far-flung lands was regarded as an extremely respectable vocation, and compensated for the privations of the climate, the vast number of sea-miles from home and family, and jealous and argumentative merchant colleagues. We should not overlook, either, the intense pride that consuls of the time took in serving their country.

When a consular vacancy occurred, the first activity might well be the local British merchants meeting in someone's home in the humidity and the heat to suggest one of their number as the new consul for the port. Sometimes the Foreign Office was happy to accept the suggestion, following the long tradition that a British consul abroad was the leader of the local British residents, and appointed to keep them motivated and in good order. Sometimes, however, when the Foreign Secretary was not happy with the merchants' nomination, or, more likely, he had someone in mind whom he wished to place in the consular service, he had no hesitation in appointing him. We do not know which method resulted in Robert Hesketh's appointment in 1812 to Northern Brazil, but, as we have noted, his usefulness would have been enhanced by his fluency in Portuguese, acquired as a boy in Porto. For the twenty years in which he occupied the Consulate in his port, São Luis, his authority never seems to have been questioned by his fellow-merchants and residents, and he was regarded by all as efficient, sensible, and loyal. But the system of local nomination was less successful in Pará. When Robert, doubtless at the suggestion of the local merchants, nominated Henry Dickenson, one of their number, as Vice-Consul, this was accepted without demur by the Foreign Office, but, as we shall see, turned out to be disastrous. More successful was Robert's later nomination of his brother John to the same post.

Sometimes, a suitable candidate was moved from elsewhere, as Henry Augustus Cowper was from Pará to Pernambuco in 1841. Cowper's earlier career had faltered in Cartagena in Colombia, when he had been accused of misappropriating public funds, but a lengthy campaign by his relatives to clear his name overcame even this blot on his honour, and he followed John Hesketh as Consul in Pará. Cowper had had the advantage of serving under his father in Pernambuco. Family connections often weighed favourably with successive Foreign Secretaries. William Warre was nominated by the Porto merchants to succeed his uncle, John Whitehead, in Porto in 1802, and their judgement was endorsed without question by the Foreign Office of the day. It was by no means unusual to come across families like the Pennells, the Cowpers, and, of course, the Heskeths, who provided several consuls or vice-consuls.

Unlike their colleagues in the diplomatic service, however, consular appointees rarely seem to have been close relatives of Foreign Secretaries or the offspring of close political allies. They came from a surprisingly wide spectrum of middle-class society, and from all over Great Britain. John Whitehead in Porto, for instance, came from Ashton-under-Lyne near Manchester, in the foothills of the Pennines, Augustus Cowper's family seem to have been based in Newcastle-on-Tyne, and the Heskeths, of course, came from Liverpool.

Whatever the route to a name, the foreign government in question had to be consulted. It was rare, but not unknown, for them to raise objections, but it must have been pleasing to John Hesketh to receive support from the President of the Province of Pará when he was appointed Vice-Consul there in 1824. The President, we are told, was happy to support the appointment, "owing to the general Esteem in which he is held by all the Inhabitants of this Province in consequence of the propriety of his Conduct."[34] Events would later show that "all the Inhabitants" was an overstatement, and that a few never came to terms with the appointment of the new Vice-Consul.

The appointment of a consul was announced with the full authority of the Monarch. In 1852, Robert Hesketh's successor in Rio de Janeiro, John Westwood, was announced in these words:

> Victoria, by the Grace of God, Queen ....Whereas we have thought it necessary for the encouragement of Our subjects trading to Brazil to appoint a Consul to reside at Rio de Janeiro, to take care of the affairs of Our subjects, and to aid and assist them in all their lawful and mercantile concerns; now know Ye that We, reposing especial trust and confidence in the discretion and faithfulness of Our trusty and well-beloved John Julius Collings Westwood, Esquire,... we appoint him .... to aid and protect Our Merchants and others, Our subjects, who may trade with, or visit, or reside at Rio de Janeiro aforesaid..."

Vice-Consuls seem to have received their Commissions from their supervising consuls. John Hesketh's Commssion was issued by his brother, Robert:

> "The undersigned Robert Hesketh Esquire ... do hereby make known unto all the constituted Authorities in the said Province of Pará, and unto all His Britannic Majesty's Subjects who may reside or appear in the said Province, that with the sanction of His Britannic Majesty's Secretary of State for Foreign Affairs I have nominated constituted

and appointed ... John Hesketh Esqre. to be British Vice-Consul at Pará in the stead of Henry Dickenson Esquire..." ...

Having received his Commission, perhaps John Hesketh was not unusual in his loyal response: his appointment as Vice-Consul, he wrote, "will give me the opportunity of serving my country, and meriting the esteem of my Gracious Sovereign."[35]

The Commission would normally have been followed by a letter from the Foreign Secretary giving instructions to the new appointee; Robert Hesketh seems to have been unusual in 1812 in attending the Foreign Office in person before taking up his appointment. Perhaps he was home on leave, but he later wrote appreciatively to William Hamilton of the Foreign Office reminding him of his "frequent and troublesome calls at the Foreign Office regarding my appointment in February, 1812."[36] It was only much later, after Palmerston's time, that the Foreign Office began to believe that a modicum of training might help its consuls before they embarked on their duties. When Robert was moved to Rio de Janeiro in 1832, he received no further instructions, but was told that his previous experience of Brazil and the consular role would be sufficient to enable him to carry out his very extensive duties.

Given the paucity of instructions from the Foreign Office, it is not surprising that consuls broke the unwritten rules on occasions. Mr. Watts of Pernambuco, in spite of long experience, irritated the Foreign Office considerably by ordering without permission an expensive royal coat of arms for the British Church in his port. His offence was compounded by his dying before the bill was paid to the firm of London iron-founders he commissioned to produce it. And we shall see later how Henry Dickenson totally misunderstood his duties in Pará in the years before he was dismissed for "improper Conduct".

Having taken up his duties, it was the consul's duty to acquire an office and appropriate furniture. The consul was expected to arrange this himself, if necessary buying the office equipment from his predecessor, if he had one. Most consuls seem to have had an office separate from their residences, and separate from any commercial premises they may have occupied. It was important that consular offices were close to the quays of the port, as most of the consul's work consisted of visiting ships, their crews, and dealing with customs-house officials. The offices were doubtless chosen for their convenience rather than for reasons of national prestige, though the flag seems always to have been flown, as it is today. Sometimes, some British citizens felt that there was a mismatch between the needs of British prestige and of

Eighteenth-century merchant's house in São Luis

economy. We are told that the consular office in Rio after Robert Hesketh's time was "up two flights of wooden stairs above a third-rate cook-shop".[37]

Another necessity was the consular uniform. In the 1840s, the full-dress uniform was elaborate: a blue coat with silver embroidery, silver-plated buttons, a white kerseymere waistcoat, blue cloth trousers to be worn with boots and black silk stockings. The undress uniform was, of course, slightly less splendid, with a plain blue cloth coat with a velvet collar, buttons embossed with the sovereign's initials, and a buff waistcoat. Both versions of the uniform were worn with a hat and sword, and all items were obtainable, we are told, from Mr. Smith of 12, Piccadilly. Both undress and dress uniforms must have made for warm wearing near the Equator, but, elaborate as they were, they were plain compared to some of the military and court uniforms invented by the new Empire of the Brazils. John Hesketh was obviously not too keen to follow this tradition, and when the consular uniform changed in the late thirties, he announced that he would wear out the old one. The inventory of his property compiled after his death includes a trunk containing John's uniform.

The consul's residence was likely to have been in a somewhat more pleasant area than his office, and further away from the port. Robert Hesketh's house in São Luis is likely to have been high up in the steep streets above the quay, and until 1835, John had a spacious one-storey residence in Belém south of the city, surrounded by a pleasant and fruitful garden. A traveller in 1828, Lieutenant Henry Lister Maw, described it after he had been to dinner, but it was apparently too far out of the city for John and his wife to offer him full-time hospitality. The house was wrecked in the convulsions of the Cabanagem Rebellion. When Robert had given up his commercial activities, and made the enormous financial sacrifice of going to Rio de Janeiro, he rented a "small cottage on a steep hill". Later on, especially after he married in 1837, his address became more prestigious, and his children were all born within the city, either in Caminho Velho or in Rua da Infante.

We have no information about the house owned by William Hesketh in São Luis, but it is likely that it would have been near the old quay in the old-established part of town in what is now the *Cidade Velha* (the "Old City"). If so, it would almost certainly be one of the old colonial houses which still exist, with their living quarters on the balconied first floor. Gilberto Freyre tells of the local junta's attack in 1824 on the house of a "Mr. Hesketh", halted only when a British warship threatened to fire on the town; but it is likely that it is Robert's rather than William Hesketh's house that is referred to.[38] The Navy was more likely to take a strong line after an attack on the Consul's house rather than on that of his merchant brother. Wherever he lived, William was obviously settled and happy in the town. He stayed there even after his retirement from business until his death in 1856, although his will was proved back in England.

Robert's life in São Luis must have been comfortable. He was doing well in business, and being paid a perfectly reasonable £1,000 per annum, together with his Consular Fees. From a financial point of view, Robert Hesketh's translation from Maranhão and Ceará to Rio de Janeiro could not have been timed more unfortunately. The former British Consul-General in Rio, Henry Chamberlain, was notorious throughout the Foreign Service for the vast remuneration he received. It was said that between 1814 and 1820, he earned the total sum of £57,567, partly from his very high salary, and partly from the Fees to which he had become entitled.[39] Successive Foreign Secretaries had been determined to reduce this exceptional sum, and when further economies were demanded in 1831, the posts of Consuls-General were the first to be axed. The new Consul-General in Rio, Mr. Pennell, who had inherited from Chamberlain many of his advantageous terms, was forcibly retired, although the blow was softened by a handsome pension of £675 p.a. "H.M. Government has decided to abolish the role of Consul-General in Rio de Janeiro, and to appoint a Merchant Consul with a small salary to transact the Consular Business at that Port."[40] The "small salary" they had in mind was £300 p.a. The House of Commons must have been delighted at cutting so much expenditure at a stroke, for Mr. Pennell's basic salary was the very considerable sum of £1500 p.a. It was, however, a decision born out of political necessity, and lacked any real practicality; the "Merchant Consul" in question was Robert Hesketh, who had to spend the next fifteen years restoring the salary of the post to a more realistic level, albeit with the help of very sympathetic Foreign Office officials.

The abolition of the posts of Consuls-General was not the only dramatic cut in salaries proposed for South America. The Consul in Bahia was to have his salary reduced from £1,200 to £800 p.a., and the Consul in Pernambuco was to have his £1,000 salary reduced to £500. Robert Hesketh's salary of £1,000 was to be similarly halved.

This may have encouraged Robert to feel that his contribution was not very highly valued. He had now been in post at Maranhão for nearly twenty years, and was beginning to feel that further promotion was passing him by. In 1831, he wrote a dignified complaint to the Foreign Office:

> "I am now the Senior Consul in Brazil, and even in the Continent of South America, and although others much my juniors have been promoted to more southern ports, increasing thereby their Emoluments and making an advantageous change in Climate, I have never had the good fortune to be promoted from my original Post.... When Your Lordship considers that Maranham is situated almost under the Equator, seriously injurious to the Health of all Europeans, and that it is in every respect expensive, I trust that Your Lordship will consider me to have established a fair claim to Promotion to the first vacancy in any of the superior Consular Appointments in Brazil or in Europe."[41]

If Robert Hesketh thought there was any method in the madness of consular promotions, he was mistaken. No-one in London had any responsibility for ensuring that merit was duly rewarded. Indeed, the very idea of "Merchant Consuls" implied that their appointment in a specific port was for life. It was not easy for a successful merchant to abandon his established business and go elsewhere, ands to start up a commercial operation all over again. Foreign Office thinking was that it had no need to have the slightest regard to the promotion prospects of its consuls. Nor was it particularly concerned if salaries were cut dramatically, for it naïvely assumed that merchants could always spend more time on their commercial activities, and make up any financial shortfall through their trade in exports and imports.

Unfortunately, however, Foreign Office policy had become seriously illogical. By the end of the eighteenth century, the concept of the "Merchant Consul" was well-established throughout the consular service, although it was not supported by all the commentators. D.B. Warden's views on the concept of mercantile consuls[42] were shared by George Canning, who, when he came to the Foreign Office in 1822, developed his plans for a totally salaried service in the Consular Act of 1825. He was strongly supported by William Huskisson, who had studied the nature of the consular service, rather than adopting, as some did, an approach which saw economy as the only relevant virtue.[43]

Canning's new philosophy reached Robert Hesketh in late 1825, in a letter from Canning's major-domo, Joseph Planta. There were profound personal implications for Robert:

> "In the new arrangements for the Consular Service, the principle will, in all practical cases, be adopted, that British Consuls shall not be in any way concerned directly or indirectly, in commercial pursuits. ... Mr. Canning is informed that you are engaged in (extensive) Commercial Pursuits at the place of your Residence. As Mr. Canning has ... had sufficient cause to approve the manner in which you have executed the Consular Functions at Maranham, he is not anxious at once rigidly to apply the principle laid down in his despatch in your particular case... He directs me, however, to request that you will maturely consider what is stated in his Despatch; – and that you will report to him (fully, though of course in confidence) the nature of your concern in commercial business and your intentions as to continuing it in order that he may judge whether your private engagements will be compatible with the due execution of the Functions of your publick situation."[44]

Kind and measured though the convoluted language was, it was clearly an instruction for Robert either to abandon his business affairs or to resign. His reply informed Canning that he had carried on a "Commission Business" called "Robert Hesketh and Company" at São Luis ever since his arrival there in April, 1812, selling on commission British manufactured goods, and purchasing and shipping cotton to Liverpool. He explained that for the last eight years he had taken less of the responsibility for running the firm, and his two partners, who were his brother William and their friend, William Wilson, had conducted most of the business. However, even his modest exercising of the joint functions of consul and merchant was not always appreciated by competitors, who wrongly assumed that his consular role gave him some sort of commercial advantage. He had found that the "assiduity and interest so long devoted to this Consulship" had produced a satisfactory result, and so he had therefore decided "to retire from my commercial Establishment" with effect from the end of 1826.[45]

Robert fulfilled this promise, and therefore ceased to be a merchant consul from the beginning of 1827. Unfortunately, Canning's "principle" soon ran foul of economies, and the House of Commons evinced a new enthusiasm for mercantile consular appointments, based entirely, it would seem, on the equally powerful principle of reducing expenditure. Canning's principles were further undermined by very considerable cuts in consular salaries. There was a sizeable number of consuls throughout the world who were not merchants, and the new arrangements must have placed many of them in considerable financial difficulty. Robert was now, of course, of their number. The Foreign Office wheeze of abolishing the Consul-General in Rio and replacing him with a merchant consul was of little use to Robert Hesketh. But, having agitated for "the next vacancy", Robert could scarcely refuse the Consulship in Rio when it was offered, however poor the remuneration, and however unrealistic the expectation that he would once again be a merchant consul.

Robert therefore accepted the appointment as Consul in Rio de Janeiro, and arrived to take up his post in October, 1832, a victim of official inconsistency. Nevertheless, he set to with a will, quickly developing excellent relationships with his diplomatic superiors, playing a very large part in the commercial life of the part, and acquiring a sturdy reputation for his work against the Slave Trade.

That was not the end of the story for him, however. He agitated politely to have his salary raised. In 1833, for instance, an F.O. Memo was very supportive of him:

> "The salary of former Consuls has been from £2,500 a year to £1,500, independently of Fees. Mr. Hesketh is a very efficient Consul and an old Servant, and what he addresses respecting the difficulty of re-engaging in trade, and of the little time his official Duties would allow him to devote to it – are worthy of consideration."[46]

Palmerston, caught within the toils of his Government's *volte-face*, could only add with some obvious sympathy: "Sorry – cannot increase. P 21/8– 33."

But Robert's pleas were more successful later on, and he managed to edge up his salary by increments of £100 from time to time. In 1836, his salary had risen to £400, and in 1843, it was raised to £500. Sir Henry Ellis, an experienced negotiator of treaties, was sent to Brazil in that year on a special mission to persuade the Brazilians to renew the 1826 Treaty with Great Britain. His mission was unsuccessful, but he obviously got to know Robert Hesketh well. After his trip, he took up the cudgels on Robert's behalf, calling him "a very useful adviser", and "capable and zealous", and asking the Foreign Office to "do something for him".[47] In 1846, the Foreign Office produced a long Memorandum on the subject of Robert's salary, reviewing its history.[48] The Consulship at Rio, it said, "is by far the most important, as well as the most laborious in Brazil ... the duties of the Consul therefore are in fact those of a Consul General with all the attendant responsibility and expence. He is of course constantly consulted and referred to by the Minister [the Envoy] on matters connected with commerce & from his long experience of Brazil has always been found a valuable adviser to the Mission". His responsibilities, especially with regard to the abolition of the Slave Trade, would make it quite improper for him to engage once more in trade."

The Memorandum recognised that there was a further problem: the lack of any clear salary structure in the Foreign Service had resulted in many anomalies, with consuls at now unimportant ports receiving salaries quite out of proportion to the amount of work and responsibility they had to undertake. While Robert Hesketh, the senior consul in South America, was trying to raise his salary from £500 p.a., Mr. Ryan, the querulous Consul at the much less busy port of Pará, was receiving the same amount, and the Consul at Bahia was receiving £800, as was the Consul at Buenos Aires, who had much less work to do than Robert. The Memo suggested raising Robert's salary to at least £800 to match the Bahia and Buenos Aires posts. Lord Aberdeen, now Foreign Secretary, accepted the argument, commenting at the bottom of the Memo: "This appears to be just and proper. Abe."

All Consuls received, in addition to their salaries, Notarial Fees – small sums for issuing documents, and Consular Fees, which were related to the cargoes of British ships using the port. The system had, as with the salaries of Consuls, been allowed to grow up with little attempt at consistency or central control, and systems of charging varied greatly from country to country and even from port to port.

There were three basic systems in operation:
1. A fixed charge on all vessels, or
2. A fee based on each £100 of imported and exported goods, or
3. A levy on tonnage.

British consuls in Brazil adopted the second system. There were, of course, advantages and disadvantages to each system, and there were frequent complaints from merchants both in Britain and abroad about the inconsistent approach adopted by the Foreign Office. Parliament made attempts to tackle the issue in the 1830s, but without much determination or success.

Whichever system was in operation, Consular Fees could amount to a considerable amount of money, and a disproportionate amount of the total remuneration of a consul. Robert was getting an average of £1,181 p.a. in Fees from 1812 to 1818 at Maranhão, which was then a busy port, exporting vast quantities of locally-grown cotton. When Robert arrived in Rio in 1832, the Fees were £1,000 p.a., but they declined in subsequent years to £770 in 1835, and to £575.15s.0d. [£575.75p.] in 1844. Whilst the Foreign Office liked to take them into account in its estimation of salaries, it is clear that fluctuations in trade made it an unreliable measure. A sensible approach might have been to reduce the amount of Fees and their corresponding importance, and increase the basic salary, but the economy-minded legislators of the Commons never even gave the idea consideration.

It was also possible for a consul to supplement his salary in other ways – by acting as an agent either for Lloyds, the shipping agent, or for the Post Office in a few places. Robert had been the Lloyd's Agent in Maranhão, though he was clearly aware that, where a conflict of interest might arise, his first duty lay with his consular duties. In Rio, the British Post Office maintained an agency until late in the nineteenth century. One particular diplomatic problem at the Rio Post Office caused Robert a good deal of difficulty, and he subsequently took over responsibility for the good behaviour of the Post Office staff, receiving an annual fee for his trouble.

So, by one device or another, Robert raised his paltry salary in order to support his growing family. After he married Georgiana Raynsford in 1837, children arrived at frequent intervals, and by 1848, when Georgiana left Brazil for the last time, Robert and she had seven young dependants.

In his role of Consul at Maranhão and Ceará, one of Robert's responsibilities had been the oversight of the port of Belém, on the Amazon delta. It was over five hundred miles from Maranhão, and lay further north-west along the northern coast of Brazil, and was eighty miles inland from the Atlantic coast. Belém was the capital of Pará Province, and the natural marketplace for the vast range of forest products from the Amazon. Trade with Belém had slowly but steadily increased up to the end of the eighteenth century, but there was as yet no significant single product to catapult Belém into a major port. Only after the discovery of the uses of rubber – Goodyear invented the vulcanising process in 1844 – did *borracha* make Belém rich and prosperous. Before that, it was the export of timber, especially brazil-wood, and of the numerous food and drug products of the forest that kept the port busy. But increasing British interest in trade with the Amazon made it desirable to appoint a consular agent there, and in 1813, Robert suggested the appointment of Henry Dickenson.

Dickenson was strong-willed, imperious, and independent, and made full use of the miles and sailing-time that separated him from his superior in Maranhão. Robert Hesketh tried to seek his co-operation and support, but signally failed, and in 1824, with full support from the Foreign Secretary, Robert sacked him. The last straw had been an attempt by Dickenson to set up a British cavalry troop, completely at odds with every Foreign Office principle, in which British ex-patriates were expected to behave appropriately in their adopted countries.

The Vice-Consulship at Belém was therefore vacant. The British merchant community was small, and some of its members based up the Amazon hundreds of miles from Belém. Some of the merchants had worked hand-in-glove with Dickenson, and were therefore unsuitable and quite unacceptable to the Foreign Office. The only suitable candidate was a merchant who had moved out to Belém from Liverpool in 1819. By 1824, at the age of 33, he had established an import and export business in Belém. He was, of course, John Hesketh.

Robert knew the dangers of appointing his younger brother in place of a prominent and long-established resident. He was aware of Dickenson's propensity for making trouble, and of the likelihood that he would not forgive the man who had sacked him. Robert wrote to the merchant community in Pará firmly laying the blame for Dickenson's disobedience where it belonged: "If my instructions ... had been followed, then all this would have been unnecessary. He ignored my orders."[49] It was in full knowledge of this background that John nevertheless accepted the post, and with it, a life of some trouble and strife.

His appointment was fully supported by Mr. Secretary Canning, who noted that the appointment was to be "in the room of Mr. Dickenson", and conveyed to Robert "the approbation of Mr. Canning in regard to the conduct you have pursued ..."

However, political storm-clouds were gathering in Belém and the wider province of Pará, with a rebellion in 1823, another in 1831, and the most vicious of all Brazil's nineteenth century rebellions from 1835–9. John Hesketh's task was to protect British people and their property through all this troubled period.

In spite of George Canning's new emphasis on paid consuls and vice-consuls, John did not receive a salary for the first four years of his vice-consulship. He *did* receive a small amount of Notarial Fees during that period, and presumably a fairly small amount of Consular Fees, though Robert does not mention it. We shall look at John's financial misfortunes in a later chapter, but a disastrous commercial deal in 1829 left him in serious financial trouble. Robert made the case to the Foreign Office for a regular salary for John, and secured agreement not only to a salary of £200 p.a., but also to the payment of £800 in back-pay. The Treasury, however, refused to accept this, and John was allowed only £300 of back-pay for his four years of salary-less employment. Not only had he been unpaid, but he had had to spend his own money to allow him to fulfil the role of Vice-Consul: he swore on oath that he had expended a sum of 1450 *milreis* (over £180) on extra accommodation, the employment of a clerk, and stationery, all of which he needed to carry out his consular duties.

The events of the Cabanagem brought great stress to John, but also made his superiors aware of the value of his service, and almost straight after-wards, he was made up to full Consul. He then received a salary of £300, but later occupants of his post seemed to have fared better, with Robert Ryan receiving £500 upon his appointment in 1842.

It was standard diplomatic practice at the time to require each repre-sentative of a foreign government to be in possession of an "Exequatur", a document expressing the host government's permission to operate in its territory. When Robert took up his post in Maranhão, he signed the appro-priate "Procuration" in São Luis, but sent his brother William on the lengthy trip to Rio to acquire the "Exequatur" itself. It was soon realised in 1826 that John was the only British consular or diplomatic agent in Brazil not to possess an Exequatur, and John Bidwell of the newly-formed Consular Department in the Foreign Office wrote to Robert in Maranhão to ask him to ensure that an Exequatur was obtained.

Obtaining an Exequatur, particularly when John was so far from Rio in Belém, was a formidable task, but it seems to have been achieved without too much difficulty or expense on this occasion. It was a different story in 1836 when John was appointed as a full Consul in Pará. The Brazilian Government was now charging considerable amounts to issue the Exequatur – 138 *milreis* (£18) including fees to the Office of the Secretary of State, the

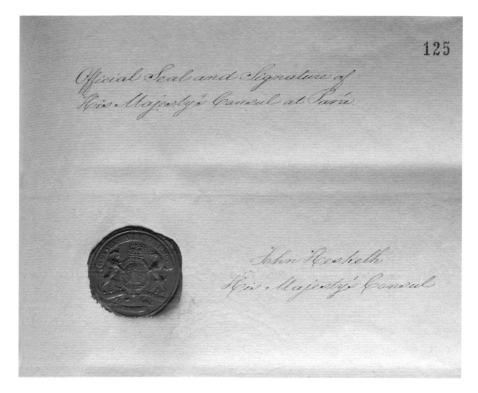

John Hesketh's official consular seal and signature

Office of Justice, the Chamber of Commerce, and 10 *milreis* for a Seal and sundry documents. The British Mission in Rio became agitated about this, and complained to Viscount Palmerston that Brazilian diplomats and consuls based in Great Britain got their Exequaturs free, but the Brazilian Government would not budge, and John had to pay. It was only later that his outlay was refunded by the Foreign Office.

Once the Exequatur was obtained, the consul or vice-consul could establish himself in his port, and could be there for many a long year. Leave of Absence was rare, had to be requested, and involved some financial sacrifice. A consul on leave had to pay from his own pocket for a deputy, and had to share the Fees obtained in his absence. But the decision as to his deputy was the consul's own, and all he had to do was to let Rio and the Foreign Office have a name. After his arrival in Maranhão in 1812, Robert Hesketh's first Leave of Absence was in 1817, when he returned to England, nominating his brother William as his deputy. His stay in England was affected by poor health, and he wrote to the Foreign Office early in 1818 regretting that he could not come to London, as he was ill in Liverpool. After his return to health and to Maranhão, he did not leave his post for a further eleven years. In asking for Leave of Absence in 1829, he says that he had not been more than "2 leagues" (six miles) from his house in the previous eleven years.

His 1829 Leave of Absence began in Belém where he visited his brother, John. The occasion was not a happy one, for it involved Robert's trying to sort out John's disastrous financial affairs. Robert paid out an enormous sum to help his brother – £5,140 – and he seems to have supported John's growing family with a further sum. Only then was he able to sail for England; there he wrote to the Foreign Office on his brother's behalf, pleading for a proper pay settlement for John.

Robert's next application for Leave of Absence was in 1836, after his move to Rio. It followed an unpleasant bout of illness, which his doctor called "a severe attack of inflammation of the Liver, with acute Dysentery". He was too weak to get up for most of March, 1836. His illness was compounded by his anxiety over John and his family, who were now refugees in Maranhão, and by his own financial worries – his Consular Fees were £300 down on the previous year. He sought permission to spend a few days in the cooler conditions of the Organ Mountains, a day's travel west of Rio, and then, on the advice of his doctor, asked to be allowed to return to England in the summer. Having pondered, however, on the financial implications of taking Leave of Absence – he would have to pay his deputy £150 during his absence – he seems to have decided to stay put, and returned to his post on 17 May, 1836.

Almost all the consuls and diplomats in Brazil complained about the climate and its sapping effect on their health. Robert seems to have lasted longer than most, but some complained early in their residence in Rio. W. G. Ouseley, who was Secretary to the Legation from 1832 to 1846, sent his family to the United States to live and be educated, partly because of the climate, and partly because Rio was so expensive. But the prize for the longest Leave of Absence goes to Hamilton Hamilton, the Envoy Extraordinary in Rio, who was absent from his post, mostly at home in England, for three years. Palmerston's patience, never his strongest point, was sorely tried by Hamilton Hamilton in all sorts of ways: by Hamilton's insistence that he have a steamer to take him and his luggage down from Portsmouth to Falmouth, by his insistence on a warship to take him out to Brazil ("beneath the dignity and the dignity of this country to go otherwise than in a man-of-war"[51]) and, above all, by Hamilton Hamilton's reluctance to return to Rio. In spite of the Hamiltons' absence from Rio for so long, Robert and his wife were friendly with them, so much so that they named their second daughter after Mrs. Hamilton, whose Christian name was Maria. The Heskeths reversed the names for their daughter, and called her "Hamilton Maria".

Robert's next Leave of Absence was not until 1847, when he returned to England, and Palmerston granted him a further six months' extension of his Leave. Some of Robert's official correspondence at this time comes from Titchfield, in Hampshire, from his newly-acquired house there. Robert returned home with the intention of setting up an English base for his wife and their children, for their next child, Hanbury Bold, was born in Titchfield on 26 July, 1848. Robert had had a recurrence of his medical problems, and he submitted a medical certificate dated 25 November, 1848, diagnosing stones on the bladder. He had obviously had a lithotomy operation, and his doctor, Dr. John Havers, F.R.C.S., recommended a further period of convalescence in England before he returned to Rio. He was back at his post in Brazil by April, 1850, and stayed there until his retirement in 1852. He left his wife and their children in Hampshire, and there is a census record of one of their sons, George – aged 11 – attending Stubbington House School near Fareham in 1851. Sadly, Hanbury Bold, the youngest child, died in May, 1852, before Robert retired permanently to England.

John Hesketh seems to have had even fewer opportunities for Leave of Absence. He was married to a Brazilian, so the attractions of returning to Great Britain would have been correspondingly less, and his only recorded visit to England was in 1836, after the flight of the Belém residents to Maranhão when the rebels took over the city. The foreign residents fled in September, 1835, and John was in London the following summer, keeping the Foreign Office informed of the progress of the Rebellion in Pará, and asking for restitution for his considerable losses. He was in Liverpool with his wife, Margarida, on 26 July, 1836, and back in Pará by the beginning of December that year.

The third Hesketh brother, William, who was a merchant in Sao Luis, Maranhão, had various spells as Robert's deputy during his absences from his post. His letters to the Foreign Office are straightforward and clear, and he seems to have held the fort quite adequately. He often calls himself "His (or Her) Majesty's Deputy Consul", though this seems not to have been the official designation. He had to deal with the Consulate through periods of disturbance in the province. Palmerston was obviously happy with his work, for he sent William a note of commendation:

"I have pleasure in signifying to you my approval of your conduct during the period that you have had charge of the Consulate."

Buoyed by this approval, William chanced his arm when Robert was transferred to Rio de Janeiro. William applied for the vacant post in Maranhão, but claimed to have found the £375 p.a. salary inadequate, and suggested that he would be happy to be appointed as full Consul at Maranhão, provided the salary was increased to £500 a year, which was the amount Robert had received towards the end of his time there. "No resident Merchant of Respectability acquainted with the duties of the Office would accept the post of Consul at Maranham at the salary of £300". Unfortunately for William, one did – John Moon, one of a family of merchants established in São Luis, and, like William, hailing from Liverpool.

The Monarch's pleasure at the appointment of a new consul was doubtless genuine, but the details of the appointment, together with salaries, fees, and allowances, were all left to the Foreign Office, and, as we have noted, the frequently changing direction of the political wind in London could be felt strongly in the foreign ports where the "British functionary" worked. Robert seems to have given his all at a time when the Foreign Office possessed strong leadership, but lacked system or consistency. Some years later, Lord Palmerston was asked whether improvements could be made, but could think of none. Any of the Hesketh brothers could have made some useful suggestions – that the Foreign Service would have benefited from a proper system for making appointments and promotions, from a consistency of approach where salaries and fees were concerned, and from steadiness and continuity of policy at its head. Mere consuls were, of course, never asked for their opinion, and, unlike H. Augustus Cowper in Pará in 1840, the Heskeths never had the front to take the initiative and make such suggestions. It is remarkable that diplomats and consuls served their country so well, given these official failings. Certainly, there is no hint of bitterness or resentment in any of the Robert's or John's communications with London – they simply got on with the task in hand.

6

THE EMPIRE OF THE BRAZILS

"... a rich, powerful, happy, and independent Empire ... Nature has adorned the face of this most favoured child." (Cowper, British Consul in Pará, 1841)

When Robert Hesketh arrived in Maranhão to take up his new post at São Luis in April, 1812, Brazil had just embarked on a period of dramatic change. After four centuries of colonial slumber, Brazil was on the move to nationhood.

In 1494, the Convent of Santa Clara in the small northern Spanish town of Tordesillas had hosted a meeting, where an agreement brokered by the Pope was reached. This set a line from north to south in South America, to mark out the division between any new territories acquired by the Kings of Spain and Portugal. Only six years later, in 1500, the Portuguese adventurer Cabral and his thirteen ships crossed the Atlantic, landed in Brazil, and named their new discovery the "Island of the Holy Cross". It soon became known as "Brazil" or "The Brazils" after one of its first exports – brazilwood. The Portuguese were not long alone – the French followed, setting up a settlement near what is now Rio de Janeiro, and establishing São Luis in the north. The Dutch also arrived to review the new continent, but were quickly squeezed out. So the Portuguese were left in possession of the field, and the Brazils were set fair to provide unlimited and vast wealth for perpetuity to the little home country on the west of the Iberian peninsula. The new colony was divided into "Captaincies", all being made responsible to Lisbon, without much in the way of co-operation or federation being required or encouraged. The consequences of that policy were to reverberate well into the Heskeths' residence in Brazil.

The country was not uninhabited – the early European settlers met clusters of Indians living all along the coast. There was at first no major conflict with the colonists, and it was only later, when the tribal hunting fields further inland were annexed by the newcomers for the raising of cattle, that some Indian tribes provided an aggressive challenge. But the Europeans possessed a secret weapon – contagious disease – which began to make serious inroads into the Indian population, the first epidemics in 1562–3 setting the pattern for two more centuries of reduction by contagion. Other European activity had a malevolent or at least a mixed effect on the Brazilian Indians. They were often chased and captured by the *bandeirantes* – freebooting white hunters – who enslaved or sold them. Others were collected together in the villages known as *aldeias* set up by the Jesuit fathers in order to educate, civilise, and Christianise them in a proper European fashion. This level of organisation was not always appreciated by the Indians, who frequently deserted the *aldeias* and resumed the freer life of the forest. After the Jesuits' forced departure from Portuguese dominions in 1759, there were many other attempts to find ways round the King of Portugal's prohibition on enslaving the Indians. The combined effect of these activities over the next four centuries, was to diminish their numbers quite dramatically. Those who remained lived on in many parts of inland Brazil, and Pará was unusual among the Brazilian ports in having the Indians as a regular feature of daily life. Many came to Belém in canoes to sell their products, and after a time a fair number settled in the vicinity of the city.

More obvious in the other ports of the North, the North-east, and Rio were the black African slaves. Almost every traveller in the nineteenth century who touched at Rio, or who travelled from the coastal cities of the north into the interior, mentions first of all the striking numbers of black slaves from Africa working and living in Brazilian cities. In the Heskeths' time, every third inhabitant of Brazil was a slave snatched from the barracoons of East and West Africa, and then brought over the Atlantic in appalling and dangerous conditions to serve the needs of a nation used to having all its physical work done for it. In Rio and the other cities, some slaves were given some flexibility, franchised to make money for their owners, but others carried out every physical task Brazilian society required, from carrying goods ashore from the ships in the harbour at Rio de Janeiro to carrying out the back-breaking toil involved in growing and transporting coffee or rice. Scarcely anyone in Brazil in the early nineteenth century could imagine civilised life without the slaves, and it took until 1888 for slavery to be finally abolished in Brazil. There has been no lack of attempts to count the number of slaves brought over to Brazil from the sixteenth century onwards, and estimate vary, sometimes widely, but four million seems a likely figure.[51] Nor was there a let-up in the trade in the Heskeths' time in Brazil, for the attempts of Great Britain to pressurise Brazil into abolishing the trade seemed only to encourage it.

Slavery had become an integral part of Brazilian life as soon as the need for intensive agriculture manifested itself. After the first exports of timber, the cultivation of sugar was developed, estates or *fazendas* being established

African slaves bringing coffee down from the mountains to Rio de Janeiro

behind the ports of the north-east coast. The developing European taste for sweet drinks soon ensured a regular export trade, and the level of Brazil's production swiftly put paid to lesser sugar economies, like that of Madeira. Sugar required a great deal of physical effort: to clear the ground, to plant the canes, to cut them, to crush the cane, and then to process the juice. Steam was not widely available for the process until almost half-way through the nineteenth century. Until then, all labour was provided by the bodies of slaves.

In the eighteenth century, coffee began to ease out sugar as the main Brazilian export crop, and again, the slaves carried out the back-breaking tasks of clearing the ground, planting the bushes, caring for them, picking the beans, preparing them for packing, and then conveying them to the ships which would carry them to Europe. In Maranhão and the surrounding areas, cotton, which had been formerly grown for home use only, began to acquire a large export market. Robert Hesketh and Company in São Luis was one of the small group of British firms to take advantage of the new trade.

All these export crops depended on the availability of very cheap labour. In the 1820s and 1830s, as well as later, attempts were made to attract European immigrants to Brazil to provide the manpower for the growing Brazilian economy, and even though some considerable communities of Germans and Italians and others were founded, European immigration did not succeed to any great extent until much later. Certainly, until the supply of African slaves dried up in the 1850s, few in Europe, however hard their plight at home, wanted to become white slaves. The Irish seem to have been particularly unlucky. Shipments of Irishmen seem to have been regarded with particular disdain by the Brazilians, and even an attempt to build up an Irish battalion to augment the Brazilian Army in 1826 foundered on the rock of Brazilian apathy. Their quarters by the idyllic beach of Praia Vermelho near Rio did not disguise the terrible food and the neglect of their welfare.

So the labour of the slaves was the engine that drove the bulk of Brazilian production. But there was one kind of product that had excited the Portuguese in the seventeenth century and beyond – gold, and to a lesser extent, silver. The precious metals had been discovered in the region north of Rio called later *Minais Gerais* – "general mines". Vast amounts of gold and silver were produced, and shipped over the Atlantic back to Portugal. Not all of it stayed there, and there seems to have been a lucrative trade in smuggling Brazilian gold into many other parts of Europe, including Great Britain.

With all these products, and with the realisation on the part of nearly every Brazilian that the country contained untold resources, Brazil began to look rather too large for its small European parent nation to handle. Throughout the eighteenth century, there were very strict prohibitions on trade with the rest of the world. Only Portuguese merchants and Portuguese ships were allowed to carry the wealth of Brazil back to Europe. But back in Portugal, much of the trade was in the hands of merchants from many European nations. The British had a pre-eminent position in Lisbon and Porto, but others like the French, the Germans, and the Dutch also played a significant part. We have already noted that the Hesketh brothers' father, John, working as a wine merchant in Porto, was offered some of the first cotton to cross the Atlantic, and passed it on to his uncle William in Liverpool, to see if there was a market for it.

The British influence on Portugal had a long history. The political fortunes of the two countries began to be linked in the fourteenth century, and well before the Methuen Treaty of 1703, there were other treaties. The Methuen Treaty had encouraged both trade and mutual defence between Portugal and Great Britain, though the latter, larger and more powerful, undoubtedly wielded the upper hand. In the mid-eighteenth century, the Marquis of Pombal, in charge of Portuguese government policy and practice, made a determined attempt to defend and develop the Portuguese economy. "The English," said Pombal, "had firmly bound the nation in a state of dependence."[52] Almost everyone in Portugal wore English woollens and used English domestic goods, which were exchanged for Newfoundland fish caught by the Portuguese, and for Portuguese wine.

Not that the relationship between the two nations was entirely one-sided. Pombal was not to know that when the French threatened to overrun Portugal fifty years later, only Great Britain was willing to save it. And it was this event which, in many senses, propelled Brazil forward, and removed it from the power and influence of Portugal. The oversized adolescent was about to come of age, and the Heskeths had a good view of the process on both sides of the Atlantic.

In 1802, John Whitehead, the British Consul in Porto, Portugal, died, and was buried with affectionate ceremony by the merchants of the city, and a dignified monument erected in the middle of the new British Cemetery. John Hesketh, Robert, John, and William's father, was one of three to sign the will, and was doubtless present at the funeral obsequies. That peaceful moment was not to last, for, in spite of the defeat of the French and Spanish fleets at Trafalgar, and Cochrane's commando raids on French communications in northern Spain, Napoleon's armies were occupying the Iberian Peninsula, and threatening to overrun Portugal. Napoleon gave João, the Prince Regent, an ultimatum: imprison the British in Portugal or face the consequences. João, acting for his mentally-ill mother, Maria, did neither. Instead, encouraged by the British Government, he made extraordinarily speedy plans to leave Portugal. Within four days, he had assembled thirty-six ships, fifteen thousand people, and the contents of his Treasury and of his Royal Library. He boarded his flagship, the "Principe Real", which carried no less than sixteen hundred people. On the 29 November, 1807, the vast fleet, accompanied by four British men-of-war commanded by Admiral Sir Sidney Smith, left the River Tagus, and sailed out into the Atlantic bound for the Portuguese colony of Brazil. They were only just in time, for the French arrived in the capital to see the topsails of the Portuguese fleet receding into the distance.

After a very difficult voyage, with storms tossing the ships about, little food, and outbreaks of smallpox and lice affecting the noble but overcrowded passengers, landfall was finally made in late January at Bahia. João and his court then sailed south, arriving in Rio de Janeiro in March, 1808. The transfer of the Court, and, with it, the whole panoply of the state, was an extraordinary event, unparalleled in history.

There is little doubt that João and his court thought the stay in Rio de

A Royal procession in Rio – distributing the Host to members of the Court

Janeiro would not be of long duration, but João, for all his reputation for caution and hesitancy, made some fairly speedy decisions that would have a profound effect on the course of Brazilian history. The first, which he made with astonishing speed on his first landfall in Brazil, was to announce that henceforward, Brazilian ports would be open to foreign trade. In a stroke, this removed much of Brazil's colonial status, and gave it the same trading position as the occupied mother-country. The second decision was equally momentous – to develop the rusty administrative mechanism of the colonial capital into the full-blown machinery of a national government.

The result was that Rio de Janeiro instantly became a capital city. Palaces, monasteries, and convents were quickly converted for royal and governmental use, and the organs of government were quickly established. There was no shortage of bureaucratic manpower, for jobs had to be found for the hundreds of court and public functionaries who had been landed on the Palace Stairs on the Rio waterfront. A vast building programme began, both of public buildings and of private dwellings. One of the best witnesses to this rapid growth was the English merchant, John Luccock, who visited Rio in both 1808 and 1818. His breakdown of the population in 1808 shows the unbalanced nature of Rio society in that year. He lists no fewer than a thousand court officials, and a thousand public functionaries, together with seven hundred priests and five hundred lawyers. Even larger was the number of slaves in the city – twelve thousand – to serve the varied physical needs of this new community. When Luccock again surveyed the city in 1818, the infirm Queen Maria was dead, and the Prince Regent, João, had been crowned king. The people of Rio were by now quite used to living in his capital city. The population had doubled, but the city had become cleaner, and a more efficient police force had been organised. Women were no longer hidden behind the *gelosias* or shaded balconies, which had been officially banned on the grounds of security, and new colleges, schools, and hospitals had been built. A Botanical Garden had been established, and the Customs-House enlarged. New country-houses were being built over a wide area. "Even scavengers [refuse-collectors] were now and then seen in the streets."[53]

Elsewhere in Brazil, however, matters were less satisfactory. Rio's growth and prosperity were envied by Bahia and Pernambuco to the north, who resented the diminution in their own roles. The cities of the far north, São Luis and Belém, were so far from Rio de Janeiro, that it was quicker to sail to Lisbon than to the new capital. They both had many merchants and military men, who saw themselves as entirely Portuguese. They looked askance at the new developments, and saw no reason why they should re-align their loyalties to Rio. It was only forty years since Pará had given up its own independence, and its hinterland of Amazonia provided it with a strong power-base, particularly as other nations were eyeing its rich resources with great interest.

São Luis de Maranhão had prospered over the previous decade or two, largely because of its cotton and rice exports, and was now the fourth most important port in Brazil. Its garrison was composed largely of Portuguese soldiers, who were unwilling to kow-tow to the edicts from Rio. As early as 1817, Robert Hesketh was reporting on the atmosphere in São Luis: "all [are] sighing for an amendment, at the same time fearing the inevitable risks to Life and Property in a revolution."[54]

These tensions and disagreements, and many more besides, were to accompany the Brazilian colony on its journey into nationhood, and though outright national revolution never occurred, Brazil remained an unsettled and quarrelsome country for the next forty years, a period coinciding almost exactly with the time that Robert, John, and William Hesketh lived and worked in Brazil. The Hesketh brothers had plenty of opportunity to observe the birth-pangs of one of the largest nations on earth. Every region, including Rio de Janeiro itself, suffered at one time or another from civil and military strife. The underlying source of tension was the question of Brazil's own destiny – colony or kingdom – but each region had its own distinctive mix of political, religious, and social complaints. Portuguese-born were set against Brazilian-born, monarchist against republican, rich against poor, black against white, freeman against slave, radical against traditionalist, centralist against seceder, Catholic against free-thinker, and all against foreigners. Sometimes strange alliances occurred, with Catholic priests, for instance, leading the radical camp, and white men leading blacks into rebellion.

It was unfortunate that the armed forces were hardly adequate to deal with any military or naval crisis across this vast land. Soldiers were small in number and badly paid, and there was a marked class division between officers and men. The officers were largely Portuguese-born, and the men black or mulatto. The Portuguese navy was inefficient and poorly trained, and had never fought a successful engagement in Brazilian waters. This military weakness contributed to the numerous revolts, risings, and disturbances which afflicted all parts of Brazil in the first years of its independence. The Heskeths became personally involved in the disturbances, in spite of their best efforts to remain suitably aloof from Brazilian politics.

1821 marked the end of the fairly beneficent reign of João VI – the historian Leslie Bethell calls it "enlightened absolutism"[55] Joâo had been put under enormous pressure to return to Portugal. The clamour for his return redoubled after the end of the Napoleonic Wars in 1815, and he eventually felt he could resist it no longer. He was encouraged in this by two of his sons, Pedro and Miguel, who stood to gain by his departure. It has even been suggested that Pedro played some part in fomenting the civil unrest which preceded João's decision to go home. In the end, João bowed to the inevitable, at the same time being aware that Brazil could never return to its former docile state. In Robert Southey's words: "So heavy a branch cannot long remain on so rotten a trunk."[56] It was, writes Alan Manchester: "emancipated, economically, from the decadent mother-country"[57]. It was not long after João VI returned to Portugal, again in a British warship with four thousand followers, that the Cortes, the Portuguese parliament, began to pressurise Pedro, whom João had left in Rio, to return home and obediently to exercise the functions of a crown prince. They added to this some gratuitous insults to the Brazilians – one speaker said it was "a land of monkeys, of little negroes gathered from the shores of Africa, and of bananas".[58] But Pedro was not to be bullied, and had a taste for the dramatic. Only eight months after his father's departure, on 9 January, 1822, Pedro announced that he was staying – the *Dia do Fico* ["I Shall Stay Day"], and the following

September, he uttered the fatal cry beside the Ipiranga brook near São Paulo: "Independence or death".

And so a great nation was born. All three Hesketh brothers were established in Brazil at this point, and nowhere in their letters home is there any hint of unease with this turn of events. Their attitude was shared by most Britons and certainly by the British Government. Commerce with Great Britain was likely only to benefit from the independence of Brazil. But the atmosphere of all Brazilian cities was tense. Consul Parkinson describes the tensions in Pernambuco in 1825 as the British envoy, Sir Charles Stuart negotiated with the Emperor Pedro about the independence of the nation: "A very anxious feeling here persists re Sir Charles Stuart – the Portuguese residents openly exult... whilst the Brazilians are downcast at the bare thought of the Emperor of their choice compromising their new dignity and independence by anything of the nature of a coalition with Portugal."[59]

At home, Canning did not discourage the declaration of the independence of Brazil, although he hoped it would steer clear of the revolutionary and anti-monarchical fervour displayed by almost all of the Spanish colonies in Latin America. He sent Sir Charles Stuart first to Lisbon to acquire the right to represent the Portuguese, and then to Rio, to negotiate a settlement between the mother-country and its rumbustious and over-grown child. Stuart emerged with an agreement – under which Brazil had to pay two million pounds sterling to Portugal for the loss of its profitable colony. And so – slowly – Portugal and the world accepted the *fait accompli*, and Brazil could get on with its nation-building.

True to his word, Pedro I did stay, at least for ten turbulent years. During that time, he wrote a Constitution, created an elected Assembly, dissolved it, made war in the south, spent a deal of time riding and hunting, spent just as much time with his mistress, Domitilla de Castro e Melo and their children, was credited in some quarters with hounding his first wife, Princess Leopoldina, to death, and married again. Barely out of his twenties, he finally faced the fact that he too must go home to Portugal to settle the succession after his father's death in 1826. There he became involved in a protracted war with his unprincipled brother Miguel, who had taken advantage of Pedro's absence to claim the Portuguese throne.

But Pedro left behind a small son – also called Pedro. Regents were hastily appointed, and Brazil now had a Brazilian-born heir to the throne, and, at last, an end to the acrimonious dispute about the crown with Portugal. That did not create instant peace in the new empire, and the ten years between Pedro I's departure in 1831, and the accession of Pedro II in 1841, were one of the most disturbed periods in Brazil's political history.

Regent succeeded Regent, and only the crowning of the fifteen-year old Pedro II in 1841 achieved some political calm and stability.

If the Hesketh brothers had been of almost any other nation, their working lives would have been less complicated. But Great Britain managed to get itself embroiled in Brazilian affairs in a way that had profound implications for British diplomats and consuls, affecting not only their daily work, but sometimes their personal safety as well. Wellington had saved Portugal by stopping the French in their tracks in the hills and pine-woods of Torres Vedras north of Lisbon, and then driven them before him back to their native land. The British Navy had taken responsibility for escorting the Portuguese court to Rio de Janeiro. British political support remained a strong feature of Portuguese and Brazilian life. "With England's friendship," said the Marquis of Barbacena in 1825, "we can snap our fingers at the rest of the world".[60] But British support was at times an uncomfortable burden.

Great Britain, moreover, was not entirely philanthropic in its motives. There is not the slightest doubt that Castlereagh, Canning, Palmerston, and the Earl of Aberdeen, the four great Foreign Secretaries of the period, were not interested in adding Brazil to the British Empire – in any case, the latter concept had not yet been invented. But they *were* interested in doing all they could to encourage British commerce with the emergent nation. The "Treaty of Alliance and Friendship" of 1810 and the separate "Treaty of Commerce and Navigation" set the tone, and resulted in special lower tariffs for British products in Brazil, not matched by corresponding tariff reductions in Britain for Brazil. Indeed, to protect Britain's colonies in the West Indies, Brazilian sugar and coffee were not allowed into Great Britain at all. But freedom of worship was guaranteed to British subjects in Brazil, and a packet-boat service was set up between the two countries. Initially, only British warships were allowed in Brazilian ports, and there were restrictions on Brazilian involvement in the Slave Trade. A further Treaty in 1817 gave the British Navy privileges to stop and search vessels for slaves, which remained the issue most likely to inflame Brazilian opinion. The post-independence Treaty of 1826 protected British merchants, British consuls, and British trade, and in theory at least committed the Brazilians to abolishing the Slave Trade by 1829. A great deal of time and effort in the Foreign Office was spent on the relationship with Brazil, as well as on the development of the new Spanish republics of South America.

There was, however, a cost to all this. The Brazilians began to get the impression that Great Britain was only interested in her own welfare. The modern Brazilian historian José H. Rodrigues talks of "ignominious treaties", dominating Brazil, "harming her interests, threatening her, obtaining concessions and privileges that would be inconsistent today", but he also adds that "it was also on Great Britain that her independence and her sovereignty depended."[61]

As British pressure on Brazil's involvement in the slave trade mounted, the Brazilians developed a distinctive way of dealing with Great Britain. Consul Pennell in Bahia was aware of the technique: "Brazilians seem to regard the Treaties with England on the Slave Trade as the dictation of a superior authority, from which it is lawful to escape, rather than as compacts, which they are bound to enforce."[62] "Polite inertia" was the approach. A regular theme of the consuls' despatches to the Foreign Office was the way in which the provisions of the treaties were ignored, often by the Juntas in various ports not following the agreed tariffs on imported goods. There was strong feeling against France too, whose powerful navy was much in evidence, but it was the British who seemed to touch the rawest Brazilian nerve. Jozé de Rocha said in 1842: ""If there is today a generalised & highly popular idea in the country, it is that England is our most treacherous & persistent enemy".[65] That was written at a time when tempers were running high in Brazil over the insistence of Great Britain that Brazil should abolish its Slave Trade. The feeling was particularly strong in the ports where merchants made fortunes out of importing slaves, exactly the ports where British consuls were active every day.

This brave defiance, at odds with wiser counsels, has nevertheless left its mark on Brazil's attitude to nineteenth-century Great Britain. It is, therefore, not entirely surprising for a modern Brazilian historian to maintain the ambivalence of the Brazilians of the time. José H. Rodrigues, in "The Foundations of Brazil's Foreign Policy" (1962) makes the rather extraordinary observation that "Brazil never betrayed her interests except on paper"![64] Great Britain placed a lot of reliance on the paper of the Treaties, and saw Brazil's cavalier attitude to its solemn promises as a sign of moral decadence.

Committed to it, the Hesketh brothers found Britain's anti-slavery campaign particularly painful, as we shall see in a later chapter. Even before this issue became so large a bone of contention, anti-British feeling sometimes welled up. Carvalho was the leader of an anti-Rio revolution in Pernambuco, and when the revolution was overthrown, saved himself by taking to a raft and sailing out to sea. As luck would have it, he was picked up by H.M.S. "Tweed", and the British were then accused of sheltering a fugitive from Imperial justice.

Brazilian feeling about the British was complicated by the fact that its infant Navy was staffed and led very largely by British sailors. It was a famous British sea-captain, Lord Cochrane, fresh from his triumphs on the other side of the continent, in Chile and Peru, who took over the Brazilian Navy in 1822. He actively encouraged British seamen to desert and join the Brazilian Navy ships. With his usual mixture of efficiency and trickery, he snuffed out anti-Imperial feeling all the way north from Rio as far as São Luis and Pará. In spite of this, there was inevitably doubt about the commitment of the Admiral to Brazil, doubt not removed when Cochrane sailed the Brazilian frigate "Piranga" to Portsmouth without Brazilian permission, citing rather unconvincingly the condition of her masts and spars and the direction of the wind. In view of this, it is not surprising that Brazilian confusion about its Navy's nationality continued, and has even bedevilled later history.

Brazil, rising from the somnolence of its colonial past, was certainly not a dull place to be in the early nineteenth century. Representing a great but unpopular ally in a turbulent new society had its excitements and its pressures. The vicious Cabanagem Rebellion in Pará may well have contributed to John Hesketh's early death in 1838, but Robert and William lasted longer, living through the end of the Regency in 1841, the beginning of the reign of the young Emperor Pedro II, and the passing of the Queiroz Law in 1850, which was the first effective Brazilian measure against its slave trade. Robert retired to England in 1852, but William stayed in Brazil until his death in 1856, when peace had begun to settle on the young Empire. The end of the 1880s saw two significant events – the total abolition of slavery in Brazil in 1888, and the ousting of Pedro II as Emperor the following year, with a republic set up in 1891.

Ahead lay the industrial development of the fifth largest country in the world, the gradual exploitation of its mineral wealth, and the controversial destruction of vast swathes of its rain-forests. Ahead too lay unrest over land reform, the continued contrast between the fortunes of the rich and the poor, and the authoritarian regimes of the twentieth century. By 2022, two hundred years after its independence was declared, it is to be hoped that Brazil will be able to fulfil the hopes that its founders had, of peace and prosperity, or as the national banner has it, of *Ordem e Progresso*.

7

THE CONSUL'S DAILY LIFE

"...There was little glamour in being a consul, but there was also little work at any but the most important ports." C.R. Middleton.[65]

The Hesketh brothers may have enthusiastically agreed with the first part of Middleton's rather sweeping conclusion, but probably not with the second.

There is no doubt, for example, that at Rio de Janeiro the Consul was run off his feet, largely because of the volume of British shipping entering and leaving the port. This meant that the quantity of goods entering and leaving the Custom-House was also very considerable, especially as Rio served as a staging-post for exports destined for many other parts of South America. Rio was also a natural stopping-place for ships bound for India, for the east coast of Africa, and for Australia and New Zealand. Ships bound for these distant places called in at Rio for water and other supplies before heading for the Cape of Good Hope and the Indian and Southern Oceans. In addition, the determination of Great Britain to force Brazil into abolishing the Slave Trade brought with it a great deal of work for the Consul. Politics too had their effect: the presence of the Imperial Court and of the Brazilian Government in Rio meant that the British diplomatic representatives in the city needed accurate and speedy commercial information – who better to ask than the local Consul, who had been a merchant himself?

The other Brazilian ports, whilst not suffering from these particular pressures, had their own distinctive activities. Of the three Hesketh brothers, John in Belém probably had the smallest number of British ships arriving and leaving his port, and consequently the lowest level of trade. At the same time, he had a particularly difficult group of merchants to deal with, and responsibility for the safety of the British community and their property in an almost unbroken series of rebellions and revolutions. This political turmoil naturally depressed trade, which accounts at least in part for the lower level of trading between Great Britain and Pará.

In São Luis, the level of trade was higher than in Belém, but political instability again took its toll, and the Consul in Maranhão also had the supervision of the Vice-Consul in Pará, which during Henry Dickenson's tenure of the latter post, caused Robert Hesketh a great deal of extra work.

Nevertheless, it is generally true that some ports did not offer a great deal of regular work, as long as not too many crises occurred. It is also true that the Foreign Office was not speedy in its reaction to changing patterns of trade, and there are cases on record during the nineteenth century when some consuls in ports which had lost their earlier commercial importance led a very peaceful and untroubled life, often at an unrealistically high salary. Nevertheless, even a consul in the sleepiest of tropical ports had to fulfil some basic duties.

The first duty, as we have seen, was to send regular despatches back to the Foreign Office. There were difficulties, however. Castlereagh's requirement that a despatch should be sent every week could only be complied with if there was an available ship heading to Britain or at least to Europe. There were regular packet-boats travelling out from Falmouth to Rio de Janeiro, São Luis, and Pará, but inclement winds, rough seas, damage to boats, or even enemy hostilities, for instance in the American War of 1812, could interfere with the arrangement. If the consul worked in a smaller port, there was no guarantee that a ship would be available on a regular basis. The Foreign Office's insistence that each despatch should have a single subject meant that several despatches might need to be sent at the same time. The National Archive Records contain many letters that are simply elaborate acknowledgements of the receipt of official memos or circulars, but others deal with a very wide range of subjects, from revolution to taxes, and from church matters to British burial grounds. The despatches, it will be recalled, had to be written on standard-sized paper, and written in black ink. The lack of carbon paper, or of any other copying device, meant that every despatch sent had to have a copy kept in the Consul's Office, and that meant that either the consul had to copy it out, or, if he was lucky enough to have a clerk, get him to do it. The vast majority of the despatches sent by the Heskeths, some of them of great length, were penned by themselves.

Another regular requirement was the writing of six-monthly Naval and Trade Reports. The Naval Report, many examples of which exist in the Foreign Office records, required a careful note of the name of every ship entering and leaving the port, with the name of its Master, the number of its crew, its tonnage, its cargo, and either its originating port, its destination, or both. Details of Ships of War had also to be noted down, along with other official ships such as Packets and convict-ships. Summaries of ships from particular nations were often appended, and it is curious to see representatives of the shipping of such long-superseded countries as the Two Sicilies, Genoa, the Hanseatic League, and Tuscany. Ships trading under the Brazilian flag feature very frequently, and it is easy to forget that this was, at the time, the only practical way for contact to be kept up between the far-distant provinces of this vast land, with its three-thousand mile coastline.

The Naval Report, which must have given some useful information if anyone at the Foreign Office had the time or inclination to analyse it, was matched by a Trade Report, which clearly must, in some cases, have taken some considerable time to write. It analysed trends in commerce, noting down products which were imported or exported in particular strength, and compared the volume of trading with different countries. There are years, for example, when John Hesketh in Belém was noting an upsurge in trade with the United States, or perhaps a decline in trade with France or Great Britain. The Foreign Office saw itself as merely a post-box for the Trade Reports, and passed them on largely unread to the Board of Trade. There is some doubt as to whether the latter took full advantage of the information they contained.

Another regular duty was the calling and administration of meetings, usually for the merchants working in the port. In the Foreign Office records, there are many examples of the minutes of local meetings, often again about such subjects as the local British or Protestant church, the British burial ground, or the British Hospital, if there was one. Every commercial firm in the port seemed to have a view on these non-commercial matters, perhaps understandably, for they were expected to raise at least half the revenue locally for their maintenance. In times of crisis, meetings were often called at very short notice, with the minutes being required to be sent back to London at the earliest opportunity. The minutes make it plain that these meetings were not always peaceful or harmonious affairs. Not only did the consul have to chair the meeting and often write up the minutes himself, but he had to represent the position of His or Her Majesty's Government – not always sympathetically heard by the local merchants – and try to steer the meeting to a realistic and proper decision. At its best, the consul's skill in chairing the meeting was appreciated, as it was in Rio in 1841, when a vote of thanks was conveyed to Robert Hesketh after a difficult meeting, it being proposed that "thanks at this meeting be given to the Consul for his attentive and impartial conduct".[66]

The consul was usually the channel for informing the local British community of news from back home. Back in Portugal, for example, the British Consul in Porto acknowledged the death of King George III's daughter, Princess Amelia, in 1787, and reported that "I communicated this Event to His Majesty's faithfull subjects in this City, who with me sincerely take part in the General Affliction upon the sorrowful Occasion."[67] In 1798,

Crispin, British Consul in Lisbon, reported: "The Princess of Brazil was yesterday safely delivered of a Prince, at the Palace of Queluz" near Lisbon[68] – significant because this prince was the future Prince Pedro, destined to be the first Emperor of an independent Brazil. In Brazil, the consuls announced the news of the death of King William IV in 1836, and the accession of Queen Victoria. In 1842 Henry Dickenson seems to have made up for his former improper conduct by a fine show of patriotism – flying the Union Jack, "brilliantly" illuminating the Consulate and his house – on the occasion of the birth of a son to Queen Victoria – the future King Edward VII.[69]

The Consul's fellow-merchants will doubtless have kept him up to the mark where the administration of fees was concerned. Especially if he was also a merchant, he would be well aware of local difficulties, and might spend a great deal of time negotiating with the officers of the Custom-House. In 1822, Robert Hesketh reported from São Luis that the 1810 Treaty between Great Britain and Brazil was not being properly observed, and that there were problems with the costs of anchorage, with importation fees, and with the effective protection of the lives and property of British citizens. British citizens and their consuls are frequently to be observed quoting the articles of the 1810 and later Treaties, and comparing their provisions with the reality of provincial practice. Given the increasing unpopularity of Great Britain and its policies during this period, it is easy to see how distance from Rio might encourage some political point-scoring against its "favoured nation" status. In 1830, William Hesketh, temporarily in charge in São Luis, voices complaints from resident merchants there that, firstly, dues had increased by up to 100% or 150% following instructions from Rio earlier in the year, and, secondly, that the local Junta was requiring payment of the dues in a specialised form – ¾ in silver, which had to be proved, causing a delay, and ¼ in copper coin, which was notoriously easy to forge, and which had consequently lost much of its value. The result was that British merchants were not paying the 15% laid down in the Treaties, but 20%, which gave them no advantage over any other nation, contrary to the 1810 Treaty.

Another duty of the consul was to administer and account for the "Contribution Fund". Each port had its Fund, to which the local British merchants were expected to contribute fairly handsomely, and which was in some ways a relic of the time when the merchants in a foreign port paid for their own consul. Robert Hesketh explained the São Luis and Pará arrangement in a letter to the Foreign Office in 1819.[70] "At both Maranhão and Pará, one-fifteenth of the Fund's annual income went to the Consul-General in Rio. As questions had been raised in the House of Commons about the vast sum the Consul-General, Mr. Chamberlain, was already getting from other sources, this extra contribution does seem a little unnecessary, but time and custom had hallowed it. One-third went to the Consul himself in Maranhão, and in Pará, one-third was shared between the Vice-Consul there and the Consul in Maranhão. That added up to 6/15ths. of the total, leaving 9/15ths. to finance chapels, hospitals, burial grounds, and any other local facility. The usual arrangement was that the British Government would pay half of any approved expenditure, though it is obvious from their sometimes suspicious tone that local communities of merchants experienced in financial matters were quite capable of some creative accounting. A frequent cause of difficulty was that the local merchants, having met for a meeting, like businessmen of any era, could not see why they could not make an instant decision, forgetting that the Foreign Office had to be asked for its agreement – a lengthy process. The British community in Rio got itself into considerable difficulty on several occasions in relation to their Chaplain. They decided at one point to increase his salary to the very handsome sum of £700 p.a., which was far more than the Consul himself was getting. The Foreign Office strongly disapproved, and refused to pay its 50% of the increase. On another occasion, they arranged for an appointment board to decide who their next chaplain was to be, quite forgetting that they needed the approval of the Bishop of London, as well as that of the Foreign Secretary.

Robert Hesketh seems to have presided over a very successful Contribution Fund in São Luis in the 1820s, so much so that he was asked in 1826 to reduce the scale of the Fund by sending to His Majesty's Exchequer moneys in the Contribution Fund, and to sell some investments they had made.

The Contribution Fund also helped to pay for the "Judge Conservator" in the larger ports. This was an arrangement, agreed by treaty, whereby the British community was regulated by its own judicial officer. The idea was not new, and had been part of the British-Portuguese alliance arrangements for several centuries. France had a scheme even more beneficial to its citizens, who were judged not only by their own judicial officer, but also according to French law. Rio and São Luis both had British Judge Conservators during the period, and the Consul was responsible for their appointment, their efficiency, and their pay. The Judge Conservators were generally, but not invariably, Brazilian lawyers, and their judgements did not always please those British who were brought before them. Rio had a British Judge Conservator for some time, until he was ousted after seeming to take the side of Portuguese slavers and slave-owners during the 1840s.

We know that the Judge Conservator often had a legal officer to help

The *Alfandega* or Custom-House in Belém

him, as Judge Francisco Paulo Pereira Duarte did at Maranhão in 1826. In that year, the Foreign Office issued instructions to the South American consuls at Bahia, Pernambuco, and Maranhão about the arrangements for Judge Conservators in a circular.[71] In Maranhão, the Governor seems to have had some influence over the local British Judge Conservator, and Robert Hesketh was not pleased when, without referring to him, the Judge Conservator was ordered to investigate what had happened to the clothes of six deserting seamen from the ship "Return". The Judge Conservator ordered the forcible boarding of the ship, and the restoration of the clothing to the men.

Pará had no Judge Conservator, although John Hesketh wrote to the Foreign Office in 1830 to enquire about the possibility of appointing one: he was smartly reminded that the details he sought were in the 1826 Circular. It turned out that a copy of this Circular had been sent only to his superior in Maranhão, and he had therefore not seen it.[72] In the event, a Judge Conservator was not appointed in Pará, and the local British community seems to have got used to using the local courts – to the profound disapproval of Consul Robert Ryan in the 1840s, who thought it was quite undignified for British merchants to be suing each other in Brazilian courts[73] In 1837,

Charles Coleman, a British merchant in Pará, was accused of *estelionato* (fraud), and instead of being referred to an unbribable Judge Conservator, had it suggested to him by some locals that he bribe sixty possible jurors in his case with 500 milreis each (£62.50), which would have cost the merchant the total of £3,750.

Brazil did not much like the system of Judge Conservators, and tried to abolish it unilaterally in 1835, but the Foreign Office was adamant that the system was part of the agreed Treaty obligations to which Brazil had signed up, and the system survived for many more years after that, though it continued to be a bone of contention.

The consul was also responsible for another official duty – the keeping of records on births and marriages. This seems simply to have involved a declaration of the authenticity of the Chaplain's signature where a British Chaplain was at work, as at Rio. Elsewhere, the consul was authorised to conduct a marriage if no clergyman was available. The recording system does not seem to have been very efficient, with consuls having to be reminded at regular intervals that they must send back details. There are no records of marriages in Pará during John Hesketh's time, and there is apparently no record of his own marriage. As it was to a Brazilian girl, it may well have been conducted in a local Roman Catholic church. His children do not seem to have been baptised, at least in a Protestant church, and one of the first things that John's elder sister, Louisa, did when three of his sons were sent back to her in Liverpool was to have them promptly baptised according to the rites of the Church of England.

Most consuls will have quickly built up their expertise as a result of very close daily contact with merchants and seafarers, as well as years of their own experience of business. Consular duties were heavily biased towards the trouble-free maintenance of good commercial activity. Much of their time seems to have been spent meeting ships' masters, and advising them on the strict Brazilian port and custom-house procedures. No-one could come ashore until the "health-boat" had visited the newly-arrived ship, to check that no contagious disease was on board. A French visitor in 1830, Jean Narcisse Metayer, described this process, which he called *La Santé*, and which involved a doctor, his assistant, and two negro soldiers.[74] Then the customs officers would make an official visit. This could be a cheerful occasion – Koster gives an account of a very convivial visit in 1815 to a British brig which had just arrived in São Luis: "As the brig came up the harbour, we received the health and custom-house visit. It was composed of several well-dressed men, some of whom wore cocked hats and swords, and all of them ate much bread, and drank quantities of porter."[75]

Unloading the ship and transferring the goods to the Custom-House was strictly regulated, and there was a rigid set of rules over fees. For much of the period, British ships should have been charged only 15% duty on imports, whereas other nations had to pay 20%. Insisting on their rights as guaranteed by treaty cannot have made British merchants immensely popular, either with the local politicians or with merchants of other countries, and much must have depended on the diplomatic skills of the consul to keep matters calm. The Hesketh brothers seem for the most part to have retained the goodwill of the local juntas, though Robert had some trouble with the local regime in São Luis during the commotions of the 1820s, and John had to enter fairly spirited protests on occasion. One of the last problems he had to deal with before his death concerned what he saw as the highly prejudicial treatment by the Custom-House officials of a British mulatto captain in Belém.

The consul's daily life must, therefore, have been much preoccupied with ships and their officers, and with custom-houses and their officials. But it is obvious from the consular letters that dealing with the local British community was just as time-consuming, and sometimes more stressful. The local British church, the local British hospital, and the local British cemetery, all took up a great deal of the consul's time. Letter after letter, meeting after meeting, concern church matters, from lofty discussions about the appointment of a new chaplain to the cost of new pews and pulpits.

The British had not long been allowed to have their own churches in Portuguese-run territories; indeed, in Portugal, the seventeenth century had seen persecution of British residents by the Inquisition, the banishment of at least one chaplain, and rumours of British children being kidnapped to be brought up in closed institutions by the Roman Catholic Church. Matters in Brazil were more relaxed, and it was accepted that foreign residents were allowed to build their own places of worship, providing that the churches looked like normal houses and did not have bells to summon people to worship. After the influence of the Inquisition waned in the eighteenth century, the authorities in Portugal had adopted the same approach. The Anglican church of St. James in Porto, hidden still by high walls and locked gates, was built to resemble a secular building, and was given the same proportions as the ballroom of the Factory House in the town centre. The effect is light and airy, without any of the gothic gloom of many churches of the time in England.

The Anglican Church in Belém was not built until 1913. Like the British Church in Porto, it was built within the grounds of the British Burial Ground there. During John Hesketh's time in Belém, the Burial Ground was situated on the very edge of the town on the road to the village of Nazaré, and carved out of the jungle. Nowadays, the city of Belém, with its 1.6 million people, has expanded round and far beyond it. A row of railings separates the well-tended cemetery and the church from one of the busiest thoroughfares in the city. The Burial Ground, which had existed since 1815, caused plenty of problems for the consul, but there was no chaplain there during John Hesketh's tenure of the consulship. The problems in Belém tended to be caused by arguments about who was eligible to be buried within its bounds. Though the British residents paid for its upkeep, Americans, Germans, and other non-Brazilians were buried there. This occasionally caused resentment, and there was a very unseemly incident after John's time in 1855, when Archibald Campbell, one of the leading British merchants, aided by the American Consul, broke down the gates in order urgently to bury an American tourist, Mr. Chaffee[76] Belém did not have a British hospital, and so was spared the funding problems associated with that.

São Luis also had no chaplain during Robert Hesketh's time as consul, though it did have a British Burial Ground, and, for a short period, a hospital. Its British Burial Ground had been established in 1816, and continued to be used for many years, and Robert Hesketh and his successors there found frequent occasion to write home about it. One particular problem was again nationality. The "Buryal Ground" crops up in a letter of 1827, when Robert wrote home to ask if there was any official policy about access to the cemetery.[77] The cemetery had been formerly open to all Protestants, especially the citizens of the United States, but the body of an American sailor had recently been refused admission, and the Committee was anxious to find out whether a portion of the Burial Ground could be laid aside for non-British Protestants. Sadly, with the decline of British trade and therefore British residency in the city, the Burial Ground seems to have been neglected, and its location forgotten. The likelihood is that it was incorporated into a larger municipal cemetery.

Rio de Janeiro, with its large British community, had greater ambitions. It had a chapel, later a church, and a Burial Ground which still exists, together with a chaplain. Luccock's map of 1820 also indicates a British hospital near the waterfront·

The provision of an Anglican Chaplain for the British community in Rio caused innumerable problems over a long period of time for a succession of consuls in the city. We shall examine later the difficulties surrounding the employment and resignation of the Rev. Mr. Crane, a subject requiring the skills of Anthony Trollope to do it full justice. The appointment of Mr. Crane's successor, the Rev. Arthur Maister, seems to have gone altogether more smoothly. When he arrived in Rio in 1833, he had the support of the Bishop of London, responsible in those days for ecclesiastical appointments abroad, and of the residents. Lord Palmerston, who had been much irritated by earlier events, was greatly relieved, and Maister survived as Chaplain until 1839, carrying out his pastoral duties, including Robert Hesketh's own marriage in 1837, and the subsequent christening of the first of his children.

Palmerston's impatience with the independently-minded merchants and with the clergy is obvious from his replies, and church affairs must have taken many long hours to sort out both in Brazil and in Downing Street. Later in his life, when Palmerston was Prime Minister, his dislike of making ecclesiastical appointments was so great that he handed over much of the responsibility to his son-in-law, Lord Shaftesbury. The occasional problem caused by Protestant missionaries in Brazil seems small beer by comparison. A certain Mr. Youd, busy on the borders of Brazil and Guiana trying to convert good Roman Catholics to Protestantism, caused profound irritation to the Brazilian Government, and he is frequently mentioned in the Foreign Office records, but the British Government, although not sympathetic, eventually decided that it could not legally prevent his earnest missionary zeal.

Eternal life might create headaches for the consuls, but its portal, death, also gave them problems. Consuls were expected to have records on all British citizens who had expired whilst in their territory, especially those who had died intestate. Enquiries about the welfare and destination of their property came from relatives, sometimes many years afterwards. A Mr. Sheely died in Brazil early in the 1820s, and his relatives wanted to know what had happened to his property. Eventually, in 1839, came the reply, that it had been left to his daughter, who then married a Mr. James Thompson, who, according to the law of the time, took possession of it. Robert Ryan, Consul in Pará in 1842, criticised his predecessor, John Hesketh, for allowing the Campbell brothers, merchants in Pará, to administer the effects of late and intestate British citizens, but the reply came back from London that, though consuls were to be aware of the arrangements, they had no automatic right, according to the 1827 Treaty, to take over the administration of the effects of the deceased. John Hesketh had therefore acted properly.

Rather more pressing were the dignity and demands of the British Navy. The records have many examples of the difficulties when one proud martial power met the representatives of another. As a result of a series of disputes in Pernambuco about flags, cannon salutes, and precedence, not helped by the tactless attitude of Mr. Parkinson, the Consul there, an "Instruction" came out in 1825 from Mr. Secretary Canning:

"When the Captain of one of H.M.'s Ships of War being a Post Captain shall signify , in writing, to the Consul his arrival in the Port at which he resides, the Consul.... shall take the earliest opportunity of waiting, in Person, on the Commander of the Ship, and of affording him any Assistance which he may require; and that the Captains of Ships of War arriving in Foreign Ports where Consuls reside, will have directions to furnish a Boat to convey the Consul on board and reland them, on the Consul notifying his wish to have a Boat so sent for him."[78]

In busy ports, that procedure could result in a large expenditure of time, and the consul would have to undertake such duties dressed in his official uniform, with its frock coat, cocked hat, sword, and sash in crimson and blue.

Less prestigious folk might occupy much of the consul's time too. Merchant seamen seemed to be particularly adept at getting themselves into trouble, either as a result of mutiny or of yielding to the blandishments of the Brazilian Navy. Many were the difficulties caused by British merchant seamen deserting their ships, and taking the Emperor's *milreis*, and the consul was expected to use the judgement of Solomon. Disease on board ship was common, and often contagious and fatal, and the consequences of that were the responsibility of the consul. Henry Augustus Cowper, promoted from Pará in 1841, was much praised for his efforts in countering an outbreak of disease in his new port of Pernambuco. Indiscipline on board was a common occurrence, and the consul in the receiving port would have to rush out to the ship to sort out the difficulties. There are references to Second Mates attacking the Master, and there are also cases when the consul judged the Master himself to be partly or wholly to blame. The brig "Ceres" of Whitehaven had discipline problems on its voyage out to South America, but Robert Hesketh judged the Master, Captain Clements, to be largely responsible, as his procedures were slack and his paperwork was not in order.[79] Another Master was fined £5 for not ensuring the crew had signed the Ship's Articles, and the money was remitted to the Greenwich Hospital for Seamen, which still exists. Other distressed British citizens were sometimes stranded on the shores of South America, and expected the consul to be available and willing to help. We shall look later at the case of the irresponsible Mr. William Willstood of Liverpool, who abandoned sixty of his fellow-countrymen in the jungle.

And so the list of daily duties went on. The trickiest were those concerned with the safety of British residents, and relationships with the local provincial government. As we shall see at Pará, the safety of British residents was one thing, and their conviction that they were safe was quite another, and good judgement and public relations were both essential weapons in the consul's armoury. Equally, the elaborate and courtly epistles in Portuguese which flowed from the provincial government often hid sharper challenges, and there were occasions, as at Maranhão in 1824 and 1826, when the consul's own safety was at risk. Again, history was repeating itself, for the Portuguese authorities in the old country had threatened with imprisonment the consuls in Lisbon and the northern Portuguese port of Viana do Castelo in the years before the French invasion. In the early years of the new Brazil, political attitudes amongst the Portuguese who still governed the new Brazil were much the same. It was important for the consul and the British subjects for whom he was responsible to behave impartially, and to steer clear of local politics.

In view of all this, it is difficult to agree completely with Alan Manchester that there was little work to do in some ports. Even if all had gone well all the time, there was a sufficient range of responsibilities to keep anyone occupied. Naturally, everything did not go well all the time, and the consul had to be adept at solving the diverse problems that arrived, often literally, on his doorstep. In addition to this he had to keep in good odour with his diplomatic superiors in Rio, look after the foreign dignitaries like Prince Adelbert of Prussia, who visited Pará during Richard Ryan's time as Consul, keep an eye on explorers like Schomburgk on the Oyapock River in 1837, deal with the odd shipwreck and its cargo, and remember to use the right-sized paper in despatches.

It therefore seems a little unfair of Harold Temperley in "The Foreign Policy of Canning" to refer to consuls as "a miscellaneous and often undesirable set." C.R. Middleton said that "Ministers envisioned the Consular Service as little more than an organisation for collecting data on the trade and industry of the powers."[87] This could hardly be true, if they carefully read the many despatches from consular ports. Moorhouse, writing about the modern Consular Service in "The Diplomats", seems to reflect more accurately the situation in Brazil in the early nineteenth century – consuls, he says, are "Martha to the Marys of the Chanceries", nursemaids to the merchant navy, and solvers of a huge variety of human problems. Miscellaneous they may have been, but they were often also men of remarkable versatility and resource. They were out of sight of ministers, and often out of mind, but later chapters will show the wide variety of problems addressed by the Heskeths in their own ports, and the impressive range of skills needed to represent the British Government abroad.

SECTION II

PLACES:
SÃO LUIS DE MARANHÃO

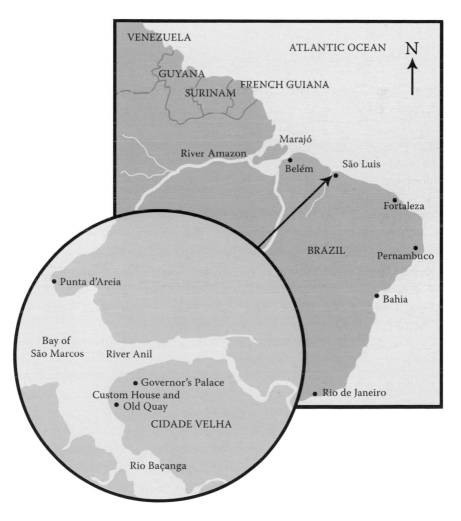

Map of São Luis – main features c.1820

8

SÃO LUIS DE MARANHÃO

"... a short description of the place particularly as its rapid increase of commerce and advantageous situation are equally unknown." (Robert Hesketh)

The city of São Luis de Maranhão, or Maranham as the British usually called it, was founded first by the French in 1612, who gave it the name of their patron saint. After a brief Dutch appropriation of the new settlement, the Portuguese invested it in 1644, and throughout the seventeenth and eighteenth centuries it became the leading port on the north coast of Brazil. Its status at the start of the nineteenth century, as the fourth largest of Brazil's trading ports after Rio, Bahia, and Pernambuco, encouraged the British Government to decide to appoint a Consul there in 1812 It took the rubber boom in the later nineteenth century for Pará, its northern rival, to surpass São Luis in commercial importance.

Today, both São Luis and Belém have been challenged by Fortaleza in Ceará to the east. In spite of its shallow anchorage, Belém is still an important port, owing its importance now not only to its exports but also to its position on one of the main arterial waterways of the Amazon. São Luis's commercial buildings survive, and it consequently maintains much of its historic air. São Luis may yet again enjoy prosperity, for there has recently been enormous investment pouring into various projects in its hinterland, to develop aluminium processing and the extraction of iron ore. The Brazilian space project is also on the doorstep, at Alcântara along the coast to the west.

São Luis's renovated buildings are attractive and colourful, and have been restored to something like the state they would have been in when Robert Hesketh arrived in 1812. He has left a very detailed description of the town at that period in one of his first letters back to the Foreign Office.[80] Robert's impressions can be compared with those of Henry Koster, who visited the town a short time later in 1815.[81] Robert's account, dated in November, 1813, is contained in a long private letter to William Hamilton, Under-Secretary at the Foreign Office, who had dealt with him nearly two years earlier, when Robert was preparing for office. His aim was, he says, to "gratify the curi-

The old Quay at São Luis, now only used by local ferries

osity of the Noble Lord at the head of Foreign Affairs", but Robert also felt
that the rapidly increasing importance of São Luis's commerce made it
necessary for London to know a little more about a hitherto unknown area.

After explaining that "Maranham" means "a large river", he suggests that
this might be a reference to the Amazon. The various mouths of the world's
second longest river are, however, many miles up the coast, and it is more
likely that the word refers to São Luis's own rivers, the Itapicuru and the
Pindaré, which are large enough. He says he does not know much about the
early origins of the city, but he does know that Maranhão and Pará were
separated administratively in 1774, nearly forty years before his arrival in
São Luis.

He obviously remembered his own arrival in the town from the sea. The
approach from the Atlantic remained difficult, and it was all too easy, in the
days before detailed charts were prepared, to mistake the two openings in
the low sandy coast – the Bay of São Jozé to the east, and the Bay of São
Marcos. The latter offers open water, and a good anchorage opposite the city
itself, which is built on an island. The approach from São Jozé was navigable
for the small boats of the time, but they had to negotiate a narrow channel
never more than two hundred feet wide, and lasting for all of eleven miles to
the north of the island, before emerging into the roadstead off the city.
Today, the plane from Fortaleza follows this channel as it drops down to the

airport at São Luis, and it is easy to imagine how worrying it would be to the sailing-boat captain, unfamiliar with the coast, to be in so narrow a channel. Koster mentions that the brig he arrived in took the São Marcos channel, but "with the lead going".

The island of São Luis has at its heart the *cidade velha*, the old city. It is protected from the Atlantic by another island to the north, across the River Anil. Today, a bridge connects the *cidade velha* with the northern island, where many of the new buildings and businesses are developing. In Robert's day, the island to the north boasted defences at Punta d'Areia at its north-western tip, with a small fort equipped with twenty old guns, a signal post, and some other guns on a low hill. Today, Punta d'Areia, with its fine beach, is a small holiday resort, with elaborate condominiums being built along the shore.

Although São Luis was a busy harbour at the time, the ships which brought European manufactured goods and took back Maranhão cotton were quite small, most not more than 200 tons. Lord Cochrane, whose part in the history of Maranhão was short but dramatic, was the first, he tells us, to take a large line-of-battle ship into the harbour. Following his famous ruse in 1823, when he pretended he had a large Brazilian fleet with him, he sailed his flagship, the "Pedro Primeiro", into the roadstead, and anchored opposite the Governor's Palace.

Smaller ships, Robert tells us, even if they eventually made it safely into the harbour, had to be careful along the coast. For six months of the year, from August to January, the current along the coast was very strong along the low sandy shore, and sailing-vessels found it hard to proceed to the east against the prevailing current. This made the journey to Pernambuco, Bahia, and Rio de Janeiro a long and tiresome one, and must have increased the sense of isolation felt by São Luis and its western neighbour, Pará. During the rainy season from February to July, the current eased, and encouraged a greater coasting trade. The lack of accurate charts made all sailing in the area hazardous, and it was only when British and French naval hydrographers prepared accurate charts, and steam-powered vessels began to arrive, that some of São Luis's natural disadvantages were overcome. Unfortunately, by that time, its importance as a commercial port was on the wane.

Another difficulty, according to Robert, was that the harbour entrance was enclosed by two rather unstable sand-banks, and he suggests that only the building of moles or "keys" would guarantee the viability of the port. At the time he was writing, the shifting sands limited the anchorage to "15 large sail of Merchantmen". They were well-sheltered from the sea, but needed to be anchored so as to swing with the tide. If they were anchored bow and stern, and were thus immobilized, the sun caused great damage to their seams and structure.

The tide's rise and fall was considerable – Robert says it was twenty feet, and Koster eighteen feet. The old quays, cobbled still and now usually empty, still exist, as does the elaborate warehouse nearby. The buildings of the old town rise behind it, with the Governor's Palace and the Cathedral occupying some of the highest ground on the bluff overlooking the port. The old houses have changed little since Robert's day. They are windowless at ground level, but have brightly-painted tall doors which are flung open at the start of business each day. Inside, São Luis's shopkeepers stock their wares and conduct their business. On the next floor above, family life takes place, with balconied rooms overlooking the street. Some rooms face inward to a small space perhaps a metre or two wide shared with another room. Today, as then, one street, the Rua da Estrêla, is planted with mango trees, which offer shade during the day, and a pleasant area to sit under in the evening. Robert's description of the town in 1813 is less flattering: "The best houses … generally adjoin the meanest thatched hovels…. This indiscriminate mixture of whitewashed and mud walls, of tiled and thatched roofs, gives the town a very shabby appearance … the best public buildings here … have been built by the Jesuits." Koster's description of the city a year or two later is very similar. He says the streets "are mostly paved, but out of repair" (still true today). "The houses are many of them neat and pretty, and one story [sic] in height. The lower part of them is appropriated to the servants, to shops without windows, to warehouses, and other purposes…. The family lives upon the upper story; and the windows of this reach down to the floor, and are ornamented with iron balconies. The churches are numerous…."

Robert also comments on the temperature: 82° Fahrenheit in the morning and 86° during the afternoon, with the heat more oppressive in the rainy season, when thunderstorms are frequent. In spite of the heat, Robert says that fevers are rare, a benefit of the sea-breezes, he supposes. São Luis had its outbreaks of Yellow Fever later, but not on the scale of Pará or Rio.

The island of São Luis was not cultivated to any great degree in Robert's time. He complains of the "indolence" of the inhabitants, which meant that the island had to import all its vegetables. The real agriculture took place to the south, where the planters burned down areas of brushwood and forest to grow a crop of rice or cotton or Indian corn, leaving the half-burnt trunks in place, and growing the crops "promiscuously" between them. Most of this development took place along the rivers, which were many, and which offered easy transport and access to the interior. The best cotton, however, was grown to the west of Sao Luis, near Alcântara, which was, he says, "a

A square in São Luis, showing its characteristic houses

pleasant town", and which would rival São Luis, were it able to boast a harbour. From there, Robert has been told, rivers connect with Pará to the west.

To the south, vast plains provide breeding for cattle, Robert believes, but it is obvious that he has not yet explored the interior. He knows, however, that a few beaten-dirt roads link the province with Bahia, "366 leagues" away (1100 miles), and with Pernambuco, Minais Gerais, and Pará. The journey to Bahia begins with a river-trip south-west on the Itapicuru river for two hundred miles, and the whole trip takes six weeks. It was not given to British consuls to take that sort of time away from their ports, and Robert must hardly have left the vicinity of São Luis until he returned to England in 1817.

São Luis itself was not noted for the number of its Indians, but they were numerous in the surrounding country districts. He has been told that the Jesuits "made slaves of the Indians or Aborigines". After the expulsion of the Jesuits in 1759, the Indians spurned their recently-acquired domestication, and "returned to their former barbarity and natural indolence". Robert was not the only European visitor to Brazil who looked askance at the Indians' apparent lack of economic productivity. The Indian view was always that "economic activity" was an alien concept and that growing and catching enough food to survive was ambition enough. Their relations with the planters were poor, and Indian attacks on the newcomers were answered with aggression from the planters, who attacked the Indians' houses – "this gradually gave rise to the warfare that at present exists between the planters and the Indians." He has heard that some of the Indians are cannibals.

At any rate, the Indians were not suitable for menial or manual labour, a conclusion reached throughout the Brazilian Empire in the nineteenth century, if not earlier. So, the climate being what it was, alternative labour was required. The answer seemed to be slaves from Africa, "without which a sensible decrease in the annual produce of exports would take place instead of the present increase".

This statement of Robert's, doubtless repeating the accepted wisdom of the economic controllers of Maranhão, neatly summarises the well-established Brazilian defence against the abolition of slavery. Robert and the British Consulate got themselves into a little bother over their ownership of two young slaves, a situation from which George Canning had to extricate them. In his defence, it is worth remembering that Robert later spent his most mature years in Rio as one of the most active workers against the slave trade. As was so often the case, there was widespread agreement about the need to abolish the transport of slaves from Africa, but there were many ticklish questions to tackle about the status and treatment of those already enslaved or already in Brazil. These questions existed too in the British West Indies, and there were thirty years of frustration and disturbance there before the full abolition of slavery was effected.

In his introductory letter, however, Robert shows himself aware of the complexities involved in shipping thousands of people across an ocean to work in servitude. "The planters," he says, echoing a common belief in nineteenth-century Brazil, "appear generally to treat their slaves well". Nevertheless, in spite of this and of a diet of "cassada" (cassava) and salt beef, there are a great number of deaths among the slaves when first introduced to the country – a result, he thinks, of the "unwholesome air that exists in all woody places in this climate". Later on, in Rio, Robert was to write passionately and powerfully of the state of the Africans when they first arrived in Brazilian ports, describing their fevers, their small-pox, their eye diseases, and their mental depression. For now, however, he limits himself to the observation that "perhaps a more delicate treatment with the female slaves might render them more fecund and thus by increasing the population gradually diminish their importation." Robert was right, up to a point, for the question of slave fertility was a problem wherever slaves were imported – in the West Indies as well. The free trader and the humanitarian fought for supremacy in Robert at this stage, and he comments: "The trade is inhuman, but a sudden annihilation of it would undoubtedly produce a break in the present increasing trade of the place." Robert says later in his letter that five-eighths of the population of Maranhão consists of slaves – 30,000 out of 48,000. The proportion of black to white and Indian in Maranhão continued to be high, especially as there was a tendency in the mid-nineteenth century to send unruly slaves north to Maranhão from Rio and São Paulo as a punishment. The present-day population and culture of São Luis still shows its origins, with its festivals and its music heavily influenced by African tradition. In 1813, the population was boosted by a regiment of Portuguese soldiers a thousand strong: their presence was to create real problems ten years later, after Brazilian independence had been declared, and only decisiveness and lack of punctilio on Lord Cochrane's part rid the province of their presence and their influence.

In 1813, the trading activity of São Luis was predominantly in exports, and Robert bemoans the fact that the import side of the trade was much less noticeable, and much less profitable. He blames it on the social background of the early settlers, who were convicts, and "not very enlightened". The two staple exports were rice and cotton, especially the latter. He speaks of 70,000 bags of cotton being exported from Maranhão in 1811, and the trade increasing by 5,000 bags every year. His own firm, Robert Hesketh and Company, as it was called in the early days of his residence there, was very profitable at this stage, and exported considerable quantities of cotton to Liverpool, where it was received by his brother Thomas, ensconced in one of the offices in the Cotton Exchange near the waterfront.[82]

In his introductory letter, Robert tells the story of the birth of the Brazilian cotton trade. He credits its beginning to John Burford, a ship's surgeon born in 1708, who settled in São Luis, first of all growing and exporting ginger, and then developing the technique of tanning leather with the bark of the mango tree, and exporting the tanned hides to Lisbon. He was also the first to grow China tea in Brazil, the forerunner of a much larger experiment in Rio in the next century. At this stage, no rice was exported – it was used as currency – nor cotton. When Burford sent two bags of cotton to Lisbon in 1759, he was threatened with violence by the locals, and fled to Lisbon, where the Marquis of Pombal, conscious of cotton's potential, protected him. Experimental samples of cotton were by now being sent from Brazil across to Lisbon and Porto, and similar samples were being sent from the southern United States to Britain. There was therefore some competition between Maranhão and North America; both of which used slave labour to produce the cotton crop. There was, however, enough European trade to keep many exporters busy and prosperous, and to keep the cotton-mills of Lancashire turning. The trade also brought in considerable revenue for the provincial Junta, who, says Robert, use the money to defray "all the military expences at Pará". Shillington and Chapman, in their study of trade between Great Britain and Portugal[83], give the date of the first export of cotton as 1767. They say that by 1790, cotton worth £9,190 was being imported into Great Britain, and that muslin was first made in 1780, thanks to the availability of fine Brazilian cotton.

Henry Koster's arrival in São Luis in 1815 was striking. When his ship arrived off the port, there was no pilot in evidence, so he joined the Captain in one of the ship's boats to fetch one. They were soon halted, however, by a warning shot fired from the fort, and ordered back to their ship. They had infringed one of the strictly-kept regulations of all Brazilian ports – that they should await the visit of the port health and customs authorities. This, as we have seen, was a sociable affair, which did not hide the insistence of the Brazilian authorities on the strictest protocols when a ship arrived from overseas. Behind the sociability was an iron fist, for he says the Governor "ruled with most despotic sway". It was even obligatory to remove your hat when passing in front of the governor's palace. But he speaks more warmly of his meetings with the merchants and planters.

Koster gives figures which illustrate the nature of São Luis's export trade. In 1812, twenty-nine British vessels left the port on their journey back to Great Britain, a number exactly matched by those of other countries. By 1815, the number of ships sailing to Great Britain had risen slightly to thirty-two, but with forty-nine now sailing for ports elsewhere in the world.

This level of activity created a small British community in São Luis. In 1826, there were fifty-seven British citizens living in the town and the nearby country districts. In addition to the Consul, there was a doctor, ten merchants organised in seven separate commercial establishments, seven-teen clerks, five planters, twelve mechanics, five carrying out the varied roles of auctioneer, boatman, and storekeeper, and six women. Of these British citizens, forty-five were based in the city itself, and the remaining eleven men and one woman lived "in the country". São Luis seemed to have been lucky in its doctors. Dr. Hall served for many years there during the first years of Robert's consulship, and a Dr. Arbuckle was there in the 1830s, when the traveller George Gardner stayed with him for three weeks.[84]

The shortage of European women was typical of many South American consular ports, and was common elsewhere. For British ex-patriates, it meant either a long period of bachelorhood (as in Robert's case), or marriage to a Brazilian (as in his brother John's case in Pará), or one or more unofficial liaisons (as in their brother William's case). As it was, only six of the English male community in Sâo Luis were married, four to English women, and two to what he calls "natives" – local Portuguese or Brazilian women.

Robert Hesketh's service as British Consul in São Luis, which lasted twenty years, saw the town at the height of its prosperity, but it was also a time of political instability. Its troubles did not, however, equal the cataclysm that overcame Pará in 1835 and 1836, and it was Maranhão that offered refuge and safety to the British fleeing from the blood-letting in Belém. For the Heskeths, it always offered a base, for even when Robert left the port for Rio in 1832, William remained, frequently in touch with the rest of his family.

ROBERT AT MARANHAM

"The importance of the Province has increased very rapidly..." (H. Koster, 1815)

Nine years after Robert Hesketh arrived in São Luis in 1812, he appeared in the pages of the *Estatistica histórico-geográfica da Provincia do Maranhão* ("Historical and Geographical Statistics of the Province of Maranhão") of 1821. The author says that "Roberto Hesketh" is the most successful of the foreign merchant in the province, paying into the Custom-House a total of 37,268 reis in dues on the cotton he was exporting. This was well over half the contribution of even Antonio Jozé Mireilles Ferreira, the most successful Portuguese-born merchant, who had been established there for a long time.[85] So his work as British Consul and his part-time job as the Lloyd's Agent in Maranhão did not apparently harm his commercial prospects.

Perhaps partly because he was so busy as a merchant, few consular letters from him have survived from this early period, except the very long one quoted in the last chapter. His next surviving letter dates from 1816, and is an enquiry about the charging of Consular Fees, a subject he returns to regularly later on. The growth of the cotton trade with Lancashire meant that there was a gradually increasing number of British ships shuttling between the port and Liverpool, with plenty of work for Robert to do. He will have had to keep in touch with the other six British firms established in São Luis, and to superintend the operation of the Hospital and the Burial Ground, and keep up good relations both with the local Junta, and with other local consular colleagues. There was, for a relatively small port, a large cadre of consular officials and agents from other countries. The United States had stationed a consul there, and there were vice-consuls from Russia, France, Spain, and the Hanseatic towns.[86]

In Robert's case, his younger brother, William, was a useful deputy. The first time William deputised for Robert was in early 1817, when Robert called on him to look after the Consulate. On 3 January, 1817, Robert informed the Foreign Office that the Consul-General in Rio, Henry Chamberlain, had asked him to go to Rio de Janeiro. He was about to set off, would be away for up to four months, and had appointed William as his deputy.

There were several occasions later when William stood in for him, usually for far longer than on this occasion. It seems surprising that the Foreign Office was not more interested in the identity and qualities of consular surrogates, but it was often happy as long as it had a name – any name – to write to in the absence of the regular consul. It was obviously not fazed by the fact that the name was that of the consul's brother; indeed, family connections were a perfectly acceptable way of promoting talent, and ensuring consistent standards. William seems to have taken his duties seriously. Only later did *hubris* interfere with the smooth course of his consular career.

The precise reason for Chamberlain's invitation to Robert is not made clear, but Robert's mind was certainly full of the challenges posed by the slave trade as he left Maranhão. He reported to the Foreign Office in a letter sent from Bahia on 27 February, that there were "nefarious proceedings with slave vessels on the Northern Coast of Brazil".[07] Up to the date of his departure from São Luis on 22 January, he had little definite information, but he had heard just before he left of a small Portuguese schooner, the "Pomboa Felis", which, though damaged, had landed twenty-three African slaves on the coast near Guimarães north-west of São Luis. On board his transport to Rio, he had "accidently [sic] ...managed to get on board one of the crew of the "Pomboa Felis", who had told him of a second schooner about to land slaves from a prohibited port, presumably in Africa. He had left details with the Deputy Consul, but was full of praise for the local Portuguese government in Maranhão, who so far "were unexceptionable in their desire to punish the offenders". It sounds likely, therefore, that the Consul-General wanted to discuss the question of slavery, especially in view of the fact that the Secretary of State for Foreign Affairs, Viscount Castlereagh, had recently agreed with all the European nations at the Congress of Vienna that they would take a common line in combating the transport of slaves. It was also the case that Chamberlain had not yet met Robert, who was the furthest-flung of his three consuls in Brazil. Robert also seems to have taken the opportunity to "settle some affairs of a most vital importance to my private interests".

Robert arrived back in Maranhão by 11 May, doubtless feeling a great sense of commitment to the cause of British diplomacy. He was therefore not ready for a letter he found waiting for him in his office. It was from the Foreign Office, and it was a stern rebuke. He was told that he should not simply have announced that he was off to Rio. The behest of the Consul-General was not enough – he should have sought and obtained permission from the Foreign Office in London. The practicality of writing back to

The Custom-House in São Luis, situated only a few yards from the Quay

London, and then waiting several weeks for a reply seems to have escaped the administrators. In his grovelling letter of apology, Robert said that he "had the mortification to learn... that I have been guilty of a great irregularity in departing from this place without leave from Lord Viscount Castlereagh."[88] He hopes he may be forgiven. And obviously he was, for it was not mentioned again, at least in the official correspondence.

Less than three months later, on 7 August, 1817, Robert asked for permission to return to England, partly for reasons of health, and partly in connection with his business.[89] As far as we know, Robert had not returned to England after his father's death in 1815, and this was probably therefore his first visit home for five years. His letters to the Foreign Office are from Liverpool, in February, 1818, and then from Gloucestershire.[90] He conducted his business in Liverpool, which probably meant discussing the fortunes of the family firm with his brother Thomas, and sailed back to Brazil from there, but in between his spells in Liverpool, he spent some time in Cheltenham, doubtless "taking the waters". Cheltenham was in its heyday as a spa town, and many of its elegant buildings date from that period. He says that he had visited London, but he had not been able to see William Hamilton at the Foreign Office. Since then, he had been ill and confined to the house for six weeks, but he had obviously recovered sufficiently by 9 April to plan his return to Maranhão at the end of the month. Quite what his health problems were is not made known, but his later medical troubles were mostly to do with his liver and kidneys. "Taking the waters" at the Pump-Room in Cheltenham suggests an early onset of his later more serious troubles.

When he returned to his post in São Luis, he had a series of problems to deal with. The first was William Willstood of Liverpool. Suffused with the Romantic spirit of the age – it was only twenty years since Coleridge and Southey had been planning their Utopian "pantisocracy" on the Susquehanna River – he had bought a steam-engine, and persuaded sixty English people, including women and children, to sail with him for Maranhão to set up a saw-mill and a sugar-plantation. As they established themselves on the Pindaré river near Monção, the local merchants shook their heads at this ill-conceived project. They were right. The naive party arrived in Brazil in October, 1817, but almost immediately got into trouble. Some of them deserted, there were other difficulties, and eight of the party died – five adults and three children. William Willstood's response to all this was to desert the project himself, and he fled back to Liverpool, leaving a large number of the immigrants penniless and stranded. They had not secured from Willstood any kind of written contract, so they appeared in São Luis at Robert's office, registering themselves as "distressed British subjects". Robert used the Maranhãao Contribution Fund to give them financial help, and to pay for the passage home for those who wanted it, but he was concerned about the precedent the whole project was setting. He wrote to the Foreign Office asking them to dissuade others from hatching similar plans.[91]

Robert also had several problems in the port of São Luis itself. The Master and crew of the British ship "Caledonia" were imprisoned for some time for infringing the local regulations, and Robert wrote to the Foreign Office to say that he was doing his best to ensure that visiting British sailors behaved well while in the port, and that he was supplying a translation of the Port Regulations to every British ship, in order to prevent other British mariners getting into the same difficulties.[92]

He had also had to intervene in the case of two young British clerks from the town, James Haddon and Henry Moon, who had been put in jail for visiting a newly-arrived British ship before it had received its regulation visit from the *Juiz de Fora*, the immigration authority. After a fortnight, he had secured their release on bail, but the case was still ongoing five months later, when Robert wrote to say that "His Excellency", the Governor, was inclined to pardon Haddon and Moon[93] Presumably they *were* pardoned, for Henry Moon was part of a well-established Liverpool merchant firm that continued to flourish in Maranhão and in Rio de Janeiro. John Moon, Henry's brother, became British Consul in Maranhão when Robert left in 1832.

There was also some anti-British feeling in the port, based on the issue of counterfeit coinage. The problem of "false coin" was a regular one in the first few decades of Brazil's independent existence, and it caused damage not only to the Brazilian economy but also to trade and commerce generally. In November, 1818, Robert wrote to the Consul-General in Rio telling him of the problem in Maranhão, and of the accusation by a Portuguese resident that British ships were importing counterfeit coins made in Birmingham. As a result, several British ships had been boarded and searched by soldiers, but nothing had been found, and Robert was inclined to think it was a rumour specifically designed to damage British trade in the port.[94] The Brazilian Government's understandable desire to rid itself of counterfeit coinage was to cause a serious problem some years later for one British merchant in Pará.

Robert's other major problem was one that continued to haunt the Hesketh family for the next twenty-odd years – Henry Dickenson. Dickenson was a merchant in Pará, who had married a wealthy Brazilian woman, and had thus come into possession of her estate and her slaves. He was clever, well-spoken, and well-educated, and of the small number of British merchants in Belém in 1813, he seemed the most suitable to be appointed as Vice-Consul there. Robert's suggestion that Dickenson be appointed was readily agreed to by the Foreign Office, and Dickenson duly received his Commission from the King.

It was a decision Robert and successive Foreign Secretaries lived to regret. After causing many difficulties, Dickenson was eventually sacked, and earned Canning's and Palmerston's profound antipathy. He still managed, however, to come back to the role time and again, in the absence of other suitable candidates. He antagonised almost every one of his successors, and he and his English-based brother kept the clerks at the Foreign Office busy for years. But it was on John Hesketh's life that he had the most profound effect, and that story deserves a chapter of its own.

Robert's complaints about Dickenson first surface in the official correspondence in 1819, though Robert was clearly unhappy about him for some time before that. In his letter to William Hamilton at the Foreign Office, he complains that Dickenson has not fulfilled his duties, causing "considerable Inconvenience to the Consul-General and myself".[95] There is "a want of regularity" in Pará, and the Office Returns have been neglected. Later on, he says that Dickenson has not sent in any returns for the whole of the previous year. He has "in one instance, totally neglected my instructions; which lately was the cause of much trouble, and the motive of a Sloop of War being sent down to Para by His Excellency the Governor of Barbadoes"[sic].[96]

The root of the trouble seems to have been Dickenson's resentment at being supervised from Maranhão, and at the fact that his salary was less than that of Robert in São Luis, although it was still £400 per year. Dickenson was also resentful of the fact that some of the Pará Consulage fees were paid to Robert in Maranhão. Robert tried to mollify Dickenson by offering him the whole of the Consulage fees formerly paid to Maranhão, but it was not enough to turn resentment into cooperation. The situation was exacerbated by the arrival in Belém the following year of John Hesketh, Robert's brother. Dickenson immediately assumed that Robert intended to supplant him as Vice-Consul with his newly-arrived brother. "He has most unaccountably supposed that I wish to supersede him, and appoint my Brother who is lately arrived at Pará from England. However, I beg leave to assure you, that no such idea has been entertained by either my Brother or myself."

Castlereagh wrote back in support of Robert, assuring him that his conduct has been "perfectly correct", and the "remonstrances you have made to Mr. Dickenson on this irregularity appear to have been called for by his misconduct." Castlereagh also approved of Robert's "just and liberal" action in fining Dickenson half his fees as a punishment for his disobedience and non-compliance with his orders.[97]

Viscount Castlereagh's support for Robert only seems to have made Dickenson's attitude more obstreperous. From that time onward, Dickenson, whilst still being only a Vice-Consul, behaved as if he were Consul, and not responsible to Robert, or even to the Foreign Office. When a revolution broke out in Pará on 1 January, 1821, Dickenson did not even inform the Consul in Maranhão. Dickenson had some support in Pará, and Robert told Hamilton to expect a Memorial [a petition] from Pará urging the appointment of Dickenson as Consul there, and was pessimistic about the future. He thought it unlikely that Dickenson would "alter his ideas and intentions".

Castlereagh's reply gives Robert the option of appointing someone else, but Robert was in a cleft stick, knowing that there was no one else in Pará with the ability and competence to take on the role – except, of course, his brother John. *That* course of action was effectively ruled out at least for the present by Dickenson's tactic of predicting it. The fact that Robert delayed for five more years before dismissing Dickenson and appointing John, demonstrates how clever a move it was. But eventually, Dickenson went too far, and could not prevent the sword falling on him in 1824.

In the meantime, Robert had maritime matters to attend to. HMS "Icarus" arrived in Maranhão in January, 1821. In accordance with the accepted practice, the "Icarus" fired seventeen guns, but only fourteen were returned from the fort at São Luis. Nowadays it is hard to take with due seriousness the many disputes that erupted between visiting naval ships and the Brazilian port authorities over such matters as the precise positioning of flags and the number of guns fired on a ship's arrival in port. There were problems not only at Maranhão, but at Bahia, Pernambuco, and, very frequently, at Rio. Brazilian sensitivities were always finely-tuned, and the British Navy was equally sensitive about the respect it considered due to its ships, its flag, and its officers. While seeming trivial to us, these disputes were seen at the time as politically significant, often requiring the intervention and wisdom of British consuls and diplomats.

The shortfall of three guns ought to have warned Captain Eliot of the "Icarus" to exercise great caution. Instead, he allowed one of his officers to go on board a British merchant ship before the latter had received its Health Clearance visit. The Portuguese authorities in the port responded immediately by ordering HMS "Icarus" to leave within twenty-four hours. Eliot was prepared to comply, but realised that the tides were all against a safe exit to the open sea. However, the fort was manned, ready to fire, and a Portuguese Sloop of War in the port prepared to use its guns against the "Icarus", so Eliot took his ship out of the Bay of San Marcos, and into the Atlantic on the neap tide, when no pilot would normally take a ship out. Fortunately, Eliot was successful, and the "Icarus" made it safely out to sea.[98]

There were also frequent problems with British merchant ships. In 1821, the British merchant ship "George" called in at the port, and then sailed south. When it returned some time later on its way back to Liverpool, it was with an almost totally different crew. This suggested to Robert that its crew had been improperly off-loaded, and when he discovered one member of the crew, John Holly, who had been dismissed, he arranged for him to return to England on the British brig "John". When he reached Liverpool, Holly was to swear an affidavit in the Town Clerk's Office about the treatment of the crew.[99] Equally irregular was the replacement of the Master, Edmund Willstood, with his name-sake William Willstood, a name we have already met, though whether it was the same individual who had led sixty people to Maranhão, and then deserted them in 1818, is not clear.

More sinister was the arrival of the Dutch schooner "Aurora" in the port in December, 1822. Rumour had it that it was waiting for another vessel to arrive with a cargo of African slaves, so that it could transport them to Surinam further up the coast. The "Aurora" departed suddenly, in company with a Portuguese ship that allegedly had one hundred and eighty slaves on board.[100] Whilst it was not a daily occurrence, the arrival of slavers from Africa was not unknown in Maranhão at this period. It did not reach the scale Robert met with in Rio de Janeiro twenty years later, but he nevertheless informed the British naval commander in the Leeward Islands, Sir Henry Ward, K.C.B.

Meanwhile, political change all over Brazil was quickening in pace. It will be remembered that the departure of João VI for Portugal in 1821 was followed by the "Cry of Ipiranga" in September, 1822, when João's son, Pedro, proclaimed the independence of Brazil from Portugal. In the north, tensions had been rising both in Pará and in Maranhão. A revolution in Pará in February, 1821, was followed by a more peaceful change of government in Maranhão two months later, and a new Junta of seven members was set up in March, 1822. But the tensions created by the declaration of independence were building, and there was trouble in Bahia and Pernambuco. In the northernmost ports of Maranhão and Pará, there was strong support for Portugal, and a notable presence of Portuguese troops and administrators. But there were others who supported Pedro and his newly-declared Empire, and conflict between the Portuguese and those who considered themselves primarily Brazilian was inevitable.

Matters came to a head in 1823, when the Junta in Maranhão had still not declared for Pedro and independence. Their hand was forced by one of the most outrageous tricks in history.

Thomas Lord Cochrane had been rapidly promoted in the British Navy at the time of Nelson, when he had exhibited skill, daring, and ruthlessness in fighting the French and the Spanish. He had then ventured into politics, where he allied himself with radicals like Burdett and Hunt in the House of Commons. But he was implicated in a financial scandal, and to escape this, he took his experience and his gifts abroad, first to Chile and then to Peru, in both of which countries he was appointed Commander of the Navy, and played a considerable part in their fight for independence from the Spanish. Cochrane left the service of Peru in a huff, because he claimed not to have been paid what he had been promised – a recurring *leitmotiv* in Cochrane's career. He travelled to the east coast of South America, where the new Emperor of Brazil, Pedro, was very happy to take up Cochrane's offer of service, and handed over the slender resources of the fledgling Brazilian Navy to him in March, 1822. Cochrane inspected the nine ships available, and set off up the coast to quell a rebellion in Bahia. His first attempt at marine warfare was disastrous, and Cochrane realised he had to concentrate his best seamen – mostly British and American mercenaries – in his best ship, the "Pedro Primeiro". Assisted by his mostly British captains, he returned to Bahia, defeated the rebellion, and restored the province to the Empire.

Aware that a fleet of Portuguese ships was making for Maranhão, he outsailed them in the "Pedro Primeiro", and arrived off São Luis in June, 1823. Knowing that the Provincial Government was expecting the Portuguese fleet to arrive, Cochrane decided to meet their expectations by flying the Portuguese flag. The Portuguese brig "Don Miguel" came out of the port to greet him, and its Master, Captain Garção, went on board. He was shocked to discover that the big warship was in fact Brazilian, and that he was facing the Commander of the Brazilian Navy. The "Don Miguel" was seized, and Captain Garção was sent back to the port, firmly believing that the rest of the Brazilian fleet was shortly to follow its flagship. In fact the "Pedro Primeiro" was quite alone.

Cochrane's flagship entered the river, and anchored in a prominent position opposite the fort. The authorities, by now convinced that their pro-Portuguese cause was hopeless, came on board, accompanied by the local Bishop, and somewhat reluctantly pledged their loyalty to Pedro and

Thomas Lord Cochrane

THE EARL OF DUNDONALD.

FROM A PICTURE BY JAMES RAMSAY

the Empire. The Portuguese troops in the town were not quite so quick to capitulate, but a shot from the "Pedro Primeiro" over São Luis's rooftops soon convinced them. The Portuguese flag was hauled down for the last time, and replaced with the new Brazilian flag. This act was performed by Captain Pascoe Grenfell, another ex-British naval officer in the service of Brazil.

Over the next days, there was increasing surprise and suspicion when the rest of the Brazilian fleet did not arrive, but Cochrane continued his pretence, and the Portuguese troops were disarmed and packed off back to Lisbon. Cochrane had an election of sorts, and a new pro-Brazilian junta was elected. Grenfell was sent off in the "Don Miguel" – now renamed the "Maranhão", to Pará to repeat Cochrane's trick. Grenfell arrived in Belém, claiming that Cochrane and a large Brazilian fleet were even then sailing up the river to the city, and the ruse worked again. The junta vowed its loyalty to the Empire, and Grenfell returned to Maranhão, claiming that the only blood spilt there was his own – he had been shot in the arm during an assassination attempt. The truth was much more unpleasant, as we shall see when we come to Pará.

Meanwhile, Cochrane was having trouble with the new Junta. They wanted to punish those Portuguese who had stayed on, and pressed Cochrane to confiscate Portuguese property. He refused, and protested vigorously when the new regime brought irregular troops into the town to imprison Portuguese citizens, even those who had committed themselves to the new Brazil. Cochrane was suspicious of the Junta's motives, for several of them owed the same Portuguese merchants considerable sums of money. The Junta also awarded the troops, who had behaved themselves in a thoroughly disobedient and disgraceful way, a gratuity forcibly financed by the Portuguese merchants.

Cochrane was very unhappy about all this, and ordered the election of a proper government. The election took place, and Miguel Ignacio dos Santos Freire e Bruce, a Brazilian of Scottish extraction, became President.

Perhaps of more immediate concern to the British Consul, Robert Hesketh, was that Cochrane was very dissatisfied with the quality of his own crew, which, he felt, needed more British expertise and involvement. W.H. Koebel says his officers tried to persuade the British crews of merchant ships in the harbour to desert and join him, and an armed guard had to be kept on board the merchant ships while Cochrane's boats circled their prey.[101] Robert would certainly have objected to that, though we have no record of his protests to Cochrane.

Cochrane left on 20 September for Rio, which he reached on 9 November, presented himself to the Emperor, and was promptly made Marquis of Maranhão. Cochrane admitted he had exceeded his orders – "The powers I had taken upon myself to exercise....were, no doubt, in excess of those conferred by my orders" – but no-one who knew Cochrane would have been surprised by that.[102]

Meanwhile, Robert, who was present in São Luis throughout these events, was preoccupied in keeping the British community safe amidst the general mayhem. Only one British citizen seems to have become politically involved: James Wood. He chartered a ship for a political group opposing the President, and received money for it, but Robert quickly packed him off back to Great Britain, putting him on board the British brig "Crisis", which was bound for Liverpool.[103]

Robert's other letters during 1824 speak of São Luis itself being quiet, but of disturbances continuing in the province at large.[104] In August, food was scarce in São Luis, and there was widespread alarm about the conduct of the resident troops, but the British community was left unharmed. In September, the party opposed to the President was gaining ground, and now held what Robert calls "the mountains", a goodly distance south of the city. Later in the month, one hundred and twenty of the troops from São Luis were killed in a battle with the troops of "the country party". Disturbance and alarm continued, with opposition to the President and his troops growing throughout the next two months. It was obviously time for Lord Cochrane to come back and reassert his control.

Cochrane paid a second visit to São Luis at the end of 1824, over a year after his first. He arrived in the frigate "Piranga" on 9 November, to find anarchy reigning in the province. The leaders of the army had risen against the President, Bruce, and claimed to represent the Empire. Bruce was accused of setting up a dictatorship, and of keeping the province in a ferment in order to support the cause of the pro-Portuguese party in Rio. Law and order was obviously breaking down, and Cochrane took action, arresting and imprisoning Bruce's troops.

In his autobiography[105], Cochrane quotes verbatim two letters he received at this time, just before Christmas, one from the French Vice-Consul, and one from Robert, both expressing concern about the danger to their own citizens of the disturbed state of the Province. Robert's letter speaks of "violent party intrigues... barbarous warfare...[and] merciless outrages", but adds that "the resident British, by general and firm perseverance in a strictly neutral line of conduct, and by calm endurance of not a few unavoidable ills, succeeding in averting from themselves the chief weight of those evils to which all the remaining population were exposed." However, some of the

British community had been openly threatened, including, it would seem, Robert himself, for there is an interesting story in Koebel's book:

"An instance of this [attacks on foreign residents] occurred in 1824 at Maranhão, where the house of a Mr. Hesketh, an English merchant, was forcibly entered by the local authorities. As a hint concerning the unwisdom of such procedure, His Majesty's sloop of war "Eclair", which happened to be at the port, shifted her berth so as to approach the shore and control the place with her guns. In the meantime, an apology was obtained from the local authorities for the occurrence. But the Junta felt itself outraged at the action of the British, and seriously debated as to whether it would not confiscate the "Eclair's" rudder in punishment of this too close and too unceremonious approach!"[106]

So it was with genuine feeling that Robert told Lord Cochrane that "I may be allowed to assert that Your Lordship's presence in this Province for the time being is indispensable for the tranquillity and security of all its inhabitants."

Cochrane's reply to Robert is preserved in the Foreign Office records.[107] It is in Portuguese, of course, for whilst Cochrane was writing to a fellow-Briton, he was in the service of the Empire of Brazil. Cochrane says he has found in Maranhão animosities and opposition to the Emperor, but also "a total want of confidence in regard to personal security" among "the respectable classes". Robbers and assassins are at large, and "every evil which attended the Portuguese Colonial Government exists in an aggravated degree." He concludes that Bruce cannot be left in control "without imminent danger of internal warfare."

Again, Cochrane took action. Miguel Bruce, the President, was told that Cochrane could not move his squadron from the port while Bruce was in power, as he anticipated that the lower orders of soldiery would get out of control and seize power. He therefore suggested that Bruce withdraw from office, and take up Cochrane's offer of a free passage to Rio, so that the Emperor himself could decide Bruce's fate. Bruce, faced with Cochrane's squadron, as well as with his well-known propensity for "exceeding his orders", wisely accepted the offer of the free trip, and peace gradually returned to Maranhão. Cochrane was, of course, accused of dismissing him, but, with his usual silver tongue, explained that he had "suspended his functions merely till His Majesty's pleasure should be known."

Cochrane's high-handedness with his fellow mariners left Robert with a serious problem, after a boat from the Brazilian frigate, the "Piranga", boarded a British merchant brig, "Minerva", in March, 1825, to collect the wages of a former member of the crew who had left to join the Brazilian Navy. Captain Chambers, the Master, told them to return the following day, but an argument broke out, and one of the visitors tried to stab Chambers. The crew of the "Minerva" came to the rescue, and there was a pitched battle on the deck, in which the "Piranga's" crew took a severe beating, and one of them fell overboard and was drowned.[108]

Chambers was arrested, imprisoned, and then let out on bail, but was still threatened with severe punishment, even though he was not on deck when the man drowned. The British community held a public meeting to protest at the threat to Chambers, who had been sentenced to eight years' banishment in the Rio Negro district of the Amazon, which Robert called "sickly". The sentence could be commuted upon payment of a hefty fine (almost a thousand milreis – £125), and this is doubtless what happened. Robert's earlier plea for Cochrane to stay in the port had been successful, but after the "Minerva" affair he must have had some feelings of relief at seeing the "Sea Wolf" and his ship weighing anchor.

Cochrane put it about that he was sailing for Rio, but he never got there. The "Piranga" was next spotted sailing into Portsmouth harbour back in England, flying the Brazilian flag. Cochrane's autobiography is profuse in its explanations, blaming causes as various as defective masts, spars, and the wind for his unforeseen arrival several thousand miles from his supposed destination.[109] The Brazilian Government was, of course, furious, and a vigorous protest was made to Great Britain. Cochrane himself regarded that as the end of his service in the liberation of the Empire of Brazil, but, as usual, left others to tidy up the mess his actions had caused.

Meanwhile, back in Maranhão, Robert was continuing with his usual duties. He reports that trade was surprisingly buoyant, in spite of the "Commotions". Brazilian and Portuguese trade was down, but trade with France was improving, trade with the United States was double that of 1823, and trade with Britain was strong. The "London", 351 tons, had arrived from Liverpool with fish and butter, and the "Nevis", 154 tons, and the "Eliza", 246 tons, had also arrived from Liverpool with merchandise, all of them due to take back "cotton wool", or bales of raw cotton.[110]

1826 came, and with it another tricky problem for Robert Hesketh. Although the transport of slaves had been prohibited to British citizens from 1807, the slave trade had many years to run in Brazil before it was finally abolished. The small British hospital in São Luis had acquired two slaves in the early 1820s with moneys from the Contribution Fund. Robert seems to have realised with a start in 1826 that this was an improper state of affairs, and he wrote to Canning, the Secretary of State for Foreign Affairs, to ask for his help and advice.

Canning was horrified, and John Bidwell, the newly-appointed head of the Consular Department, wrote:

> I am directed by Mr. Secretary Canning to instruct you to declare to them their immediate and complete emancipation, and to render it authentic by some formal Document." Canning went further: "HM's Government, however, in making these poor persons free, does not intend to throw them upon the world, so that they may fall into distress and thence again probably into Slavery. You will enquire whether their services can be made useful in any British Hospital which may be established at Maranham, and should that be the case, you will offer to them at a fair and liberal [rate], for their free labour. If their service should not be required in this way, you will seek out for them elsewhere some employment where they will be comfortable and well-treated, you will see to the fact of their being so treated, by personal examinations each half-year and you will, until you can get them settled, make some arrangement for their maintenance, including the expense thereof as an item in the account of contingent Expenses for which you will have to draw upon His Majesty's Treasury."[111]

Robert had touched a raw nerve in Downing Street – given the bold and public stand the British Government had taken against slavery, it would not do to have two slaves discovered in a British community in Brazil bought and paid for out of official funds. The two slaves, called Jozé and Raimundo, and both aged 18, were freed as soon as Canning's instructions reached São Luis. They were both keen to continue to work at the hospital with Dr. Hall, "to whom they are much attached". Robert, obviously in a state of some embarrassment, promised to continue to look after their welfare.

The British Hospital in Maranhão, supervised by Dr. Hall, was based in a rented house, and had an average of about fifty patients a year. Robert gives an illuminating list of the equipment. It was not always in the best of condition – there were ten chairs, with five other broken chairs; there were only six beds, one of which had a broken leg, and three lacked canvas bottoms. There was a little linen, but only three pillow slips. There were eight spoons, but only two knives and forks. There was only one bed pan, one urinal, one lamp, and one tea pot, and, alarmingly, one "Injection Syringe". If equipment was scarce, funds were scarce too, and medicines expensive. In spite of this, the medical treatment was obviously effective, for the word "cured" is written against every name on the list of patients. One of the patients mentioned was one of Robert's own clerks, Samuel Lowden, who had been ill with fever. Most of the patients were, however, visiting British seamen. Though Maranhão continued to have a doctor, the hospital itself closed soon afterward for lack of funds.

Robert's embarrassment at having to admit that the British Hospital had bought and employed two slaves, was soon followed by a telling-off from London for something else. It concerned the case of James Johnston, a British merchant at São Luis. In April, 1826, Johnston was in his office at the port, when a Portuguese called Senhor Faria came in to settle a bill he owed for the conveyance of freight in the "Pará Packet", which sailed from Falmouth to the ports of São Luis and Belém in Pará. Faria, according to Johnston, acted "in an insulting way, and attempted to defraud the Captain". Faria used "intemperate language", but Johnston replied with "some sort of personal Violence". The incident was witnessed by Johnston's Portuguese and British clerks. Later that day, a soldier arrived at Johnston's office with a warrant for his arrest. The clerks told him Johnston was out, and the soldier went away. Johnston sent for the Order for his arrest, and then went to Robert for help. While they were discussing the incident, an officer arrived from the Governor, and Robert accompanied Johnston to the Palace. Unfortunately, the President was out, and Robert and Johnston left. Johnston then received a letter from the President requiring him to write an apology, and he was summoned again to the Palace for an interview with the President. On this occasion, Robert, whose relationship with President Barros was not good, did not accompany him. Johnston was briefly imprisoned, but the President then changed his mind and released him.

So, in the end no lasting harm was done, but Canning rebuked Robert for not accompanying Johnston in his examination before the President.[112] Robert's reason for leaving Johnston to face the music alone was that he would "have been exposed to personal insult". He had received "an insulting letter" from the President, and he says that he had heard that he was to be arrested a few days later.

Then, suddenly, the President's attitude changed, and Robert was invited to a levee, "where I was received with the most pointed attention and marked respect".[113] This change of attitude might well have had something to do with what happened next. In June, 1826, the old enmity between what might be called the "Portuguese" Brazilians and the "Brazilian" Brazilians had flared up yet again, and with no Cochrane this time to sort things out, anarchy was again threatening the province. Twenty of the Brazilian party had been arrested and put on board several Brazilian Navy ships anchored in the port, and units of the army had been deprived of their artillery. The President was fearful of being assassinated, and asked Robert, the American Consul and the French Vice-Consul if they would allow seamen from British, American, and French merchant ships to be armed, landed, and employed as guards for his person and his government.

This suggestion was, of course, an impossible one, and in company with the American and French Vice-Consuls, Robert refused. Canning offered "his entire approbation of your refusal to comply with the request made to you by the President", and then, in a statement of the proper diplomatic position that Henry Dickenson in Pará might have done well to heed, said: "It is no part of the duty of H.M. Consuls abroad to interfere, or to authorise the interference, of British Subjects in any internal dissensions of the country in which they are resident."[114]

Another dispute between the British merchants and the local authorities in São Luis occurred in 1827, when a Portuguese Brazilian clerk, Jozé Baptista de Souza, employed by Messrs. Willstood and Bingham, was forcibly enlisted in the army. Formerly, clerks in the employ of British firms had been exempt from military service, and Robert sent details of the case to Robert Gordon, the current Consul-General in Rio, so that he could make representations to the national government there. As was usual in almost all disputes between British merchants and the Brazilians, the Imperial Government did not yield an inch. Their communication was sent rather oddly to "The People of the Republic of England", a mode of address which might well have caused widespread alarm in Britain if it had been taken seriously. The reply asserted that the exemption applied only to British-born clerks, and that the clerk concerned, required to join the local Militia, had refused to buy his own uniform, and had therefore, as a punishment, been enrolled in the Regular Army. It went on to say that if the exemption applied to all clerks working in foreign business houses, they would lose 120,000 men, an unbelievably high figure.[115] São Luis was a flourishing port, but it had only seven British mercantile establishments, with, perhaps, a maximum of thirty clerks, many of whom would have been British, and therefore unavailable to the Brazilian military.

In fact, Robert's Trade Report for 1826 paints a picture of comparatively modest levels of trade. In the last six months of the year, sixty vessels had called at the port to bring in or to take out goods. Half of these were Brazilian, coming from other ports in the Empire. Seven were British, twelve American, eight Portuguese, two French, and one Genoese. Whilst the number of British vessels was smaller than usual, Robert was happy that the Brazilian appetite for British manufactured goods was growing – "The

Population [is] becoming annually more habituated to the use of them".116 Robert, only a few degrees south of the Equator, will have hoped that the British cargoes of manufactured goods did not include, as they did elsewhere in Brazil, ice-skates and warming-pans. The ingenious Brazilians were able to convert these cold-climate goods into knives and ladles for sugar-mills respectively.

In 1828, Robert, who had not left his post since 1817, asked the Foreign Office if he could return to England during the following year.117 The Earl of Aberdeen, who was now Foreign Secretary, agreed to the request in February, 1829, "but provisoe [must] be made at your expence, for the discharge of the Consular Duties during your absence".118 The letter took time to come, and it was June before Robert was able to leave for Pará on his way home, leaving his brother, William, in charge as "H.M.'s Deputy Consul". It was the effectively the end of Robert's work in São Luis, and his return there was brief, before he was promoted, in importance if not in salary, to Rio de Janeiro. When he left in 1832, he had served twenty years in Maranhão, the last ten years of which had been troubled almost constantly by the political strife between the old and the new Brazilian orders. If Robert thought that Rio would provide a statelier or calmer life, he was adrift of the mark. As he left São Luis, news came of privateers off the port, flying the flag of Buenos Aires, and after his departure, the British vessel "Admiral Benbow" was plundered, and three of its crew murdered by a pirate schooner. It was the shape of things to come.

10

WILLIAM HESKETH – H.M. DEPUTY CONSUL

"...[He} acted with great zeal, and in a manner perfectly satisfactory both to this department and to the British mercantile interests of that Place." (Foreign Office Memorandum)

While Robert sailed north along the coast in 1829 on his way to Pará, William Hesketh was settling in once more to the Consul's Office in São Luis. He must have been very familiar with it, popping in on many occasions to see his elder brother, Robert, to discuss matters relating to the family business. Heskeths, Wilson, & Co. was the most successful of the seven British firms now established in the port. In 1829, on his journey home via Pará, Robert was rising forty, and William was thirty-five. Their youngest brother, Thomas in Liverpool, was thirty, and had bought himself a house at the bottom of the hill in fashionable Mount Pleasant, where he lived at No. 5, a site now occupied by a concrete car park. Later on, Thomas moved in with his sisters at No. 91, Mount Pleasant, now a hotel. William, however, was to retain his loyalty to his adopted home in Brazil.

William's Will[119] gives us some interesting information about him. Though he lived much of his sixty-two years in Brazil, he seems to have visited England and Liverpool quite regularly, for his two friends, William Bingham and John Clark, both merchants in Liverpool, testified to having been "well acquainted" with William for some time before and up to the time of his death. They testify also to having seen him "write and subscribe his name" on many occasions. The will was proved at home in England, together with an undated codicil, but his executors were two close friends and colleagues in São Luis – William Wilson, a partner in the family firm, and Henry Season of Skarbo and Season, one of the other six merchant establishments in Maranhão. William calls both Wilson and Season "partners", so there may have been some commercial link between Heskeths, Wilson, & Co. and Season's firm.

William wrote his will on 27 July, 1835, over twenty years before his death. Given that most people in the nineteenth century seem to have

Rua de Estrela in the heart of São Luis

written their wills only when staring death in the face, it is possible that William was sick in 1835, perhaps with yellow fever, and not feeling confident about his chances of survival. In his will, he left £100 to his god-daughter, Livia Wilson, the daughter of his partner, William Wilson. He also left a third of his estate to his "natural daughter", Thomozia Rosa da Coureirão. William appears never to have been married, and it is not clear who Thomozia's mother was. Certainly she would have been either Brazilian or African, and, if African, either free or a slave. Thomozia's possession of a second name, and of a Portuguese family name, suggests that her mother was Brazilian, for slaves rarely seem to have had more than one Portuguese name given to them. Thomozia would have been comfortably off when she grew up, but, sadly, the codicil to the will announces that she has died. It is a pity that William did not date the codicil, and it is therefore impossible to know how old she was at her death. Her first name is not a common Portuguese form, and it is possible that William named her after his younger brother in Liverpool.

A rather surprising item in the will concerns Alfonso, " a negroe [sic]... belonging to my firm of Heskeths, Wilson, & Co.", who is to be given his freedom on William's death, "as a reward for his faithful service". It is to be hoped that William granted Alfonso his freedom long before his eventual death, though it is strange that William did not alter his will accordingly. We have already seen that two slaves were owned by the British Hospital in Maranhão in 1826, and hurriedly given their freedom when Robert raised the issue with George Canning, the Foreign Secretary. Heskeths, Wilson, & Co. was, of course, a private firm, and therefore not subject to the same sensitivities as a public institution like the Hospital, but Robert must have found it rather embarrassing to be linked, however tenuously now, to a firm that owned a slave, at the same time as he was working to expose and stop the trade in slaves from Africa. Perhaps this is one reason why he was glad to give up his mercantile interests in Maranhão in 1826.

In the codicil, Thomozia's share of William's estate was allocated to Robert Hesketh, who had been left the residue of the estate even when Thomozia was alive. The will contains touching testimony to the closeness of the family, and to Robert's central role as eldest brother. In his will, William says that he is "entirely indebted to him for the success that has attended me through life and for his brotherly love and affection towards the whole of his family".

In the event of Robert's death, William's estate was to be divided between all his brothers and sisters. Of those who were based in Liverpool, Harriet died in 1833, Thomas in 1840, Louisa in 1845, and Mary Ann in 1856. Their brother, Henry, who was in California, also died in 1856, and John, who was in Belém, died in 1838. William himself was, therefore, one of the longest-lived of the family, and only Robert outlived him for any length of time. Had Robert died earlier, there would have been no one left to inherit William's money.

When William arrived in Brazil, the firm of Robert Hesketh & Co., as it was then, was growing fast at this time and, as we have seen, reached its pre-eminent position amongst foreign merchant firms in Maranhão by 1821. We know that William took over the consulate in 1817 when Robert went to Rio to see the Consul-General, so William must have been well-established in the town by this time, and an automatic choice for acting as Robert's deputy. William was again left in charge when Robert returned to England in 1817.

William's letters to the Foreign Office are neatly written and very businesslike, although he was capable of a fine turn of phrase on occasion. He seems to have played a central part in the institutional life of the British community in São Luis, acting as the Treasurer of the Contribution Fund, and serving on the committee of the Burial Ground. There was therefore plenty of responsibility remaining for him when Robert returned in 1818 after his furlough. Robert did not leave his post again for eleven years, but when he did so in 1829, William was again there to deputise. By now, Robert had withdrawn from "mercantile pursuits", and the name of the firm expanded to "Heskeths, Wilson, & Co.". Robert says he has "entrusted the Duties of this Consulate to Mr. William Hesketh"[120] On this occasion, William's tenure of the office lasted far longer than before, for Robert left Maranhão in July, 1829, and did not return until early in the new year of 1832. He had been intending to return several months earlier, but had been kept in Liverpool by contrary winds until November, 1831, and the voyage to Maranhão had then taken the exceptionally long time of forty-three days.

In Robert's absence, William duly reported on trade. He noted that the largest number of vessels in the port in the first half of 1829 were British, with American ships ranking second. By the end of 1830, however, there were problems affecting foreign trade with the province.[121] William's fellow-merchants were complaining that though taxes had been high, they had recently been raised even further by 100–150%, on the orders of the Imperial Government in Rio. The problem was exacerbated by the local Junta's insistence that all bills be paid according to a fixed formula: ¾ in silver, and ¼ in copper. The inconvenience of this arrangement was made worse by the time taken to prove the silver, and by the fact that the copper coinage was fast depreciating. The overall effect of this was to raise the duties paid by the British merchants to 20%, far higher than the 15% long ago agreed by treaty. A copy of his letter in Portuguese to the Junta still survives. Quite how this problem was resolved is not recorded, though there were constant problems in almost every Brazilian port throughout the next twelve years over the 15% tariff awarded to Great Britain in the 1810 Treaty, and over problems raised by the supply and value of the coinage. The semi-independent status of the provinces also meant that policy throughout the Empire of Brazil was often inconsistent, at least until new orders arrived from the capital. From the evidence of the Foreign Office records, it would seem that British merchants were quick to question changes in policy and complain.

Six months later, in June, 1831, political events in Rio were beginning to affect the whole country. Dom Pedro I's abdication, as we have noted, left his young son, also called Pedro, to inherit the Empire. Pedro's tender age (he was five) meant that Regents had to rule Brazil for the next decade. The consequent political turmoil affected every part of Brazil, including Maranhão. William's comment on the situation in Maranhão shows the way that the underlying tensions in Brazilian society, such as the tension between the Portuguese and those native to Brazil, came to the surface immediately the

abdication was announced. He had "advised British merchants not to interfere with 'contending parties'. The "Brazilian party" was demanding the
resignation of the Military Governor, and other European officers were
deposed. The troops were beginning to show signs of insubordination, and
the City Militia – mostly Portuguese – had been disbanded and banished.
The President, Jozé de Arajo Viana, was still popular, but "the violent
Brazilian and coloured population" was causing trouble, headed by no other
than the President deposed and sent to Rio seven years earlier by Lord
Cochrane, Miguel Ignacio dos Santos Freire e Bruce As a precaution,
William had informed the British Naval Commander-in-Chief in the West
Indies of these events.[122]

William's next letter[123] was about the escalation of violence between the
two parties. An armed mob had demanded the sacking of all European-born
personnel from public office. "Respectable Brazilians are panic-stricken,"
reported William, and being brow-beaten by the extremists. So far, "Public
tranquillity.... has been scrupulously preserved... but it is not to be expected
that a Mob of Mulattoes joined to a mutinous Soldiery can be long kept
from committing excesses." William suspected that trouble was being
fomented deliberately, so that the northern provinces of Brazil could secede
from the Empire.

By the end of October, 1831, the province was calmer, and the troops
were more orderly, with fresh reinforcements having arrived from Caxias to
the far south of Maranhão. The Revolutionary Party's demand that European army officers be dismissed had been strongly rejected by the soldiers
in the ranks. William blamed "the Federal Party" in Rio for the unrest, and
said that there were "secret Clubs of People of Colour" set up throughout
the province. "Subversive notions have been insidiously promulgated among
the lower classes, especially the mischievous doctrine of Equality and Division of Property." He pondered on the population statistics. There were
eighty thousand slaves in the province, with a further fifty thousand who
were black, mulatto, or Indian. There were only twenty thousand whites,
with a mere eight hundred troops to keep the peace. This all added up, said
William, to a keen threat to the lives of the whites.[124]

Three weeks after this letter, trouble again surfaced, with an "armed
Revolutionary mob" demanding the deposition of the President and the
Commander-in-Chief, and threatening to pillage the city, and kill all Europeans. The President asked for the help of British merchant crews docked in
the harbour, but William refused, in line with the established British policy
on non-interference, and following his brother's example of some years
earlier. The situation was only defused when the rest of the resident troops

refused to back the revolutionaries. The police initially rebelled, but then back-tracked, and were pardoned.[125]

William was well aware that his abiding concern throughout all this time was the safety of British lives and property, and he seems to have kept the British community out of the limelight, and out of danger. The ominous signs of future trouble, however, were laid out for all to see: a strong and prosperous Portuguese presence in the province, a very large and resentful underclass, an unreliable army, and a lack of strong leadership both in the capital, Rio de Janeiro, and in Maranhão itself. Though Maranhão did not have its revolution until 1839, the same ingredients were present in Pará in 1835, where they had altogether a more vicious and serious outcome in the Cabanagem Rebellion (see Chapter 15)

Meanwhile, for William as for Robert and John, the abandonment of Canning's fine plans for a salaried and full-time consular service was disastrous. The handsome salary of £1,000 which Robert had been receiving for many years was halved, and the Foreign Office, under strong pressure from the Lords of the Treasury, announced quite blithely that the new salary, £500, "together with the authorized fees, will form an adequate remuneration."[126] William's spirits will certainly have flagged at this news, but things were to get worse. William had been undertaking the responsibilities of the consulate at Maranhão since Robert's departure on 12 July, 1829, though for some reason the Foreign Office later calculated it from 10 October. William had performed well, according to a Foreign Office memo of May, 1832: "In the period of his acting Consulship, Mr. Hesketh acted with great Zeal, and in a manner perfectly satisfactory both to this department and to the British mercantile interests of that Place."[127] In spite of this, Palmerston decided to pay him at a rate of only £300 per annum, and offeed him a total of only £375 for the eighteen months' work he had done in Robert's absence.

William was an experienced businessman, and was not, of course, happy at being short-changed, and wrote immediately to complain.[128] Palmerston replied in May, 1832, holding out the hope that William might get a further £200, which would at least have brought him to the £500 per year to which Robert had been entitled. But Palmerston was leaving office, and took the easy way out of leaving the final decision to his successor.

By this time, Robert had been offered and had accepted the post of Consul at Rio, also on a salary of £300 p.a., and William was quite prepared to accept the permanent position now available at Maranhão. But, having done the job for eighteen months, he felt that £500 was the least he would accept for what was a stressful role. He complains that superintending the Slave Trade regulations was a duty "peculiarly obnoxious to the merchants whose interests are so tied up in it. The Consul is subjected to the ill-will and violent passions of the Brazilians engaged in it." In spite of this, William claimed that he has acted with great zeal in the matter.[129]

Falsely buoyed by a supportive letter from Palmerston, William then went further, and at that point made a tactical error. Though he clearly wanted the job, he decided to hold out for the salary of £500. "No resident Merchant of Respectability," he wrote, "acquainted with the duties of the Office would accept the post of Consul at Maranham at the salary of £300."

As we have seen, someone did. It was John Moon, whom William must have known very well. He was a member of another well-established British firm in Maranhão with links to Lisbon, and with a branch in Rio; Henry and John Moon & Co. On 29 November, 1832, a letter arrived in São Luis: "The King has been graciously pleased to appoint John Moon Esq. to be His Majesty's Consul at Maranham", at the controversial salary of £300.[130]

By this time, things had moved on. Robert had briefly returned to Maranhão and taken over the Consulate again, only to leave for Rio on 7 July. William had gone to England, and it was from London that he carried on his complaints to the Foreign Office. When Robert left, he appointed his other partner, William's close friend, William Wilson, to the Consulate for the few months while a new appointment was made.

William could, one suspects, have counted on the new post if he had not held out for the £500. He must have known that the wind from the Foreign Office was not blowing kindly. Robert had, after all, just accepted, however reluctantly, a much more onerous role in Rio at the very low salary of £300 p.a. At the same time, the Foreign Office, and Palmerston in particular, seem to have acted in a rather unprincipled way. Having decided to halve the original salary of £1,000 per year, they then took it down further to £300 per year, and offered William only £375 for at least eighteen months' work, when, even at the low rate of £300 p.a., it might have been £450. The Foreign Office archives do not record William's final settlement, though one assumes that Palmerston's successor will have been no more sympathetic: Maranhão was, in any case, a distant port, and it was hard for William to protest after the event, and after the work had been done. With all his commercial experience, William should not have been surprised that the Foreign Office would be quite happy to settle for the lowest expenditure possible.

Palmerston was, of course, under tremendous pressure from the House of Commons over consular and diplomatic spending. Members, irate at the steep rise in total costs, took little note of the international political changes which had caused so many new appointments in, for example, South America. Their attention was only on the total cost. The Foreign Office archives contain many internal documents from this period, with countless attempts at calculating possible reductions in consular and diplomatic salaries. The losers were always going to be those members of the service who were too distant from London to complain effectively, and who had no direct family influence on those who ran the Foreign Office. Consuls were always, in any case, going to have less lobbying power than their colleagues in the diplomatic service. Palmerston could not be but well aware of the problems, but, in one of his less glorious moments a few years later, maintained that he could think of no improvements that could usefully be made to the Foreign Service. If Canning had been supported, or perhaps had lived longer than 1827, the logic of his 1825 reforms would have benefited the service immensely, with salaried representatives who had no extra mercantile responsibilities, and a proper career structure. The chaos and lack of direction obvious in the Foreign Office at this time damaged Britain's interests, as well as damaging the Hesketh family amongst many others. Palmerston and his colleagues were guilty, at the least, of poor management, and, at the worst, of cynicism.

William returned to Maranhão, doubtless sadder but wiser. The firm of Heskeths, Wilson, & Co. was still flourishing in 1837, when they were represented at a meeting of the Maranham Burial Ground Committee.[131] At a further meeting of the Committee in January, 1838, the firm is said to be "in liquidation".[132] Later that year, the Consul at Maranhão, John Moon, became ill, and William Wilson again stepped into the breach, becoming Acting Consul once more. He served throughout much of the Balaiada Rebellion in 1840, until John Moon's brief return to duty in December, 1840. Moon only served for a further year, asking for leave again in November, 1841, and leaving Maranhão for the last time in February, 1842. He again left William Wilson in charge. Moon died in Lisbon on 29 May, 1842, and was succeeded not by the long-suffering William Wilson, but by Robert Falconer Corbett, from Belém.

William Hesketh must have watched all these comings and goings with close interest. He could not claim that he had not had his chance, but he was not the first to find that sticking to his principles did not do much for his career. The liquidation of the family firm in 1838 seems to have left him comfortably off, as his Will attests. He did not return home permanently, and seemed content to live in retirement in Maranhão. Some of his brother John's children came to live in Maranhão in the mid-1840s, presumably at his house, or at least in close contact with him. John's mother-in-law also moved to Maranhão in 1845, so it is likely that he continued to play a large, avuncular part in the life of the family. By this time, John and his wife were dead, and Robert was far away in Rio de Janeiro, with William the last repre-sentative of the older generation of Heskeths in northern Brazil.

Today in São Luis, there is little evidence of the English influence so strong in the port in the early nineteenth century. The British Consul, now Honorary, works from Fortaleza in Ceará, which has become the dominant port on the north-east coast, and there are no obvious traces in São Luis of the Consulate, the Hospital, or the British Burial Ground, about which there were so many meetings and so many letters. The denomination of São Luis as a World Heritage Site has provided money to restore the old, picturesque buildings – known locally as the *Projeto Reviver* – but it has also frozen the old town at a particular time in its history. The quay and the big warehouse on the waterfront survive, but the quay is empty of cotton bales, the ware-house has become a museum, and the business quarter has moved over the River Anil to the new part of town. There are no large ships sailing into the tricky harbour – only small pleasure-boats scuttling over the bay, perhaps to the town of Alcântara, which is the site of the Brazilian rocket-launching pad. King Cotton has given way to the Space Race.

SECTION III

PLACES:
SANTA MARIA DE BELÉM

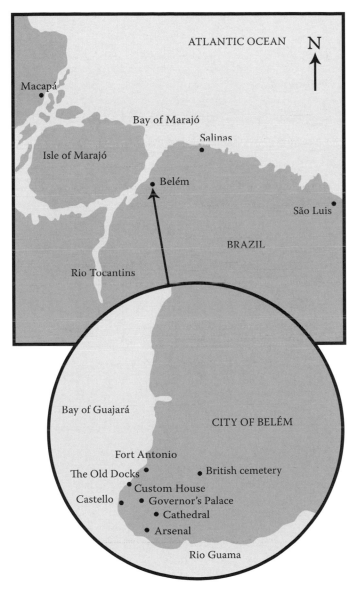

Belém – main features c.1835

11

SANTA MARIA DE BELÉM

"...o terra de ricas florestas,
Fecundadas ao sol do ecuador... ('Hymn of Pará' – Arthur Porto)

("Land of rich forests, Fertilised by the soil of the Equator...")

The city of Santa Maria de Belém was founded in 1616, not long after São Luis, by Francisco Caldeira. Its discoverer had set out from the newly-settled colony of Maranhão; three centuries later, the two towns were still closely linked in trade, transport, and politics. What was happening in one was always a matter of concern and interest to the other. In the early nineteenth century, their successes and their tribulations followed a parallel track.

There were some geographical similarities, too. Both lay close to the dangerous and tricky north coast of Brazil, with its equatorial weather and its perilous tides. Both cities controlled the entrance to a vast river-system. Both lay at a great distance from the rest of Brazil, with Rio de Janeiro several weeks' sailing-time away. But there were differences, too: São Luis lay only a mile or two from the Atlantic coast, with a shallow harbour, whereas Belém lay 80 miles (120 kilometres) from the coast, and its harbour was spacious if not deep.

Belém was named after the royal enclave of the same name in Lisbon, which, in its turn, was a rendering of the name of Christ's birthplace. For much of its history, it has also been called Pará, although that term is properly reserved for the province as a whole, which was the largest in Brazil, and included the major part of the great Amazon basin. The site on which the city was built offered a ready opportunity to erect a fort or two, a naval arsenal, a cathedral and several other churches, a bishop's palace (for it soon merited a bishopric under the archiepiscopate of Lisbon), a Governor's Palace, and a Customs-House, all along or near the waterfront. In 1819, when John Hesketh first arrived there to run his mercantile business, there was still dense forest surrounding the city. There was also a great deal of fertile land around it, and along the banks of the rivers which formed the Amazon delta. The province's products were many and various, most

The city of Pará (or Belém), with the Custom-House on the left, and the *Castello* on the right

growing in the forest: cocoa, corn, rice, cinnamon, coffee, sugar, India rubber, nuts, and drugs of many kinds. By the middle of the nineteenth century, Pará was exporting all these, along with tapioca, balsam, capivi, anatto, isinglass, cotton, sarsaparilla, cloves, copal, vanilla, and many hard-woods. It was also exporting hides in some quantity, for the vast island of Marajó, 120 miles long and as large as Switzerland, lay across the Bay of Guajará from Belém, and produced large herds of cattle.

Pará's rubber boom was some years off. Charles Goodyear was already busy with the process of vulcanisation in 1839 and 1840. His work was to change Belém for ever. Augustus Cowper, John Hesketh's successor as Consul in Pará, suggested that there were many minerals to be exported, "if the people were not so ignorant", and talked about gold deposits[133], but his optimism has only recently been fulfilled, with the development of mineral extraction plants in the province. In 1840, two years after John's death, the population of the city was only thirteen thousand, of whom a third were free men and women over twenty-one, a third were slaves, and a third were children. There were also over four hundred people who originated in other countries, twenty-five of them British. At a time when the steam-engine was powering a vast number of industrial processes in Great Britain, there were still only two steam engines in the city, one used to prepare rice, the other used in a sugar-mill. There was a poor standard of elementary education, according to Cowper, and only the Portuguese inhabitants possessed any degree of education. He had a low opinion of the city's priests, who were "unrivalled demagogues; they are the cause of disturbance, and have immoral habits." Trade, which had been growing encouragingly in the early 1830s, had been dealt a harsh blow by the Cabanagem Rebellion later in the decade, and was only recovering slowly again in 1840. The province was divided into four regions, twenty-six parishes, and a hundred and seven districts, and was headed by a President appointed by the Emperor for a period of three years. The Provincial Assembly had limited powers, and was elected by only three hundred and twenty men out of the total population of four hundred thousand people.

There are numerous accounts in existence of Belém in the mid nine-teenth century, for it was a popular starting or finishing point for the increasing number of expeditions up the Amazon. William H. Edwards, for instance, set off from New York in February, 1846, for Pará, on the "Undine" in the company of the American Consul to Pará, Mr. Smith and his wife.[134] After twenty days, they saw the blue-green water of the Atlantic Ocean change to the muddy-brown waters of the Amazon. They steered past the two great sand-banks, the Bragança and the Tigoça, and sailed past the settlement of Salinas, with its broad, white beach and its dangerous breakers. Normally, ships took on a pilot here, but the "Undine's" captain decided to trust to his own skill, and proceeded up the river against the current and the tide, to begin the 24-hour trip to Belém.

On the right stretched the long island of Marajó, and on the left, a series of long, low islands. They passed tall trees, clearings, and haystack-shaped huts, and then threaded their way past the islands that lie twenty miles north of the city. They reached Belém at 8 o'clock at night, and anchored opposite the town. "It was too late for a visit, and we turned in, impatient for the morning. All night long, church bells were ringing, and clocks striking, and, at inter-vals, we could distinguish the notes of a bugle, or the loud cry of the patrol."

The next morning, they awoke to find that they were anchored amongst ships of many nations, river-boats, and canoes loaded with all kinds of produce. "Fine-looking buildings, of three or four stories height, faced the water, all yellow in colour, and roofed with red tiles. Vast cathedrals and churches covered with the mould of age, shot up their tall spires, their walls and roofs affording sustenance and support to venerable mosses and shrubs of goodly size. Garden walls were hung with creeping vines, like ancient ruins. Vultures were leisurely wheeling over the city, or, in clusters, upon the housetops, spreading their wings to the sun. Mid the ringing of bells, and the discharge of rockets, a long procession was issuing from the church of San Antonio, and a Babel of sounds, from dogs and parrots, and strange tongues, came over the water."

After the formalities of a visit from the port doctor and a custom-house official, they went ashore, past the files of canoes drawn up above the high-water mark:

> "The more fortunate occupants, who have sold their wares, are variously engaged; some sleeping; others, preparing their morning meal; others, combing and arranging their luxuriant tresses.... and others, the most of all, chattering with their neighbours, or screaming in shrill tones to friends on shore. Here are negroes of every shade and colour, from the pure Congo, to the almost pure whites; some buying, some selling. There stands one, with his basket of coarse cotton cloth and his yard-stock; and close by, an old wench is squatted by a pot of yellow soup, the extract of some palm-nut. Here are strings of inviting fish and piles of less captivating terrapins; coarse baskets filled with Vigia crabs, the best in the world; and others of palm-leaves, fashioned like a straw reticule, are swelled out with the delicious snails. Monkeys, fastened to logs, entice you to purchase them by their antics; and white herons, and various other wild birds, by their beauty. Everywhere, and most numerous of all, are the fruit-dealers, and for a mere nothing, all the luxuries of the fruit-prolific clime are yours ... the singularly neat appearance of the women, each dressed in white, and with a flower in her hair, and you remember that it is a holiday. Oddly-dressed soldiers mingle among the crowd; inquisitive officials peer about for untaxed produce; sailors, from vessels in the harbour, are constantly landing; gentlemen of the city are down for their morning stroll, beautiful Indian girls flit like visions, and scores of boys and girls in all the freedom of nakedness, contend with an equal number of impudent goats, for the privilege of running over you."

The naturalist, H.W. Bates, approached the city from the same direction two years later, in 1848, at the end of a voyage from Liverpool.[135] He was travelling with Alfred Russel Wallace, the co-propounder with Darwin of the theory of natural selection. His captain took on a pilot at Salinas, and then sailed down the river, which was thirty-six miles broad at its mouth, and was still twenty miles broad opposite Belém. Higher up the river, other

The Market Wharf.

The Market Wharf in Belém in the nineteenth century

rivers joined it, especially the Tocantins, which was sixteen hundred miles long, and ten miles broad at its mouth.

Belém is "built on a low tract of land, having only one small rocky elevation at its southern extremity... the white buildings, roofed with red tiles, the numerous towers and cupolas of churches and convents, the crowns of palm trees reared above the buildings, all sharply defined against the clear blue sky... The perpetual forest hems the city in on all sides landwards, and towards the suburbs, picturesque country houses are seen scattered about, half buried in luxuriant foliage."

He met the consignee of the vessel, Daniel Miller, who was soon to be appointed Consul, and went for an evening walk:

"There was "ringing uproar" everywhere, with the sounds of cicadas, frogs, and toads. After traversing the few streets of tall, gloomy convent-looking buildings near the port, inhabited chiefly by merchants and shopkeepers, along which [wandered] idle soldiers, dressed in shabby uniforms, carrying their muskets carelessly over their arms, priests, negresses with red water-jars on their heads, sad-looking Indian women carrying their naked children astride on their hips... we passed down a long, narrow street leading to the suburbs... The street was unpaved, and inches deep in loose sand ...The houses were mostly in a dilapidated condition, & signs of indolence and neglect were everywhere visible."

Everywhere he was conscious of the "overpowering beauty of the vegetation", with sturdy mango trees, and "here and there, shooting above the more dome-like and sombre trees, were the smooth columnar stems of palms, bearing aloft the magnificent crowns of finely-cut fronds."

Twenty years earlier, before the Cabanagem Rebellion had severely damaged the city's buildings, Lieutenant Henry Maw and his navy colleague Edward Hinde had approached Belém from the south.[136] They had crossed the continent from Peru, following the Amazon for the whole of its course. At Santarém, eight hundred and fifty miles up the river, Maw and Hinde had been imprisoned by the Military Governor, and were still seething with indignation. They were in no mood for sightseeing, and, upon their arrival in the city, made straight for the Vice-Consul, John Hesketh, to make a formal complaint to the Governor. Later on, however, when Maw had received the apology he sought, he had time and patience to describe the city. The Custom-House, was "large, well-built, and apparently commodious... with a distinct quay, with a broad flight of wooden stairs leading up to it." The houses were large, and "most of them well-built. The streets are also broad, and some of them paved." Maw noticed that the River Guama opened into the bay of Guajará just below the city, and beyond the Naval Arsenal. "The principal building in Pará is the palace, a large square two stories high, having a large balcony of the second story [sic] ornamented with large wooden figures at the outer part, and palm-trees between the windows." The palace still exists, and was to form the backdrop for a significant murder six years later.

The next two eye-witnesses, two more naval officers, W. Smyth and F. Lowe, arrived in Pará shortly before that murder. The city was already in a very unsettled state. They were welcomed by the merchant community, but could not but be aware of the violent undercurrents within the city. They stayed in a rented house, but it was not safe to go out at night, and their social life and their knowledge of the city suffered accordingly. They did, however, notice the locals' habit of keeping "boa-snakes", presumably anacondas, in their houses, to deter vermin. In a warehouse belonging to Mr. Smith, the same American Consul who returned on the "Undine" in 1845, "we saw a very large one, which was between fifteen and eighteen feet long; he said it was perfectly tame, and that he never supplied it with any food, and as it never did any mischief, he supposed it caught a sufficient quantity of rats for its support. When we saw it, it was partly coiled around a cross-beam fixed to two uprights, which had been placed there for its use. It had recently cast its slough, and the brilliancy of its colours was inconceivably vivid."[137]

Herbert H. Smith, another American, was in Belém much later, in about 1880, but also commented on "the never-failing beauty of the vegetation in the outskirts", and described the Rua dos Mercadores, still one of the main streets, crowded with stands selling Açai juice, the distinctive Pará beverage, and noted that the Indian canoes were being gradually replaced with steam-powered vessels. He enjoyed the morning sun, the afternoon rain, and the beauty of the evenings.[138]

Today, Belém is a much larger city, and it has long ago driven back the dense jungle. But many of the nineteenth century travellers' observations remain true. The waterfront, active during John Hesketh's time, and even more so during the rubber boom, still bustles, with the *Ver-o-Peso* market, and the *docas* (the docks), which have been cleaned up and turned into an attractive mall of shops and restaurants. One of the two forts still exists, and contains a museum of pre-Columbian artefacts. The old buildings nearby – the palaces and convents – have largely been restored to their earlier glory, and the churches are as well-thronged as ever. The nearby harbour is crowded with fishing-boats, which putter up and down the river. The open-air market nearby is large and odorous, and the centre of the city is still crowded. The pavements are as imperfect as they were a century and a half ago. Açai stands are still plentiful. The religious festivals are still kept noisily and enthusiastically, and processions are announced by firecrackers and clouds of pyrotechnic smoke. The Naval Arsenal has been attractively restored, and is still the local headquarters of the Brazilian Navy. The weather is still warm and wet, often at the same time. There is still a British Consul in the city, though he is now "Honorary".

A thriving export and import trade remains, though the docks are further down the river nowadays, and modern exporters and importers do not have to deal with the bartering system which obtained in the 1820s and 1830s. In those days, Brazilian currency was a very uncertain and unreliable medium for business – Maw goes as far as to say that there was in 1829 "no circulating medium". The troubles of the 1830s played havoc with European trade to Belém, and the slowly-growing commerce of the 1820s did not recover until the 1840s. Richard Ryan, the British Consul from 1842 to 1850, was gloomy about the prospects for trade, commenting on the "yearly increasing indolence & apathy of the higher classes of Brazilians", and criti-

The Naval Arsenal in Belém

cising the "inferior & ignorant men running the Province".[139] But Ryan did not reckon with the rubber boom. William Scully, writing his Brazilian guidebook in 1868[140], shows a table of the number of ships and total tonnage, which was greater than that of Maranhão, though it was only a tenth of the fast-growing trade of Rio. He says that the harbour of Belém is safe, but is only used by smaller vessels, of 150 to 300 tons. Larger steam-ships had to moor further down-river.

The inhabitants of Belém in the early nineteenth century "present the most varied & curious mixture of races", according to Alfred Russel Wallace.[141] In 1755, sanctions against intermarriage had been abandoned in Pará, and this, along with the fact that most Portuguese immigrants were young and single, had meant that a century later most Belenos were of mixed race. With the eye of a biologist Wallace describes "fresh-coloured Englishmen, ... the sallow American, the swarthy Portuguese, the more corpulent Brazilian, the merry Negro, and the apathetic but finely-formed Indian." The Indians and the slaves wore little – "simply a pair of striped or white cotton trousers, to which they sometimes add a shirt of the same material." The white inhabitants, however, "generally dress with great neatness with linen-clothes of spotless purity. Some adhere to the black cloth coat and cravat." The women and girls "on most gala occasions dress in pure white, which, contrasting with their glossy black or brown skins, has a very pleasant effect; and it is then that the stranger is astonished to behold the massy gold chains and ornaments worn by these women, many of whom are slaves." Children seem to wear very little, if anything at all.

The European women were, according to Maw in 1829, very reluctant to venture out alone. "When a lady goes to visit her neighbour, she is carried in a hammock slung to a pole, with a large cloth thrown over to prevent her being seen." As the years went by, however, the visitors noted changes. Wallace observed, twenty years later, "On moonlight evenings till eight o'clock ladies walk about the streets and suburbs without any head-dress and in ball-room attire", and Herbert H. Smith, in 1880, noted that the ladies of Pará were not shut up as much as those in other Brazilian cities. Smith also makes a rather enigmatic observation about the merchants: "In large transactions, the Pará merchant is governed, perhaps, rather by a wholesome regard for the law than by any abstract reasoning." This comment finds an echo in earlier criticisms that the British merchants in Belém were excessively litigious.

Belém always possessed a substantial number of Portuguese merchants who suffered greatly in the troubles of the 1830s, but the other foreign merchants were never numerous. Mr. Harrop was said to be the first foreign merchant to have settled in Belém, but a more substantial group arrived at about the same time as John Hesketh in 1819. Most, if they married at all, married Brazilian women, often from wealthy families, and they inherited not only fine houses, but also a coterie of family slaves. Some prospered mightily, often at the expense of their colleagues, and, far from working closely together, they seem to have created an atmosphere of distrust and disharmony. We shall shortly meet many of these quarrelling ex-patriates, who caused their Vice-Consul, John Hesketh, a great deal of trouble. Consul Ryan, after his arrival, reported to the Foreign Office: "It is painful to have to report to Your Lordship that I found the few British merchants resident here in almost open hostility towards each other... The almost total want of good feeling that unfortunately exists here between the resident British Merchants proves to me the absolute necessity for having a Judge Conservator to prevent the constant recurrence of exposing in the National Tribunals, by petty actions, the rancour that exists between them."[142]

It is tempting to transfer Bishop Heber's words from Ceylon to Pará: "... every prospect pleases, and only man is vile." The personal hostilities of the British merchants, and the first rumblings of the political cataclysms of the 1830s, were lying in wait for John Hesketh from Liverpool, who sailed into the port in 1819, doubtless full of high hopes and ambitions.

JOHN HESKETH – COUNTING HOUSE TO CABANAGEM

"... the opportunity of serving my country, and meriting the esteem of my Gracious Sovereign" (John Hesketh, 1824)

Louisa Ann, the wife of John Hesketh of Porto, gave birth to their fourth child on 9 May, 1791. He was twenty-one months younger than Robert and Louisa, the twins. His parents called him John after his father.

John the younger was seven years old when his mother died after the birth of her youngest child, Thomas. He was sixteen when the French invaded Portugal in 1807, and he and his family fled back to England.

We know that John was himself a merchant in Liverpool in 1818, for Gore's "Directory of Liverpool" has him living at 18 Gloucester Place, off Kensington, a long road that rises from the city centre and up towards Prescot and the rest of Lancashire. His "counting-house" address is Molyneux Place, Water Street, right in the heart of Liverpool's commercial quarter, and in a street which led directly down to the banks of the Mersey. In earlier editions of the "Directory", Gore mentions other John Heskeths. In 1810, for instance, there is a John Hesketh who is listed as "Accountant", with an address at 21 Princes Street, just off Water Street. Another John Hesketh is listed in the 1811 edition, described as a "Collector of Property Tax", with an address in Great Crosshall Street, further away from the river, and close to the present site of St. George's Hall. In 1814 and 1816, Gore lists a John Hesketh who is a "Bookkeeper" with an address at 35 Lime Street, again only a step away from the other addresses. It is difficult to be certain whether these are all the future British Consul in Pará, but it would not be surprising if John, with his facility for accounting, had not tried various roles within the financial sector before acquiring the resources to set up as a merchant. He would almost certainly be importing and exporting goods, maybe including some from Maranhão, where Robert and William were already well-established.

By 1818, John's youngest brother, Thomas, was nineteen, and thought capable of running the Liverpool end of the family business. Maybe Robert

Drawn by G. & C. Pyne.

Engraved by R. Aco...

WATER STREET. 1828

Water Street, Liverpool, where John Hesketh had his office, in the early nineteenth century

and William thought the time was ripe for expansion, and that Pará, further up the northern Brazilian coast, was a suitable site for another branch of the family business. When Robert had to come to John's aid a decade later, the implication is that John was running a separate business, although, of course, they may have co-operated. There was less cotton produced in Pará than in Maranhão, but the Amazon forest provided a whole range of desirable goods. John took up the challenge, and was established in Pará by 1819. When he arrived in Brazil, he was twenty-seven or twenty-eight, considerably older than Robert and William had been when they began their careers in South America.

As far as we know, John had not married in Liverpool, but once in Pará he lost no time in losing his heart to an attractive young Brazilian, Margarida de Mattos, and they were married fairly rapidly. There is a later suggestion by Cowper, his successor, that Margarida was only fourteen years old when they married. Although it would have been unlikely in England, the marriage of a twenty-eight year-old man with a fourteen year-old girl would not have been so exceptional in South America. Girls were expected to assume adult responsibilities early in Roman Catholic Brazil. It is certainly true that by 1824 they had two children, a boy and a girl, for it was in that year that the family appeared on an application for passports made to the Governor of Pará by the then Vice-Consul, Henry Dickenson. John and Margarida were presumably married in one of the many Catholic churches in Belém, though we have found no records. Margarida was the daughter of Dona Francisca Leonarda de Mattos, and we know that she had at least one sister, probably younger than herself. The identity of her father is not certain, for de Mattos is a common surname, but a likely candidate is a distinguished military man, Colonel João Henrique de Mattos, who was born in Barcelos on the Rio Negro in 1784, became Military Commandant of Cametá, Vigia, and Macapá in the 1830s, and was later well-known for his survey of the resources of the Amazon. He published his report in 1846, the *Relatorio do Estado de Decadencia em que se acha o Alto Amazonas* ("Report of the State of Decadence in Alto Amazonas"). He died at the age of seventy-three in 1857 on the Rio Cucui. If indeed he was Margarida's father, he would certainly have had to live away from his family for almost all his career. There is a later reference to a Colonel de Mattos in a letter written by the British Consul, Samuel Vines, in 1856, about the intestacy of both John Hesketh and a Mr. Dickson. De Mattos was involved in the legal proceedings following the death of Mr. Dickson, who is described as his son-in-law. It is tempting to speculate that Mr. Dickson had been married to Margarida's sister, and that John Hesketh was therefore also Col. de Mattos's son-in-law.

By a stroke of luck, we have at least some indication of Margarida's appearance, and of her relationship with her husband. Lieutenant Henry Lister Maw, whom we have already met, finished his journey down the Amazon at Pará on 19 April, 1828.[143] His incarceration in Santarém meant that he was keen to report the facts to the local Vice-Consul, and, as a result, he got to know John Hesketh well. His first dinner invitation was to John's house, and he gives a long description of the event. He speaks of being introduced to Mrs. Hesketh, her mother, and an unmarried sister, who lived with them. "Mrs. Hesketh," said the young Maw, "had been, and still was, pretty, and appeared much attached to her husband."

The two children John and Margarida had before 1824 had been joined by others by the time of Maw's visit in 1828. Maw went for dinner a second time, and says that he often called at John's house on his way back after an evening's ride. "On one of these occasions, I was talking to Mr. Hesketh respecting snakes, with which he said his lawn and garden were infested, and on the following morning, he sent me a snake upwards of seven feet long, which had been killed in his children's nursery during the night."

Eventually, John and Margarida were to have eight children: a girl whose name does not feature in the records, John – the eldest boy, and six other brothers – Robert, William, Henry, Thomas, Mariano, and James. Maw describes the house they lived in until the Cabanagem Rebellion of 1835-6. "Mr. Hesketh's house has no second storey, but is well-built, containing several large well-furnished rooms, with a broad veranda on two sides, which in a climate like Pará, is a most desirable appendage. Between the house and the road is a large lawn, that keeps the former sufficiently retired; there is also a garden in which Mr. Hesketh amuses himself, having a taste for botany."

We have some information about how John and Margarida's house was furnished, for when Dona Francesca, Margarida's mother, left for São Luis in 1845, she left an inventory of John and Margarida's property [Appendix II]. The inventory describes the contents of "a country-house with gardens planted in the street of St. Joseph", which was the last house John Hesketh and his wife lived in. It lists considerable stocks of cutlery and crockery, and, in a country which tended to furnish its rooms rather sparsely, a reasonable amount of furniture.

Maw also describes the dinner-party in some detail. The ladies spoke only in Portuguese, which left Maw and his companion Hinde compelled to talk to the Englishmen present. But he devotes a several lines to Margarida's unmarried sister: "The ladies, however, were not wanting in attendants, particularly the unmarried sister, who had a variety of beaux, whom she managed rather skilfully, noticing their attentions more of less according as superior favourites were absent or present. From what I afterwards heard and saw, I suspect the brother of Mr. Campbell was the prime favourite, although lameness from an accident prevented his being of the party. The young lady had taught herself to play upon the piano, which she performed with a considerable degree of taste, accompanying the instrument with her voice." The Mr. Campbell referred to must have been Archibald Campbell, whose involvement with the Heskeths continued for many a long year, not always happily for the family. Maw himself sounds as if he was in danger of becoming one of Margarida's sister's "beaux".

He also comments on the menu:

"The dinner was sumptuous, and a variety of rich wines were on the table, but there was one dish, although it was considered a luxury, did not accord with my taste – it was a stew made out of a land tortoise. Such a mess," he concludes rather tartly, "might be well enough up the Marañon [the Amazon], in lieu of a dried monkey, but when "carne vaca", or roast beef, was to be had, it did not appear to be desirable."

The quality of John's wine-cellar is not surprising in view of the fact that both his father and his grand-father had been wine-merchants. Maw describes going to a funeral a few days later, at which many of the British merchants were present. The service was read by one of the oldest, as Mr. Hesketh, who generally officiated, was unwell. One trusts the cause was not the tortoise stew.

If Maw is to be believed, John was living well, with a loving and attractive wife, a fast-growing family, and a pleasant and spacious house. By this time, he had been in Pará for nine years, and his business affairs must have been going fairly well. He had survived the first of several political crises in the province in 1821, when the regular troops in Pará briefly rebelled. When news of Pedro I's declaration of independence came in 1822, there was a whole range of reactions in Pará, from the enthusiasm of those who saw themselves primarily as Brazilians, to the bitter opposition of those who were Portuguese, and who wanted to keep Pará as a dependency of Lisbon.

Passions continued to run high, and in October, 1823, there was widespread disorder, with looting of both Brazilian and foreign property, and threats to kill the foreign residents. The arrival in the port of Captain Pascoe Grenfell, sent by Admira Cochrane, the head of the Brazilian Navy, initially calmed tempers down, especially after he had repeated Cochrane's ruse of pretending the rest of the Brazilian Navy was close behind him, and thus obtained the loyalty of the local Junta.

But Grenfell's arrival was the signal for the pro-Brazilian party to settle old scores, and some of the troops joined them in attacking the property and persons of what Dickenson called "Europeans", although they were almost certainly largely Portuguese. Drink fuelled the disorder, and the rioters threatened to annihilate all whites. Grenfell landed his crew, and restored order, disarming the mutinous troops. Next morning, he had five of the mutineers shot. The rest of the mutineers and rioters, numbering over two hundred and fifty, were imprisoned in the hold of another ship. During the following night, there was so much noise, quarrelling, and disturbance below decks, that Grenfell ordered the hatches to be opened, and a volley of fifteen muskets to be fired into the hold. When day broke, it became obvious that there had been a terrible loss of life below decks. Only four of the two hundred and fifty-two were left alive, the rest having sustained terrible injuries, with many of them being crushed to death.

After this horrific incident, order was restored, but news of the disaster produced a very black mood in the city, with wild talk of revenge. The town of Cametá, not far from Belém, rose in protest, and threatened resident Europeans, whom they blamed for the loss of life on the Brazilian Navy ship. The Vice-Consul at Pará at the time, Henry Dickenson, wrote a rather panicky letter to Robert Hesketh in Maranhão reporting the Grenfell incident, and then listing a series of atrocities that had been reported from the interior.[144] According to these rumours, some Europeans had been "mutilated to death", others had been roasted alive, and still more tied back-to-back before being plunged into the river. These rumours, which do not seem to have been verified, were enough to send panic into the minds of the British residents. Dickenson wrote to the provincial authorities in early 1824, asking whether their safety could be guaranteed.[145] The answer was decidedly unsatisfactory, the Government maintaining that it could only guarantee European safety as long as Grenfell, with his two ships, was in port.

Dickenson did not report, however, an extremely embarrassing incident that had occurred in the middle of December, 1823. HMS "Eclair", with Captain John in command, arrived off Pará, to find, to his astonishment and anger, that His Britannic Majesty's Vice-Consul, Henry Dickenson, had organised a cavalry corps, composed of members of the British merchant community, as a response to the perceived threat to the Europeans. This rash action broke every rule of residence in a sovereign foreign country, and was quite unprecedented. Captain John was very clear about the stupidity of this action, and gave Dickenson and his fellow-hussars twenty-four hours to disband the cavalry corps, or be forcibly disarmed. Dickenson backed down. When news of this incident reached Robert Hesketh in Maranhão, it confirmed all his worst fears, and strengthened his determination to sack Dickenson. He told the Foreign Secretary, Canning, that Dickenson and some British merchants in Pará had "identified themselves with a beaten party [so] as to render themselves as much apprehensive for their safety as the party themselves."[146] This must refer to the pro-Portuguese party, who were regarded by the insurgents and by the pro-independence Brazilians with the most violent hatred. Dickenson's action, according to Captain John, was "the cause of great bad will in the port".

John Hesketh does not seem to have become involved in any of this; indeed, he would certainly have been fully aware of his elder brother's many reservations about Dickenson. John's name is one of many appearing on a general statement of anxiety about the disturbed situation in 1823, but he did not play any part in the cavalry corps fiasco.

Two months later, in February, 1824, Dickenson, still under pressure from his fellow-merchants, wrote another panicky letter, this time to Canning in London telling him that nine hundred residents of Belém had left the city, as the Government of Pará was quite incapable of governing the province. Believing a force of six thousand men was threatening Pará, he organised a ship to evacuate the British residents and some Portuguese. Dickenson applied to the Governor for passports for all the British residents then living in Belém His list includes John Hesketh and Mrs. Hesketh, together with two children, one a girl, and the other a boy, and a *preta escrava*, a female African slave. Dickenson timed the departure of the ship to coincide with the departure of the two Brazilian men-of-war, and so, on March 3rd., the British brig "Mary Donaldson" set sail from Pará for the safety of Barbados with the all the British residents on board, with only two exceptions: Mr. Gibbs, who went with his brother to Cayenne, and John Hesketh, who stayed behind with his family, believing that Dickenson was greatly exaggerating the danger.

As he left, Dickenson sent a letter to John Hesketh, appointing him as his deputy while he was in Barbados. He had not, however, asked John Hesketh first. Dickenson must by now have been aware of the strong likelihood that he would be dismissed for the cavalry corps incident, and perhaps decided to anticipate it and the appointment of John in his stead. His letter to John was churlish – "I give you permission to act in my absence. P.S. I hope that you may have cause to be satisfied with your resolve." This was not a promising approach, and when news of the nomination reached the ruling Junta, they refused to agree to it. Robert Hesketh wrote to them from Maranhão asking them to agree to John's acting as deputy, but his letter did not reach them in time. Dickenson's action had again made it awkward for Robert to

The Belém waterfront today

appoint John immediately as his successor, and it was much later in the year before he could proceed with the appointment.

Meanwhile, in Barbados, Dickenson received a letter from John, who was still in Pará.[147] It was written only a week after Dickenson and the others had fled. John began by declining the role of deputy, and chided Dickenson for listening to rumour-mongers within the British community. Doubtless with much satisfaction, he was able to announce: "Since you departed, there is great quiet here, and the rebellion has been completely crushed in Villa de Conde." Twelve rebels had been killed, and the rest had fled into the woods, leaving their ammunition behind. Eight days later, on 18 March, he again wrote to Dickenson announcing that it was "very tranquil here", and that food supplies were excellent – two of the local giant-sized canoes had arrived carrying eighty cattle, and other supplies were arriving by sea.[148]

John's cheerful assurance that all was well back in Pará, and that the flight to Barbados had been totally unnecessary, was not well received by Dickenson in Bridgetown. Nevertheless, he set sail again for Pará in April with the British residents, on board two British naval vessels, the frigate HMS "Eden" and the sloop "Scout". When he arrived in Belém, Dickenson had to admit, doubtless through gritted teeth, that the town was much calmer, and that the rebels had disappeared.

Dickenson had now been responsible for two disasters in four months – the cavalry corps incident, and the apparently unnecessary flight to Barbados; his days as Vice-Consul were clearly numbered. With the full support of Canning, Robert sacked Dickenson on 24 November, and appointed his brother as Vice-Consul in Pará in his stead. Canning wrote to Dickenson on 27 November, asking him to turn over his office to John, together with the archive and his consular seal.[149] He also wrote to the British merchants in Pará, announcing the new appointment, and admonishing them for their interference in local politics, and warning them against a repetition.[150] He reported all this to the President of Pará, who said that he was pleased at the new appointment, "owing to the general Esteem in which he is held by all the Inhabitants of this Province in consequence of the propriety of his Conduct." Presumably the refusal to agree to John's nomination as Dickenson's deputy was entirely due to the slipshod and improper mode of approach Dickenson had employed.

The official notice by Robert Hesketh of the appointment of John as Vice-Consul dated 27 November, 1824, did not spare Dickenson's blushes: "With the sanction of His Britannic Majesty's Secretary of State for Foreign Affairs I have nominated constituted and appointed ....John Hesketh Esq[re.] to be British Vice-Consul at Pará in the stead of Henry Dickenson Esquire; and I hereby make known to all to whom it may or shall concern, that all the Powers granted unto the said Henry Dickenson to act as British Vice-Consul at Para are rescinded..." Dickenson, after ten years of awkwardness and obstreperousness, was now dismissed, but did not disappear from the scene. He continued to live in Pará for the next thirty years, causing difficulties to consul after consul. Even the disapprobation of Canning and the declared instruction of Palmerston that Dickenson was never again to exercise authority under the Crown were not enough to stop him popping up time and again to exercise consular functions. His staying-power and his audacity seem quite remarkable, and, supported by his brother in England, who bombarded the Foreign Office with strong letters in his support, he continued to irritate Foreign Secretary after Foreign Secretary. His career is so breathtakingly shameless that a separate chapter is devoted to him.

For the meantime, however, John had no alternative but to accept that his disgruntled and discomfited predecessor was a daily feature of life in Belém. Dickenson's earlier prediction that Robert Hesketh would appoint his brother in his place had now come true, largely because Dickenson had made it come true. Small wonder that John gravitated towards the other major merchants in the town – the Campbells.

Vice-Consul Dickenson's list of those applying for passports in 1824 is a complete guide to the British community living in Belém or nearby. [151][See Appendix I] Of the forty-five people listed, thirty-four are British or married to British citizens, and eleven are listed either as slaves (*escravos*) or servants (*criados*). There are only two families with children, the Gays and the Heskeths, and one other married couple, the Dickensons. Perhaps surprisingly, there is one lone woman, Mrs. Poole, accompanied by her son, and one single woman, Maria Southby. The rest of the list is composed of single men, twenty-one in all. Several on the list lived some distance from Belém. Edward Holland lived in Cametá, on the west bank of the Tocantins River, and Edward Jeffreys, who acted as agent for John Gay, one of the merchants based in Belém, lived and worked in Santarém, eight hundred and fifty miles up the Amazon. Smyth and Lowe, travelling through Santarém in 1835, also met Jeffreys. Gay himself died in 1828, a few days before Maw reached Belém. Maw comments that the widowed Mrs. Gay "was not in affluent circumstances". From their positioning in the list, we can assume that many of the single men lived together in larger households. Robert Corbett and James Henry Weetman, for instance, seem to have lived with the Dickensons, and the Campbells' household contained three slaves or servants.

It is perhaps very surprising that so many of the British merchants, including John Hesketh, had slaves sixteen years after the British Government had banned the involvement of Britons in slave transportation. But it was not until 1838 that Great Britain finally banned its citizens from any involvement in slavery. In any case, the situation in Brazil had hardly changed. There were many slaves already in Brazil who could be legally bought and sold, and no provision was made for their automatic manumission. Dickenson and John Hesketh were both married to Brazilian wives, whose families would have owned slaves perfectly legally for a century or more, and their British husbands doubtless would have found it hard to justify the dismissal of long-serving slaves who had become part of the family. Nevertheless, the British Government's insistence that Brazil abolish the slave trade sits badly with the fact that its representatives in Belém owned slaves. There seems to have been a distinction made between transporting slaves, which was understood by all Britons to be prohibited, and owning them after they had been landed in Brazil.

The British merchant community in Pará was, therefore, quite small, and predominantly a bachelor one. The shortage of British women was very marked, and John's status as a family man must have marked him out as different. It may even have created jealousy. The fact that he lived some distance from the centre of Belém may also have added to the relative importance of those who lived in the city itself. The Campbell family, for instance, had a large house by the river, and this establishment was often seen as being at the heart of the British community. Later consuls were told in the rather sly way that was characteristic of the way the British residents in Pará dealt with each other, that John Hesketh was very friendly with the Campbells, and allowed them privileges beyond their deserving. Ryan, Consul in Pará from 1842 to 1850 says "I am led to believe from report that the men [James and Archibald Campbell] had great influence with him, and as they were generally Creditors on the respective Estate, they so managed, and got the liquidations... into their hands."[152] The Foreign Office, however, was not happy with this imputation of undue partiality, and defended John Hesketh's behaviour, declaring to Ryan that John had done nothing wrong. John Hesketh must have been in a difficult position, hated by Dickenson, and trying to get on with at least some of what Samuel Vines, Consul in the 1850s, called "a Party of turbulent English residents", though to be accurate, some were Scots! We shall see what an uncomfortable time John Hesketh had, and how the "turbulent English residents" made his role painful and troublesome.

JOHN HESKETH AT WORK

"Mr. John Hesketh is a very efficient Consular Agent, & on the occasion of the recent disturbances in Para, exerted himself very creditably for the protection of British interests."(Lord Palmerston's note, 8 August, 1836)

John Hesketh first occupied the Consular Office in Pará towards the end of 1824. One of his first letters back to the Foreign Office was about yet another political crisis in Pará, this time offering a rather more substantial threat than the one that had scared Henry Dickenson earlier in the year. On 11 May, 1825, less than six months into his post, he wrote to Canning, reporting a violent insurrection in the province, and expressing his fears: "...as the insurgents are proceeding to massacre all the European subjects in the Province, there is reason to apprehend that the British may ultimately share the same fate."[153]

The signs of a larger and more dangerous conflict were already there – the anti-European feeling, focused on the Portuguese, but extending without too much nicety to other Europeans; the violent threats of massacre; and the organisation of rebellion across the whole of the vast province. This time, John seems to have been less sanguine, and arranged for the fast-sailing schooner "Blackbird" to take an urgent message to the Commander-in-Chief of the British Naval Squadron based at Barbados, asking for assistance.

The Commander-in-Chief in Barbados was quite used to receiving requests of this kind. Almost every consul and vice-consul in Brazil wrote at one time or another, some frequently, asking for a man-of-war to be sent to safeguard British lives and property. The French seem to have contacted their navy in much the same way. The Commander-in-Chief usually responded sympathetically, but, of course, when sail was the only method of propulsion, everything took time. The request would take up to a week to reach Barbados, arrangements would then have to be made to provision and send a suitable ship, which would take a further week or two. When the ship finally arrived, the British were much cheered, and then, when it was time for the ship to leave, they were despondent. The British merchants were, of course, convinced that the only safe approach was to have a British naval presence permanently in every port, especially their own. During disturbed periods of Brazilian history, this is just what seems to have happened. The British Navy was, at this time, becoming the largest in the world, and had almost a thousand ships, but they were increasingly needed in all parts of the world, had to be re-fitted from time to time and to be provisioned regularly, which meant that they had to return to their base, in this case the West Indies.

By the late 1830s, there were signs that the Navy was less enthusiastic in its response to every cry for support, and the Foreign Office sometimes had to tread very warily in passing on requests to the Sea Lords. British residents had begun to assume that the might of the Navy would always be available whenever any local problem surfaced, and the gradual introduction of steam-powered vessels at the time encouraged them to expect an even more rapid response. The Foreign Office was also aware that sending a British naval presence into a troubled port sometimes had political ramifications, and even Lord Palmerston, who is nowadays credited with a taste for gunboat diplomacy, was surprisingly sensitive and cautious on the issue. The merchants always linked in a close embrace the concepts of "British lives" and "British property", as if they were equivalent, and the Foreign Office does seem to have taken its responsibility for the welfare of British trade very seriously. However, when the situation got very perilous, it was naturally the lives that were saved first.

However, on this occasion, the crisis in Pará calmed down, at least for a time, and the British residents remained safe and secure. There is no report of a ship being sent to Pará in response to John's letter, and we can assume that the merchants' sense of panic soon subsided.

Later that month, however, a disturbing case of the ill-treatment of a British merchant came to light. Edward Holland, who lived and worked in Cametá, some distance south of Belém on the west bank of the Tocantins river, had been supplying the Brazilian Government with various goods for some time, but the last consignment had not been paid for, and he was owed 120 milreis (about £15). This was not a vast sum even then, but Holland decided that he had to make a stand. When asked for more supplies, he refused, unless the local judge, Pedro Paulo Figueredo, gave proper security for the payment. Figueredo responded with fury, and imprisoned Holland in the local barracks, ordering a military force to break open his stores. Fortunately, wiser counsels prevailed, and the order was not carried out, but Holland himself was sent to prison, put in irons, and treated with some cruelty. Only when John Hesketh intervened was he released on bail, and sent to Belém for trial. There he was acquitted of any offence, but no order for restitution for his sufferings was made.[154]

John Hesketh had written to Robert in Maranhão about the matter, and Robert reported the facts to London. He felt it was "an unjustifiable arrest and severe Treatment suffered by Mr. Holland at Camita (sic) in that Province." [155] He was astonished that the Brazilian provincial authorities had not taken action against the judge concerned. Canning was equally appalled, and ordered the Consul-General in Rio to put the case before the Brazilian Government, "so that the displeasure of the British Government might be made known to the judge, and effectual reparation be made."[156] The Brazilian Government seems to have acted with promptitude, and ordered that the judge should be punished for acting beyond his powers, and recommended that proceedings be instituted against him for compensation.

Robert was congratulated by Canning on his handling of the Holland case – "Mr. Canning directs me to express his approbation of your conduct in this affair". But the approbation obviously extended to John Hesketh as well. The case is remarkable for another reason. In all the claims brought by British citizens in Brazil against the Brazilian Government, it seems to be one of the few that were dealt with speedily and sympathetically by the Brazilians. The usual response, even when the individuals concerned were strongly supported by the British Government, was delay, prevarication, and often a refusal to accept any responsibility. This seems to have been particularly true in the Imperial Regency period of the 1830s. Perhaps this case benefited from being dealt with early on in the life of the new nation. Later on, other factors came into play – especially the unpopularity of both the French and the British amongst most classes of Brazilians. Both countries were seen as using their economic power to enforce their will against Brazil. Great Britain became especially unpopular because of its stand against the transportation of slaves, and one suspects that the Brazilian Government's tardiness in settling claims against it was partly to avoid giving the impression to its own people that it was at London's beck and call. Holland himself lived on to continue his trading activities, and his name crops up in lists of merchants based in Pará for a considerable time afterwards.

John Hesketh seems to have carried out his work with commendable enthusiasm, but his mood must have been affected by his increasing financial difficulties. Britain's lack of an overall policy for the payment of consuls and vice-consuls, even in Canning's time as Foreign Secretary, had resulted in John's not being paid any sort of salary. This is odd, for his predecessor, Henry Dickenson, had certainly had a regular salary. John had obviously expected some sort of payment, for in December, 1828, he complained that he has not received any salary for the previous four years. He would have received a share of the Fees earned in the Consulate during that period, but these only averaged, according to Robert's later calculation, £168 p.a. His outgoings, on the other hand, amounted to an average of nearly £200 p.a., consisting of extra rents, and the provision of a clerk and stationery. According to Robert, John's time and efforts were fully devoted to the office of Consul. The demands of British ships and their trade required him to attend his office daily, and there had been much "Anxiety and Labour ...., the consequence of the long-protracted State of Revolution and Anarchy".[157] John had also, according to his brother, spent a great deal of time and effort to identify and counter the activities of illegal slave-dealers. Entertainment costs must also have been significant – Lieutenant Maw was only one of the increasing flow of British visitors who were being attracted to the Amazon. In addition, by 1829, he was, said the bachelor Robert, "burthened with a Wife and five children". All this in one of the most expensive towns in the world. This conscientious activity had left very little time for his mercantile activities, and he seems to have neglected them for most of the first four years of his consulship. Small wonder, then .that he was heading for financial disaster.

John himself wrote to the Foreign Office in July, 1829:

> "Finding myself in most reduced circumstances and in Considerable Debt with a Wife and Family of five children, I am forced to represent my distressing situation in this Foreign Place to your Lordship in the hope that some allowance from His Majesty's Treasury for the Expences incident to the Office of Vice-Consul and for the Labour I have undergone in fulfilling its Duties."[158]

John seems to have decided to restore his financial fortunes by redoubling his efforts as a merchant, but, according to Robert, this proved disastrous, and he lost a great deal of money. Robert blames it on John's dividing his time and effort between trade and the "increasing Duties of his Office", but perhaps John's desperate attempts to make as much money as possible opened him up to undue risk, and one of his ventures spectacularly failed. There is no mention of a cargo lost at sea, so we must assume John had perhaps speculated on a particular cargo, and failed to sell it at a profit. Whatever the reason, John was deeply in debt.

Who was to blame? As we have seen from Maw's account, John seems to have lived well, with mention of "fine wines" at the dinner-table, and generous menus. As the son of a successful Porto wine merchant, John might have had tastes beyond his pocket. And, although there was always much to do for a consul at any seaport where British merchant ships docked, Pará was not at that stage the busiest port in Brazil. John seems to have taken his duties very seriously, and perhaps devoted too much time to them. Perhaps the antagonism of Dickenson and his friends made John feel that he had to spend a great deal of time on the consulship to prove to them that he was worthy of the position.

Robert too must take his share of the blame. He was responsible for the payment of the Vice-Consul at Pará, and it is curious that he did not take up the cudgels on John's behalf at a much earlier stage. Perhaps Robert felt rather guilty about his failure to support John's case, and he certainly paid hugely from his own pocket to help his brother. But London politics were also a major culprit. The four years of non-payment of salary coincide, ironically enough, with Canning's attempts to reform the system of paying consuls, by giving them a salary, and thus freeing them from the need to trade as merchants. If Canning's reforms had been successful, and had been persisted with, John's conscientiousness in the consular service would have been rewarded. But Canning moved on from Foreign Affairs to become Prime Minister, before his death not long afterwards, and there was no-one to continue the reforms. On the contrary, the House of Commons took the opportunity to embark on a campaign of pressure to reduce the cost of consuls abroad. This involved pressing consuls and vice-consuls into mercantile pursuits all over again, a policy directly opposed to the one Canning had instituted only a year or so earlier.

On his way home to England in December, 1829, Robert went first to Pará. He was appalled at John's "distressed situation", and spent a great deal of his own money in trying to restore some financial equilibrium. He says that he gave John over £1,000 to pay off his most urgent debts, and "by this step secured him in a short time a Dwelling and Garden, the cultivation of which, with some assistance from me, provides a temporary support."[159] This sounds as if John had not been able to continue to afford the house that Maw describes in his account of his visit a year earlier, and that Robert secured him a cheaper alternative. A contemporary print shows the house of "the English Consul" on the waterfront in the middle of the city; but this may have been John's Consular Office: the later Inventory of John's possessions says his house is in the Rua Josefa, which is slightly south of the city centre.

Robert therefore supported John's claim for regular remuneration. In a letter from London six months later, Robert again mentions the sum of money he had given to John – he states that it was £1,080, and says that he has also lost the sum of £4,060. Quite why this sum was also lost is not clear

The Rua Sáo Josefa today – John Hesketh lived here from 1836

from his letter – it may be that he had been asked by John to invest in his ill-starred enterprise. Certainly, it made large inroads into the fortune Robert had built up in his years in Maranhão.

The Earl of Aberdeen, now Foreign Secretary, was not unsympathetic, and in his letter of 8 May, 1830, he announces that he is to pay John £200 p.a. This was £100 less than the sum suggested by the Consul-General in Rio, but Aberdeen sugared the pill by saying that John was also to receive payment in arrears for four years, totalling £800.[160] In spite of this promise, Aberdeen and the Foreign Office did not cover themselves in glory, for a further letter was sent to John telling him the Treasury would not agree to four years' back-pay, and would only pay arrears from 1 January, 1829. Knowing this would be a disappointment, Aberdeen raised John's salary to £300 p.a. Whether John received any of this pay is not clear, for almost a year later, the Foreign Office was again revising its offer, and in April, 1831, he was back down to £200 p.a. once more.[161] It is remarkable that John's motivation remained as high as it did. This episode strongly suggests that the Foreign Office was not adept at, or even interested in, maintaining the morale of its far-flung consuls.

John meanwhile carried on with his duties, but never seems to have prospered financially. He may not have risked being involved in "mercantile pursuits" again, and the troubles of the 1830s in Pará hit trade so badly that his Fees, which were levied on British shipping using the port, plummeted. His Fees for 1833 were less than £15. He was insolvent at his death in 1838: At a meeting after his death, his creditors agreed to forego their claim on his estate, in view of the penniless state his children had been left in. His background as a young man was in finance, but he does not seem to have been able to make much money himself. Perhaps he is not the first accountant to be unable to balance his own books. However, the chaos and inconsistency in official policy regarding its consuls could not have helped a man already under pressure in a disturbed and expensive part of the world, and responsible for an awkward group of expatriates.

The case of HMS "Pickle" exemplifies John's difficulties with the merchants. As we have seen, in 1824, he was one of only two British merchant to stay in Belém during political disturbances, and he had been right – peace had soon returned, and no harm was done. But at the beginning of May, 1832, the British Schooner of War, HMS "Pickle", was in port in Pará. Its commanding officer, Lieutenant Stopford, was running out of provisions, and had announced to the Vice-Consul, John Hesketh, that he would shortly be leaving for his base in the West Indies, in order to re-provision his ship.

The city had been in a state of disturbance for some time, with *Conego* [Canon] Baptista Campos, a local priest who was also an influential journalist, fighting a campaign against the Portuguese in the province. Some public officials had been removed, some assassinations had taken place, and there were cases of robbery against the Portuguese. On 2 May, 1832, realising that HMS "Pickle" was due to leave, a small group of British merchants, seven in number, and led by Archibald Campbell, met to write to John Hesketh to ask him to delay the departure of the schooner, "for the protection of our property".[162]

John Hesketh wrote back to them the following day, after HMS "Pickle" had sailed:

> "Gentlemen, In answer to your note of yesterday, I have to remark that deeming the causes which led to your meeting to take into consideration the disturbed state of this province, of some importance, I accordingly wrote to the commander of HM Schooner "Pickle" requesting him to delay his departure until the same should be examined into. But upon various enquiries that I was enabled to make, I found that the grounds for alarm were not sufficiently urgent to justify my making a case sufficiently strong to induce Lieut. Stopford to exceed the positive orders of the Commander-in-Chief of His Majesty's Naval Force in the West Indies."

John's assessment of the political state of Pará was again good, and he wrote to the Foreign Office on 3 May reporting that all was quiet in the city and the province. But the British merchants were not at all happy. They met again on 4 May, again at Archibald Campbell's house, to fulminate against John Hesketh's refusal to accede to their demands. They seemed to have taken no cognisance of the ship's need for new stores, and spoke of the "risk incurred to themselves from the neglect of the British Vice-Consul, John Hesketh, Esq.". They explained that they had been unable to attract a large number of signatures to their letter to the Vice-Consul because time had been so short. Nevertheless, they decided to report him to the authorities in London. They drew back from a full-frontal assault on Lord Palmerston, and wrote instead to the Privy Council for Trade in Whitehall, whom they thought would be more sympathetic. The complaint was strongly worded: – "His unwarrantable Conduct and total neglect to our interests, caused us to represent the circumstance to a higher quarter... and it being the general wish of the English Residents, that the same be presented by you, beg to request that you be good enough to do so, and trust that your influence may be the means of preventing a recurrence of such Conduct on the part of a Person placed here and paid, to watch over the interests of those connected with this Trade."[163] The reference to his pay might have caused John's lip to curl.

The Office of the Committee of Privy Council for Trade sent the letter to Sir George Shee, one of the two Under-Secretaries at the Foreign Office, asking him to put the matter before Lord Palmerston, "that His Lordship may take such steps as shall appear to him to be proper, with the view, as far as may be practicable, of relieving the Parties from the State of Apprehension in which they appear to be placed."[164] This obsequious circumlocution was hardly the sort of approach to impress Lord Palmerston, and nothing appears to have been done to discipline or rebuke the erring Vice-Consul, except that enquiries were made of the Navy to see whether a ship could be sent to Pará on a permanent basis. The local naval commander, Vice-Admiral Colpoys, said he would send a ship to Pará, but added: "I think it would be highly inexpedient to station a Vessel at all seasons on that dangerous Coast".[165]

And there the matter rested, until the much more dangerous events of 1835. John Hesketh doubtless was hurt by the complaint that had been sent over his head, and the merchants may have felt equally frustrated by their lack of success in having him disciplined. Archibald Campbell was at the heart of the trouble, but seems to have decided to let bygones be bygones, for he and John Hesketh were soon working together quite closely.

Meanwhile, John had to concern himself with matters maritime. The British brig "George Canning", a regular visitor to Pará, arrived one day in September, 1834, with an incorrect manifest. It was carrying a large number of cotton spools, five hundred dozen in each of three boxes, making a total of eighteen thousand spools. Unfortunately, the manifest said there were fifteen hundred boxes – a staggering total of two hundred and sixteen thousand spools. The Brazilian port authorities fined the master of the "George Canning" the vast sum of 8,220 milreis, over £1,000. This would have destroyed any profit that might have been made on that particular trip, and John wrote to the President of the Province, Senhor Bernardo Lobo de Souza, arguing that the problem had been caused by a "casual mistake", and that a distinction ought to be made between that and deliberate fraud.[166] The Brazilians were, however, fierce in matters of detail, and the Master of the "George Canning" seems to have had to pay the fine.

On an earlier voyage home from Pará to Liverpool, in 1833, the "George Canning" had carried one Robert Roy back to England on John Hesketh's orders. On the voyage, he had attacked a member of the ship's crew, Jeremiah Jones, cutting and maiming him. Roy had then been sent to Pembroke Gaol, and eventually to Newgate in London, but later released for lack of witnesses.

Robert Roy was a lucky man, for, in addition to his attack on Jeremiah Jones, he had been involved in an appalling instance of bestiality on board the brig "Margaret Richardson" of Glasgow, as it lay at anchor off Pará. We are told that on the evening of Christmas Day, 1832, in the sight of three visiting Customs officials, he had repeatedly copulated with a sow, "in contempt of the dignity of man", and with "monstrous transgression of the Laws of Nature, and of Public Morals, and the shameful scandal of the crew". It was not unusual for consuls to have to deal with cases of moral turpitude on merchant ships, but John found this case particularly repugnant and difficult to deal with, and he took great pains to provide the British authorities with sworn affidavits from the Customs officials and the crew. Normally, that would have made it possible to try a defendant in a British court, but it seems that on this occasion, the system failed to deal adequately with Robert Roy.[167]

Less distasteful, but lasting much longer, was the case of Captain John Hislop. Hislop was a British merchant based at Santarém, the next significant port up the Amazon from Belém. He travelled widely throughout Amazonia, and early in 1833 was in the town of Itaituba, 150 miles up the Tapajós river. When he returned from his business trip in February, 1834, he was carrying a large amount of money – 4,520 milreis – about £530. The money was in the form of copper coin, until then the coin of the realm. Hislop was astonished and dismayed to find that, during his absence, copper coinage had been entirely substituted by paper money. The Brazilian Government's difficulties with counterfeit coinage had caused it to announce the change quite suddenly to avoid further forgery and criminal speculation. They had given a period of only ten days after the publication of the edict for copper coins to be handed in and certificated, so that they could be changed for the new money. The ten days had long expired when Hislop returned to his home at Santarém, staggered by the news that his fortune was now worthless.

He was understandably upset, but set about reclaiming the value of his copper currency by petitioning the *Câmara Municipal* – the Town Council – to grant him the necessary documents so that he could exchange the coinage. They felt they could not do so, as the Imperial Government had been quite explicit about the rules. They recommended that Hislop apply to the Provincial Government in Belém, but he was again rebuffed. Hislop's only path lay now to Rio and the Imperial Government itself. To do this, he needed John Hesketh's help. John wrote a letter very supportive of Hislop to the Envoy Extraordinary, H.S. Fox, asking him to take up the case with the Government there.[168]

Even with such high-level advocacy, the claim was not settled, and Hislop was still trying to get satisfaction of his claim four years later in 1838. It is possible that Hislop never recovered the value of his coinage. There is an interesting reference to Hislop a few years later in Alfred Russel Wallace's account of his time in Pará from 1848–1852. Wallace visited Santarém in the late 1840s, and was introduced to "Captain Hislop, an old Scotchman settled here for many years".[169] Hislop arranged a house for Wallace and his companions to rent, and invited them to dine at his table as long as they were in the town. "In the evenings, some of these [local officials] and a few of the principal traders used generally to meet in front of Captain Hislop's house, which was in an airy situation overlooking the river, where they would sit and smoke, take snuff, and talk politics and law for an hour or two." So, whether or not his claim was settled, Hislop seemed to have survived as a merchant.

Back in 1835, John Hesketh was about to face his biggest test, the Cabanagem Rebellion. John's part in it seems to have made Lord Palmerston thoughtful about consular roles in northern Brazil. After John's claims for compensation for his losses had passed before him, Palmerston wrote a note dated 25 June, 1836, asking his subordinates: "What sort of Vice Consul is Mr. Hesketh, when and by whom was be appointed, and what was he before."[170]

The answer is also dated June, 1836, and says: "Mr. John Hesketh is a very efficient Consular Agent, & on the occasion of the recent disturbances at Pará exerted himself very creditably for the protection of British interests." Palmerston made an instant decision, with a note dated 29 June, 1836: "Make him Consul and give him 300L a year."[171] In early August, a formal letter was sent to John, who was at that time in London, informing him that "The King has been graciously pleased to promote you to that situation."[172] The letter, presumably a standard one, mentions some of his duties: "Your duty [is] to avail yourself of every favourable opportunity for collecting & transmitting to me any useful or interesting information relating to Commerce, Navigation, Agriculture, & any other Branch of Statistics." He was to be paid the £300 salary, and he was to be allowed to follow "mercantile pursuits", perhaps by now a painful topic with John.

John arrived back in Pará with his family at the beginning of December, 1836, six months or so after the rebels had fled Belém. The city was badly damaged, trade was almost non-existent, and his own house was destroyed. In addition, he returned to a new problem – the activities of the French. The Government of the soldier-President, d'Andrea, was accusing France of harbouring rebels during the recent Cabanagem Rebellion, and of encouraging runaway slaves. He also accused the local French Vice-Consul of having links with both the insurgents and the local Indian population. John, for his part, had heard from his commercial contacts that the French were encroaching on Brazilian territory. His information suggested that the French were building a fort in "Guiana" – a general term at the time for the northern coast. John wrote to the Foreign Office immediately in a letter dated 9 December, 1836. He followed it up with another letter on 28 December, a fortnight later, saying that the French were taking advantage of the "helpless state of this Province to enforce their Claim.[173] He admitted that the land they had occupied on the northern coast of Pará was of little use commercially, apart from allowing the smuggling of cattle to and from the island of Marajó, but he feared that this was a precedent for occupying the whole of the northern bank of the Amazon "to the Injury of navigation of that river, and by consequence to the British Commercial Interests in this quarter."

John would have known that the dispute about French encroachment had a long history, and that the French claim depended upon the identification of the position of the Oyapock River, which supposedly divided French from Brazilian territory. Southey, in his "History of Brazil"[174], dates the dispute about what he calls the "Wiapoc" from 1687. The French were now claiming that the Oyapock was not the major river that today divides French

Guiana and Brazil, but a small river on the island of Marajó. A French map exists in the Foreign Office archives supposedly illustrating this claim, which, if accepted, would have given the French possession of a large tract of land which included one of the major mouths of the Amazon and half of the vast island of Marajó, and brought them within striking distance of Belém itself. Whatever the French intentions, John thought he had reported as much as he could, but carried on a correspondence with the Pará authorities about the matter. .

The British Government responded to this warning in September, 1837, saying that when Brazilian borders were being negotiated after João VI came to Brazil in 1808, the French had agreed that the River Oyapock would form the northern boundary of Brazil, and that Brazil would extend from the Oyapock in the north to the *Prata* (the River Plate) in the south. So this was, they declared, "an open act of hostility which could never be supposed between Friendly Nations without a previous declaration of war."[175]

But then everyone in London seems to have forgotten the matter – surprising in view of Palmerston's long-held suspicion of the French. It was a letter to Palmerston from McCalmont Bros. about their losses during the Cabanagem Rebellion which raised the issue again. They quoted John Hesketh as saying that the French were still encroaching on Brazilian territory. Palmerston seems to have registered the problem more effectively this time, and wrote to John Hesketh, "Endeavour to ascertain the facts of the case."[176] There was no direct criticism from Palmerston of John's apparent failure to alert the Foreign Office to the problem, but John was obviously disturbed that he had appeared to have failed to do Palmerston's bidding. He wrote immediately to Palmerston, enclosing his original 1836 letter, and to the British mission in Rio, pointing out that he had warned London eighteen months before. "Being apprehensive of the possible misconveyance of my communication to Your lordship of the 28th. December, 1836, and the same may in a manner be prejudicial to the Public Service, I have taken the liberty of forwarding Copies of the Correspondence ... to Her Majesty's Mission at Rio de Janeiro."[177]

Perhaps John was being over-sensitive, but his appointment as Consul was recent, he was obviously motivated to do well, and, though he had numerous problems in Pará with members of the British community there, he had up to now had the full support of the Foreign Office. He knew the matter was viewed as being of great importance in London, and this hiccup in communication might well have added to the sense of pressure that he felt.

The matter did not end there – two months later, Hugh Goodair, one of the leading British merchants in Belém, was writing to the Foreign Office, announcing that "The French colony at Mapá [about ten miles north-west of Amapá] is said to be increasing wonderfully; they have two Steam Boats running between there and Cayenne constantly; besides a gift of land and the necessary utensils for tilling the land etc. they give every settler 30 dollars, and 5 dollars for every head of cattle they bring with them.... It is a pity our Government does not look into this as if they go on as reported they will soon be in possession of the best part of one of the finest Rivers. They have now constantly a Brig of War lying in the River." [178]

London listened at last, and the British Ambassador in Paris was instructed to seek an explanation "of the encroachments on the Brazilian Territory which are alleged to have been committed by the French Authorities in Guiana." The French obviously backed down, because Mapá and Amapá remained part of Brazil. The Brazilians seem to have been characteristically slow to react to this apparent interference with their territory, and seemed to have left it to Great Britain to challenge France. However, the last thing the Brazilians would have wanted would have been a battle between British and French interests in the Amazon. The vast network of rivers was a major asset to Brazil, and she was careful to regulate the commercial opportunities for both nations in the region. The rubber boom, which came later, was controlled, partly at least, by Brazil, and not solely by foreign interests, and John played some part in ensuring that the French did not acquire too much influence and power in the period before rubber became a major export from the Amazon.

The early part of 1838 was, therefore, a tough time for John. As well as his difficulties in having London acknowledge his warnings about the French, he had Henry Dickenson snarling at him over what he alleged was John's failure to help him with a court case: the Case of the Cotton Bags, dealt with in Chapter 16. He also had to take the President of the Province severely to task over the mistreatment of a British subject, the Master of the British cutter, "Plover". The "Plover" had been seized by the provincial authorities at night on suspicion of being a pirate. . The Master of the "Plover " had produced his registry documents, which were in perfect order, but the cutter was searched early the next morning, without John Hesketh's being informed. Fifty pounds of turtle shell was removed by the *Juiz de Direito*, and placed in the Custom-House. The Master was now not only accused of piracy, but also threatened with a fine for not landing his turtle shell cargo in the proper way. John was furious, and all his upset of the previous few weeks poured into a very powerful letter to the Governor. Dickenson had recently accused him of "apathy" and "supineness", but these are the very last words that could be used to describe John's fury. The whole episode, he wrote to the President, was "an Insult to the National Flag", and ""a want of courtesy to a Nation in Amity and Alliance with Brazil." He demanded the return of the cargo, the suspension of the threatened fine, and made it plain that he thought the real reason for the seizure of the "Plover" was the colour of the Master's skin. He noted tartly that "The mulatto (who Your Excellency is pleased so to term) calling himself Captain of the English cutter is a man legally appointed by the Collector and Comptroller of Her Majesty's Customs at the Island of Tobago; he presented at the Palace his Certificate of Registry and not a passport, and be his colour what it may, it was enough that he was legally appointed ... the idea that he was a pirate is absurd."[179]

A few months later, and only a month after his last letter to Palmerston, John was dead. He had not, as far as one can tell, been ill, and his sudden death on 24 July, 1838, so shocked his wife, Margarida, that she "went into a stupor", and followed him to the grave three weeks later. John Hesketh's death was reported to the Foreign Office by several senior British residents in Belém: Hugh Goodair, Archibald Campbell, Robert Corbett, and John's old enemy, Henry Dickenson. Death was not an uncommon event among consuls in foreign parts, and so the Foreign Office carried on with its business, and appointed Henry Augustus Cowper in John Hesketh's place in the spring of 1839. Cowper reached Pará by late August, 1839, just over a year after John's death. His predecessor had been in Brazil for nineteen years, fourteen of them as Vice-Consul or Consul. It had not been an easy posting, and John must often have reflected on the way in which his elder brother, Robert, seemed always to have prospered while he struggled. John's life in Pará was greatly influenced by three factors – the Campbell family, the Cabanagem Rebellion, and Henry Dickenson, and to these now we turn.

14

THE CAMPBELLS OF BUTE

"[We] took leave of Mr. Campbell with those feelings of regard and respect which his genuine kindness and constant Attention to us while at Pará ... had produced."(Lieut. Maw, 1828)

Ettrick Bay lies on the western coast of the island of Bute in the Firth of Clyde, looking across the Sound of Arran to Goat Fell. It is a beautiful spot, only a few miles from Rothesay, Bute's only town. Today, a few farms still dot the slopes above the broad sweep of the bay; two hundred years ago, there cannot have been many more. The view across to the Isle of Arran is superb, but Ettrick Bay could not have offered enough otherwise to support three ambitious young brothers who were born and brought up there. And so, after a false start in Glasgow up the Clyde, the Campbells sailed for Brazil.

In 1824, the three – James, Archibald, and John – were living in Pará. A letter from Mr. Liddell of the Greenock Chamber of Commerce, written in 1838 to put forward the claims of Archibald Campbell for the Pará Consulate, asserts that Archibald arrived in Pará in 1826, but Mr. Liddell appears to have got his dates wrong, for all three names are in Dickenson's passport list of that year. There is a strong implication in Maw's book that John Campbell was in Pará during his visit in 1828. After that date, there is no further mention of John in the records, so he must have either died or returned home soon after 1828. Only two other brothers – James and Archibald – were in Pará after that time. They were younger than John Hesketh, James being born in 1800, and Archibald in 1802. Samuel Vines, British Consul in Pará from 1852 to 1857, tells us that Archibald first became a clerk with a mercantile family in Glasgow.[180] He apparently set up in business on his own account, but ran into financial difficulty, "and never made any settlement with his creditors in Scotland". Vines accuses Archibald of fleeing to Brazil to escape his commitments, and goes even further, accusing him of inducing "parties to consign goods taken from Glasgow", which, he asserts, is "Criminal in British Law". Vines was an excitable man, and given to making rather wild claims of others' wrongdoing, so this may be an exaggeration, especially as thirty years had passed since the events he complains of. But there

The Isle of Arran from Ettrick Bay, Bute, where the Campbells were born

exists enough evidence from the later history of John Hesketh's family to agree that Archibald Campbell was, at the very least, a sharp businessman.

James was the elder brother, however, and, judging by Lieutenant Maw's account, had been the longer in the Brazils, and was regarded as the senior of the two, at least in the late 1820s. Neither of the surviving Campbells can have been in Pará for much longer than John Hesketh, if, indeed, they arrived before him. James Campbell would have been only nineteen years old in the year in which John arrived, and so it is likely that they settled in Pará in the very early 1820s. They must have prospered exceedingly quickly, for by 1828 they owned a substantial property in the heart of Belém, as well as trading with other places up-river in Amazonia. When Maw was introduced to them by John Hesketh, there was no doubt about their importance in the community. The first mention of them in his book[181] relates to a snake: "I was told by Mr. Campbell at Pará that an acquaintance of his being over at Marajó [a very large island opposite Belém] during the rainy season, and riding up towards a small bridge that was partly under water, he observed something apparently moving on it. Riding up, he saw part of the body of an enormous serpent, that was crossing, neither the head nor tail of which were at that moment visible, being hid in the Montaña or bushes on each side of the bridge. Mr. Campbell is too good an authority to doubt." Maw, perhaps blinded by Campbell's story-telling, forgets that this story is being told at third-hand.

Maw says that James Campbell was "one of the earliest British residents in Pará", but this can hardly be true. Samuel Harrop was said to have been the first, and we know that Henry Dickenson had been Vice-Consul since 1813, and even John Hesketh probably preceded James Campbell. James was, said Maw, the head of one of the principal mercantile houses. He immediately offered Maw and his companion, Hinde, accommodation in his house, with "that hospitality for which he is celebrated in Pará". Campbell then introduced him to others of the British community, to the American and French Consuls, and to "several of the principal natives", doubtless including the rich Portuguese, Senhor Pombo, after whom Archibald later named one of his sons.

James showed Maw and Hinde round the Campbells' commercial establishment: Maw tells us that it consisted of the three brothers, "and some young men who acted as cash-keepers and clerks: there was also a Brazilian clerk to carry on business with the natives. With the enterprise of the British merchant, Mr. Campbell had pushed his negotiations up the Marañon [the Amazon], and some of its nearer tributaries, and had even been himself as far as the Rio Negro, but such was the want of a regular communication, that his returns were uncertain, and some of his speculations had not proved beneficial in consequence." He had therefore begun to curtail the range of his commercial activities, although he owned several river-craft that were sent to trade in various directions. In spite of this check to his ambitions, Mr. Campbell was apparently very optimistic about Brazil's future, and very fond of contrasting the current state of the province with its enormous potential.

Maw comments too on the exotic pets housed in the Campbell residence – a pet *onça*, which he calls a tiger, but which was more likely to have been a jaguar. It was allowed to live indoors, and was provided with a den, a collar, and a chain, and was washed every morning by a servant. When Maw was there, it had disgraced itself by eating Paraway the parrot, "almost without notice". One of Mr. Campbell's brothers kept two "kings of vultures", but one had recently fallen off its perch and expired.

Maw and Hinde dined out with John Hesketh and others, but were often found dining with the Campbells. He tells us of two incidents that occurred on separate occasions during dinner, which would have been in the middle of the day. In the first, which happened soon after their arrival in Para, one of Gay's children burst in upon the company to say that her sister had died.

The company were shocked, particularly as her father, Mr. Gay, the merchant, had himself died only a few days earlier. Maw tells us that he sat up with the body of the girl in the company of a young man who lived with the Campbells, "Henderson", who must be George Henderson, who was still living there twenty years later, but at that time dependent on the Campbells for his welfare. In the second incident, a man rushed in during dinner, and pressed Campbell's hand to his forehead. Apparently he had acted dishonestly in a deal with Campbell. Campbell had sued him, and the man had been imprisoned. Campbell had only agreed to the man's release on condition that he acknowledged his wrong-doing. "Mr. Campbell's firmness in this case had produced a considerable sensation, which was likely to have a beneficial effect on the mercantile men." There are frequent references in the Foreign Office records of the Campbells going to law to further their commercial concerns, and some of the consuls found it shocking and unacceptable that they should sue other merchants, especially fellow Britons. Consul Ryan said of him in 1842: "The almost total want of good feeling that unfortunately exists here between the resident British Merchants proves to me the absolute necessity there is for having a Judge Conservator to prevent the constant recurrence of exposing in the National Tribunals, by petty actions, the rancour that exists between them, but which is principally caused by the House of Archibald Campbell, whose chief seems to take pleasure in endeavoring to degrade his Countrymen by dragging them before the said National Tribunals."[182]

But back in 1828 Maw could see no fault in James Campbell, and sums up his and Hinde's departure from Pará in a rather turgid paragraph "Hinde and myself took leave of Mr. Campbell with those feelings of regard and respect, which his genuine kindness and constant attention to us while at Pará, and the opinion that evidently existed respecting him, as a British merchant, among his own countrymen, foreigners, and natives, had produced."

Seven years later, Smyth and Lowe, also naval men, were repeating Maw's and Hinde's journey down the Amazon, but arrived at a far less peaceful time, with a bloody revolution building in Pará. They spent a fortnight in Pará, before sailing home, and were provided by "Mr. Campbell" with a house, though the prevailing political conditions made it dangerous to leave it after dark.

In 1847, the American, William H. Edwards, was in Pará, and visited an estate thirty miles south of the River Acará, a tributary of the Tocantins south of Belém. It was owned by James's brother, Archibald, who had established a pottery there. The name of the place was Taüaü, which meant "red clay", and Campbell's manufactory was producing pots, tiles, and other earthenware objects. The estate employed eighty slaves, who were kept busy from five o' clock in the morning until two hours after dark, but with a longish break in the middle of the day. The number of slaves is credited by Consul Vines to the fact that Archibald Campbell had married a rich Brazilian woman, daughter of a "large slave-owner".

Consul Ryan had run into trouble with James Campbell in 1846. Campbell was in dispute with an American by the name of Smith over payment for a consignment of rubber shoes. Presumably Campbell had supplied the shoes, a very early example of the rubber trade in Pará, and only two years after Charles Goodyear had invented vulcanisation. The American Consul had declined to interfere in Campbell's dispute with Smith, but Ryan had not only refused to help Campbell, but, having quarrelled with him, had gone so far as to write to the United States to offer to take charge of the claim against him in the Brazilian courts, in conjunction with the then Acting American Consul, Benjamin Upton. Campbell was, of course, incandescent with fury: "... the injustice of a British Consul, seeking for and obtaining, Powers of Attorney from foreigners residing in a far-distant and Foreign Country to enforce a claim against a British Subject.... for the gratification of a petty and vindictive feeling..."[183] But Campbell's protest to the Foreign Office was to no avail, and John Bidwell in London defended Ryan, saying, somewhat unconvincingly, that he "appears to have acted in this matter as a merchant and not as Consul".[184]

This was not the first time that the Campbells and Ryan had crossed each other. In 1842, soon after Ryan's taking up his post as Consul, he was told that the Campbells had obtained the administration of the estates of deceased British subjects dying intestate. John Hesketh, he said, had apparently allowed the Campbells to act in this capacity. Ryan found this hard to accept, and ordered the Campbells to produce the relevant accounts. They refused, claiming that Ryan had no authority to demand this of them. Unfortunately for Ryan, the Foreign Office agreed with the Campbells. It cannot have helped the new Consul when the Foreign Office refused to support him in this, and told him that he was not, as Consul, entitled to claim the administration of those dying intestate. "It does not appear that the late Consul Hesketh acted wrong (sic) in permitting Messrs. Campbell to administer the effects of deceased British subjects."[185] Nevertheless, according to Consul Vines, Ryan had persuaded the police to put Campbell under surveillance.

Time did not mellow Archibald. In the last few years of his life, he became embroiled in a very unpleasant dispute over access to the British Burial Ground. Today, the British Burial Ground in Belém is beautifully kept, and open to view behind a long set of railings alongside the busy main road to Nazaré, the Avenida Serzedela Correa. It lies opposite one of the oldest cemeteries in Belém, and has its own Episcopal church, which was built in 1913. Henry Dickenson had bought the land in 1815 whilst he was Vice-Consul, and it had been developed throughout the next two decades. Residents in the 1820s and 1830s made regular subscriptions, led by Robert Hesketh in Maranhão and John in Belém. A list of graves with inscriptions dates from the 1870s, and includes mostly British and American names, with the odd Dutch one. The list says that "others have no inscription."[186] It was used for all Protestants dying in this Roman Catholic city.

After his arrival in 1852, Vines seems to have taken a severe line on who was to be allowed to be buried there, and on fees. The first inkling of trouble came in 1854, when the Campbells and others wrote a "Representation" to the Foreign Office, complaining that Vines had been acting "threateningly" over the Burial Ground, and was not allowing some merchants to attend meetings.[187] Vines replied that he had only excluded those who had made no financial contribution, and hinted that the "Representation" was an attempt by the Campbells to cause trouble for him, and that their avowed aim was to get rid of him.[188] Tempers flared when a German lady died and needed to be buried. The Treasurer, James McDermott, asked for the fee for the burial, but none was forthcoming, and so McDermot refused to hand over the key to the Burial Ground, apparently with Vines's full support. Campbell, in line with his usual policy of involving the local authorities in British affairs, asked the President of the Province to force open the gates, but he wisely refused to become involved. It would appear that the body was eventually admitted for burial, and Vines was advised by the Foreign Office to employ rather more of "a liberal spirit".[189] But Campbell seems to have played a central part in opposing Vines.

Six months later, in May, 1855, an American visitor, Mr. Chaffee, who was visiting Pará, and was lodging in Archibald Campbell's house, died suddenly. The hot climate made burial an urgent matter, and Archibald Campbell appears to have taken matters into his own hands, in conjunction with H.B. Dewey, who, though an Englishman, was the American Consul in Pará. They refused to pay the burial fee of 160 milreis (about £20), and broke down the gates of the Burial Ground to admit the body. Vines was furious, and threatened to have the body disinterred. This time the Brazilian author-ities were involved, and Dewey's action was reported to the United States Government as well. Flurries of diplomatic letters went between Pará, Rio, London, and Washington; Washington instructed its Consul not to repeat the exercise, and Vines was told that, though he was right in law, he should

The Campbells' grave in the British Cemetery in Belém

be "circumspect and moderate", and should attempt to calm down the excitable British residents, and not allow the Brazilian authorities to be involved in matters affecting British property.[190]

Vines's hard line cannot have helped his reputation in London, but he was not dismissed, as Campbell apparently intended, and Campbell became a resident in the Cemetery himself when he died in October, 1858, aged 56, joining his brother James, who had been interred there only nine months earlier. Their grave, which also contains Archibald's two sons who died in their twenties in 1868 and 1869, is one of the most prominent still.

But perhaps it is Archibald Campbell's conduct after John's and Margarida's deaths in 1838 which might most interest us. He became involved in the administration of their estate, and was later accused of acting dishonestly towards the heirs – John's and Margarida's children. The matter involved the children themselves, Consul Vines, the Foreign Office, Robert Hesketh, and the Brazilian legal system, and gave rise to a persistent rumor in the Hesketh family for the next 150 years that a Campbell had cheated the Heskeths out of their money. We shall look at the truth of the rumour in a later chapter, but it is safe to say that Archibald, the younger brother, became the most prominent of the two remaining brothers in Pará, and seems to have acquired his considerable wealth, not only through his marriage to his rich Brazilian bride, and through his commercial and manufacturing activities, but also through some business dealing that could at least be described as astute. He also seems to have become a *bête noire* to the Consuls who succeeded John Hesketh. James Campbell, the elder brother, though he lived on in Pará nearly as long as Archibald, is rarely mentioned in the Foreign Office records after 1846. Archibald seems to have become the more prominent and the more aggressive of the two. With Archibald Campbell setting the tone so forcibly, the British community in Belém certainly seems to have deserved its reputation for awkwardness and litigiousness, and the fractious relationships with a succession of British Consuls contrasts with the generally positive atmosphere in Maranhão and Rio de Janeiro.

15

THE CABANAGEM REBELLION

"... terrible work in this unfortunate place..."(letter from a Belém merchant to his brother, 1835)

In 1755, King José I of Portugal, under the influence of the Marquis of Pombal, issued a new law, decreeing that the Indians of the Amazon should retain "the liberty of their persons, goods, and commerce." If this law had been consistently observed over the next century, it is likely that the Cabanagem Rebellion would never have occurred. For its non-observance was one of the root causes of a bloody and dangerous conflict.

The seeds of the uprising had been sown long before. Epidemics of European diseases had cut down the Indian population whenever and wherever they came into contact with the Portuguese, and this prolonged and insidious attack by contagion was accompanied by the pressing of many of the remaining Indian men into forced-labour battalions, only a short step away from slavery As the lot of the Indians steadily deteriorated, they were aware that many of the Portuguese immigrants were becoming very prosperous. The contrast between the welfare of the Indians and of the Portuguese–born became even more obvious when groups of Indians moved to the vicinity of the growing towns along the Amazon river system. Many Indians came to live in cabins (*cabanos*) on the river-banks near Belém and on the island of Marajó, eking out a poverty-stricken existence. They were easily roused to hatred of the rich, whether estate-owners or merchants. Though the majority of the rich were Portuguese by birth and loyalty, numbers of other Europeans began to find their way up the rivers, setting-up estates and trading-posts. Some of these *brancos* – whites – were uneducated, and some unscrupulous and cruel. Sometimes the provincial government's policies towards the Indians ignored their wishes and their long-established way of life, and were quite at odds with the 1755 proclamation that Indians were never to be enslaved. It was thus hardly surprising that the Indians regarded all Portuguese, and by extension all white foreigners, with suspicion. A more surprising and particular hatred was reserved for those whites who were freemasons. Not only had the Roman Catholic Church set its heart against freemasonry, but those within its society – prosperous white men – met in secret. Those outside – the Indians and the poorer whites – were naturally suspicious of its motives. All these factors fed a volcano of resentment that finally exploded in 1835.

The Cabanagem was born out of violence. Pará had seen uprisings in 1821, in the wake of the liberal revolution in Porto, and again in 1822. It did not help that the province was tricked into loyalty to the Empire in 1823 by Grenfell, and that, on 16 October, 1823, Grenfell had shot five rebel soldiers, and imprisoned two hundred and fifty-three prisoners on board the "Palhoço", with all but four being found dead next morning.

Only a year later, in May, 1825, there was what John Hesketh called "a violent insurrection", part of it focused on Cametá on the Tocantins river, and John wrote once more to the British Naval Commander in Barbados, asking for help. The insurgents were, he thought, threatening the lives of Europeans in the Province, and he feared that the British might eventually share the same fate. For the moment, however, this apprehension was not fulfilled. But the tone of protest and of violence had been set.

In 1831, as the Empire reeled from the abdication of Pedro I and his return to Portugal, there was further disturbance. There were uprisings in Santarém, Marajó, and Cametá, and the soldiers mutinied in Belém. On 2 June, some soldiers attacked the Arsenal, captured arms and ammunition, and released prisoners. The mutiny was quelled after eight hours of disorder, with help from the crews of Brazilian naval ships off the port. The avowed cause was twenty months' arrears in military pay, but John Hesketh, in spite of his own experience of arrears of pay, did not believe that was the main motivation – its main purpose, he said, was "subversion and commotion".[191] Three months later, in September, the President of the Province, the Visconde de Goiana, was deposed, on account of his supposed backing for the Revolutionary Party, and sent packing to Rio. Further down the coast, Maranhão was also suffering at this time from "commotion".

In April, 1832, there was a short-lived rebellion in Manaus fifteen hundred miles up the Amazon. The garrison mutinied, and in June the surrounding region of Rio Negro declared itself independent of Pará. By August, both rebellions were put down, but an atmosphere of insecurity and defiance had been created.

Meanwhile in Belém, on 18 May, there was again, according to John Hesketh, "much insubordination" to the will of the Rio government. "An indiscreet individual – Joaquim Affazo Talles [or Galles] … in a misconceived plan of supporting the authorities … assembled some thirty persons in his house, and offered resistance to a Patrole [sic] of the Municipal Guard sent with a warrant of search."[192] All thirty were shot. In June, the island of Tupinambaranos downstream of Manaus was attacked by rebels.

In Belém, one of the leaders of the 1823 rebellion, Canon João Batista Gonçalves Campos, was editing *"O Paraense"*, an influential periodical in the province. His voice was on the side of those wanting justice for the poor, but it did not rule out the idea of vengeance on their oppressors. When the Bishop of Belém issued a Pastoral Letter against freemasonry in 1834, Campos published it more widely, to the disapproval of the provincial authorities, and had to flee to the River Acará south of Belém. He died at the end of 1834, after cutting himself while shaving, but his work had been done. The Bishop himself had been accused of "subversive doctrine" by the new President, Bernardo Lobo de Souza, whom we shall meet again on the steps of the Governor's Palace.

Campos's flight to the River Acará was to the *fazenda* or plantation of Felix Antonio Clemente Malcher, an infantry officer who had been one of the five-man Junta running the province in 1824. He had combined with two sets of brothers who were either white or mulatto , and who were virulently anti-Portuguese. The Vinagre brothers were rubber workers from the River Itapicuru in Maranhão, and the Nogueira brothers came from Ceará further east. Their two main representatives, Francisco Pedro Vinagre and Eduardo Nogueira, who called himself "Angelim" after one of the hardest woods in the Amazonian forest, were both to reign as rebel presidents during the Cabanagem, the rebellion of the *cabanos*.

In mid-October, 1834, the President sent a party of soldiers under Sergeant Nabuco to Malcher's *fazenda* on the Acará, to investigate rumours of rebellion, and to arrest one Vicente Ferreira Louvor Papagaio, who was accused of publishing seditious papers. The soldiers were ambushed overnight and killed by Vinagre, Angelim, and a man called Gavião. In reprisal, the President, Bernardo Lobo de Souza, sent three hundred troops led by Captain James Inglis to Malcher's *fazenda*. They burnt it down, and captured Malcher himself, bringing him back to Belém to be imprisoned in the Barra Fort along the waterfront. On 3 November, one of Vinagre's brothers, Manoel, was killed by a *juiz de paz* (justice of the peace).

A few weeks later, on 7 January, 1835, the rebellion broke out in earnest. In John Hesketh's words: "On the 7th. Instant at three o'clock in the morning, a sudden insurrection broke out in this City, which began by the Soldiers at the Barracks shooting their own Officers; being then joined by the malcontents of the River Acará; they proceeded to murder the President of the Province and the Military Governor."[193] The President, Lobo de Sousa, was shot on the staircase of his own palace by one Domingos, who

The Governor's Palace in Belém, where the President of the Province was murdered in 1835

called himself *Onça* ("jaguar"), and the Military Governor, de Silva Santiago, by Filipe *Manda-Chuva* ("big shot"). The bodies of the Military Governor and the President were mutilated, and dragged in triumph round the streets of the city. Several prisons were then opened and the prisoners let out, and, says John, "the scene of Massacre which ensued was truly horrible." In particular, many of the Portuguese shopkeepers of the city were slaughtered. Amid the carnage, Malcher was hailed as President by the insurgents, and he appointed Vinagre as Military Governor. Perhaps surprisingly, Malcher and Vinagre began by promising their loyalty to the Empire of the Brazils.

John went to see Malcher the following day, 8 January, to ask whether British lives and property would be respected. Malcher gave him that assurance. By 14 January, John was reporting that the city was in a state of "comparative tranquillity", but was urgently asking the British Navy for the presence of a British warship.

In spite of Malcher's assurance that he was loyal to the Empire, John had heard that "the new Government runnounced [sic] all allegiance to the Regency during the minority of the young Emperor", and he thinks it likely that the rebellion would lead to a separation of the provinces of Brazil. This possible outcome preoccupied John much in the next few months, until he had even more urgent matters to think about. "If the Regency cannot resist this act of insubordination, the Province is lost to the Brazilian Empire, and by a progressive course of misrule, will ultimately fall under the power of the Negro Population to the extinction of the white."[194]

In spite of the rebel president's reassurances, there were almost immediate problems for the foreign residents. On 2 February, the French Consul, M. Denis Crouan, had his house surrounded by armed soldiers, and he was accused of harbouring a fugitive councillor. He was insulted by Malcher "by the most gross epithets such as 'rebel', 'mutineer', and 'shelterer of criminals and assassins'." He was ordered to be imprisoned on board a Brazilian warship, and then put under house-arrest. M. Crouan complained to his government, and it was not long before two French brigs of war, "D'Assar" and "Cuirassier", were on their way from Brest to right the wrong.

John was already by this time convinced that the Province would secede from the rest of Brazil. He speculated a few days later that the Province would be a valuable acquisition to the British Empire, and the inhabitants would welcome British rule, rather than endure the present state of anarchy. This kind of thinking was unrealistic: not only was Palmerston not interested in the acquisition of territory, but John grossly underestimated the tumult and horror that was to follow.

For behind the scenes, Malcher and Vinagre were seriously at odds. Malcher imprisoned some individuals in defiance of Vinagre, and the two men became instant enemies, one backed by the mob, and the other by the undisciplined soldiery. On 19 February, Malcher's followers took possession of the *Castello*, a small fort on the waterfront, and Vinagre's followers took possession of the arsenal. Fighting broke out between 11 a.m. and noon, and continued till nightfall. As the fighting began, the foreign merchant ships situated opposite the city quietly slipped anchor and moved a mile downstream out of harm's way, leaving some Brazilian ships of war off the port.

Early next morning, the battle began again. Malcher, finding himself hard-pressed in the fort, went on board one of the Brazilian brigs of war, the "Cacique", leaving a small party behind occupying the fort and the nearby military hospital. John Hesketh's account of the battle is cool but telling: "Vinagre's party, having stationed field pieces and some larger pieces of ordnance in different parts of the town facing the river, a brisk fire was kept up between these and the Vessels of War in the harbour, who from the beginning fired into the town, doing much mischief to the buildings and wounding many of the inhabitants; this continued during the whole of the day and the night following."

On 21 February, Malcher put up a flag of truce, requesting that the Council be convened, in order to find out their views. Fighting stopped, and the members of Council met, and decided to depose Malcher, proclaiming Vinagre as both President and Military Governor. While the meeting was in progress, some of Malcher's followers stationed at the hospital began firing again, and another brief but fierce exchange took place. During this battle, Vinagre's men took the *Castello* and the military hospital, and summarily shot everyone they found there. Malcher was arrested, and imprisoned on the "Bella Maria", a Brazilian schooner. On 26 February, a week after the conflict began, Malcher was ordered to be taken as a prisoner to the "Barra" fort, but, as he came ashore, he was shot by his guards, and his corpse, like that of his predecessor, was dragged in triumph round the city.

John then tells us that Malcher, with a party of armed men, had boarded all the merchant ships in the harbour, and forced into boats all the Brazilians and Portuguese he could find, and put them to work defending the *Castello*, where many of them perished. The Masters of all the British ships had written to John Hesketh complaining of this "insult offered to the British flag". John's other concern was with the property and lives of the British residents, and he promised to "watch with unceasing assiduity any infraction of these rights as far as respects British subjects". It is certainly true that at this stage no British lives were lost, and British property seems to have escaped unscathed. Nevertheless, John was obviously very concerned at the unsettled state of the province, although he might have been reassured that Vinagre and his Extraordinary Council, meeting on 21 February, again promised their allegiance to the Empire and obedience to the Regent's orders. Vinagre was violently anti-Portuguese, and therefore supportive of the Empire, even in its present unsatisfactory guise of the Regency. But his loyalty often wavered, being strong in theory, but weaker when it came to the point of handing over his hard-won power. But for the moment, Vinagre was all that stood between "tranquillity" and murderous chaos.

Vinagre's own safety was by no means assured, for almost immediately an anti-Vinagre party plotted to assassinate him. John reports on 7 March: "All here is anxiety and alarm, a constant dread prevailing of a pillage likely to take place if they put down the present President, Vinagre, & there is a party forming for that purpose."[195] The British were, however, cheered two days later by the arrival of HMS "Dispatch" off the port. She came up at night, and Captain Daniell, her commander, said that some of the "Indians" – the *caboclos* – retreated as she approached. Captain Daniell quickly found John Hesketh, and together they went to see Vinagre, again to seek "the strongest assurance that the persons and property of British subjects should be held sacred, and that any attempts to molest them should be punished."[202] They received their assurance, though both men were far from certain that Vinagre could deliver on his promise, for he had annoyed many of his followers by refusing to allow them to carry out a general plundering of the town. Having sized up the situation, Captain Daniell agreed with John Hesketh that HMS "Dispatch" would stay "until affairs assume a more settled aspect". They were both being over-optimistic, for the three months that Captain Daniell and his crew stayed in Belém saw fierce fighting. For the moment, however, the usual courtesies prevailed. On 13 March, four days after the arrival of the "Dispatch", President Vinagre came on board, followed a week later by the Portuguese Consul and a party of Portuguese merchants. Vinagre, in spite of his rebel status, went on board the Brazilian frigate in the port, receiving the official 21-gun salute. At the end of the month, the growing number of vessels arriving in the port to protect the foreign residents was augmented by the French brig, "L'Oreste", which had sailed from Martinique.

At the end of March, Rio de Janeiro finally reacted to the bad news from the north, and appointed a new President for Pará, Manoel Jorge Rodrigues. He was ordered north with a Brazilian naval squadron of four ships, commanded by Commodore John Taylor, who, like Cochrane, was a Briton in the service of Brazil. He was to call first at Bahia, and collect there a regiment of five hundred regular soldiers. When Taylor arrived in Bahia, however, the spirit of mutiny was abroad there too, and only two officers and six men agreed to accompany him. The authorities in Bahia took no action against the rest of the five hundred soldiers who had refused to answer the bidding of the Empire.

Meanwhile, in Belém, the uneasy peace continued. On 24 March, rumours reached the city that the President of Maranhâo was preparing an expedition to put down the rebellion, and more Indians were brought into the town to strengthen the defences. On 17 April, two more Brazilian ships arrived off the port, the frigate "Imperatriz", and the brig "Constância". They brought very few soldiers, certainly not enough to mount an attack upon the rebels, who were now very well-entrenched in the city. The Brazilian squadron now consisted of a frigate, a corvette, three brigs, and three schooners.

A political drama now began to unfold. A Vice-President was elected, with the theoretical power to take over the presidency of the province. The successful candidate was Dr. Custodo Correa, who was based in Cametá three hundred miles to the south of Belém. At first, Vinagre said that he would yield his powers to a properly-elected person, and a schooner was detached to Cametá, to bring Dr. Correa to Belém to assume his powers. Vinagre's second thoughts began almost immediately, however, and he armed more men, and, it was alleged, sent two armed boats to waylay and murder the new Vice-President. The Brazilian Admiral, Pedro da Cunha, heard of it, and sent boats in the night to head off the assassination attempt. A skirmish occurred in which several lives were lost, but Correa arrived safely at the Brazilian fleet on 4 May, accompanied by a substantial armed force of his own.

Also on 4 May, Captain Daniell was informed by John Hesketh that Vinagre had seized several cases of muskets from the Custom-House. The muskets belonged to one of the English merchant companies, Inglis McCalmont & Co., and Vinagre declined to pay for them. Captain Daniell and John Hesketh again visited Vinagre, and Daniell's elegant threat that he would "depart from the neutrality which I had hitherto observed", persuaded Vinagre to restore the arms to the Custom-House, and not make any more attempts to interfere with British property.[196] Nevertheless, it did not escape the notice of Vinagre's party that muskets were readily available, even though the Custom-House itself had been closed for the previous fortnight, with trade at a standstill.

On 11 May, a third President was elected, a Senhor Picanza. Pará now had three presidents, but no "tranquillity", for the next day, the battle entered a new phase. An Indian fired on the "Imperatriz", and the Brazilian ship replied with a broadside. It was ten o'clock in the morning, and the start of a disastrous day for the Brazilian government authorities.

The whole of the Brazilian naval force now fired on the guns in the town, and Vinagre's men replied. The firing went on until 2 p.m., when Pedro da Cunha, the Brazilian Admiral, ordered a landing to be made. Boats, said Daniell, "pushed off from the ships and effected a landing abreast of the anchorage of the Dispatch, and opposite a large building used as a custom-house and barrack.". A letter from one of the British merchants to his brother[204] takes up the story: "In the first instance they made the attempt at a place where it was almost impossible to get on shore, where not a vessel could fire to protect their landing; and where they were exposed to the fire of at least four times their number." Nevertheless, the first hundred who landed, most of them Germans from the "Imperatriz", were gaining ground, and driving the insurgents back at the point of the bayonet. All would have gone well had the next wave of troops landed and fought their way forward. But, faced with the withering fire from the windows of the barracks, they aborted their landings, and tried to go back to their ships, some trying to manoeuvre their boats back into the river, and others jumping overboard and swimming back. This left those still on land dangerously unsupported, and many of them were shot down in the streets, others killed as they tried to relaunch their boats.

Some of the survivors made it as far as the "Dispatch", the French man-of-war schooner "Bernaise", and an English merchant brig, the "Creole", which were all moored nearby. Their crews had been helpless spectators of the vicious battle, but they now helped the survivors on board, dressed their wounds, and returned those who were able to be moved to their own ships.

Those in the landing-party who were captured by the insurgents faced a grim death. The commander of the landing-force, Major Bareto, was taken prisoner, and, according to the merchant's letter, "had his tongue and eyes torn out, the cavities filled with powder and set fire to, after which he was suspended in the air and roasted; the fellows all the time dancing, singing, and shouting the most horrid language." Another captive "was suspended by the tongue; and when by struggling he tore out his tongue, they covered him with small bags of gunpowder and then set fire to him." Others who had been killed by gunfire were cut up and some of them roasted."

At 4.15 p.m., the "Imperatriz" hoisted a flag of truce, and the firing stopped. The attempted invasion had been a disaster, with a very high death-toll. Pedro da Cunha later faced a court-martial for his mishandling of the attack. The merchant's verdict was more informal, but equally damning: "The commander of the Imperatriz is not worth a button."

The British residents had watched the battle with trepidation, and, although none in the British community had been killed, their houses had suffered considerable damage from the Brazilian Navy's bombardment. Many of them were badly hit, among them John Hesketh's house, in which, says Daniell, "eleven 18lb. shots [were] found....." John and Margarida now had seven children, most of them quite young, and the effect of this battle must have been terrifying. British commercial property suffered too, for the Brazilian barrage had holed the roof of the Custom-House, and the rain got in, and spoiled much of the stock.

The next day, Daniell persuaded the Brazilian squadron that its continued presence off the port was likely to lead to further challenges to its authority. Moving away from the port was, he told da Cunha, "the only means of allaying the excitement which existed there", and so at 2 p.m., the whole squadron weighed anchor, and drifted down the river with the current, and took up an anchorage out of range of Vinagre's guns.

The "Dispatch" stayed put off the port, with its French companion, "L'Oreste". The little fleet of foreign ships was supplemented before the end of May by three more arrivals – on 27 May, two French brigs of war, the "D'Assar" and the "Cuirassier", arrived from Brest, to demand satisfaction for the insult offered to their consul three months earlier, and "Dispatch" was doubtless pleased to see HM Sloop of War "Racehorse" sailing up the river to join her three days later. There was no doubt in the merchant's mind that the presence of the foreign ships of war was the only reason why the foreign residents of Belém were not being murdered in the febrile atmosphere which followed the Brazilians' unsuccessful landing. There seems to have been a cordial atmosphere between the British and French vessels, for the two French brigs hoisted English colours on the 28th. in honour of the birthday of King William IV. Daniell also tells us that he lent John Hesketh two "blue lights" on 13 May, perhaps so that the British residents could signal for help to the "Dispatch" lying a few hundred yards from the shore.[205] The "Dispatch's" log tells us that the lights were returned on 2 June, so it may be that the Vice-Consul and the other British residents felt a little more secure by then.[197] When HMS "Racehorse" arrived, the British residents met and wrote to John Hesketh, asking him to make sure that both ships stayed in Belém: there had been an attempt on Vinagre's life on 31 May, and the merchants thought that, had it been successful, the result would have been the plunder of the city, and the murder of all the white inhabitants. The armed mob had, they said, "publicly declared that they would enter the foreign houses in case of invasion, and put to death all who may have taken refuge there"[214] John Hesketh clearly agreed, and the Commander of the "Racehorse", Captain Sir James Everard Home, also concurred, and, for the next fortnight, the two British sloops moored near each other, the "Racehorse" a little higher up the river, opposite the houses of the British and Portuguese Consuls, which adjoined each other. The little fleet was augmented on 1 June by the "Eliza", a Portuguese corvette.

Trouble now began to erupt at other places up-river, and the rebellion began to affect many areas of the Province. At this unpropitious moment, two British travellers arrived in the city. They had experienced at first-hand the unsettled state of the country. Lieutenant William Smyth and Mr. Frederick Lowe had travelled overland from Peru, where their ship, HMS "Samarang", was stationed for three months, and sailed all the way down the Amazon. When they reached Santarém, they were warned about the situation in Belém, but they decided to proceed "at all hazards", as they were anxious to return to England. They were particularly warned about a Creole called "Jacco", who had murdered a great number of Portuguese. Shortly afterwards, they met Jacco, who took them into the nearby house of a Welshman, Mr. Davies, who was a manager for the Campbells. As they drank Davies's coffee, with Davies obviously very nervous of his visitor, Jacco told the naval men that he had "a great respect for the English".[198]

Smyth and Lowe reached Belém on 29 May, reporting to Captain Daniell, who took them on shore, and introduced them to the Messrs. Campbell and to James Blashfield. They only stayed in Belém for a fortnight before shipping out on the "Creole", which left for England on 14 June. All the Brazilians and Portuguese who were able to had already fled, and those who were unable to flee had taken refuge in the houses of the British and American residents. According to Smyth and Lowe, the Campbells had nearly forty of these refugees living in their house. They also came across an Austrian botanist, Dr. Natterer, who had lived for seventeen years in Belém. He too had been threatened, and eventually fled, leaving all his specimens to the mercy of the insurgents, who destroyed them all.

While Smyth and Lowe were in Pará, the news got out that Vinagre, fearing the imminent arrival of Taylor's Brazilian squadron, had secreted £40,000 in silver, an astonishingly large sum, on board an American schooner, the "George", and that he proposed to join it and flee to the United States. There was a sharp reaction from Vinagre's irregulars to this apparent betrayal, and his house was surrounded by his "friends" the night before the schooner sailed. The following morning, the "George" sailed without him, and Vinagre publicly proclaimed, in an echo of Pedro I's "Cry of Ipiranga", that he would be staying in the city.

"L'Oreste" left on 9 June, saluting the British Consul, John Hesketh, with the customary nine guns as she sailed north down the river. Then it was the turn of the "Dispatch" to prepare for departure: all the consuls went on board to say farewell, and John Hesketh handed over a letter to Captain Daniell, to be given to Vice-Admiral Cockburn in Barbados, thanking him for the support the British residents had received from the Navy on the West Indian station. "Dispatch" left on 14 June, and must have cleared the mouth of the Pará River just before Commodore Taylor and his Brazilian squadron hove in sight, with the new President on board, Marshal Manoel Jorge Rodrigues. Although it had taken three long months for him to arrive in Pará to take up his post, he was now about to embark on one of the shortest tenures of any provincial president in that era of short presidential reigns. He came with a limited force of soldiers, and four Brazilian naval vessels.

After his long voyage, and after his difficulties in securing enough soldiers to attempt the restoration of legal authority in Pará, Commodore Taylor cannot have been confident of victory. There were too many well-organised rebels to attempt anything like Grenfell's trick of twelve years before. He had a frigate, the "Campista", a corvette, and two other small vessels, and one hundred and eighty soldiers, the vast majority acquired when he put in at São Luis. His little fleet joined up with the Brazilian ships already in the river, giving Taylor a flotilla of two frigates ("Campista" and "Imperatriz"), two corvettes ("Regeneração" and "Defensora"), two brigs, and two schooners of war. With the benefit of a good view of the port from HMS "Racehorse", Sir James Everard Home takes up the story:

> "On the second day after their arrival, [22 June] the Commodore, having the President on board, brought his ship within a mile and a half of the town, leaving the squadron off Fort Barra, During this time, great preparations were made on shore for a vigorous defence of the City, Three heavy guns were mounted on the Citadel [the Castello] in addition to four that had been there from the beginning. Vast quantities of ammunition was [sic] removed from the Train to the Citadel & Fort St. Antonio.....The shops and Custom House were shut and the merchants embarked their Books & Papers."[199]

The rest of the squadron, except the "Imperatriz", which had run aground in the shallow waters, came up the river and moored next to Commodore Taylor's "Campista". After some tricky negotiations, which lasted three tense days, Vinagre was persuaded to go on board the "Campista" on the morning of 25 June, accompanied by the leading military and civil leaders of the city. "At 1 p.m.," says Home, "the President, having Vinagre and his staff with him in the Boat, disembarked with a force of 180 troops, who had been collected by the squadron from Bahia and Pernambuco and 300 Seamen, 120 of which were English [i.e. British seamen in the Brazilian Navy], and took up their possession [sic] in the palace, after which the families that had embarked returned again. The next morning, the 26th., he was installed, after which he took possession of the citadel, and on the day following, Fort Antonio."

News of this apparent success was rather tainted by the information that two field-guns had been stolen the night before, and two more had disappeared from in front of Vinagre's house. Nevertheless, the Train – the collection of field-guns and gun-carriages – was handed over to Taylor the same evening. He loaded the guns of Fort Antonio on board the "Campista", and spiked the guns of the citadel. He threw them over the ramparts, against, according to Home, the wishes of the President. There are more than a dozen long gun-barrels still on display outside the citadel, perhaps including the very ones that Taylor threw over the walls, and, interestingly enough, they bear the names of British foundries.

The ramparts of the *Castello*, scene of much of the bloodiest fighting in 1835

For the legitimate forces of the Empire, so far, so good. The "Indians" began to withdraw from the city, accompanied by Antonio Vinagre, the ex-President's brother, and Eduardo Angelim. Francisco Pedro Vinagre, however, stayed in the city, doubtless nursing his resentments – his attitude to the Empire was always ambivalent, but Rodrigues made no immediate attempt to have him arrested. Home and the British residents were alarmed at Rodrigues's seeming lack of urgency and decisiveness. Rodrigues mounted a guard of twenty men on the Train during the day, doubling it at night, but it took him until 18 July to set up and organise a Civil Guard.

And then came reports of attacks and atrocities in the area surrounding the city. An American estate was plundered and destroyed, and on 25 July, news came that the town of Vigia, sixty or so miles north of Belém, had been attacked on the 23 June by the insurgents, and whites singled out for particular attention. Two Jewish residents and a Frenchman were murdered, in circumstances of what Home called "horrid barbarity".

On 27 July, John Hesketh received a letter from President Rodrigues, asking for help in defending the city against anticipated attack. He called Great Britain *"Uma Nação das mais aliadas do Brasil"* ("a nation in the closest alliance with Brazil"), and begged for the assistance of the seamen and marines of HMS "Racehorse". John Hesketh immediately called a meeting of the British merchants, at Home's suggestion, "to know in what manner their lives and Property could most effectively be preserved," said Home, "giving it as my opinion that the most effectual way of accomplishing that end, as no nation was to be respected more than another, and as they came for the entire extirpation of the White Inhabitants, to land and oppose them by force."[200]

The merchants agreed, and that evening Home and Hesketh, together with Archibald Campbell, went to see the President to report on their meeting, but also telling him at the same time "that before we took any part for the protection of the City, which was filled by British property under one form or another, either by goods or Debts contracted by the Brazilians and Portuguese to the English, it was absolutely necessary that he should take some steps himself, and remarked to him that it was well known that many houses in the City contained a vast quantity of arms and ammunition, and that Snr. Vinagre himself was daily walking the streets at large." Furthermore, according to John Hesketh, the insurgents had been allowed to leave the city with their guns.

The point was taken, and Vinagre was arrested the following morning, together with his senior colleagues, and imprisoned on the "Imperatriz". The town was searched for weapons, and nearly four hundred "Stand" of weapons were found secreted in private houses, all fully loaded. In Vinagre's house alone was a cache of twenty stand. This seems to have resulted in a rethink about the threat offered by Vinagre and his forces, and he was put in irons on the 30 July, and moved to the hold of the corvette "Regeneração", where he remained a prisoner for many months.

Vinagre's brother, Antonio, was furious to hear of his brother's detention, and wrote on 2 August from Acará to the President. It was a bellicose letter, threatening an immediate attack upon the city by four thousand men if his brother were not released. It met with no reply, of course, but events were being set in motion. On the 13 August, two "blacks" – presumably former African slaves – came into the town, having deserted from the insurgent forces. They brought a great deal of up-to-date information: Antonio Vinagre's forces had occupied an estate no more than ten miles from the city, where they were massing for the attack. They had all dyed their clothes red, and great efforts were being made to amass as much gunpowder as possible, and it was being collected at a point fifteen miles from the city. The gunpowder had originally been in barrels, but it had destroyed the hoops and staves of the barrels, and was now lying in great heaps loose on the floor.

The roof of the powderhouse was in poor order, and let the rain in, and this had caked the gunpowder together. With scant regard for their health and safety, the rebels dried it in the sun, and then carried it in pocket-handkerchiefs to their headquarters. The two deserters also said that the attack on Belém would take place on the following day. Fort Antonio, in the east, would be the apparent target, but the main force would attack the Palace in the centre of the older part of the city. According to Home's account, "they intended to destroy all whites of whatever nation they may be, whether English, French, or otherwise."

Acting immediately on this information, Home ordered his seamen and marines ashore, where they proceeded to occupy the substantial property shared by the Campbells and James Blashfield, slightly to the north of the citadel. This building had eight windows facing the street, and an interconnecting door, and also had an exit on to the riverbank. The building had been unanimously agreed as a rendezvous for the British community if an attack occurred, and as a suitable embarkation point. The position was a good one, for it commanded a view of the main street from Fort Antonio to the Train, and any attackers approaching would also have to run the gauntlet of soldiers firing from the windows of the Barracks adjoining. The marines took over a house on the opposite side of the street, the Rua Açougue. Meanwhile, Portuguese seamen and marines from the "Eliza" landed, occupying the Portuguese Consul's house which was next to John Hesketh's, and the premises of Messrs. Inglis and McCalmont opposite. The President's forces occupied two buildings – the Government Palace and the Military Arsenal.

Early the next morning, between five and six o'clock, two more ex-slaves arrived, one of them wounded, and reported to their master that the insurgents were advancing, and would reach the town between ten o'clock and noon that morning. At nine o'clock, the alarm was sounded, and many of the population rushed down to the shore and lined the beach, hoping to be taken off. The British residents embarked on the "Racehorse" with their account books and some items of property. The foreign residents left their houses in considerable haste – an American newspaper account of the attack speaks of the English Consul – John Hesketh – having to leave without his books and papers, and an American merchant, Mr. Upton, having to jump out of his counting-house window, and run to the shore without his hat.[201] If John Hesketh left without his papers, he did at least manage to get his large family on board in time.

There was one exception to the general exodus – Henry Dickenson. He remained on his *engenho*, his estate out of town, reversing the situation of 1824, when he had fled and John Hesketh had stayed. His activities during the next few months are of great interest, and caused both Dickenson and John Hesketh a great deal of trouble.

There were only three hundred men in Antonio Vinagre's attacking party, taking on almost the same number of Government troops, aided by four hundred others, either foreign seamen and marines, or volunteers. The three hundred attackers were, however, received with sympathy and support by some of the inhabitants, and the attackers patiently worked their way into the city, taking advantage of the structure of the houses. They approached from the village of Nazaré, to the south-east of the town, along a street that is today one of the city's chief thoroughfares. The residents still in their houses and the refugees on the ships in the harbour heard the bugles and muskets of the advancing army at noon, and the President's troops retreated to the Palace. The invaders took their time, barging their way into the houses on the outskirts in small parties of two or three, according to Sir Everard Home. They cut their way through into connecting houses, and thus gradually took over the streets and squares. They fired from the windows, and killed a great number of the male inhabitants. The victims often did not see their killers, and this, we are told by the American newspaper account, produced panic among the remaining inhabitants.

The rebels targeted the foreigners' houses, which were full of property stowed there, and there was, we are told, a great deal of pillage. The American Consul, Mr. Charles J. Smith, who was a close friend of John Hesketh, had his house broken into and its upper windows were used to fire at the British marines who were occupying the Campbells' house.

Soon, Antonio Vinagre led his troops, together with a field-gun, towards the Palace, and a party of defenders, led by the President's son, was sent out to meet them. The defenders captured the gun, but then had to retreat, and in the fighting, the President's son was killed, and Captain Eyre, another British member of the Brazilian Navy, was severely wounded. On the rebel side, their leader, Antonio Vinagre, was killed. The firing went on till dusk, when it ceased, only to begin again at first light the next morning.

By half-past eleven the next morning, the insurgents had moved close to the British positions. Home, who had lost a man killed and two others injured, could see that the time would soon come when the rebels would have possession of all the houses along the river, and would be able to fire at will at anyone trying to escape to the ships. He therefore ordered his marines from the house across the street, and then all of his men back to the "Racehorse". They made safety without further loss, and Home ordered the ship's guns to concentrate on an alley to one side of the slaughter-house in the Rua Açougue, and the guns of the "Campista" concentrated on the other side of the building. But the President, according to Home, lacked decisiveness, and it was the evening of that second day before he ordered his men to take possession of empty houses in the town, or ordered them to try to retake the houses the rebels already occupied. This warfare, said Home "continued with very slow but certain success on the part of the Indians until the evening of the 22nd., during which time three most violent attacks were made upon the train without success, and except that building they had possessed themselves of all parts of the town, to the houses forming the Palace square, a space of about 11 acres of land."

In the afternoon of the 22 August, Commodore Taylor came on board the "Racehorse", and said that embarkation was necessary. By midnight, President Rodrigues had fled on board the "Campista", and the boats of the "Racehorse" and one from the "Campista" had taken on board the two hundred and fourteen men manning the Train. When the other defenders heard this news, there was a mass exodus from the town, and by six o'clock the next morning, as many as six thousand people had embarked on the ships of the Brazilian squadron and the foreign ships. It took the insurgents till eight o'clock that morning to realise that the Train was abandoned, said Home, "when a scene of horror succeeded passed [sic] all description by the murder of those who had taken sanctuary in the churches, and those that had remained in their houses."

At noon, the "Racehorse" weighed anchor, and sailed down the river with the merchant ships, anchoring in the Bay of San Antonio. The Brazilian squadron also sailed, anchoring about three and a half miles down the river, which it began to blockade. Thus Belém was lost.

Back in the city, Eduardo Angelim became the fifth President of Pará in eight months. John Hesketh, with his family and the other British residents and many other refugees on board HMS "Racehorse", wrote sadly to the Foreign Office: "I am sorry to say that my surmises have unfortunately been too truly verified, being myself just now a refugee on board HMS Racehorse, Sir James Everard Home, Bart., Commander, together with all the British residents, to avoid the dismal fate that awaited us on shore."[202] Both he and Home planned to wait in the river, and then, when provisions were running low, to make for Maranhão to the east, where a sizeable British community existed, including John's brother William.

However, information seems to have reached the "Racehorse" that the new rebel President was, in John's words, "inclined to show a friendly disposition to British subjects", and so Home got permission from Rodrigues to return up-river to Belém, together with the merchant ship "Pará Packet", and two American schooners. Two other British merchant ships, the "Alexander" and the "Stranger", followed them. It was a bold and dangerous decision to take, particularly with so many refugees on board, and with so volatile a situation in the city. However, they were received with surprising civility by Eduardo Angelim, and they were able to load "all the property belonging to the British merchants which had escaped the plunder of the insurgents, exempting such bulky articles as could not conveniently be transported."[203] Pottery was, for instance, regarded as too heavy to be rescued. Also left behind were the two Englishmen, Dickenson and Corbett. Home tells us that "Mr. Dickenson, an English gentleman who holds the office of Auctioneer, and who is married to a lady of the Country, and his partner Mr. Corbett, who is agent for Lloyds, having determined to remain on shore, have received powers of attorney from the different gentlemen respecting the property left behind." As always with Dickenson, this piece of apparent prudence was to cause all of them a great deal of trouble when the Cabanagem Rebellion was over.

At noon on 6 September, Home and his little fleet set sail down the river once more, passing the blockading Brazilian squadron. Home reflected on the result of the successful attack by the insurgents: "The Province of Para is in my opinion for ever lost to the Brazils; they sent for its recovery the strongest Power they could Muster, both Naval and Military, and they have been beat." He said that Eduardo had decided to call the new flag "The Independence of the Amazons", and had decided "to beg the protection of Great Britain"[204] Echoing the earlier thoughts of John Hesketh, Home thought that this might have its advantages, especially for navigation, and that the soil was rich, and "the climate the finest in the world".

The immediate situation was, however, dire, and Home soon decided to take his overcrowded ship and its refugees to the comparative safety of Maranhão. The presence of the "Racehorse" had undoubtedly saved the mass murder of the British community. The rebellion had cost many of them, including John Hesketh, their homes. One British civilian – Mr. Gay, one of the merchants – had been shot and killed while attempting to defend his property, and HMS "Racehorse" had lost one man killed and two wounded. The lot of the British was comparatively fortunate, for others of the six thousand refugees who had boarded the ships during the attack met with various fates. Some found their way to Cametá, which remained free of the rebellion, but which was regularly threatened. Others put ashore on various islands in the river, where they succumbed in great numbers to disease. Politically and militarily, there was stalemate, as Commodore Taylor and his Brazilian Navy ships remained at anchor down the river. On board was the erstwhile legal President of Pará, Rodrigues, and the erstwhile illegal President, Vinagre. At the end of October, 1835, the new rebel president, Eduardo published a manifesto which again proclaimed that he and his government were subject to the Brazilian Empire. At the same time they ignored the Brazilian Government blockade, whose effect was in any case minimal, because the rebels needed very little in the way of supplies from the outside world beyond the mouth of the Amazon.

* * *

It was near the mouth of the Amazon that the next tragic incident occurred. Before the outbreak of the rebellion, the murdered President, Bernardo Lobo de Souza, had ordered from the Campbell brothers a sizeable quantity of arms from manufacturers in Great Britain: two thousand muskets and bayonets, a thousand pistols, five hundred carbines, and five hundred cavalry swords. They were loaded on to a British brig of 126 tons, the "Clio", in Liverpool, whose owner was based in Montrose in Scotland. Totally ignorant of the state of affairs in Pará, the ship, with a relatively small crew captained by another Scot, George Reid, set sail across the Atlantic. It reached the Brazilian coast on 30 September, 1835, a fortnight after the "Racehorse" sailed past the same point on its way to from Belém to São Luis de Maranhão.

At Salinas (now Salinopolis), east of the Amazon entrance, the "Clio" hove to beyond the wild breakers and sand-dunes of the coastline, and sent a small party ashore, led by the mate, to enquire about a pilot to take the ship up to Belém. They were greeted by a middle-aged American, John Priest, born in Massachusetts, but who had lived in Salinas for fifteen years, plying his trade as a carpenter. Unfortunately, the mate let slip that part of their cargo consisted of arms destined for Belém. From that moment, their fate was sealed. Priest and the local *Juiz de Paz* (magistrate), Manoel Maria Montero, who acted as Governor of the small community, collected a group of local Indians, and they all agreed that the ship could not be allowed to proceed to Belém. It would, in any case, be intercepted by the blockading Brazilian Navy. The mate and his colleagues were kept on shore overnight, and the Captain encouraged to land the next morning. Once he was on shore with two young members of his crew, Alexander Paton and a seaman called Lloyd, Priest and a party of Indians went out to the "Clio" and brought her in nearer the shore.

They then turned on the crew remaining on board, and murdered all of them, with the exception of the cook, who tried to swim ashore. But he was no match for the breakers, and drowned. On shore, the Captain was stabbed

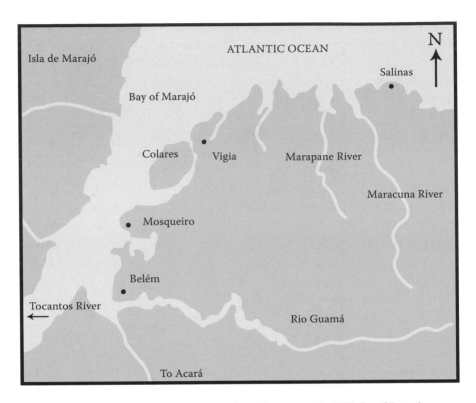

The area around Salinas, which saw the murder of the crew of the "Clio", and Paton's escape

to death, but the two young seamen escaped, and fled into the jungle. After wandering around for two days, they finally headed west, and again passed Salinas in the distance, and saw the ship aground, surrounded by people carrying her cargo ashore. On 6 October, they arrived on the banks of the Maracuna river, which was, says Paton, about two hundred yards wide. They agreed that they had no alternative, and plunged in to swim to the other side. When Paton got to the other bank, he waited for his companion, who was not a strong swimmer, but Lloyd did not appear. Paton waited for some time, but had to assume that Lloyd had drowned. He pressed on, swimming another large river, the Marapane, and eventually got to the town of Cintra, where he recognised food, domestic articles, and weapons that had been taken from the "Clio". Eventually he was taken to Vigia, on the banks of the Pará River. Whilst he was there, word of his survival reached Everard Home, who had returned to the Amazon, and, at the beginning of December, he was rescued by the "Racehorse" and became a crucial witness in the case against Priest, Montero, and the villagers of Salinas.

Later on, the British Envoy to Rio, Hamilton Hamilton, summed up the episode by saying that the "Clio" was "seized off Salinas in September, 1835, on her voyage to Pará, by the Insurgents in that Province".[205] It is true that many of the weapons the "Clio" was carrying found their way to Belém, and the insurgents eagerly swapped their antiquated muskets for the new guns, but the rest of the cargo, as well as the personal possessions of the crew, including their bedding and a black and white dog, were simply stolen. Many of these objects were found in the houses of Priest and Montero. Whilst Priest and Montero were obviously aware of the insurgency, they had taken no part in it, and the seizure of the "Clio" and the murder of her Captain and crew seems to have been an opportunistic act of piracy by a local group led by the American. Certainly the taking of the "Clio" was not endorsed by the rebel President, Eduardo. The subsequent action taken by the British Navy did cause considerable political difficulty, however, and sometimes continues even now to be misunderstood in Brazil.[206]

When Paton told his story to Everard Home, and the fate of the "Clio" was communicated to the headquarters of the West Indian squadron, there was fierce anger and indignation. Vice-Admiral Sir George Cockburn was furious, saying that "so shocking and atrocious an act as that which has been perpetrated on the " Clio" ought not to be allowed to remain ... unnoticed and unrevenged."[207] He therefore ordered the Senior Officer at Barbados, Captain Charles Strong, to take his ship, HMS "Belvidera" and two other ships, HMS "Rainbow" and HMS "Snake", to Pará. Strong was ordered to find out, firstly, if the Brazilian authorities were back in power in Pará, and, if so, demand the immediate apprehension, trial, and punishment of those responsible for the fate of the crew of the "Clio". If Eduardo were in power, he was to be encouraged to do likewise, and it was thought likely that the presence of a British squadron off the port of Belém would influence him. If, however, there were no authority operative in Pará, and only if this were the case , "the senior officer is to take such steps as the force at his disposal and the nature of the country at Salinas and its neighbourhood may enable him, by landing hostilely at Salinas, and taking and seizing as many of the inhabitants as he may be able to capture, by destroying the houses and property he may find there ..... to prove our determination under no circumstances of any country, to allow an act of the monstrous nature of that perpetrated on the Clio".

Sir George Cockburn's fury was understandable, but his third alternative was fraught with potential political and diplomatic difficulties. He did, however, add that the Senior Officer must always bear in mind "that if there be an adequate responsible authority established in the country, his first efforts for redress must be with such authority." Fortunately, Captain Strong took this point, and decided in early March, 1836, to sail up the Pará River to see Eduardo about the matter. He approached President Rodrigues on board the Brazilian blockading squadron for permission to go to Pará to see Eduardo, but there was first delay, and then refusal. With the confidence that British naval power exuded so naturally in those days, Strong decided to ignore Rodrigues, and sail up-river to Belém. His decision reverberates still in Brazil. Strong takes up the story:

> "At 11 o'clock I sent the first Lieutenant Wood ... to Eduardo the President who occupied the palace, requesting an answer without delay. Lieutenant Wood informed me on his return that my letter was read through an interpreter, in the presence of a great number of people, who, when they came to that part of it where satisfaction was demanded, called out "Satisfaction does he want? Give it to him with powder and ball." Eduardo, however, harangued them, and pointed out the justice of their case – and sending me word that an answer should be returned either that afternoon, or the next day." [208]

Eduardo said that he would have come on board and paid his respects, "only the people would not suffer him to do so." Nevertheless, Strong was pleased with Edward's reaction, and received the following day a letter written on Eduardo's behalf by the Provincial Secretary, Ignacio Lima, ordering the authorities in Salinas to deliver up to Strong "the American John Priest, as well as all others that may have taken part in the plunder and death of the English vessel that was seized there."

Strong sailed back down the river, eventually capturing Priest and Montero, and sent them to Maranhão with HMS "Snake". The Governor there sent them for trial, but no sentence was passed, Brazilian law being adjudged to require that all those suspected of the offence should be tried together. They never were tried; Priest died in captivity in late 1836, and Montero was later released, to the anger of the British Government.

Much was made of Strong's refusal to obey Rodrigues, and he was accused of high-handedness and failing to respect the authority of the Emperor of Brazil, but Palmerston defended him stalwartly: "HMG will never suffer British subjects to be outraged with impunity", adding rather provocatively, "he must remark that if a Govt. is too weak to cause its own authority to be respected in its own territory, and by its own people, it must not be surprized that foreign powers should take upon themselves to redress wrongs that may be inflicted on their subjects."[209]

The "Clio" incident is often associated with accounts of the Cabanagem, largely because of its timing, but it was at most an act of criminal opportunism, and although Strong's actions offended the Brazilians, they were intended to bring criminals to justice, regardless of the political situation in Pará. It was the offence to the British flag and to the peaceful course of British trade that motivated Sir George Cockburn and the Navy, rather than any attempt to interfere in the rebellion against the Rio de Janeiro government. And, for the second time, Eduardo seems to have treated the British with reasonableness and some degree of favour.

* * *

Meanwhile, John Hesketh and his family were exiled in São Luís. John's brother, William, was, of course, long established in the town, and undoubtedly supportive of his brother and his large family. Margarida may also have had relatives in São Luís, for her mother, Dona Francisca Leonarda de Mattos, eventually left Pará to go to São Luís in 1845, and would have been unlikely to have left her home for an unknown place without having some friends or relatives there. It did not take John long to realise, however, that he was in a very difficult financial situation. He had lost his home in Belém for the second time, had no possibility of earning money through mercantile activity while he was exiled from his post, and at a time when the rebel government in Pará was scaring away trade. For the second time in six years, he was in serious financial trouble.

This was the time when he received the letter from Lord Palmerston criticising his handwriting and syntax. The letter left London before the end of July, but did not reach John until he had arrived in Maranhão in October. Palmerston's criticisms were met by John with an admirable humility[210] And, judging by John's surviving letters to London, he certainly seems to have made an effort to improve his handwriting.

At the same time, however, he had even more serious concerns. He wrote to Palmerston privately in his new "larger and rounder Hand": "I humbly beg to lay before Your Lordship's the peculiar and distressing circumstances of my situation, & in consequence of the distressing events in Para, which have forced the retreat of myself and the British residents to this Place.... having in consequence been obliged to abandon the Property there I possessed, and from which I derived pecuniary competence for the maintenance of a numerous family, for whose subsistence I am now obliged to trust to my limited pay of Two Hundred Pounds a year". He points out that he has had to depend upon the liberality of his relatives (doubtless William and Robert), has worked in Pará for eleven years, five of which brought him no pay, and has received only a limited amount of fees, at an average of $150 p. a. He ends: "It is with feelings of reluctance I am forced to lay my case before Your Lordship, but the untoward events which have subjected me to this course will [surely?] plead my cause. And I sincerely hope that taking what I have above stated into consideration, His Majesty will be graciously pleased to sanction an addition to my annual pay."[211]

When this letter reached London in February, 1836, Palmerston reacted with some sensitivity. He acknowledged the letter "representing the distressed circumstances in which you are placed by the recent events at Pará, and requesting that some additional allowance be made to you on that score", but asked for further details.[212] John's reply in June[213] listed his losses:

    1. House.   £4166.13s.4d.

    2. Personal Property   £833. 6s.8d.

    3. Extra expences of flight to Maranham £238. 0s.0d.

In August, eight months after he had complained of being almost penniless, he received a reply, penned by Fox-Strangways, one of the Permanent Under-Secretaries, awarding him £360 for his Personal Property and the expenses of fleeing to Maranhão.[214] There was to be no compensation for the very much larger loss of his house.

In his letter to the Foreign Office in June, John had asked to be made a full Consul, and, again, Palmerston reacted sympathetically, asking his officials for more information about John. It seems a little strange that Palmerston appeared not to know anything about a man he had recently rebuked for his handwriting, but the reassuring answer encouraged Palmerston to write another note: "Make him Consul and give him 300L a year."[215]

John was by this time in London – he had friends there – and then travelled back to Liverpool, where he doubtless visited and perhaps stayed with his sisters, Louisa and Mary Ann. Harriet had died in 1833. He could hardly afford to bring his family over, but there is mention of the arrival of "Mr. and Mrs. Hesketh" in Liverpool, and it may well have been the first time that he had been able to introduce his wife Margarida to his English family and friends.

John and Margarida were back in Pará by the beginning of December, 1836, reunited with their children. While he had been away, there had been momentous events in Pará. Eduardo Angelim was no longer the President. His rule as President had lasted slightly longer than that of his immediate predecessors, until May, 1836. The Brazilian blockade of Pará does not seem to have been very effective, and it was only when the strong and sometimes ruthless hand of Brigadier Francisco José de Sousa Soares d'Andrea was employed that Brazil recaptured its lost northern province. Rio made him

President, and he was given two and a half thousand troops He recaptured Belém with no resistance on 13 May, 1836, and the rebels abandoned the city they had taken with such bloodshed eight months earlier. D'Andrea pursued the rebels with vigour, as they once more established themselves on the River Acará three hundred miles south of Belém, and in other areas of Amazonia. The rebel troops were routed, and in July Eduardo was wounded, and finally captured at Lago Real on the River Pequeno on 20 October, 1836.

By the end of the month, Angelim was back in Belém, this time as a prisoner. Hamilton Hamilton in Rio struck a triumphant but perhaps inappropriate note: – "The celebrated mulatto chief Eduardo has been captured." The Rio Government was, of course, delighted, and the report of the Minister of Justice speaks of "brave troops", and "the intelligence and great activity of the President". But there were still problems, for d'Andrea's very thoroughness was fomenting trouble. He pursued the rebels with great diligence and sometimes cruelty throughout the province, and Hamilton Hamilton expressed his reservations in October, 1837: "The Province of Pará is still in a most deplorable position, and presenting abundant elements of conflagration. The rebellion, it is true, is put down, but the whole population is in an extreme state of penury and wretchedness, and the President, d'Andrea, however qualified to command as a military man, appears little suited to fill the chair of civil magistrate, and still less capable of healing the wounds inflicted by intestine warfare."[216] It was, in fact, another three years before an uneasy peace settled on Pará, and only after an amnesty for those who had fought with such violence against authority. Eight hundred *cabanos* accepted the amnesty in March, 1840.

Vinagre and Eduardo were taken to Rio, but released in the early 1850s, and both returned to Pará. Vinagre died in 1873, and was buried in Belém, and Eduardo "Angelim" died in 1882, and was buried beside his wife in Barcarena, south of Belém.

H.S. Fox, the British Envoy in Rio, called Pará "the ill-fated province". The Brazilian historian, Salles, called the Cabanagem Rebellion "one of the most profound, most serious, and most characteristic of the Regency phase".[217] It does not seem to have been influenced from outside to any great degree, and had little intellectual animus, apart from its hatred of wealth and position. It had no connected aims, and was, perhaps surprisingly, not interested in the abolition of the slave trade or of slavery itself. Indeed Eduardo Angelim put down a slave revolt which broke out during his brief tenure of the presidency. Perhaps, as John Hemming suggests, the insurgents themselves did not know what they wanted, once the hated Portuguese and the foreigners had been ousted from the city.[218] The rebels were for Catholicism, Pará, the Emperor, and liberty, and against the Portuguese, some (but not all) foreigners, and freemasons. Their stand against the Empire kindled fires elsewhere, and the decade after 1835 saw rebellions in most parts of Brazil. None of them, however, matched the Cabanagem for the violence of its blood-letting. John Hesketh and his fellow foreign residents were undoubtedly fortunate to escape with their lives, if not their property. When they returned by slow degrees to Pará, they found their trade largely destroyed, and a familiar figure in a position of some influence – their former Vice Consul, Henry Dickenson. He had escaped the rebels, and was apparently none the worse financially for the Cabanagem. His financial prosperity had been gained, however, at the expense of his fellow-merchants, and it was to be left to John Hesketh to try to sort out the problems Dickenson created with such facility.

HENRY DICKENSON

"A gentleman ... of high character" (Samuel Vines, British Consul in Pará)

Henry Dickenson was born in Lancashire, possibly near Bury, for he claimed later on to be on friendly terms with the family of Sir Robert Peel, who came from that town. He was certainly living in Pará by 1813, for the newly-arrived British Consul in Maranhão, Robert Hesketh, thought fit to appoint him as Vice-Consul in Pará in 1813. Robert himself had only arrived the year before, and did not receive his own Commissionn until November, 1813. In that month, he wrote to the Foreign Office asking for approval for Dickenson's appointment. Whether Robert met Dickenson face-to-face before recommending his appointment is not clear. If he had, there is no doubt that the impression Dickenson would have created would have been a good one, for he was initially impressive. Much later on, we learn from Samuel Vines, British Consul at Pará in the 1850s, that Dickenson was "a gentleman of extensive practical knowledge, possessing perfect acquaintance with the French and Portuguese languages, of high character and position as a British merchant in this city".[219] We learn from Robert Ryan, British Consul in the 1840s, that Robert Hesketh had told him that Dickenson "possessed gentlemanly manners".[220] He and his brother, I. Pargiter Dickenson, claimed to possess that highest qualification of the Victorian job-seeker – connection. Ryan says that Henry Dickenson gave out "that his family in England have great influence with the Right Honourable Sir Robert Peel, Her Majesty's First Minister and Secretary of State" So it is perhaps not surprising that Robert Hesketh was impressed enough by Henry Dickenson in 1813 to make him Vice-Consul, especially as there were apparently few other suitable candidates.

After Dickenson's appointment was made, he seems to have given Robert little opportunity to continue to make positive comments. The next reference to Dickenson's performance comes in 1816, when there was an exchange of letters between Robert Hesketh and Henry Chamberlain, the Consul-General in Rio. Chamberlain's reply[221] makes it clear that relations between Dickenson and the Provincial Governor of Pará had been strained. Chamberlain says his conduct "has been marked by a degree of Warmth and Pretension in which it is quite impossible that he can be supported by me". He suggests that "if this Government were to make a serious Complaint against Mr. Dickenson's Tone and treatment of their Governor, and his assumptions of rights and powers not vested in any Consul whatever, and directly at variance with the Paramount authority of the state, I am afraid that I should be unable to appease the Minister by my Offers of Satisfaction short of an Intimation to you ....that you should appoint another Vice Consul." Chamberlain also suggests that Dickenson has been prepared to break Brazilian law, for he explains that His Majesty's subjects are answerable to the laws of Portugal or Brazil, and that Dickenson's powers as Consul are restricted to settling disputes between his countrymen, and protecting British lives and property – "He has no power to do more."

So Dickenson was accused of arrogance and assumption, as well as an imperfect understanding of the limits of his official powers, together with a considerable insensitivity. To these faults was added, we later learn, a total refusal to supply reports and returns as required. In 1819, Robert Hesketh wrote him a letter preserved in the Honorary Consul's office in Pará, saying "that it is now a considerable length of time since I most earnestly requested you to bring up and forward the returns from your office..." Earlier that year, Robert had written to Viscount Castlereagh, the Foreign Secretary, about Dickenson's "misconduct". In addition to his treating the local authorities with contempt, there was "a want of regularity" in Pará. Dickenson's refusal to send his Returns "has occasioned considerable Inconvenience to the Consul-General and myself ... and he has, in more than one instance, totally neglected my instructions."[222] This had resulted in a Sloop of War being sent from Barbados, unnecessarily, according to Robert.

Since his appointment, Dickenson had been regularly receiving his salary, £400 per year, together with half of the Consulage Fees at the port. We have seen that Robert Hesketh shared his entitlement to some of the Fees at Pará with Dickenson, in an attempt to make him "a satisfactory and equitable allowance".[223] It is interesting that £400 was twice as much as John Hesketh received from 1829 onwards, and that John's first four years as Vice-Consul produced no pay at all. It was also £100 more than Robert himself received in Rio on his first appointment as Consul there in 1832.

Relationships between Dickenson and Robert Hesketh in Maranhão were therefore at a low ebb when John Hesketh arrived in the port on the Amazon in 1819. Dickenson's prickly response, suggesting that Robert Hesketh intended to sack him and appoint his brother instead, will not have helped relationships with the new arrival, and Robert indignantly refuted the idea: "no such idea has been entertained by either my Brother or myself."

This unsatisfactory state continued for the next three years. Dickenson was obviously still not sending in his Returns, for the Pará statistics are not included in his Trade Returns for 1822. "I presume," said Robert, "[that] Vice-Consul Dickenson has not been absent from Pará since the year 1815", but Robert had no Returns to prove it.[224]

In 1823, Robert wrote to the Foreign Office about the Pará Contribution Fund. Even though Vice-Consul Dickenson had received a considerable sum of money from the Contribution Fund, he had not sent in any returns, in spite of being specifically requested to do so. This must have meant that he had kept the whole of the third due to be shared between Robert and himself, and even the fifteenth due to the Consul-General in Rio.

December, 1823, however, saw Dickenson make his most egregious blunder. The setting-up of the Cavalry Corps was discovered when HMS "Eclair" arrived in Pará, and its commander, Captain Hope Johnstone, found to his astonishment that the foreigners in the port had enlisted themselves in an illegal military unit. His prompt action in having it disbanded will not have enhanced either Dickenson's reputation or his authority. It is clear from Captain Hope Johnstone's account that Dickenson himself was personally involved, along with a fair number of the British merchants, though not all. Hope Johnstone was obviously furious as well as amazed at this attempt to interfere with Pará's politics.

Dickenson's excuse for flying in the face of every accepted principle of residence abroad, and every tenet of the consular code, was the volatile political state of the province, and it was not long before Dickenson orchestrated a mass departure from Pará by the British residents. Robert Hesketh claimed that Dickenson and his friends had allied themselves too closely to "a beaten party", and were, as a consequence, in fear of their own safety.[225] In view of Dickenson's previous history of involvement in the politics of Pará, this would not be surprising. Trouble in Pará had begun the previous August, when the underlying tension between the pro-Portuguese and the pro-Brazilian parties erupted in violence. The arrival of Captain Grenfell and the resulting deaths of a large number of dissidents on board the "Palhoço" stirred up a good deal of hatred of Europeans. The British residents feared retribution; and thus was born the misconceived plan to form a private police force, in the shape of the Cavalry Corps, to ensure what Dickenson called "the maintenance of sound order". Their case, according to Dickenson, was bolstered by events down the river in Cametá, where the rebels, Dickenson asserted, had mutilated and massacred numbers of Europeans. Policing, even in times of civil disorder, was, of course, the responsibility of the local authorities, but deprived of the Cavalry Corps and faced with the withdrawal from the port of the small Brazilian naval fleet, he decided to abandon Belém. He chartered the brig "Mary Ann Donaldson", and, having acquired passports for the British community, set sail on 3 March, 1824, in company with the Brazilian squadron, and a schooner sent by the Government of Cayenne. Altogether, over a thousand people left the city, the British contingent sailing to the safety of Barbados.

Dickenson's evacuation of the foreign residents, it will be remembered, did not include John Hesketh and his family. Dickenson's graceless and unsuccessful attempt to nominate John Hesketh as his deputy in his absence must further have increased the hostility between them. Doubtless with some quiet satisfaction, John reported to Dickenson in Barbados that "since you departed there is great quiet here, and the rebellion has been completely crushed in Vila da Conde, with twelve rebels killed, and the rest fleeing without their ammunition into the woods. Food supplies were plentiful, with canoes from the island of Marajó bringing eighty cattle, and other supplies arriving by sea.[226]

Given the antipathy that Dickenson encouraged back in 1819 when John had first arrived, this latest series of events was not calculated to cement their friendship. Dickenson's behaviour had been high-handed and ill-judged. He arrived back in Pará in mid-April, leaving his family in Barbados. Even he had to admit on his return that the province was peaceful.

Robert Hesketh had now had enough of Dickenson's behaviour, and decided that he must be replaced. Dickenson had strengthened the case for John Hesketh as his replacement by nominating him, albeit inefficiently, before his flight to Barbados. The response of George Canning, the Secretary of State for Foreign Affairs, was very supportive of Robert:

"The reasons which incline you to believe that the Resumption by Mr. Dickenson of the Vice-Consular functions would be injurious to the Interests of His Majesty's subjects, appear to be well-founded, and I approve of your intention to appoint Mr. John Hesketh to be British Vice-Consul at Pará in place of Mr. Dickenson."[227] In November, 1824, the appointment was made, and John's Commission sent to him. The Foreign Office, in a letter of 27 November, instructed Dickenson to hand over to John Hesketh his office and all his official documents. Dickenson seems to have obeyed.

Canning also thought that something needed to be said to the rest of the British merchants in Pará. Robert was therefore instructed to admonish the rest of the British community, and warn them against interfering in any way in local politics; it was important to ensure that local people and the local authorities maintained the best possible relations with Great Britain. Robert told them that if his instructions had been observed, all this disturbance would have been unnecessary.[228]

The British community's abortive flight to Barbados and the appointment of John Hesketh must have produced great loss of face for Henry Dickenson. There is no record of his immediate hostility to John, but the 1830s provide plenty of examples of deep-dyed resentment and animosity – not that his relationships with most of the later Consuls were any more peaceful.

We have no further information until 1828, when Maw and Hinde, ended their cross-continental journey in Pará.[229] As well as dining with John Hesketh and his family, they also mention dining with "Mr. Dickinson [sic], formerly His Majesty's Vice-Consul". They tell us that Dickenson has purchased an *engenho* – a plantation a short distance up the river. Mr. Dickenson has married a Brazilian lady, whose sister is the widow of another English merchant, and who lives with her. Both the lady and the plantation figure in later events. We are told that his wife was from a rich Brazilian family, and owned a great number of slaves, most of whom would have been occupied in working on the plantation. Robert Ryan, who quarrelled with Dickenson in 1846, speaks of his wife's numerous family, and that he was by then "a considerable Proprietor of Slaves, and ... a violent defender of Slavery in this country." Ryan says that he had been in the country for "nearly thirty years" – in fact it must have been nearer thirty-five – had been married to his Brazilian wife for much of that time, and "it is only natural that he has imbibed the ideas of those with whom he has been so long associated, & forgotten altogether those he possessed in his native land." Certainly, Dickenson showed no enthusiasm for sending Robert Hesketh his annual return on the number of slaves imported into Pará, and, soon after John took over in Pará, Robert asked him to send him the figures for 1825, and "also any earlier years you can find".[230]

Henry Dickenson does not seem to have played any part in the British merchants' protest against John Hesketh in 1832, when the latter was asked to keep HMS "Pickle" in Belém for several more days in the middle of another political crisis in Pará. John Hesketh's refusal to do so infuriated some of his merchant colleagues, but Dickenson, perhaps having learnt his lesson from the flight to Barbados in 1824, took no direct part in the protests. Or, of course, he may have been away from Belém at the time, and staying at his *engenho*.

The Cabanagem rebellion of 1835–6 was too cataclysmic an event to leave Dickenson untouched. Indeed, it gave him novel opportunities for making money, and, eventually, for quarrelling with John Hesketh. The previous chapter plotted the course of the Cabanagem's bloody conflict, and how the defeat of the legal regime of President Rodrigues necessitated the rapid evacuation of the provincial capital. This time, John Hesketh left, and Henry Dickenson stayed.

Dickenson wrote to his brother, I. Pargiter Dickenson, in London in September, 1835, a month after the bloody battle of Belém, when the city had been overrun, and most of the other Europeans had fled. "All the British residents are resolved to go except myself and my old fellow-labourer Corbett ... the only ones whose property consists chiefly of slaves, lands, copper-mining.... I am living at present under the protection of the Bishop, a very old friend of mine."[231] Dickenson was fortunate that the *cabanos* held as one of their guiding principles their support for the Roman Catholic Church, and that being protected by the bishop was a piece of great good fortune. "Corbett" was Robert Falconer Corbett, the Lloyds' Agent in Pará, and almost always associated in earlier records with Dickenson, until his appointment as British Consul in São Luis in 1842.

Dickenson was, however, struck by the damage inflicted on the city and the province by the Cabanagem conflict: – "To walk through this once-happy, well-thronged, and prosperous place is heart-rending... I trust to God, that never-failing source of consolation to the distressed, that it may be permitted to me to write to you again, where and when if at all he only knows." The stress of his situation must have told on him, for there is no other record of his sounding either so unsure of himself, or so dependent on the mercy of God.

The *cabanos'* occupation of Belém lasted for a further seven months, and Dickenson soon saw opportunities. How we interpret his conduct depends on our reading of his character. According to his brother, he was "instrumental in the saving of Property belonging to Merchants of various Nations which had been abandoned by them, & had been left to the mercy of the Insurgents."[232] Dickenson treated with the insurgents, and made "an ostensible purchase of it [the property] at a low rate". When the Cabanagem was over, and the merchant community returned, they found that Henry Dickenson was the apparently legal owner of their houses and property. Many of them were not pleased when he presented his bill for their purchase. Expecting thanks, Dickenson was taken aback by their ingratitude. His complaints were reproduced with interest in his brother's frequent letters to Lord Palmerston. The Foreign Office summary of the situation suggested that Dickenson's "Proceedings however are stated to be viewed with Jealousy [Lord Palmerston has written here "Not unnaturally, I think"] both by the legal Authorities who are now again in Possession of Pará, and by several individuals who far from thinking themselves that Mr. Dickenson rendered them any real service, are loud in their complaints against him for demanding the repayment stated by him to have been incurred of expense on their behalf."

However, Lord Palmerston had to be seen to examine the ethics of the matter thoroughly, and wrote to John Hesketh instructing him to examine the situation, and, if he found that Dickenson's claims were "founded in equity, you will use your best endeavours to protect him against loss or inconvenience". At this point in the draft, whoever, Palmerston again added a comment in his distinctive handwriting: "If on the other Hand it should appear that he is attempting to take undue advantage of those of his countrymen who quitted Pará, you will report to me the Circumstances which may lead to such a conclusion. P." It is not hard to detect here a mind already made up, an impression strengthened by a further comment in Palmerston's hand, presumably for his Under-Secretary's benefit: "I always look with suspicion upon men who are clamorous & abusive without evident cause, & such Mr. Dickenson in England has been."

I. Pargiter Dickenson certainly seems to have spent a lot of time and ink on his increasingly ranting letters to Palmerston, the main burden of which was that his brother Henry had been abandoned in Pará during the Cabanagem Rebellion. Palmerston reminded him that his brother had stayed behind of his own volition, whereupon I. Pargiter Dickenson, feeling "great indignation at the letter he has received", wanted to know "whether the protection of the British Government is to be considered permanently, as it appears to be at present, wholly withdrawn from its subjects remaining resident in Pará."[233] Palmerston countered by wanting to know what the "protection" consisted of, and, after another blast from Dickenson, delivered himself of a lecture. Palmerston's reply to Dickenson shows that he perhaps had a more complex personality than he is generally credited with:

"Lord Palmerston desires me to state to you that the British Government cannot prevent revolutions taking place in Foreign Countries, and that when such Revolutions do happen and when in consequence thereof, the authority of the Sovereign Power in such Country ceases to be obeyed, it is evident that the British Government cannot always secure the inviolability of Person and the undisturbed Possession of Property for British subjects who may be resident in places which thus become the Scenes of Anarchy."[234]

The letters from I. Pargiter Dickenson ceased for a while after that obviously sensible statement of policy. Palmerston did, however, add, in October, 1836, that he had "instructed H.M. Consul at Pará to institute special Inquiries in to the whole of the circumstances... and to afford Mr. Henry Dickenson such protection and assistance as the merits of the case may appear to justify."[235] Dickenson seems to have interpreted that as an instruction to John Hesketh to support him whatever the justice of his claim.

Back in Pará, most of the aggrieved residents made their peace and came to some sort of accord with Henry Dickenson, whatever they thought of his behaviour. The owners, said John, preferred to make "a sacrifice", rather than to go to law, and "accordingly paid him what he demanded."[236] One, however, did not, and the Case of the Bags of Cotton became a serious cause of conflict between Dickenson and John Hesketh. John had only been back in Belém for a little while, when he was faced with the case, which bristled with complicated issues, and was accompanied with clamour from several sides.

When the Cabanagem was at its height, the legal President, Rodrigues, had taken possession of eighty-nine bags of cotton – each bag containing 180 pounds of raw cotton – and used them for barricades for the windows of his Palace. The cotton had belonged to Vicente Antonio Miranda. After the enforced departure of the President, the bags were taken from the Palace by one Ignacio Jozé Vieira de Lima, and sold to Manoel Jozé Cavalcanti. Thirty-four of the bags were then sold on to Henry Dickenson, who might, one assumes, have been alive to the charge that he was dealing in stolen property. When Miranda, the original owner of the cotton, returned to Belém, he naturally wanted his property back. He went to the local courts to complain about the matter, and the courts ruled in his favour. Dickenson, however, refused to give back the cotton. His argument was that he had a "lien" upon the property, a right to the ownership of that property until a debt on it had been discharged. He and his brother mention the "lien" on numerous occasions, but no one else seems to have been convinced of the appropriateness of the term, given that Henry Dickenson, in buying the property from the insurgents, had not sought or obtained the permission of the original owners. He also maintained that the case was "extra-judicial", a term he never explains, but which seems to imply that he was in no way subject to Brazilian law, and that Miranda, a Brazilian citizen, had no right to have recourse to the Brazilian courts of law. Dickenson apparently based his belief that the matter was "extra-judicial" on hearing that John Hesketh had held a meeting with the President of the Province and Miranda, and that this would not have occurred if the case had been a normal one. The case was thin, especially as John Hesketh maintained that the meeting was to try and sort out an amicable solution to the problem. The President certainly did not accept the "extra-judicial" plea in his letter to John Hesketh about the matter. He refers to the property which Dickenson "affirms having purchased of the Rebels of the Province, in order to save the same for the proprietors.... this Case is entirely subject to the Law of the Country, which he is in duty bound to obey."[237]

There is a pattern emerging here, with Dickenson in 1823 heavily involved in the setting-up of a private police force, which was designed to have a vigilante role, and to ignore the sovereignty of the Brazilian state, and now wanting to be considered as a special case, owing no responsibility to the Brazilian courts. There was no Judge Conservator in Pará, and so Dickenson had to accept the authority of the local courts, and appeal to the British Consul for support. The British Consul was only likely to support him if his case was good. Dickenson seems to have believed that he was entitled to live in a kind of British bubble, where, although resident in a foreign land, he would always be protected by the force of the British Government, and be governed only by British law. Dickenson's attitude signals, perhaps, the beginnings of British imperialism. We cannot, however, blame Palmerston for it, in spite of his later reputation. He was quite clear, following the example of Canning a decade earlier, that British citizens abroad were ambassadors, not only for British trade, but also for the British nation, and that they must behave in a reasonable and law-abiding way, and subject themselves to local laws.

The affair of the cotton bags, worth, at most, 880 *milreis* (about £110 sterling), rumbled on into the new year, 1837, with Dickenson becoming ever more vituperative. When Dickenson did not produce Miranda's money, the local authorities decided to search Dickenson's warehouse in the Rua das Mercês in Belém on 23 February, giving John Hesketh the customary notice of the search. John let Dickenson know what was proposed, and pledged to be there, but also told Dickenson that "you will functionally cause your Stores to be opened, and allow such search to take place, in accordance with the Laws of this Country, unto which, by your residence in the same, you render yourself amenable."[238]

Dickenson wrote a formal protest against the search, but it was in vain. The search took place, with the Consul present, but Dickenson, having opened his doors, turned his back and walked off. He went home, and wrote to John Hesketh accusing him of a whole range of sins. He protested that the search was "unjust, arbitrary, scandalous, and malicious". He had seen a pair of scales already outside his warehouse before it was opened, suggesting that he was already adjudged to be guilty of storing stolen property, and wanted to know whether the Consul had remained during "the pretended search", because he was proposing to "represent at Home, that I saw you walk leisurely away, without caring for the result." Dickenson concluded by saying: "I have to express my utter astonishment at your want of zeal, of energy, your total supineness, Apathy, or call it by any name ... in allowing such proceedings to go on with such a Protest before you, the *Juiz* [the Judge] acknowledging the justice of such Protest, without a word interposed by you, either in the shape of advice to me, of remonstrance with the *Juiz*; true, that you said that you had a toothache."[239]

This was somewhat unfair: John had been giving Dickenson advice on a daily basis for many days before the search, but it was not advice that Dickenson wanted to hear. Dickenson continued by suggesting that his Consul was "the humble servant of the Brazilian authorities, instead of the legitimate supporter of British Interests.... I shall not cease to demand your attention to my just Claims for <u>public will I make this correspondence</u> you may rely on it, if you do not do your duty, and that this day you failed to do it is the general opinion of the natives and Foreigners." He threatens to raise questions, "even though I cause you very much trouble and perhaps some offence."[240] He then adds, rather lamely, "since no one, however wrong, likes to have his conduct public or private impeached." And he wanted to know if the Consul had given the *Juiz* a translation of his protest.

John replied on the following day, confirming that he had indeed supplied the *Juiz* with a translation of the protest. But he wanted to know how Dickenson imagined that he, as Consul, could prevent "the due execution of the regular course of Justice... Miranda considers himself to be the aggrieved party, you hold property belonging to him, and he brings an action at Law against you for the recovery of the same, now I will ask you what irregularity is there in this mode of proceeding? Is he not privileged to have recourse to an Appeal to the Laws of his own Country for the Justice of his Cause? and upon what plea do you attempt to deny him that Right?" Dickenson's argument, he concluded, was "only exceeded in presumption by its absurdity."[241] Furthermore, he had promised to write to the President on the matter, if Dickenson provided a written statement on the case, "but I heard nothing further from you on the subject until the legal Proceedings on the part of Mr. Miranda were actually commenced against you". He could hardly, therefore, be accused of laziness: "Look, sir, to your own conduct, before you judge of the conduct of others." As far as the threat to publish the correspondence was concerned, Dickenson could publish and be damned, for "it will put your character in the light it deserves."

This last was the scream of an exasperated man, and John Hesketh, when he sent an account of what he called "a correspondence of rather an unpleasant nature" back to London, apologised to Palmerston for losing his calm.

The following day, 25 February, Dickenson, having, one suspects, lost the argument, retaliated by complaining that Hesketh had insulted him: "I would willingly pass over the final paragraph of your letter as too ignoble to have come from the pen of a public Functionary's [sic]", and he proposed to "address an enquiry to Viscount Palmerston to ascertain how far innuendo affecting private character from a Public Officer of the Crown are [sic] borne out by His Lordship's sanction."[242] So it was acceptable to insult a Consul, but not for the Consul to bite back.

Then Dickensone produced his trump card in a postscript: "It may possibly be of some use to you, Sir, in shaping the course of your future publick Conduct, to know what the following extract from a letter, lately received by me from England, will inform you of." The "extract" begins by suggesting that the writer regrets not having met Mr. Hesketh, because "the parties concerned" found him "<u>lacking intelligence and zeal</u>", and his impressions of him were "that the Consul has been wanting in energy and spirit to the disadvantage of <u>British character and Interests</u> in the Brazils, but I have always avoided in addressing the Government ... any insinuation of such a feeling."

How convenient it must have been to have such an "Extract" on hand just at the right moment. How helpful that parts of the charge were already underlined, and that it was possible to hint that the writer had the ear of the Government back in London. Dickenson does not vouchsafe the name of the writer, and it is only reasonable to wonder whether the author was in fact Henry Dickenson himself. The style is tortuous and pained, as if written in the height of emotion, and the phraseology bears some similarities to the language Dickenson was himself using a few days earlier. The hint that he had friends in high places is entirely typical of the Dickenson brothers' methods, and the assumption of moral superiority, in purporting not to pass on criticism of John Hesketh to the Government, appears to be humbug. There is no other criticism of a like kind in the official records, and it must be assumed that this "extract" is fabricated for the occasion. Dickenson was shortly to be in conflict with later Consuls in Pará, and perhaps this was merely a manifestation of how deep was Dickenson's hurt at being sacked from his post as Vice-Consul thirteen years earlier. And we might also assume from his vituperativeness that Dickenson knew that he would not win the case with Miranda.

An estate up-river from Belém, similar to Henry Dickenson's *engenho*

Another curious incident involving Henry Dickenson occurred about the same time. In January, 1837, three rebels were alleged to be hiding on his *engenho* a few miles upriver from Belém. A small detachment of soldiers was sent to investigate, and on their departure from the estate, were accused of the theft of "a small amount of sugar, molasses, and rum, 192 lbs. of coffee, and 5 bushels of *farinha* [ground cassava root], a bag of approximately 100 *milreis* in copper coin, a silver tray", and some clothes. The clothes allegedly belonged to the only witnesses – two of Dickenson's slaves, and a free woman who lived on the estate. This too came to John Hesketh to sort out, though he thought the case "rests upon the somewhat suspicious [testimony] of the slaves and the free woman".[243] The officer in charge of the detachment denied the charge, and London, seeing that the total value of the theft was not great, advised John Hesketh to seek an accommodation between Dickenson and the provincial government, which presumably was done. There are, again, aspects of this allegation of theft that do not quite ring true: the exact figure of 192 lbs. of coffee is odd, given that it would have been stored in a sack rather than in carefully weighed-out packets, the fact that the soldiers allowed witnesses to see their booty, and the difficulty such a haul would have given them to transport in a small canoe. The President too was suspicious, thought Dickenson's claim rather exaggerated, and though he knew, as a brigadier, that it was not unknown for soldiers to plunder, the amounts allegedly stolen seemed large for a casual theft. There seems no doubt that the President, the Consul, and the Secretary of State for Foreign Affairs had had enough of Dickenson and his claims for the present. They must have wished that Dickenson had left Belém during the Cabanagem, and had thus been unable to carry out his various schemes supposedly designed to help his fellow residents.

John Hesketh was undoubtedly deeply upset by Dickenson's attacks on him, and it must have been pleasing later in the year to receive from the Foreign Office a commendation of his behaviour: "I am to state to you," wrote John Bidwell, "that His Lordship approves of your proceedings in the matter, & is of opinion that you have given Mr. Dickenson the full extent of support which you could properly afford him."[244] There was further support two years later, after John's death, when Henry Dickenson's brother again wrote to Palmerston, asking him to instruct the new Consul, Augustus Henry Cowper, to reopen investigations, presumably into the Miranda case. Palmerston replied very briskly, pointing out that John Hesketh had given Dickenson a high level of support, and that he could not comply with the request.[245]

Cowper, who succeeded John Hesketh as Consul in August, 1839, seems to have got on well with Dickenson during the short time he spent in Pará, but Richard Ryan, Cowper's successor, indicates a possible reason – he asserts that Cowper used to share the official dispatches with Dickenson. When Cowper proposed that he go on a fact-finding mission up the Amazon in 1840, he recommended the appointment of Dickenson as his *locum tenens* – assuring Palmerston that "both by his education and manners he is not only the most fit, but the only fit person in this city to whom the Consulate could be entrusted."[246] Cowper does not seem to have gone through with his travel plans, but in March, 1841, he received a sharp reminder that Dickenson was *persona non grata* with the Foreign Office: "Mr. Dickenson was formerly Vice-Consul at Pará, and dismissed for improper Conduct."[247] Cowper seems not to have taken the clear hint very seriously, for three months later, in July, 1841, he appointed Dickenson as his deputy before his hasty translation to the Consulate at Pernambuco. Palmerston was furious: his despatch complains that Cowper has "placed the charge of the Consulate at Pará in the hands of Mr. Dickenson, the very person whom Lord Palmerston desired you, in a Despatch of which I enclose a Copy, not to employ in this service.... You will immediately take that charge away from Mr. Dickenson, and give it to some other British subject at Pará."[248]

But Cowper was in Pernambuco, and when he wrote to Dickenson, Palmerston's instruction was, astonishingly, ignored. Even more astonishingly, the Foreign Office allowed the situation to continue for a further twelve months, until Richard Ryan arrived in April, 1842. Dickenson even got paid, eventually. He was, however, aware of Palmerston's feelings about him, suggesting in June, 1841, that he "had not the honour of His Lordship's confidence".[249] He was perhaps wise in not claiming the full consulship. John Moon, Consul at Maranhão, addressed him in October, 1841, as "British Vice-Consul, Pará", and thanked him politely for letting him know that all is quiet in Pará, and that the British residents there do not need the services of HMS "Rover".[250] Nevertheless, the next Consul, Richard Ryan, was quite clear that Dickenson had kept "forcible possession of this Consulate after Mr. Cowper's departure". But Dickenson made sure that he could not be faulted for his patriotism. In February, 1842, he told the Foreign Office that he had hoisted the Union Flag, and "caused the Consulate and his house to be 'brilliantly illuminated' in honour of the birth of a son [the future King Edward VII] to Queen Victoria."[251]

But the peace did not last long. When the new Consul, Richard Ryan, arrived in 1842, Dickenson received him with apparent graciousness. As Dickenson was in charge of the Consulate when he arrived, and there was a shortage of hotel and inn accommodation in Belém, Ryan felt he had to accept Dickenson's offer of hospitality. He had already been warned by Robert Hesketh in Rio to "keep clear of Mr. Dickenson", remarking that "although this Individual possesses gentlemanly manners, he thought it would be prudent on my part to keep him at a distance, and particularly so, when consular business was in question."[252] Ryan tried to follow the advice, and also to keep Dickenson sweet. For the next four years, he complained in 1846, he tried to treat Dickenson and the numerous members of his wife's family, with "marked friendship", and repaid the Dickensons "fifty-fold" with presents. If he thought this bought their friendship, he was mistaken. He made sure that Dickenson had no access to consular documents, and took care not to speak to Dickenson about consular affairs. Dickenson, according to Ryan, inwardly seethed, but "his dessimulation [sic] was so complete, that it kept me in total ignorance of his real sentiments towards me." Dickenson joined a "party of turbulent English residents", and eventually could contain himself no longer. There was a furious altercation in Ryan's house, which ended in Dickenson calling Ryan a liar, with the result that Ryan ordered him out off the premises. History was repeating itself.

After this, we hear little in the official records of Henry Dickenson, except a request from his brother to the Foreign Office to get them to ship a collection of text-books on Yellow Fever to Pará, which was refused. The last mentions of him are from 1856, when Samuel Vines was British Consul in Pará. In October, 1856, Vines asked the Foreign Office for leave of absence, as his son was suffering from fever and ague. They agreed, and any in Downing Street who remembered must have been surprised to read that Vines was putting forward a familiar name as his deputy – Henry Dickenson, supported by Vines in the most generous terms. But Dickenson was not again to trouble the Foreign Office, for he died on 9 April, 1857, and James McDermid was appointed instead. The British Cemetery records do not show him as buried in Belém, so it may be that his body lies at his *engenho*, a few miles up the river from the city where he had quarrelled so assiduously.

Henry Dickenson had been in Brazil for well over forty years, had married into a rich Brazilian family, flourished financially, had been for eleven years the British Vice-Consul, but had also quarrelled quite seriously not only with his superior, Robert Hesketh, but with Robert's brother, John, Consul Ryan, and most of the provincial governors of Pará. He cannot have been popular with most of his fellow-residents either, especially after his "lien" on their property during the Cabanagem Rebellion. He retained, however, the friendship of his old friend and "fellow-labourer" Robert Corbett, until Corbett's translation to Maranhão as British Consul. Dickenson's proprietorship of a large number of slaves, and his strong defence of the institution of slavery, made him an increasingly inappropriate person to represent Great Britain. Indeed, as Dickenson's quarrelsome and litigious nature was creating havoc in Pará in the 1830s and 1840s, Robert Hesketh was ever more personally involved in fighting the slave trade in Rio. Dickenson certainly represented far less than he would have imagined what he called "the British character".

DEATH AND THE ORPHANS

"... the dreadful state of poverty in which the 8 orphan children of the late Mr. Consul Hesketh are left..." (H. Augustus Cowper)

The American schooner "Laura" brought John Hesketh back to Pará on 14 November, 1836. He was followed on 1 December by HMS "Racehorse", which had been held up at Maranhão awaiting suitable tides.

As he stepped ashore, John could not find a lot to be cheerful about. The Cabanagem Rebellion was over, but its effects were only too visible in the shattered city. The province was still in a disturbed state, with recent attempts having been made on the life of the new President. There was particular worry at the presence of the previous rebel President, Eduardo Angelim and his brothers, imprisoned only a short distance from the city in the Fortaleza da Barra, "un-ironed" [not in irons], and under the custody of only one lieutenant. John's house was destroyed and much of his property stolen or despoiled. There were no British merchant ships in the port, and none expected, and there was little in the way of produce from the province awaiting export. And then Sir James Everard Home, the Captain of the "Racehorse", announced that his stores were running low, and that he was intending to depart for his base at Barbados on the 14 December. John wrote to him begging him to stay until he was relieved by another ship. Fortunately, Everard Home agreed with him about the risk of the rebellion's re-igniting, and agreed to stay a little longer.

It was true that John had been newly appointed a full Consul with a further £100 p.a., but it was not enough to make a dramatic improvement in his financial fortunes. The other British merchants were in an equally desperate positon, and the province's mercantile prospects cannot have given any of them much optimism. The Cabanagem Rebellion's disastrous effect on trade to Pará was likely to take a long time to repair, and the merchant ships would only slowly return. The Consul's Fees for the whole of 1837 were to amount to the small total of only £26.17s. 1d. His wife was expecting another child in 1837, and he and Margarida would then have responsibility for eight children.

Henry Dickenson was as awkward as ever. Other merchants, as they counted the cost of the Cabanagem, began to agitate for the British Government to support them over their claims for compensation. Their battle was long and hard, with the British Government maintaining that the Brazilian response to the outbreak of the rebellion had been slow and totally inadequate, and the Brazilians countering with the argument that they had done their best, and that they could not compensate the foreign merchants unless they compensated their own citizens, and that they had no responsibility to cover losses caused in a revolution. The arguments between the nations continued into the 1840s, but the British claims were not helped by the increasingly anti-British atmosphere in the imperial capital, Rio, as the British Navy bore down on the slave trade.

The British merchants in Belém were, as usual, quarrelsome. The danger to which they had been exposed in the Cabanagem had not dulled their appetite for enmity and litigiousness When Richard Ryan arrived in Belem in 1842, he noted their "almost open hostility towards each other", and he was shocked that Archibald Campbell was beginning a series of law-suits against a fellow-merchant, Mr. Henderson, in the Brazilian courts, in "direct violation of the 3rd. Article of our Commercial Treaty". This hostility, says Ryan, tended "so much, in a Foreign Country, to degrade our National character".[253] If this was the same Mr. Henderson who had been living with the Campbells in 1828, it indicated a particularly sad falling-out.

So John cannot have had a very happy year in 1837. When 1838 arrived, it brought the dispute with the furious Henry Dickenson, the realisation that no-one in London had taken his warnings about French encroachment seriously, the need to defend Captain Hislop against charges of treachery, and the malicious treatment of the "Plover" by the provincial authorities.

After all this, and only a month after his last letter to Palmerston on official business, John Hesketh died. His death on 24 July, 1838, was quickly followed by that of his wife, Margarida. According to John's successor, Henry Augustus Cowper, writing fifteen months later, "she was so extremely attached to her husband that upon his death she fell into a stupor, from which she never recovered, and was buried three weeks after him."[254] We have already seen Lieutenant Maw in 1828 commenting on the close attachment of Margarida to her husband, but her death so soon after her husband's is nevertheless shocking. Their sudden deaths left their eight children orphaned. Some of them were very young, and certainly of an age to be taken advantage of.

The cause of John's death is not made clear in the official documents. We know from a letter written on 30 April, 1839, by Viscount Palmerston, that he had received the notification of John's death signed by Hugh Goodair, Archibald Campbell, and Henry Dickenson.[255] They had taken possession of the consular archives and John's private papers, and had written to London four days after John's death, on 28 July, 1838. Robert Falconer Corbett wrote in August, 1839, to Palmerston, protesting that his name had been missed from Palmerston's letter of acknowledgement, and claiming that it was he who had done most of the work.[256] The letter of 28 July announcing John's death is missing from the Foreign Office papers in the National Archives, although the Foreign Office's Ledger Book notes its arrival in London on 9 October, 1838. It has not found its way into Palmerston's Broadlands Papers, now held in the University of Southampton, nor does it appear in the Duke University collection of the papers of John Backhouse, who was the senior Under-Secretary at the time, and who knew the Heskeths personally. Was it standard practice not to retain distressing letters? And if so, why was it distressing to the hardened men of the Foreign Office?

It will be noticed that it was six months before Palmerston acknowledged the steps that Goodair and his colleagues had taken immediately after John's death. We know that Palmerston was away from the office during part of the six months, but it is surprising that John Backhouse or John Bidwell had not replied earlier, after hearing of John's death. The task of replying, which might have seemed difficult, or even distasteful, was left to Palmerston to deal with when he returned to the office.

A further oddity is the existence in the Foreign Office files of an "Extract" of a letter from Hugh Goodair, written on 9 August, just over a fortnight after John's death.[257] The "Extract" is clearly transcribed by a Foreign Office clerk on non-standard paper, and concerns Goodair's views on the French encroachment, bemoaning the fact that the British Government has done nothing about the French moves. Why is it an extract and not the full letter? Perhaps it contained a further account of John's death, or perhaps of Margarida's death, and was therefore considered inappropriate for retention. But Palmerston had taken careful note of Goodair's views on the French, and the British Ambassador in Paris was instructed in November, 1838, to seek an explanation from the French Government of the alleged encroachments into Brazilian territory.

Is the disappearance of these letters about John's death significant? Does it suggest that there was something irregular or shameful about his death? He could, of course, have committed suicide – we know that he was under tremendous pressure in the months leading up to his death, and his financial problems were as serious as ever. There is, however, no suggestion of this in the many later references to "the late Mr. Consul Hesketh". The cause

The British Cemetery at Belém – the double unmarked grave is the nearest to the camera

of his death was just as likely to be a heart-attack – he was 47 – or one of the many tropical diseases that troubled the inhabitants of Pará.

His burial will certainly have been in the British Cemetery in Belém, to which John had regularly contributed throughout his life there. The Cemetery still exists, and is kept lovingly by the verger of the Episcopal church which now shares its site. There remain a fair number of inscribed gravestones, but there is no gravestone marked with John's or Margarida's name. The Foreign Office records contain a late nineteenth-century list of inscribed gravestones from the cemetery[258], but many of them seem to have either disappeared or been moved, doubtless when the church was built in 1912–13. In any case, John and Margarida do not appear on this list. There is, however, a double gravestone devoid of inscription along the front of the Cemetery, behind the railings which line the street: perhaps this marks the last resting place of Her Britannic Majesty's Consul at Pará and his wife.

The account by the next Consul, H. Augustus Cowper, of the events of July 1838 goes on to say that "the lady" – Margarida – was only fourteen at the time of the marriage, and that John and she had been married for only ten years. This is obviously inaccurate, however, for the records show that he and Margarida were married and accompanied by two children in 1824, when Henry Dickenson prepared a list of residents intending to flee from Belém to Barbados. John had arrived in Belém in 1819, and assuming the two children were both his and Margarida's, must have married about 1821. If she was indeed fourteen at the time of the marriage, she would have been about thirty-one at the time of her death. We know that these two deaths caused a great deal of comment in Belém, and facts were soon twisted and altered, for Consul Ryan later appeared to believe that Margarida died three *days* after her husband, and several different dates were later given for John's death. Wilder rumours – of marital infidelity and brotherly jealousy – are still retailed in Belém, but we have found no evidence for them. The likelihood is that John died suddenly of natural causes, and that Margarida starved herself to death in her grief.

Cowper's letter[259] has as its main purpose the welfare of the eight orphan children. He heard of the problem very soon after being appointed to Pará as British Consul. Cowper had been Vice-Consul to his father in Pernambuco, and then been sent to Carthagena in Colombia. While he was there, he had been accused by Wellington, who was briefly Foreign Secretary, of misusing public funds for his own purposes. His relatives conducted a campaign to get him reinstated, and, as there remained some doubt about the justice of the original charges, John Hesketh's death provided the Foreign Office with a suitable opportunity to reintroduce him to the Consular Service. He was told in late April, 1839, to go to Jamaica whence a ship would take him to Pará. He argued about the salary, but failed to persuade the Foreign Office to add to his money beyond the £300 p.a. which John Hesketh had been receiving of late. Amidst all this, he had obviously heard about the eight orphans, for he wrote on 5 May, just before he sailed for the West Indies, to a Mrs. MacKay, of 51 Harley Street, London, informing her that a sum of money had been due to John Hesketh, and was now due to the guardians of "these poor orphans", and would be paid to anyone who could legally represent them.[260] Cowper says he had heard that Mrs. MacKay was a friend of the late Consul and his wife, and suggests that she contact Mr. Murray of the Foreign Office about the matter.

Cowper did not forget the orphans when he reached Pará in the summer of 1839, and we find him on 18 September writing his letter to Lord Palmerston, pleading their cause, in view of their father's long service to the British Crown, and saying that their parents' sudden deaths had left the children "without the slightest means of subsistence". He points out that John Hesketh had a very limited salary for the first ten years of his service in Pará, and that the province was one of the most expensive places in the world, and hopes that "Her Majesty's Government. ....might be induced to do something for them". He is worried that "the poor children" might fall upon his hands as distressed British subjects".

Cowper had obviously taken the fate of the children to heart: he described them as "unhappily suffering the bitter pangs of poverty". He had already written to Robert Hesketh in Rio about the matter, and written to Margarida's mother, Dona Francisca Leonarda de Mattos, about a meeting of John's creditors, at which the creditors had agreed to waive John's debts to them.[294] In December, he wrote to Archibald Campbell with the news that Robert Hesketh was asking for Campbell and Dona Francisca to take responsibility for the estate of the deceased Consul. Neither Cowper nor Robert Hesketh were to know that Campbell's interpretation of his duties was decidedly in his own favour.

John and Margarida had eight children. At the time of their deaths, they ranged in age from the mid-teens to a toddler – James – who had been born only a little while before Margarida's death. The eldest were a boy called John and a girl who is never named in the official correspondence. John was named after his father in the fashion of the times, and must have been the boy mentioned in the 1824 passport list, and born between about 1821 and 1824. If this surmise is correct, he was about sixteen years old when his father and mother died. In the 1824 passport list, his sister appears second, so may well have been the second child – she would have been about fifteen in 1838. The next eldest was Mariano, who was perhaps named after a member of Margarida's family, then Robert, William, Henry, Thomas and James. Henry was born in 1831, Thomas in about 1834, and James in about 1837, and so was only about one at the time of his parents' deaths. There were only six children – all boys – active in pursuing their inheritance in 1856. The youngest child, James, had died of dysentery in Crosby, north of Liverpool, in 1848 at the age of eleven. There is no mention in 1856 of the daughter, but it is likely, if she survived after 1839, that she was by this time married and depending upon her husband for financial support, and therefore with no interest in the issue of the inheritance.

Cowper's letter of 18 September, 1839, to Palmerston asking for help for the children was answered on 15 November.[262] Palmerston stated that "the Publick cannot give support to the children of Consuls, but you are authorized to pay the expence of the Passage of Mr. Hesketh's children to the place to which their Relatives may wish to send them. Mr. Hesketh's children ought to be taken care of by his own Relations." Cowper received this letter early in 1840, and let the children's guardians, Dona Francisca Leonarda de Mattos and Archibald Campbell, know of Palmerston's decision. His letter

St. George's Church, Liverpool, in Derby Square, where three of John Hesketh's children were baptized

St. George's Church, Derby Square, in 1792.

to Campbell still survives in the archives of the Consulate in Belém: – "Lord Palmerston declines making any provision for Mr. Hesketh's children, and justly observes that the relatives ought to support them, but His Lordship has authorized me to pay the expences of their passage to any port to which their friends may ask to forward them."

Dona Francisca continued to look after the children, even though she was, according to Cowper, in straitened circumstances. Some of the older children obviously decided to stay in Brazil – they spoke Portuguese fluently – Maw told us in 1828 that the ladies of the house spoke nothing else, and Brazil was all they had ever known. The first to leave was Mariano, who sailed to Maranhão on 9 April, 1840, on board the "Emulação". Cowper logged the cost as thirty *milreis*, which he calculated as £4.2s.6d. Doubtless Mariano went to join his uncle William. The consular accounts show that

Cowper paid for the passage to England of Henry and Thomas on 11 November, 1840. They made a speedy passage to England, and their aunts, Louisa and Mary Ann, lost no time in having them christened at St. George's Church, Liverpool, on 18 January, 1841. Good Anglicans as they were, they were not taking any spiritual risks, and made sure that the children were properly instituted into the Church of England.

The church register of St. George's shows a further christening, six months later, on 10 August, 1840, of Henry and Thomas's younger brother, James. Perhaps he arrived in Liverpool later, or perhaps he was ill when the two older boys were baptised. Cowper's consular records name only Henry and Thomas as sailing for England, but he quotes three vouchers, so it is likely that James travelled in the care of his brothers to England from Pará.

To his credit, Cowper was obviously much affected by the fate of the Hesketh children, for, in a wide-ranging list of suggestions he made to the Foreign Office the following month, he mentioned the need to support widows and orphans of consuls. He suggested that widows be given a life-time annuity of £250 p.a., and orphans be given £50 a year until they reached their majority at twenty-one. Palmerston was not in the least interested in these proposals, of course. Did he not say later he could find no way to improve the diplomatic and consular services? He therefore picked on one of Cowper's less important suggestions – a museum – and commented: "I think the Secretary of State and the Foreign Office have already enough on their Hands without this museum."[263]

Henry, Thomas, and James, now in Liverpool, would undoubtedly have stayed, at least initially, with their Aunts Louisa and Mary Ann in Mount Pleasant, up the hill from Liverpool's city centre. The 1841 Census shows only Thomas, aged seven, living with his aunts, so Henry and James must have been lodging elsewhere. James's death in 1848 at the age of eleven is registered as occurring in Marine Parade, one of the newly-built and very desirable villas along the sea-front at Crosby. His Death Certificate does not mention any family member present at his death, but records that Mary Hill, Aunt Mary Ann's faithful servant, was there, and it was she who reported the facts to the Registrar. So it may be that Aunt Mary Ann rented the Crosby villa in order to get the sick young boy away from the city, and sent Mary Hill to look after him.

The 1851 Census shows Mary Ann (Louisa had died in 1845) living at 91 Mount Pleasant with Henry and Thomas. Thomas was also to die young, at the age of 23 as he returned to Pará. It is a sobering thought that only one of the three sons who came to England – Henry – survived beyond his twenties, whereas all the sons left in South America survived, in spite of the wide range of tropical diseases endemic there. Liverpool's rapid growth at this time put all its citizens at a greatly increased risk of contracting cholera, typhus, or any number of contagious diseases that spread rapidly in the crowded city.

Cowper left Pará about the same time, and his permanent successor, Richard Ryan, does not mention the children until 1844. But in that year, having obviously been under fresh pressure from Dona Francisca, he explained that Consul Cowper had sent two children (he saw no specific mention of James in the records) to England, and he asked whether he could, at the public expense, send three more of the orphans to follow them.[264] Four of the eight had already left Pará, and only John, Robert, and William, and perhaps the unnamed daughter – if she still survived – remained in Belém. The response from John Bidwell at the Foreign Office was positive; Aberdeen scribbled a note saying – "This appears to be a fair request – grant it", and Ryan was authorised to give Dona Francisca the equivalent of £90, "provided that you have sufficient security that the money will be appropriated solely to the object in question."

This last phrase set alarm bells ringing in Ryan's head, with his anxieties heightened by his own financial problems. He owed the vast sum of £1300 to a contact in his previous position as Vice-Consul at Celte in the south of France, and had not succeeded in paying any of it off. He therefore responded to Bidwell's instruction with exaggerated solicitude. He had a high opinion of Dona Francisca, the children's grandmother, mentioning the sacrifice of "her entire time & extremely limited means to keep these orphans from utter destitution". In other letters, he speaks of this "worthy & highly respectable Grandmother". Nevertheless, he was nervous about handing over the money without guarantees, and wrote to ask Lord Aberdeen, the current Secretary of State, to inform the Treasury so that Dona Francisca could not claim again for the same purpose. The receipt signed by Dona Francisca still exists in the official records, countersigned by James Henderson and by – who else? – Henry Dickenson.[265]

In August, 1846, Ryan was still anxious about the matter, especially as Dona Francisca had only sent, according to Ryan, one boy to England, and taken the other two boys with her to live in Maranhão. Ryan may well have got his facts wrong, for there is no evidence of any other boy going to England between 1844 and 1846. In September, 1846, he again writes to London about the matter, admitting that Dona Francisca had not as yet persuaded all the boys to go to England. He suggests that the family had, in any case, difficulties in receiving them. This was true, for Aunt Louisa Hesketh had died in 1845, and her sister Mary Ann was no longer young.

Their sister, Harriet, had died ten years earlier, and their brother, Thomas, in 1840. Mary Ann might well have felt, having looked after Henry, Thomas, and James since 1841, that she and Louisa had done their bit. Mary Ann herself was far from well, and seems to have left Liverpool for Southampton in 1855, going to live with her newly-retired brother, Robert. She died soon after, and is buried a few feet away from Robert in the graveyard of Jesus Chapel, in Bitterne, overlooking the River Itchen and the city of Southampton.

The opportunity for Mary Ann's move to Southampton was provided by Henry's marriage in October, 1854. Now aged twenty-three, he married a local girl, Sophia Tamberlane, at Great George Street Chapel in Liverpool. He was now a Customs Officer in the very imposing Custom House behind the docks. He and Sophia left for California soon after the wedding, to see his uncle Henry, and perhaps to settle there. The Californian Gold Rush was in full spate, but sadly Uncle Henry died soon after their arrival, and the two returned to Liverpool, with their first son, also called Henry, who had been born while they were in California.

It was now 1856, and the orphans made another appearance in the Foreign Office records. Consul Ryan having died of Yellow Fever in 1850, he was eventually succeeded by Samuel Vines. Consul Vines also became involved in the saga of the orphan children and their inheritance. In 1856, the surviving sons, John, who was by now in Lima, Peru, Mariano, who was at Manaus, Robert and William, who were in Pará, and Henry and Thomas, based in Liverpool, protested that they had not received what was due to them from their father's estate. They made a "Solemn Protest", blaming Archibald Campbell, who had been appointed their guardian and the administrator of their father's estate.

While Dona Francisca was in Pará there had seemed to be no problem, but when she left for Maranhão in September, 1845, Campbell was able to take over not only the house and land their father had owned, but also his former slaves, whom he put to work with his own on his estate. The complaint was that he had not handed over a single *real* to the Hesketh orphans, and, when they made enquiries about the matter, Campbell had, according to Vines, told them that there was no money because there were heavy encumbrances on the estate. He obviously had no intention of voluntarily restoring the property and the income it produced to the Hesketh children.

On 31 July, 1856, three of the brothers – Mariano, Robert, and William – appeared personally before Samuel Vines, the latest Consul to occupy their father's role. Mariano, Robert, and William were said to be living "in this city of Pará". Henry was said to be in San Francisco, California ("one of the United States of North America"), and Thomas was said to be from Liverpool. Thomas died early the following year, his death registered as occurring on the barque "Emily" in Pará, so he must have intended to join his brothers back in Brazil. They had all appointed William, who had obviously had some legal training, as their Attorney. The other brother, John, who was based in Lima, Peru, was not present, nor specifically represented – unfortunate in view of later events. In their "Protest", they claimed that:

"Archibald Campbell ... did seize and take possession of all their father's property... on or about the 12th. day of September, 1845, and that ever since that day, he, the said Archibald Campbell, had been appropriating the profits accruing therefrom to his own use and benefit, receiving the rents from the tenants of the house and lands, and working some of the slaves mentioned in the annexed Inventory on his own plantation, with his own slaves, and hiring out others of them as domestic servants."[266]

They went on to say that Archibald Campbell had never rendered any account, and they went on to ask, "courteously", that he would deliver to them "the house, lands, plate, furniture, slaves and monies belonging to the estate of their deceased father, together with profits, interests, and rents, which have accrued during this possession of the aforesaid property." They called upon Samuel Vines to employ his functions as Consul to recover their property, and administer it on their behalf.

The "Protest" put Vines in a difficult position. He discussed the matter with the President of the Province, and then wrote to the Earl of Clarendon, by now Foreign Secretary, in October, 1856, asking for advice.[267] He knew he could not administer an estate containing slaves, and suggested manumitting [freeing] them. Altogether, the estate was reckoned to be worth £3,000 to £4,000, the house being valued at £1,200, the slaves at £1,400, and the rest consisting of interest, rent, and profits.

Vines again wrote to Clarendon, having been told that Robert Hesketh, now retired and living in Southampton, had become involved. A certain testiness creeps into Vines's tone as he discusses Robert's involvement. He says that Mariano has told him that Campbell has "conciliated Robert Hesketh by a promise to place him in absolute possession of the estate". It is now apparent, says Vines, that Robert has Power of Attorney to act on behalf of his younger, deceased brother, and that Uncle William in Maranhão, "notwithstanding his protest", has been "cajoled" to act with him. There appears to be a little professional jealousy creeping into the affair: Vines very much wants to administer the estate, resents Robert's involvement, and denies that Robert can act in any way as "Head of the family". He suggests that, if he is not given the power to administer the estate on behalf of the boys, Campbell will use the resources of the estate to corrupt the Brazilian authorities, and to deny justice to John Hesketh's children.

Clarendon obviously sensed the personal animus in Vines's attitude. He had recently had to deal with Vines in a gruesome dispute over the burying of bodies in the Belém British Cemetery, and was clearly not entirely happy trusting Vines's judgement in delicate matters. He therefore wrote back to Vines in February, 1857, telling him "Your interference in this case is unnecessary – take no further proceeding."[268] Vines wrote back rather shamefacedly on 29 April, acknowledging the advice and promised to abide by the instruction that he would take no further part in the matter.

The Law rarely moves fast at any time, and there was no danger that Brazil in the nineteenth century would prove an exception. John, the brother who had been absent from the earlier hearing, is next heard of writing in July, 1858, from Santiago, Chile, to Vines's successor as Consul in Pará, Vredenburg, complaining that the Court of Orphans in Pará has not reached any conclusion, and has therefore not yielded justice for them.[269] It is clear from Vredenburg's reply that John's brothers had settled with Campbell in 1856. They had accepted the proceeds from the sale of the house, lands, and some of the slaves, and desisted from any further claims.

Vredenburg, in his reply to John, discourages him from reopening the case. He suggests that further litigation will eat up whatever monies remain, and that the slave issue was now a very delicate one. There were only five slaves when John and Margarida had died, but they had increased to thirteen or fourteen; however, three of them were suspected of having leprosy, and the children remained unsold. Brazilian law, since 1850, had changed, and John Hesketh Junior would put himself in a dangerous position if he took charge of the slaves. After this, John seems to have given Vredenburg Power of Attorney.

However, the Foreign Office, now commanded by Lord Malmesbury, would have nothing to do with what was a family dispute, and told him to send all documents, including, presumably, John Hesketh Junior's letters, to Robert Hesketh in Southampton, and that appears to have been the last that the Foreign Office heard of the problem.[270]

The brothers must, however, have received at least some of the money due to them. Henry, the only surviving brother in England spent most of his early working career as a Customs Officer. But in 1859, five years after his marriage, and three years after the "Protest", he called himself a "Gentleman" in Gore's 1859 Liverpool Directory, and again in 1862. In the 1861 Census, when he was thirty, he is listed as "Brazilian Property Annuitant". By 1870, he has resumed a career in business, and lists himself fairly consistently as a "Commercial Clerk" or a "Bookkeeper. His return to earning a living shows that his share of his father's estate was not enough to keep him living as a "Gentleman" indefinitely. He seems to have been working well into his sixties, and he died in Formby on the coast north of Liverpool at the age of seventy in 1901, as a result of a fall in the street. His Death Certificate calls him a "Retired Brazilian Merchant", which is stretching definitions quite generously. So, even though his father was insolvent at his death, there was enough money from the sale of his estate to offer his surviving sons a reasonable income, at least for a time. It may be that Robert Hesketh obtained from Archibald Campbell further money in recognition of his eleven years' free use of the slaves.

But Campbell's unwillingness to render account to John Hesketh's children has taken a long time to be forgotten. In 2002, Henry Hesketh's great-granddaughter, Evelyn, in her eighties, was able to recall the family tradition that a Campbell had cheated the Heskeths of their money all those years ago, a story made all the more ironic because her own mother's maiden name was Campbell, though she was not, apparently, a relative of Archibald's.

SECTION IV

PLACES:
RIO DE JANEIRO

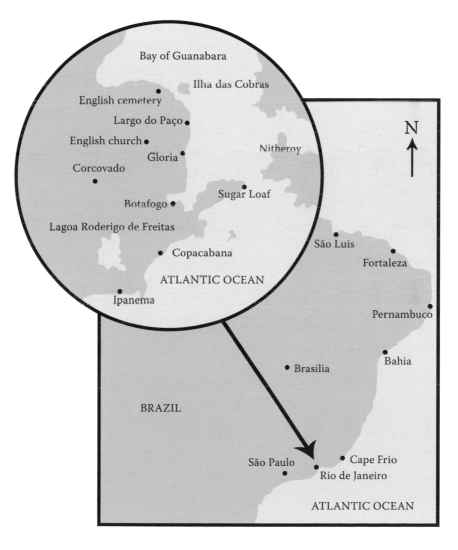

City of Rio de Janeiro in the 1840s

18

THE CITY OF SÃO SEBASTIAN OF RIO DE JANEIRO

"The bay is triangular in outline, and admitted to be one of the safest and most beautiful harbours ..." (Thomas Ewbank, 1845)

In 1817, the American frigate "Congress" was sailing south along the Atlantic seaboard of Brazil. On board was Henry M. Brackenridge, sent by order of the American Government on a fact-finding mission to South America.[271]

As the ship neared Rio de Janeiro, Brackenridge's first sight of land was of "an immense naked rock, [with] the appearance of two separate islands, from a hollow in the middle". This was Cape Frio, a familiar sight to every southward-bound ship. The "Congress" sailed on to Rio, sighting the Sugar-Loaf, as famous then as it is today, passing the islands off Copacabana beach, and watching the large number of sailing vessels entering and leaving the mile-wide entrance to the harbour. On the western side of the entrance was the Sugar-Loaf, "like a watch-tower at the termination of a high irregular rampart". On the eastern side, another granite pile, though not quite so high, and more broken. As they sailed into the harbour, they saw that the inland horizon was bounded by "high mountains in the background whose tops rose above the region of the clouds" – the Organ Mountains. As they passed through the dangerous entrance, they saw the first of two forts – Santa Cruz to the starboard, built upon a shelf of rock, with several tiers of guns, "and most formidable in its appearance", and São João on the port side, rather less impressive, nestling under the sheer granite sides of the Sugar-Loaf itself.

"As we entered the harbour, a most magnificent scene opened upon us. The noble basin, scarcely surpassed by any in the world, resembling a great lake rather than a harbour, expanded majestically, bordered by high woody mountains interspersed with rocky peaks and precipices; their ridges or spurs sloping down to the water's edge, in some places terminating abruptly, in others laving narrow vallies [sic] and a thousand beautiful coves or recesses, with sandy beaches.

The ridges, or broken grounds before the mountains, are covered with convents, churches, and beautiful gardens, while the little indents or sandy bays are occupied by elegant country seats, a great many of them constructed by Portuguese noblemen, since the establishment of the court at this place, or by English merchants who have grown rich since the opening of trade. A range of much higher mountains is seen to the north-east, probably at least forty of fifty miles distant. The city of Rio de Janeiro or Saint Sebastian is built in one of the coves just mentioned, under the mountains, the houses much crowded together."

As Brackenridge implies, there had been much building development in the decade since the arrival of the Regent and the Portuguese Court in 1808, when the English traveller John Luccock also arrived for the first time. Luccock mentions the Atlantic swell, which made entering the harbour tricky at the best of times, and then the little bay of Bota-Foga (Botafogo) to the left, "skirted by verdant and inaccessible mountains, guarded by the Sugar-Loaf and the fort of Saint John, on one side, and a smooth mass of granite on the other." He too mentions his first view of the city: its "churches and monasteries, forts and country-houses glittering in whiteness, crown every hillock."[272]

In 1828, the Rev. Robert Walsh arrived; he too mentions the Sugar-Loaf first, and then describes the "most magnificent harbour in the world......In the bay were multitudes of ships of all nations, both of war and commerce; not crowded together, but spaced over the wide expance [sic] of waters, and dotting the surface in all directions." Luccock in 1808 had been struck by the large number of vessels – fifty merchant ships and ten sail of the line in the Roads, but the number grew enormously in the next twenty years.

When the new British Consul, Robert Hesketh, arrived in Rio de Janeiro in November, 1832, he must also have been struck by the dramatic contrast in scenery from his previous port – São Luis in Maranhão. Maranhão had its hills, its sandy bars, its wide rivers, its buildings stacked up the side of the hill above the quay, but it had nothing of the stupendous scale of his new posting. Above the city, inland from Ipanema, which then boasted an iron-works, was the vast bulk of "The Hunchback" – Corcovado – not yet crowned by the massive figure of Christ the Redeemer, but impressive nonetheless – with, according to Luccock, "a romantic valley sprinkled with country-houses & gardens, to a gorge of the mountains, near the northern end of the Lagoa da Freitas – the Grassmere [sic] of Brazil."

The Bay of Rio de Janeiro, with its fleet of anchored ships

But like the other travellers, Robert Hesketh would have had to wait for the ship to be visited by the "health-boat", carrying the port physician, and by the Customs Officers, who were to become very familiar to him over the next twenty years. Looking out from the deck of the ship that had brought him from São Luis, he would have seen the whole glorious panorama – the Sugar-Loaf to the left, and then, as his gaze moved to the right, the small bay of Botafogo, with its little white houses above the shore-line, and then the beautiful bluff which was crowned by the church of Nostra Senhora da Gloria and the suburb of Catete. In front of him, he would have seen "a swarm of houses, crowding and turning through a narrow passage between two hills like troops rushing through a defile and treading on each other's heels. With the aid of a glass, a double tier of arches – the aqueduct – is seen. On the point, the arsenal is located, facing San Domingo. Immediately above the point, and behind the two hills, one of which is Castle Hill, with flag-staffs and marine telegraph on it, the old part of the city of Rio and the shipping lie." The description is that of Thomas Ewbank, who arrived in 1856, only a few years after Robert Hesketh returned from Brazil, but many parts of the scene will have been unchanged: "The immediate background of Rio, and up the bay as far as the eye can reach, consists of mountains. Nothing but sky and peaks are seen. An opening occurs in looking over the small bay of Boto-Fogo, but higher peaks behind peaks arise in the distance."[273]

At this period, there were few docks or quays approachable by the larger ships, and so most cargo and passengers had to be ferried to the landing-stage by small boats, crewed by negro slaves or Indians. Brackenridge describes the scene in 1817: "Great numbers of boats were continually moving about, rigged in a very awkward, clumsy manner, or rowed with a slow and solemn stroke, as if to the tune of the dead march in Saul. Among the watermen, a number were Indians; they wore very broad straw hats, like the Malays... On approaching the Queen's stairs, the usual landing-place, a yacht, superbly gilt, rigged like a sloop of war, and armed with brass swivels. This childish miniature is kept for the use of the queen, or rather for the sake of pageantry... Another object excited our disgust; some distance to the left of the stairs, the quay terminates in a prodigious dung-heap, the accumulation of ages from the stables of the city."

Brackenridge, having sailed from Norfolk, Virginia, in a very smart American frigate, was equally unimpressed by the Portuguese warships dotted about the harbour, which, he says, were badly-manned and not in the best order. Among them would have been the "Real Principe", which had been used to bring the Portuguese court from Lisbon in 1807/8. By 1833, when John Macdouall visited Rio, it was a prison-ship, "filthy, dark, and smelly".[274]

Only a short distance from the landing-place, and across the wide open space of the Largo do Paço, were the major public buildings of Rio, among them the Royal Palace and the Custom House. The arrival of the thousand Portuguese courtiers in 1808 had created a serious housing problem, for there were not enough palaces and official buildings to go round. The result was the use of buildings left over from the colonial era, and the need for those evicted to find somewhere else to live. The Royal Palace, fronting the Largo do Paço, was a plain building but was pressed into service for the Regent and his family. One of the four nearby parish churches was requisitioned as a Royal Chapel. Nearby was a vast and ambitious monastery, whose construction was slow. When the Regent, Dom João VI, arrived in 1808, he stopped work on the project, believing that there were quite enough monks already in Rio de Janeiro. But there were plenty of other ecclesiastical buildings, some of them very large, like São Bento, Santa Rita, Santo Antonio, São Francisco, Santa Teresa, and the Church of Nostra Senhora da Candelaria. Some of the churches were linked to monasteries, which often occupied, as they still do, the tops of hills in the city. After 1808, other new buildings quickly made their appearance, and, by the time that Robert Hesketh arrived, Rio boasted an Opera House, popular with British navy officers, especially, we are told, when a chanteuse called Louise was appearing; numerous fountains, a theatre, a library, a museum, a medical school, two hospitals, a parliament building – the Câmara dos Senadores – and the Foundling Hospital, where Rio's citizens, the *Cariocas,* could leave their unwanted infants in a swinging cradle outside the hospital, ringing the bell to warn the staff that they had a new foundling to look after. The old aqueduct had long been a feature of the city's architecture, and still acted as the city's main water-supply.

But all this magnificence was accompanied, according to early visitors' accounts, by a great deal of dirt. The streets were narrow, and in the early part of the century, had neither pavements nor drains. Luccock talks of Rio as "one of the dirtiest associations of human beings under heaven". Chamberpots were emptied everywhere, and it was not uncommon to find the dead bodies of slaves lying in the streets where they had fallen. Nor was the bay exempt – slaves were employed after nightfall to carry human waste down to the beaches, to await the cleansing effect of the next tide. By 1828, however, the situation seemed to have improved. Robert Walsh speaks of the cleanliness of the streets, and says that there were no offals or offending smells.

Luccock, who arrived in Rio only three months after the Portuguese royal court, describes the centre of the city. The narrow streets in the centre were paved with granite, but the outlying streets had no raised pavements, and a channel for waste water ran down the middle of the street. The principal street of the city, the Rua Direita, was wider than most, and ran parallel with the bay until it reached the main square, which was a hundred and sixty yards long by eighty broad, and which had the Royal Palace to the south, religious buildings to the west, and on the north, "plain houses" filled with royal servants. The eastern side of the square ran down to the bay, and there was a fine view across the anchorages and the shipping to Nitheroy opposite. The "plain houses" would doubtless have resembled Rio's other houses, and have been of two storeys, and made of the local granite. The roofs were tiled with what Luccock calls "semi-tubular tiles", which can still be seen in the city. Luccock particularly mentions the *gelosias* or "jalousies", enclosed balconies made of lattice-work hinged at the top, so that they could

The *Largo do Paço*, with the Bay to the right of the fountain, and the Royal Palace behind the square

be opened by those inside without their being seen or observed by those in the street. They seem to have provided the city's superior womenfolk, who were not encouraged to go about the town openly, with a view of the world and of their fellow-citizens. Ewbank, writing in 1856, says that the houses were built of granite, were usually of two storeys, and were all individually designed, and "not a block is uniformly built". All house entrances debouched directly on to the street, and there were consequently none of the steps or porticoes common in nineteenth-century Europe. The granite walls were often stuccoed, usually painted white, but sometimes painted with pink or blue panels. The lower windows were latticed, and those houses also used as shops rarely boasted glass windows. Like shops in other parts of Brazil, the front doors opened on to the street, were opened during the day, and bolted at night. Walking the streets in wet weather, says Ewbank, could be a dangerous exercise, for all the roofs and the balconies discharged the rain through copper spouts three or four feet long, on to the street below. The interiors of the houses, according to Ewbank in the 1850s, had none of the clutter of British and American parlours, with no carpets, rugs, curtains, and fireplaces. Instead, there were only "high ceilings, matted floors, chairs and sofas with cane-seats [and] walls papered".

Early nineteenth century visitors to Rio often complained about the lack of inns and hotels, and it seems to have been left to foreign immigrants to inaugurate the hotel trade. The first was the Hotel Pharoux on the water-front, illustrated in contemporary prints, and built and run by a Frenchman. There is also mention of an Italian inn and an establishment managed by an Englishman, as well as a French hotel in the Rua d'Ouvidor.

John Luccock gives a breakdown of the occupations of the citizens of the new capital city in 1808. The list is headed by a thousand members of the court – who were all new arrivals from Portugal, and who succeeded in operating a closed shop for the next few decades, depriving the Braziians of the opportunity of rising high in the service of the Emperor. They were joined by another thousand, who were public officers. Their task was the administration of the city, and they were joined by another thousand, more affluent, who mostly did not boast any particular occupation. There were no less than seven hundred priests, retaining the old Portuguese predilection for a large body of men of the cloth. Five hundred lawyers were apparently kept busy, as were two hundred medical men. Two thousand shopkeepers were assisted by double that number of clerks, apprentices, and commercial servants. Twelve hundred and fifty mechanics looked after the very limited amount of machinery in the city, and there were no less than a hundred vintners meeting the needs of the bibulous. Three hundred fishermen, one thousand regular soldiers, about the same number of sailors operating out of the port, and a thousand free negroes, who had been manumitted, or freed from slavery, made up the rest of the free citizens, a total of about sixteen thousand people. The free citizens were matched by almost as many African slaves – twelve thousand, for the slave trade had been supplying African negroes for several centuries already.

Luccock's list shows an unbalanced society, and goes some way to explaining much of the politics of the next fifty years in Brazil. The Portuguese, especially the upper-class refugees from Lisbon, dominated the professions and other influential roles. Native-born Brazilians were for the most part denied positions of power in the running of the city. At the same time, the slaves did all the manual work, as well as much of the incidental catering and entertainment which enlivened the streets of Rio. Some of them, the licensed slaves, acted like franchise-holders, running sometimes quite profitable businesses.

Such occupations were not to the taste of those Brazilians who were of Portuguese origin: Ewbank tells of one of the sons of an impoverished widow of Portuguese descent who refused the opportunity of a decent living working with his hands as a tradesman, preferring instead to have a very poorly-paid job as a clerk with the police, where at least he could claim respectability. Another young clerk was asked to take a small package to a nearby address. After looking at the package for some time in bemusement, he went out into the street, and handed it to the first slave he saw. He then required the slave to walk behind him carrying the package until the clerk reached his destination, and was able to deliver the package. The structure of social class in Rio based itself very firmly on the bed-rock of slavery, and we shall see later how involved Robert Hesketh was, together with his diplomatic and consular colleagues, in fighting a protracted battle against the slave trade, and against the long-established Brazilian view that there was no alternative to relying on slaves for many of their daily needs.

The treatment of the slaves at the hands of their Brazilian masters was always regarded at the time as beneficent, especially by the Brazilians, and it is still quite common to meet in modern Brazilian accounts the belief that slaves were generally treated well after arriving from Africa. There was doubtless much truth in this, but there are also descriptions of quite harsh treatment. A range of iron collars and shackles was still in the shops in Rio in the 1850s.[275] Even without the instruments of punishment, the slaves were expected to work hard. George Gardner was struck on his arrival in Rio in the 1840s by what he calls "African Blacks... nearly naked, many of them sweating under their loads, & smelling so strongly as to be almost intolerable."[276] There are also accounts of the slave auctions at the Valongo slave-market, where up to two thousand slaves were kept ready for sale. Ewbank describes the scene:

"The salesman was expatiating on a dinner-set. Another bid, and down it went. While applying his glass to a catalogue for the next article, it was forced into the crowded room close to him: *1 preto de roça de nome José, de nação Congo."* (1 plantation black named José, of the nation of the Congo.) Eyeing the lot a moment, he ordered it to mount on a stool, and there, utterly abashed, the poor kidnapped negro stands. Apparently of dullish   intellect, short, stout, and about thirty years of age, a canvas shirt and pantaloons complete his dress. No scars are visible on him, but he is shockingly disfigured with hydrocele. He is told to pull up the longer leg of his trousers, then the other, next to turn round, and, within a minute, to follow his new owner- a thin, meagre, wedge-faced old man, who bought him for 420 *milreis* [about £50]. José, from his age and build, was deemed a prime plantation-hand."

The general view of the travellers was that slaves on the plantations had a harder lot than those in the city. But city slaves covered a wide range of occupations, and were treated in a correspondingly wide range of ways. R.B. Toplin[277] gives a list of slave roles in Rio, which includes involvement in building both houses and roads, in street-cleaning, in fire-fighting, in garbage collection, in dog- and rat-catching, in nursing the sick and burying the dead, in water-carrying, and in sewage disposal. The 'licensed', or subcontracted, slaves ran businesses which paid a proportion of their takings to their owners. Some ran street-catering services, others toured the streets with products for sale, and others were street musicians and entertainers. Jean-Baptiste Debret, a French artist who lived in Rio from about 1816 to 1831, painted a whole series of street-scenes which illustrate the vast range of useful roles provided by the city's slaves.[278] Amongst them were slaves carrying very heavy casks of water, bags of coffee beans, and baulks of timber. It is therefore not surprising that the slaves' average age of death was low. Given that most new arrivals were young – Mary Karasch calculates that two-thirds of them were under fourteen or fifteen years of age[3279] – it is clear that they could not look forward to a long life. Some succumbed to the demands made on their bodies by very heavy labour, others to small-pox and other tropical diseases the slaves brought with them, others to cholera or yellow fever contracted in Brazil. A not inconsiderable number committed suicide.

There were many slaves, particularly the young men, who rebelled against their lives in Rio, and fled to the *quilombos* or encampments of escaped slaves in the countryside. Others joined in the rebellions which broke out from time to time in the ports along the seaboard. Others became accepting of their lot in life – Luccock offered two slave-girls the chance to be freed, and to go to England. They declined, partly on the not unreasonable grounds that it was cold in England, but also because they were scared to be free: "If we are freed, what shall we do with our liberty here? .... If we have our freedom, we shall have nobody to take care of us."

Robert Walsh summed up the effect that slavery had not only on the slaves themselves but upon those who owned and employed them: "I saw an African negro under four aspects of society; & it appears to me, that in every one, his character depended on the state in which he was placed, & the estimation in which he was held."

Robert Hesketh joined this complex society in 1832, at the start of a very troubled period in the history of Brazil and of Rio, its capital. The Emperor Pedro I had abdicated a year earlier, and handed over power to his five-year old son, or rather to the Regents, initially three in number, later reduced to one. British diplomats were frequently agog at the political machinations in the capital, and there were regular uprisings and rebellions. The Brazilians had passed a law in 1831 curbing slavery, but it was more honoured in the breach than the observance, and it was obvious that the whole economy of Rio still depended upon the need for slaves. It was suggested that many of the foreign merchants, most of whom were English, were not entirely innocent of the charge of abetting the slave trade by selling supplies to known slave-dealers. Many of the merchants had been in Rio for a long time, even before the ports were opened to international trade in 1808. Ewbank in the 1850s spoke of the foreign merchants as being "something like an order of monks. Nearly all are bachelors of from thirty to sixty years' standing. Their houses, like monasteries, contain no females."

That was not to be the case with Robert, but there was no denying that the foreign merchants were a significant part of Rio's social life. They were generally a close-knit group, with common business interests, and the Consul and the British Mission would have formed a natural focus of their social life. By the time Robert arrived, they were a large group – the largest of all the foreign contingents – and their lives were prosperous and well-regulated. The Rev. Robert Walsh describes going to dinner with one of the merchants, Mr. Price, who lived in the Rua dos Pescadores. The meal was timed for two o'clock, and was served on the upper floor of Mr. Price's house, in the family quarters. There was a certain amount of formality, and the host supplied calico jackets for his male guests. [280]

The Foreign Office, when committed to any degree of expenditure for facilities for the British community abroad, expected the British residents to make a contribution. In Rio, ½% was charged on all British merchandise imported into Brazil. Two-thirds of this went to the Consul-General, and one-third was allocated to "pious and charitable uses", such as a chapel, a chaplain, and a hospital. Before the 1810 Treaty, the British community had no church, but they occasionally attended a service held on one of the British naval or merchant ships visiting the port. The 1810 Treaty had allowed the British to build a place of worship, provided only that it looked like a house, had no steeple, and rang no bells. By 1819, the British Chapel was built. The Papal Nuncio had been very antagonistic, but the Bishop of Rio's attitude was more supportive, as well as more cynical.. "The English really have no religion, but they are a proud and obstinate people. If you oppose them, they will persist, and make an affair of infinite importance but if you concede to their wishes, the chapel will be built and no one will ever go near it." [281]

The British Chapel, Walsh tells us, was originally planned for the Largo da Lapa, where there was plenty of space, and a garden nearby. But the Chapel had eventually been built in Rua dos Barbonos, which, according to Walsh, was "obscure and inconvenient". It was quite large, holding 600–700 people, but by the time that Walsh visited it, eight years after it opened, it was attracting congregations of only thirty or forty regular worshippers. That may, of course, have had something to do with the Chaplain, Mr. Crane, who was not popular amongst most of the British community. Walsh also says that the Chapel was dirty and neglected. There was no lead on the

The British Chapel in 1828

portico roof, and rain was seeping in. Several years earlier, some drunks had thrown stones at the windows during a service, but the glass had not been replaced. The British community was proving the Bishop of Rio right.

Walsh's professional assessment was followed in 1855 by that of the American Ewbank, who went to a service there in 1855, only to have his republican sympathies sorely tried by the parson's rampant monarchism. The Chapel survived until the mid-twentieth century, when it was replaced by a more modern building.

The religion of the resident population of Rio was, of course, Roman Catholicism, and the travellers could not but be aware of the numerous indications of faith. There were many statues of the Virgin Mary in the streets, surrounded by curtains during the day, and lit by special lamps by night. Long and elaborate religious processions wound their way through the city on many days of the year. Funerals were also very public events, in which every passer-by was expected to join. Foreigners were expected to remove their hats when passing churches. The same obeisance was expected when royal processions passed by, and woe betide the foreigner who did not bow down before royalty as they swept through the city. The American Minister, Mr. Sumpter, got into considerable trouble in 1817, when he refused to get off his horse as the Queen's procession passed. He was threatened with violence by the Queen's guards, but stuck to his guns, and eventually received an apology from the Queen. There were also plenty of soldiers in the city. Brackenridge describes them rather unsympathetically: "We were frequently met by pairs of lazy, lounging soldiers, who, it seems, are constantly walking in the streets with their bayonets, for the purpose of preventing disturbance; their insolent deportment to the lower classes of people, gave the most certain indication of a despotic government."

In 1826, only a few years before Robert Hesketh's arrival in Rio, John Macdouall embarked on HMS "Adventure", which left Plymouth in company with HMS "Beagle" to consider the regular navigation of the Straits of Magellan. Arriving in Rio, Macdouall spent two months there on his way south. He describes the scene on the evening of a feast-day. There were fireworks, bonfires, torches, the sound of church bells tolling, muskets firing, and the the African slaves singing and dancing. Much of the population was out in the streets, and gangs of chained slaves were being led through the city.

His verdict on this noisy scene was perhaps surprising: he called it "this chaste city". We shall need to examine the life of Rio in more detail before we can decide whether Macdouall was right about its moral quality.

19

RIO – CITY OF COMMERCE AND POLITICS

"From colonial town to imperial capital" (Mary Karasch writing about Rio in "Colonial Cities", ed. Ross and Telkamp)

Every citizen of Rio de Janeiro is either an immigrant, or descended from one, for the original inhabitants, the Tamoio Indians, were either wiped out or exiled in the sixteenth century. That time saw the Portuguese as the first immigrants; they were turned out by the French, who were in their turn turned out by the Portuguese once more. Only then did a degree of stability descend as churches and forts, those two bastions of Catholic expansion, began to dominate the many hills and eminences of the young city, which was called initially São Sebastian de Rio de Janeiro. The city was misnamed from the start, for the opening in the range of coastal mountains did not lead to a *rio* or river, and was, in fact, a vast bay, largely sheltered from the boisterous South Atlantic by its volcanic mountains. Early prints chronicle the growth of the young city, as it gradually moved up the narrow ravines on the western side of the bay. The increasing size and sophistication of sailing-ships in the seventeenth and eighteenth centuries meant that many more European seamen made it to Rio and the Bay of Guanabara, and realised its usefulness as a staging-post. From there, ships sailed south to the River Plate and then to the perilous passage round Cape Horn to the Pacific; and west to the Cape of Good Hope, Mozambique, the Indian Ocean and India itself. Later on, it became an essential supply-post for the long voyage to Australia and New Zealand.

The early Portuguese involvement in the slave trade between West Africa, Mozambique, and Brazil also meant that cargoes of slaves were continually landing in the city, ready to be dispersed throughout the hinterland, where gold and silver were being discovered, and sugar and later coffee estates were developing.

But all this did not immediately create a prosperous city. Commerce was developing, mainly with Portugal and its overseas dominions and colonies, but there were limitations on the development of the city. The first was

Portuguese government policy: only in 1808 were the main ports of Brazil, including Rio, thrown open to international trade. Before that, all exports had to be shipped under the Portuguese flag, and to touch at a Portuguese port – Lisbon, Porto, or Viana do Castelo – before being allowed to be distributed elsewhere. Secondly, Portuguese finance was not always available in large quantities for the development of Rio. The disastrous Lisbon earthquake of 1755 meant that Portuguese attention and Portuguese money were being poured into the rebuilding of Lisbon rather than the growth of its colonial outpost. In the mid-eighteenth century, Pombal set up three "Companies" to develop Brazil's economy, but part of his aim was regulation and the more efficient collection of taxes from Brazil. Thirdly, the Portuguese, perhaps because they lived in a small country on the edge of Europe, were sometimes wary of allowing Rio de Janeiro to rise above its station. Rio had been the headquarters of only one of the "Captaincies" which made up Brazil, and the Portuguese made sure that the Rio Captaincy was not allowed to consider itself pre-eminent: all important matters went back to Lisbon for adjudication. This caution applied to the Roman Catholic Church too: it was slow to set its colonial offspring free, and the Archbishop of Lisbon remained the focus of all ecclesiastical power in Brazil. The Jesuits, with their strong support of the Papacy and their well-established educational programmes, had been very active in Brazil, but they were eventually considered too powerful, uncompromising, and independent. After some generally outstanding work proselytizing among the Indians, creating *aldeias* (villages), and building churches throughout Brazil, they were summarily exiled from both Portugal and Brazil by the Marquis of Pombal in 1759.

So, while Rio de Janeiro gradually grew in size and importance, it did not grow fast. Most witnesses in the eighteenth century speak, as everyone still does, of its beauty, but also of its dirt, its smells, its garbage, its lawlessness, and its mosquitoes. It was at this stage that the Brazilian Portuguese began to get used to having slaves do everything for them, and convinced themselves that there was and never would be any other way.

A fair number of merchants lived and worked in Rio in the eighteenth century – over a hundred and twenty in 1792, according to Mary Karasch[282], and not all of them were Portuguese. But only after the arrival of the Court and the opening of Brazil to international trade, did the number of merchants dramatically increase, especially from the major European trading nations of the time; from Great Britain, from France, and, soon, from the United States of America. So, although Mary Karasch argues that Rio stopped being a colonial capital only after 1850, when its institutions were well-established and good government was increasingly the rule, it would seem more reason-

Rio in 1828 – the steep valleys are already being filled with houses

able to date the change from 1808, when Brazil itself ceased to be a dependency and became, at least for a time, the cockpit of Portuguese power.

After 1808, therefore, the business of politics became an essential part of the way Rio earned its living. We have seen that a vast number of courtiers came to Rio in 1808, and that all had to be found accommodation and occupation. The show and the flummery which accompanied any official carriage or procession throughout the city will have left the inhabitants in no doubt that the royal family and their government were to be respected. When the refugees from Lisbon first arrived, they were led by Dom João VI, the Regent, whose mother, Queen Maria, was mentally ill. He became King in 1816 after his mother's death. Before he reluctantly left for Portugal in 1821, he inspired a great deal of civil engineering, all of which required large numbers of administrators. Houses, roads, and the public institutions of a capital – educational institutions, a library, a press, a museum, archives, theatres, and a botanical garden – were all developed at a rapid rate.

After João's son, Pedro, took over in 1821, he lost little time in announcing that he would stay and lead an independent nation. Whatever his faults – and they were many – idleness and passivity were not of their number. His love of horses and of women did not seem to exhaust the demands of his time, and he was very keen to direct the government of the newly-independent nation. Pedro's style was decidedly autocratic: "I will govern .... by the people not through the people". He allowed the people's representatives to meet in solemn assembly, but then dismissed them and their constitution. Until he abdicated in favour of his young son, Pedro II, in 1831, he was active, even hyperactive, in the government of the nation, and the city of Rio certainly knew it.

Even after he abdicated, the politics of power preoccupied many citizens. We have already seen that the Regency period was a time of great disturbance in Brazil, but it was not helped by the changes of personnel in the ranks of the Regents themselves, and by the frequent changes of government during those years. Rio dinner-parties would have had no shortage of political table-talk. The Brazilian historian Basilio de Magalhaes called the Regency period *uma convulção ininterrupta* [a period of uninterrupted convulsion]. But this constant preoccupation with politics was the price of Rio's growing importance. By the 1830s, it had eclipsed Pernambuco and Bahia, and was the undisputed capital of the Empire of the Brazils. Only later was its role superseded by São Paulo, and then, in much more recent times, by Brasilia.

But politics was not enough to guarantee the prosperity of the city. Industry was not as yet developed enough to provide the answer. Whilst there was a growing range of maritime services in the Bay of Guanabara, no large dockyards or graving docks were built before the middle of the nineteenth century. The ironworks at Ipanema served only local needs. The province of Rio de Janeiro had become an active coffee-growing area, but even that was not enough to maintain the economy of the rapidly-growing city. The truth was that, if Rio was to grow and prosper, it would be either in or through its role as a shipping centre. The absence of industry in Brazil meant that manufactured goods had to be brought from Europe by sea. Those manufactured goods would have to be paid for in mineral and agricultural products exported to Europe and the United States, again by sea, and the import and export trade required merchants to arrange for the goods to be ordered, conveyed, and paid for.

The flight of the Portuguese court to Rio in 1807–8 was, perhaps, the most important factor in stimulating trade. It also led directly to the 1810 Treaty between Brazil and Great Britain. The Treaty gave Great Britain an exclusive 15% tariff on its imports – 5% less than that charged to other nations, and allowed British warships exclusive use of ports in the Portuguese dominions, including Brazil. It also allowed British merchants and other residents permission to worship in their own way. At the same time, it also banned the importation of Brazilian sugar and coffee into Great Britain, for the British Government was determined that the trade of its West Indian territories should not be damaged by competition from Brazil. The 1810 Treaty was, of course, very one-sided, but Dom João was holding a weak hand, in view of the fact that if it were not for British support, he would probably have been rotting in a French jail. K. Manchester points out that the 1810 Treaty did have some advantages for Brazil – it freed her, for example, to develop an international trade: Brazil was "emancipated, economically, from the decadent mother country; in 1810, it acquired a rich stepmother." [283] But many Brazilians came to believe that, as in the nursery tales, step-mothers were often wicked.

In the years after the 1810 Treaty, an anti-English faction flourished at the Rio court, led by the politician Araujo, and perhaps encouraged by some of the haughtier attitudes of British consuls of the day. Araujo's influence was sufficient to make Viscount Strangford, who had come from Lisbon to Brazil with Dom João, sail for home in 1814. Attitudes softened to Great Britain after Araujo's death in 1817, and those years saw the arrival of a large number of merchants from abroad, the majority British. They were soon encouraging a vast number of imports: clothing and boots, hats and silks, hosiery and haberdashery, earthenware and glassware, meats of many kinds, oil, wine, and brandy. We are told that so many products were imported that the warehouses ran out of space, and goods had to be stacked along the beaches. But the trade was not all one way: ships sailed back from Rio carrying Brazil's products, among them tobacco, cotton, hides, rum, wax, timber, and gold and diamonds.

Rio also became a distribution centre for the transhipment of imports, not only to the rest of Brazil, but to ports further south in South America, to the west coast of South America, and to Africa. As a consequence, there were plenty of disputes in the port about which category goods fell into, and what level of duty they therefore attracted. The consuls of all the trading countries must have become very used to solving those problems. Just as important were the boatmen and stevedores, whose task was the unloading and reloading of ships. During the first half of the nineteenth century, that was the task of Rio's African slaves, although one contemporary account also mentions the involvement of Indians in the task.

The Bay of Guanabara and the port of Rio saw ships of many nations arriving and departing daily. As treaties with other nations were negotiated by the fledgling Empire, an increasing number of warships from the world powers anchored in the Bay. British consuls were required to send back to London regular reports of naval movements, and the activities of French and of American vessels were of particular interest. On 31 August, 1841, for instance, a letter left Rio for the Foreign Office with the intelli-

A view of Rio by John Shillibeer, R.N., from his ship "The Briton" anchored in the Bay

gence, derived from the Captain of HMS "Southampton", that the French warship "Alair" (24 guns) was in port, and that the "Gloire" and the "Tactique" had left to sail south to the River Plate. It was also known that the "Iphigénie" had visited St. Helena, and there were many French ships in the River Plate between Buenos Aires and Montevideo. Viscount Palmerston, whose fluent French did not at this stage in his career make him a Francophile, was always interested in and suspicious of French marine movements. This was the time when the French were becoming embroiled in hostilities on the River Plate, and becoming nearly as unpopular in South America as the British.

An earlier French arrival had been the frigate "Andromède", which anchored in the Bay in early 1837. The "Andromède" was carrying M. Louis Napoleon, nephew of Napoleon Bonaparte, and standard-bearer of the Napoleonic dynasty. He had been involved in a conspiracy in Strasbourg against the Bourbon government, and was being shipped to the United States out of the way. The British Envoy, Hamilton Hamilton, wrote at some length about the matter: Louis Napoleon was "sent to Rio before [i.e. on his way to] the United States so that the trial of his accomplices might be completed first." Louis Napoleon was, says Hamilton. "a mild, quiet, interesting person, little communicative, but appearing to feel very deeply the dilemma in which are placed his unfortunate friends."[284] His depth of feeling did not stop him from returning to France within the year to raise again the flag of rebellion, this time at Boulogne. He was imprisoned near Amiens, but escaped to England. He returned to France after the 1848 Revolution, and became Emperor, at least until he made the mistake of rousing Bismarck and the Prussians, who defeated him soundly. He ended his days in his favourite bolthole, England, where he died in 1873.

The list of nations represented by their warships was long. Apart from those of Great Britain, France, and the United States, there were ships from many European nations, like Denmark and Sweden, and there were even some from a landlocked country like Austria. This display of naval might induced, of course, competition, and there were sometimes tensions. In 1832, there was a pitched sea-battle between boats from a British and a Brazilian ship, in which some injuries were received. The British Navy considered that their Lieutenant McClintock was culpable, and he was reprimanded.

It is likely that the Brazilian crew involved in the fracas was largely British, for the Brazilian Navy was heavily dependent for several decades on British seamen. As Admiral of the Brazilian Navy in the early years of independence, Lord Cochrane's preference for British seamen led him to take rather extreme measures to acquire them from British merchant ships. The Brazilians were also advertising for British seamen for quite some years, often in British seaports like Portsmouth, where seamen were enjoined to meet a Brazilian contact in the bar of the "Admiral Benbow". In Pará's *Arquivo Publico*, there is a poster advertising the benefits of volunteering for the Brazilian Navy. Contracts were for three years, and passage back to England was guaranteed. Able seamen were offered forty-five shillings per month (£2.25p.), ordinary seamen forty shillings (£2), and landsmen thirty-two shillings and sixpence (£1.62p.) They were promised that there was no "rigorous discipline", and that the cat o' nine tails was illegal in the Brazilian Navy. "Steady and deserving men cannot fail to be rapidly advanced, especially if their education should fit them for a superior situation."

Rio also saw frequent visits from ships which, while not men-of-war, were chartered for government service. There were regular convict ships leaving Great Britain, and calling at Rio on their way to the convict colonies in Australia. The Brazilians were anxious to charge them duties, but an agreement was reached in 1836 treating convict ships as naval transports, and therefore exempt from duty. Other Australia-bound ships had their problems: fire, mutiny, and disease the most serious. The "Royal Admiral", for instance, left Liverpool with two hundred and eight passengers in 1839, bound for Sydney. In the course of the voyage, the Master, Thomas Frieres, became concerned at the conduct of the crew, and armed himself. As the ship neared Brazil, a fracas broke out, in the course of which one of the passengers was mortally wounded. Two members of the crew were put in irons. This left the Master short of qualified seamen, and he had to call upon the passengers to help man the ship. When the ship arrived in Rio, it was decided that it would have delayed the ship too long for the matter to be investigated there, and that any trial would have to take place in Sydney. The "Royal Admiral" was therefore sent on its way, with Commodore Sulivan, the senior British naval officer in the port, providing a naval party to accompany the ship to Australia and guard the prisoners.[285]

Other ships came in for much-needed repairs. Storms en route, or the damaging effect of the hot sun on the caulked seams of the wooden ships, kept Rio's shipwrights very busy. In 1841, for instance, the emigrant ship "Jane", on its way from England to New Zealand, limped into the Bay needing substantial repairs to its hull and to its longboat.[286] And there were ships in the harbour which were permanent fixtures there, unfit to face the ocean again. One of them was the British hulk HMS "Crescent", which was brought across the Atlantic to act as a receiving and medical station for those slaves released by the British Navy from slavers bringing them from Africa. HMS "Crescent" was anchored in the Bay of Guanabara for many a long year, and can be seen amongst the anchored ships in the view of Rio in the previous chapter.

These disasters were, however, the exception rather than the rule, and most merchant ships, wherever they were bound, proceeded on their way peacefully and in good order. Rio's trade with Europe and the rest of the world would have suffered had not most ships made it safely to their destinations.

On land, Rio's transport of goods was mostly on the heads and shoulders of slaves. Horses, sedan-chairs and mule-drawn carriages provided the only passenger-transport. The climate was, of course, warm, and there were periods of tropical disease which affected Brazilians, Europeans, and African slaves alike, and which interfered with the commercial life of the city. In 1850, for instance, yellow fever accounted for four hundred British deaths – 16% of the total British expatriate population. In addition, there were many deaths amongst the crews of British ships in the port. The yellow fever outbreak spluttered on through 1851, with another serious outbreak in 1852, when the Consul reported one hundred and twenty-four deaths among the British community in the early part of the season. Fortunately, Robert Hesketh's family was in England by this time, and so did not succumb, but many amongst the mercantile class obviously did. Consuls and diplomats constantly inveighed against the evils of the South American climate throughout the century, and frequently asked the Foreign Office for periods of furlough so that they could recover their health. It was generally granted, and some, like Hamilton Hamilton, seem to have taken full advantage. But there was generally another diplomat or consul to carry the burdens of the absent colleague, whereas the merchants might have found it more of a problem. Certainly, tropical disease was one of the hazards of the trade, and there are still many British cemeteries throughout South America full of Britons, other Europeans, and Americans who never returned to their native lands.

The Brazilian Government was always keen to recruit European workers for its industry, its agriculture, and its civil engineering projects. At one time, European immigration was offered as an alternative to the African slave trade. There were early successes – in establishing, for instance, an area of German immigration in the mountains behind Rio – but there were also failures. Macdouall describes the arrival of two Irish ships in 1826 with five hundred Irish immigrants, who were to form the basis of an Irish battalion in the service of the Empire of the Brazils. They were housed at Praia Vermelho, below the Sugar Loaf, on land now occupied by the Military Academy, but Macdouall says they were badly fed and housed, and treated suspiciously by the Brazilians. In 1828, along with a similar German battalion, they mutinied, and at least one Irish soldier was executed. Brazil, however, needed industrial expertise as it developed its economy, and immigrants from Europe arrived in Rio on their way to use their expertise in mining, or later, in the building of railways. They were, however, relatively small in number, and it was only after 1850 that a larger number of migrants arrived, so that today, Brazil has taken its citizens from almost every country on the planet.

There is still a magnificent view down into the Bay of Guanabara from the Sugar-Loaf, with the sun normally sparkling on the water, but there are nowadays very few ships to be seen. Gone is the fleet of ships at anchor that was such a feature of life in the nineteenth century. Today, only a few ferries scurry across from Rio to Nitheroy, cargo and container ships make their slow way into the Bay, and the odd cruise ship arrives to disembark its passengers for a rapid acquaintance with Rio. The Bay itself is smaller than it was, for several landfill projects have advanced the land into the Bay. What is now Santos Dumont airport, the main departure-point for the frequent planes to and from São Paulo, was once a hill overlooking the bay. Perhaps it is appropriate that in the age of the aeroplane, the Bay should still offer a departure-point for passengers. It is also true that, although Rio remains a vast and populous city, some of its commercial importance has been transferred to São Paulo and Santos, its port. Rio's heyday was in the nineteenth century, when shipping was king. And it was with shipping that Robert Hesketh and his colleagues spent most of their times and energies.

20

ROBERT'S LIFE IN RIO

"... my Anxiety to support ... the character of an efficient Publick Servant..."

"It is unnecessary for me at present," wrote Viscount Palmerston to Robert Hesketh in the summer of 1832, "to add to these Instructions, ... your long residence in Brazil has made you entirely conversant with the general Duties of a British Consul."[287] Robert Hesketh was in London in May, 1832, when he was appointed His Britannic Majesty's Consul in Rio de Janeiro, and received the standard set of Instructions. It sounds from his response as if his disappointment over the salary might have momentarily affected his enthusiasm, but he was determined to do well, as he explained rather awkwardly: "I have commenced preparations for my voyage to Rio de Janeiro, and approaching that more extended field of action, my Anxiety to support the character of an efficient Publick Servant will proportionately increase."[288] He hoped he would have "daily opportunities of being serviceable to British shipping".

Six months later, Robert had arrived back in Brazil, and taken up his post in Rio. For the next twenty years, until his retirement in 1852, he was to be an almost constant presence in the port, and to be a great influence on a succession of diplomats who followed one another as Envoys Extraordinary. He was to come to the help of hundreds of distressed British subjects during that time, to find himself a wife, and beget a healthy family.

Lord Palmerston, standing – he rarely sat – in his room in the Foreign Office in Downing Street, saw Robert's role as that of "a Merchant Consul, with a small salary to transact the Consular business". We have seen that Palmerston's description of the role owes more to the financial parameters imposed by the House of Commons than to any close understanding of the situation in Rio. One also suspects that Palmerston's attitude to Rio was tainted by his feelings about the previous Consul-General's very high income, and perhaps by some personal animus. Henry Chamberlain was well known for a certain *hauteur* of demeanour. In 1825, he insisted that the Royal Navy deliver his consular mail, not to his office near the waterfront, but to his house, which was some distance inland. The Royal Navy Lieu-

tenant refused to comply, and it was only when Mrs. Chamberlain offered to carry the consular bag that the problem was resolved.[289]

Even after Chamberlain's death, his replacement, William Pennell, received a generous salary. The House of Commons was not satisfied by this and other of the Foreign Office's attempts at economies, and Palmerston did some more cheese-paring. He decided to abolish the role of Consul-General in Rio, and downgrade it to the level of a "Merchant Consul". The expensive Pennell was given his cards, and took retirement, at a pension of more than twice his successor's full-time salary.

There was, therefore, a vacancy in Rio. Robert's timing, or his prescience, was perfect, for it was only a few months since Palmerston had received Robert's letter pleading for a new appointment. Robert was therefore fresh in his thoughts.

Palmerston consulted his junior colleagues. One of them, Backhouse, or more likely Bidwell, wrote: "Mr. Hesketh is a very intelligent, very active, very discreet, and a most excellent Publick Servant, perfectly conversant with Consular Duties, and with the General Principles of Trade, and of the Trade with Brazil in particular. After the sacrifice of his Commercial Establishment that he was required to make in 1826, the diminution of the salary there allotted to him as a compensation for it, will fall very hard upon him, and especially at a time when he might consider himself entitled by his services to advancement; and it is submitted whether if Lord Palmerston has no other Individual in view to place at Rio de Janeiro, as Consul with permission to engage in mercantile pursuits, Mr. Hesketh might not be advantageously placed at that Post." The Memo went on to point out that the Fees at Rio were about £800 a year, and Mr. Hesketh would therefore received approximately the same total as he received at Maranhão, and the "Publick Service" would gain "a good and effective officer" at Rio, a place of extensive British commerce.[290]

This was good enough for Palmerston, and he scribbled on top of the Memo "Transfer Mr. Hesketh as proposed to Rio de Janeiro, 12/1–32. P." Robert was contacted, doubtless considered his options, swallowed hard as he read of the £300 salary and of the fatuous permission to trade, but nevertheless accepted the post. A Commission was drawn up, sent on 7 May, 1832, and Robert returned to Liverpool from London, set sail for Brazil, and reported his arrival in Rio in early October.

Rio in late 1831 was a disturbed place, following the abdication of the Emperor, Pedro I. Nevertheless, Robert speedily got on with life, and soon rented a house. He wrote to Backhouse in May, 1833, reporting that he had taken "a small cottage on a steep hill".[291] This bachelor establishment seems to have satisfied him for some time, but his marriage in 1837 and the birth of his first child in October that year saw him settled in Caminho Velho in the city, where he stayed until about 1845, when he was in a house, presumably larger, in the Rua da Infante. His last address in Rio was Rua da Princeza. Lieutenant Shillibeer of HMS "Briton", visiting Rio in 1818, says that the "residence" of the British Consul was situated in the Rua Direita, near the Custom-House[292] but this is more likely to have been the Consular Office, for it lay close to the waterfront and the Royal Palace.

Robert's personal life underwent a total transformation whilst he was in Rio. He was now forty-four years old, and had so far avoided matrimony. As far as is known, he had not followed his brother William in siring an illegitimate child, but it was an inevitable concomitant of living abroad that marriageable women were at a premium, with the result that most expatriate merchants and professional men failed to marry. Not too long after arriving, however, Robert's eye was caught by a young woman called Georgiana Raynsford. She had been born in Rio in 1819, the daughter of Charles Raynsford, who came from a prominent Rio mercantile family. She had a brother, also called Charles, who in 1850 was the American Vice-Consul. It was not unusual at the time for the major trading countries to use other nationals as their representatives if need arose. Charles Junior was married to Carolina Maria Maxado, who sounds like a local Brazilian, and a record exists of the baptism of their son, Charles Alex, in February, 1850.[293]

On 5 January, 1837, forty-seven year-old Robert and nineteen year-old Georgiana were married at the British Chapel by the Anglican Chaplain, the Revd. Arthur Maister. There were seven witnesses, amongst whom were both Charles Raynsfords and Caroline Raynsford, perhaps Georgiana's mother or sister. Robert and Georgiana wasted no time in starting a family,

Georgiana Hesketh in later life, after she and her husband had returned to England

and their first child, Robert Raynsford Hesketh, was born on 18 October, 1837. He was followed by a second son, William Crosbie, in January, 1839, a third son, George, in February, 1840, and by their first daughter, Eliza Jane, in February, 1842. Henry John followed in October, 1843, and another daughter, Hamilton Maria, in February, 1845. The last child to be born in Rio de Janeiro was Georgiana Sarah, baptised in January, 1847. Later that year, Robert, Georgiana, and their family returned to England. Georgiana was not to return to Brazil, and her remaining children were all born in England.

Robert's and Georgiana's choice of names is illuminating. Their eldest son Robert had his father's Christian name and his mother's surname, William Crosbie had the name of a prominent merchant who had married into the family in Liverpool half a century before[294] but his Christian name was also shared with his uncle in Maranhão. The Hesketh Family Bible suggests that Hanbury Bold was named after one of his baptismal sponsors, Captain Bold, but the name Bold would also have been known to Robert as that of a well-known Liverpool merchant of the previous century. Henry John bore the names of two of Robert's younger brothers, and Hamilton Maria was named after the wife of the British Envoy Extraordinary. The Heskeths seem to have got on well with the Hamiltons, who had returned to Rio after their lengthy absence, and were there until 1846.

Robert must have had a dramatic change in his lifestyle after his marriage to Georgiana. There were four children under the age of five running about the house by 1843, and their tenth wedding anniversary dawned with no less than seven children around the dining-table. After an exceptionally busy day on the waterfront, or unmasking slave-traders, Robert went home to a lively nursery, and it says much for Georgiana's youth and health that she seems to have run an efficient household whilst being pregnant for much of the time. Robert's and Georgiana's children had mixed fortunes, and we shall follow them a little way in a later chapter.

Robert's major role – ministering to the needs of British trade in the port – was a full-time occupation. Certainly, he made no inroads at all into starting up his own business, and those who knew him at the Foreign Office, Backhouse and Bidwell, were not surprised, and pleaded his cause as the years went by. But Robert did pick up extra responsibilities as an extension of his normal duties, just as he had done in Maranhão. In 1850, the Foreign Office granted him permission to act as Agent for the Royal Mail Steam Packet Company in Rio, if he wished. We do not know whether he ever took up the post. In 1836, one of the Commissary Judges was on leave, and Robert offered to give up his post as Consul and act as Commissary Judge instead.

But the offer does not seem to have been taken up, and we hear no more of it. A rather more serious situation occurred in 1839. By then the so-called Mixed Commissions had been set up, attempting to bring the judicial power of two nations together to defeat the Slave Trade. They were at best patchy in their coverage and their efficacy. One of the most active was that set up in Sierra Leone, on the other side of the Atlantic. Even though Brazil was supposed to be an equal partner there, it never played a full role. The Mixed Commission in Rio also combined judges from Brazil and Great Britain, again with very mixed success. In 1839, the Proctor of the Mixed Commission Court, Mr. Shearman, resigned. His duty was to represent "the Captors" – the British Navy – in proceedings against slave-ships and slave-owners. Shearman had been threatened with assassination, presumably by the "enforcers" employed by the slave-dealers. Robert Hesketh immediately took his place, and proceedings against the six slave-ships at that time impounded in the harbour at Rio continued.

There is no mention in the Foreign Office archives of Robert's being physically threatened after this, but taking over as Proctor will not have made him popular with the Brazilian and Portuguese slaving lobby. This act of quiet courage seems typical of him, and he became a popular figure with the diplomats, envoys, and merchants with whom he worked. He was also willing in other ways. His predecessor but one, Chamberlain, had refused to draw up official letters for the merchant community, but Robert re-instituted the practice, to the pleasure of the British merchants. On one occasion in 1841, they minuted their thanks to him for his "attentive and impartial conduct".[295]

Robert was also popular with distinguished visitors like Sir Henry Ellis, who had been sent by the Foreign Office to Rio de Janeiro to try to negotiate a new treaty with Brazil. Ellis failed, but developed a high opinion of Robert's capablilities, supporting the case for a higher salary for him.The Envoy [or Ambassador] ten years earlier had also got on well with Robert. In a letter written as he prepared to leave Rio for his new posting in Washington, H.S. Fox wrote: "Upon quitting this Mission, I think it my duty officially to express to you the great satisfaction I have derived , from witnessing the active, zealous and praiseworthy manner in which you have performed the important and very laborious duties of your office of H.M. Consul at Rio de Janeiro. I feel myself greatly indebted to you for the useful assistance you have on all occasions afforded me in the execution of my own Publick duties; as well as for the constant personal civility and attention, which I have experienced from you during my residence in the Country."[296]

Fox's successor was to be on equally amiable terms with Robert, but he was a very different kind of Envoy. Hamilton Charles James Hamilton had served in Paris, and his service there had not won the full approval of the Foreign Office. His move to Rio seems to have been a case of "out of sight, out of mind". Hamilton Hamilton presented his Letters of Credence to the Emperor of Brazil in July, 1836, but it was not long before he requested leave of absence, partly on account of his ill-health and of his desire to avoid the heats of another summer, and partly because he said that his "surviving parent" had died, and he was required at home to sort out the family's affairs. Normally, Palmerston would have made the decision, but on this occasion, Queen Victoria herself was involved: "The Queen has been graciously pleased to grant you permission to return to England. Little was Palmerston to know that Hamilton Hamilton was not to return to his post for three and a half years, and was driven back only by the threats of Lord Aberdeen. Aberdeen complained about his absence in May, 1840, when Hamilton had a Brighton address.

Palmerston was back in post before long, and he decided to cut his losses by offering Hamilton Hamilton a pension. Hamilton Hamilton declined it, and announced that he would return to Rio. But he was not going cheaply. First of all, he asked for a steamer to take him, his family, and his luggage from Southampton to Portsmouth – not a great distance. Palmerston refused, and when Hamilton Hamilton pushed his luck by asking for a steamer from Portsmouth to Falmouth, Palmerston became tetchy – "Utterly impossible. Let him send them as other People send their goods and chattels". Having failed thus far, Hamilton Hamilton now declared that it was "beneath his dignity and the dignity of this country to go otherwise than in a man of war". Palmerston was not having this either, and told Hamilton Hamilton that he must "waive the deception of dignity"[297]

By some means or other, doubtless at a considerable distance below his dignity, the reluctant Hamilton Hamilton arrived back in Rio, in July, 1841, and stayed in his post until the second quarter of 1843, when he produced a sick-note diagnosing "heat and dyspepsia". But he does not seem to have come home on this occasion, and did not finally leave until 1846, when he went on sick leave, never to return. He does seem to have been genuinely ill, for Thomas Ewbank, an American who arrived in Rio in 1845, reported that "The British embassador [sic] begged the loan of a medical electromagnetic machine I had brought from the United States, and, at the request of Mr. Hamilton, I assisted the doctor in applying it."[298] The 22 year-old Astley Cooper Key, later to be a distinguished Admiral, met Hamilton Hamilton and described him with all the breezy impertinence of youth: "The Minister Plenipo'[Plenipotentiary] is a most gentlemanly man. Carmichael and myself are very intimate with him. He is a Mr. Hamilton; there is but one person between him and the Dukedom of Hamilton."[299]

An even more constant presence in Robert's professional life must have been the Chargé d'Affaires, William Gore Ouseley, who arrived in Rio soon after Robert Hesketh in 1833, but left before him in 1846. Gore Ouseley had served in various embassies in Europe as a young man, and had then spent some time as paid attaché in Washington. There, he had developed a great admiration for United States institutions, and had written a book praising them. He had also married Maria Van Ness, the daughter of the Governor of Vermont. Whether Gore Ouseley was a great admirer of Hamilton Hamilton is not recorded, but during Hamilton Hamilton's long absence from Rio, Ouseley covered for him, carrying out his own duties as well as those of the Envoy. With the benefit of hindsight, it is possible to question some of his judgements: he criticized Hamilton Hamilton, his Envoy, for supporting British claims for losses in the Cabanagem, and Ouseley's seems to have misunderstood the role of the "Belvidera" in the aftermath of the murder of the crew of the "Clio" in Pará in 1835. In both those cases, he seems to have taken the Brazilian side. He also passed on to London the view that Don Pedro II, before he was crowned Emperor at the age of fourteen, was intellectually deficient, and showed "indicators of partial imbecility"[300] He based this on the fact that his own sons, who were much younger than Pedro, were frequently invited to play at the Royal Palace with the future Emperor. The reality was that Pedro II, as an adult, was intellectually very capable, showing acuteness and balanced judgement, and the Brazilian Government certainly regarded him as capable of carrying the burdens of office at the young age of fourteen.

In less busy times, when Hamilton Hamilton was back in Rio, Ouseley found time to paint, and a set of studies of major landmarks in Rio and other places in South America was published in the 1850s.[301] He also wrote a well-informed pamphlet on the Slave Trade, from his very considerable experience alongside Robert in the harbour of Rio de Janeiro.[302] Like almost all other diplomatic and consular personnel in South America, Ouseley too had his health problems. In 1835, he wrote to the Foreign Office saying that the three years he had up to that point endured in Rio had "proved injurious to my health". He had also found living in Rio very expensive, and had taken the extreme step of sending his family to his wife's home in the United States, where the cost of living was more reasonable.[303]

Like Hamilton Hamilton and Gore Ouseley, Robert's time in Rio had its periods of sickness. He had three major bouts of ill-health whilst in Rio, one in 1836, one ten years later, in 1846, and a final one in 1851, which seems to have brought about his retirement from the consular service. In 1836, his medical notes signed by Dr. Williams and Dr. Lee diagnosed "a severe attack of inflammation of the Liver with acute Dysentery". He was ill at the beginning of the month, and wrote of being "worse this afternoon" (7 March). By the end of the month, he was feeling slightly better, and wrote a private letter on 30 March to his old Liverpool connection, John Backhouse of the Foreign Office: "I am lifted out of my bed to a sofa. I have been since rapidly gaining strength, and can now crawl about the house, but being reduced to skin and bone, am yet too feeble to be moved in a Hammock to the mountains where I am ordered by the doctor as soon as I can bear to journey."[304]

Being carried in a hammock was the standard mode of personal transport in Rio, especially for ladies, and, presumably, for invalids. A cloth was draped over the framework to keep off the sun and prying eyes. Normally, however, Robert would have ridden about on his horse. He describes to Backhouse the gradual onset of his illness: "In some months past I felt unwell, but my daily attendance at the office and riding in and out through the Sun, or Rain, was an obstacle to taking medicine in a proper and efficient manner. Besides I have been very anxious about my Brother John & his family, who are destitute refugees from Pará at Maranham, and amongst other causes of annoyance the Fees for 1835 turned out more than £300 less than those of preceding years. All this added to the daily harassing and noisy Duties of my office in the very hot season we have experienced I fear upset my Philosophy, and aggravated my predisposition to disorder in the Liver. However, I am grateful to God for this Escape, and thankful for the able Medical Assistance which succoured me."

He has been told he should have a month's convalescence in the Organ Mountains behind Rio de Janeiro. They were named after the rock formations which are a distinctive feature of the mountain-tops, and, rising to more than 7000 ft., they provided a much cooler environment for those recovering from the city's heat. A colony of Swiss immigrants had already arrived in the area in 1818, and had established the town of Nova Friburgo, where their influence is still noticeable. He asks Backhouse to pass on a request to Lord Palmerston for him to return home the following year on his doctors' advice, but also adds that, if the Foreign Office follows its usual practice, he will have to pay his deputy half his usual salary and all his fees, which will leave him to manage on £150 a year whilst he is in England – "an amount with which the cleaverest [sic] financier would be puzzled to cover the annual expences of the most economical half-pay Consul in England". Like all consuls at the time, he had to call on his own resources to make up the shortfall in his pay, and he says that he has had to draw on" the small residue" left to him after he had settled the huge loss of £4000 which his commercial connection with his brother John had involved him in. Given that his "small residue" was being eaten away by living expenses, he did not think he would be able to help John financially any more. He signs off the letter to Backhouse by thanking him "for numerous acts of Friendship", and asking to be remembered to Mrs Backhouse and all the Backhouse family.

He seems to have continued his recovery in the Organ Mountains, and he reports that he was back at his desk by 17 May, 1836. On 11 November that year, he writes to say that he has been leaving Rio occasionally for visits to the Organ Mountains to improve his health. He obviously by then had permission to visit England in 1837, but got married first in January, 1837, and presumably took his new bride to England with him, leaving Acting-Consul Grigg in charge. We know that Robert and Georgiana were back in Rio later in the year, for Georgiana's first child, Robert Raynsford Hesketh, was born in Rio in October.

For ten years after that, Robert and Georgiana stayed in Rio, with a rapidly growing family. However, in January, 1847, Robert was diagnosed with dyspepsia and urinary stones, again by Dr. George Lee, and he set out on 4 June for England, accompanied by most or all of his family. This time, they had determined to create a base in England, and they quickly acquired a house – which still exists – in the village of Titchfield, near Fareham, in Hampshire. It may be that Georgiana had relatives in the area, for Robert seems content to let her settle there, and return to Rio alone for the last few years of his service as Consul. The 1851 Census shows Georgiana living in Mill Street, Titchfield, with five children aged from two to nine, and assisted by four servants: Ann Holland, Emma Cousins, Mary Dinham, and Maria Emery. The two eldest boys, Robert and William Crosbie, were not living at home, and were possibly away at school, and the third boy, George, appears in the 1851 Census at Stubbington House School, near Titchfield.

Robert's last bout of illness during his time as a Consul was in 1851. Dr. Lee's note again mentions stones in the bladder, and blames his symptoms on Robert's long residence in the tropics. He says that an operation to remove them is necessary, but suggests that an operation in Rio would be more dangerous than the disease, and therefore Robert ought to return to England.[305] In August, 1851, Robert came home to England on the steamer "Teoish", reaching home after a very long voyage in December of that year. He did not return to Brazil, and, after his forty years' service there, stayed in Hampshire for most of the rest of his life.

21

RIO – SHIPS AND THE
BRITISH IN DISTRESS

"... daily opportunity of being serviceable to British shipping..." (Robert Hesketh)

For the best part of twenty years, Robert rode down every morning from his house in the Caminho Velho or the Rua da Infante to the Consul's Office in Rua Direita. As he neared the waterfront, he saw the Bay on most mornings sparkling in the sun, and bristling with masts as hundreds of ships lay at anchor. Some were discharging their cargo, or taking on their cargoes of sugar, coffee, or stores. Others were making their way to the special watering-point for merchant ships, to the north of the city. Others were be carrying out shipboard repairs or checking their cables or rigging. Ships of war would also be anchored in a special section of the Bay, most of them of smarter trim than the average merchant ship. Some of the ships had reached the status of hulks, and were unlikely to be sailing through the entrance to the Bay ever again, and acting either as floating warehouses, hospitals, or prisons. We have already noted the case of HMS "Crescent", brought from Britain to serve as a hospital-ship for those slaves who had been transported from Africa by the illegal slavers, and then who were released by the British naval squadron. As Robert's time in Rio went on, steamships increased in number, most of them paddle-steamers, some small and suitable only for the sheltered waters of the Bay, and others larger and sea-going, including British naval ships like HMS "Growler".

In between this large and motley fleet, smaller boats were continually threading their way to and from the larger ships, many of them making their way to the Queen's Stairs, below the Royal Palace. Some boats were manned by smart sailors, others by slaves clad only in cotton trousers and a large straw hat. The landing-place was continually thronged by seamen of all nations, milling amongst the slaves gathered at the fountain in the wide square of the Praça do Paço on the waterfront. Every day, fresh ships and their crews arrived. In the year of 1839, for example, seven hundred and fifty seven merchant ships arrived in Rio – an average of two arrivals every day.

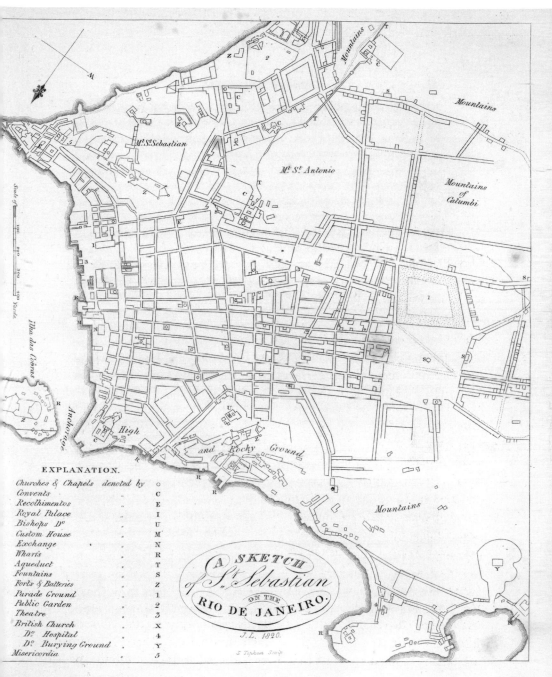

A SKETCH
of Sᵗ Sebastian
ON THE
RIO DE JANEIRO.

J.L. 1820.

S. Topham Sculp.

London Published Octʳ 1ˢᵗ 1820 by Samˡ Leigh.

John Luccock's map of Rio de Janeiro in 1818

In 1839, the largest group of visiting ships, apart from the Brazilians, were the British – one hundred and ninety-three ships, 25% of the total. American ships were also numerous – one hundred and forty-eight, 20% of the total. The next most numerous merchant fleet was that of the Portuguese, which comprised 15% of the total, and after that, smaller numbers of ships from smaller sea-going nations and the Hanseatic states of Hamburg, Bremen, and Lübeck, from the Mediterranean islands, from landlocked European kingdoms, and the odd one from the infant trading nations of South America. Robert's trading report for 1839 shows ships from Hamburg, Sardinia, Sweden, Spain, Denmark, Austria, Holland, Russia, Bremen, Tuscany, Naples, Prussia, Chile, and Lübeck, as well as from Brazil, Great Britain, and the United States. A list from five years earlier, in 1834, gives crew numbers and total tonnages from each of the trading nations. British ships tended to be of about 200 tons, Portuguese ships of half that size, and Brazilian ships of only about 62 tons, understandable in view of the fact that they were often sailing quite close to the coast and covering much shorter distances. Even the ships with the largest tonnages – those from Spain, averaging 308 tons, were very small indeed by modern standards, and, although shipwrecks and losses at sea were frequent, the vast majority of the merchant and naval fleets made it across the Atlantic in relative safety.

Robert's professional concern was with the British contingent. A British ship's master would, on his arrival in the port, report to the Consul's Office, pay his fees, and report any problems. Before that, he would have had to wait for the port health authorities to visit the ship and ascertain that it was free from typhoid fever, smallpox, or other disease, and then the port customs officials would have to investigate the cargo, and lay down the official duties payable. Robert had an interest in the smooth operation of the system, and might well have to apply his influence and his good offices when things went wrong. The consul, was, said a later consul, " a kind of dry nurse to the seafaring population".

Naval ships were not quite such frequent arrivals, but were by no means rare. In the first half of 1835, for instance, twenty-five warships arrived in the Bay of Guanabara, eleven from the Brazilian Navy, four from the American Navy, four from the French Navy, and six from the British Navy. Some were large by the standards of the day, others quite small. In the 1835 list, seven were corvettes, two were frigates, four were brigs, five were packets, four were schooners, and there was a brigantine, a tender, and one British ship-of-the-line. When a British warship arrived, Robert would have to respond to its arrival by dressing in his official consular uniform, and then embarking in the ship's boat which would have been sent expressly to pick him up, and pay an official visit to the captain. A strict protocol developed in the 1820s governed this process. Rapid and serious were the complaints if a consul in a far-flung port did not show due respect to a flag-captain of the British Navy. The British warship would be very likely to have information about naval movements, and the quarterly naval report in duplicate that consuls were required to complete was not just for innocent information – the Foreign Office was keen to ensure that the local ambassador as well as the authorities in London knew of any significant or suspicious move on the part of foreign naval ships, and consuls were carefully instructed to report such information urgently.

As well as insisting on its entitlement to the proper etiquette and procedures, the Navy could, however, be very helpful. When the "Lord Godrich" arrived in Rio in January, 1838, bound for Port Adelaide with some of the earliest colonists for South Australia, the Master reported that the voyage from Britain had been totally dominated by violent disputes between passengers. Robert took some of the passengers off the ship, and arranged for a British naval officer to sail to Port Adelaide on the "Lord Godrich" to ensure peace and harmony.[306]

Not all contacts with shipping were quite so satisfactory or productive. It was not uncommon for ships to arrive with the Master complaining of mutinous conduct on the part of one or more of the crew. Only a few weeks after his arrival, Robert was confronted by the Master of the British vessel "Exquisite", who brought before him a mutinous seaman. Robert, wishing to be supportive of the Master, had the seaman imprisoned for a time while the appropriate legal moves were being made. He then released him. A very sharp reproof was soon winging its way back to Rio from London: "It would seem from your Letter that you have exercised an authority of committing to Prison, and discharging therefrom, a British seaman, without any further trial or sentence, than your own judgement upon the circumstances of the case, the legality of which proceeding, if questioned in the Courts of this Country, will not be supported."[307] The proper procedure was, apparently, for the Master to complain to the municipal authorities. Robert did not make the mistake again. When, for instance in 1843, the "Ester", a whaler making her way south, arrived in Rio, the Master reported two mutineers to the Brazilian authorities, who then brought them to Robert, who in his turn arranged for them to be sent back to England for trial, accompanied by depositions from witnesses.[308] The "Ester" was then allowed to proceed. The same procedure was followed when the British schooner, "Jubilee", from Jersey, arrived in Rio. Three of the crew complained that the Master, Amice Hevelin, and the Mate were guilty of "abhorrent and unnatural practices", "having carnal knowledge of each other". Homosexual behaviour was doubtless not unknown in merchant ships of the time, but Hevelin and the Mate had made things worse by importuning another member of the crew, who was particularly offended because he was writing to his mother at the time. Robert collected pages of witness statements, and sent Hevelin and the Mate back home with no less than six witnesses. Robert Hesketh says he could hardly believe Hevelin and the Mate had done what they were accused of.[309]

Taking crew on part-way through a voyage could be hazardous, as Hugh Thewlis, the Master of the "Lavinia" of Glasgow, found out. He had been sailing from Glasgow for the Cape of Good Hope and then to Patagonia. As he neared the African coast, several of his crew fell sick, and he took on five new crew at the island of St. Helena when he called in for provisions. The new crew-members were a motley lot: two English sailors, an Italian, a Portuguese, and one from Heligoland, which was controlled at the time by Great Britain. They caused trouble immediately, and the Master abandoned his intended voyage, and brought the ship across to Rio. Robert was immediately summoned, took the five men off the ship, and prepared to send them back to England for trial. The Master of the ship who had been asked to take them back refused to take more than one at a time, and so Robert sent the leader of the mutineers, one John Mackenzie, on the first ship, and the rest, who were also accused of mutinous conduct, on HMS "America", where they could be suitably supervised.[310]

At least twice in his time in Rio, Robert was faced with major sea-going disasters, which resulted in large loss of life, and large numbers of distressed Britons. We shall look at the cases of the "Hibernia" and the "India" in the next chapter. Much more frequent, however, were visits to the Consul's Office by individuals who had landed up in Rio, whether by accident or design. A frequent problem concerned British citizens who had lost their jobs or who had become ill in Brazil, but who could not afford the fare home. The British Government tended to be fairly generous where circumstances justified it. A respected local family in Rio, for example, had employed a British woman, Ann Parker, as a servant for some years. Of late, her health had deteriorated, and the doctor who had examined her had recommended that she return home. The family was, however, not prosperous, and could not afford the £23 fare for her passage home. Robert, considering the facts, agreed that the British Government would pay the passage-money.[311] In 1840, William Barry, a former employee of the gold mines in Minais Gerais, was destitute, and was given the wherewithal to reach home, and, at the same time, a Mrs. Bond, whose husband had died while working as a gold miner, was paid the passage-money home for herself and her three children.[312]

The gold-mines, with their relatively easy access to Rio de Janeiro, provided many problems for the consular staff. The mining companies, sometimes Brazilian-owned, and sometimes British-owned, employed a fair number of British miners. It was usually the case that miners emigrating from Britain did not have a contract which guaranteed them a return passage. If illness struck, or they were dismissed, they often landed up at the door of the British Consulate in Rio. The cases all had to be investigated, to ensure that Government money was not being improperly used, and communication with the mine company often took a great deal of time. In 1842, one miner, Henry Kemp, left his employment at the mine, alleging that he had been badly treated. Robert had to acquire signed statements from the mine supervisor and three other British officials, who claimed that Kemp left of his own accord, having been insolent.[313] The Foreign Office was not happy to pay out for miners in this situation, and Robert was instructed in 1840 to seek compensation for any sums expended from the mine authorities. Robert was able to be more supportive of Elizabeth Ann Johns and her child. Together with her husband, Nicholas Johns, of Helston in Cornwall, she had come to Brazil, where her husband had obtained employment as a miner. He had fallen into drunken habits, and Elizabeth's situation was so insufferable that Robert arranged a passage home for her and her child.[314] His experiences with the mining companies does not seem to have put Robert off mining as an investment, and his will shows that he had shares in a number of mining operations, though none in the Minais Gerais area of Brazil, from which most of his problems would have come.

Sometimes politics produced refugees. Margaret Flein, together with her husband and their two sons, had emigrated to Buenos Aires, and owned a small farm there. The boys had been ordered to join the army of the Argentine dictator General Rosas. To avoid this, Mrs. Flein had fled with the boys across the River Plate to Montevideo, leaving her husband to tend the farm. She tried to find employment in Montevideo, and then further north in Rio Grande, but failed, and so had come to Rio and reported to the Consul's office. Robert arranged for a passage home for her and her sons.[315] Another Argentinian initiative gave Robert a headache in 1845. Thirty British subjects had volunteered for the Argentinian Navy, and had travelled out to South America. In Montevideo, which was at that time in the hands of the Argentinians, the men had been examined by a medical officer, and found to be unfit for the arduous tasks involved in going to sea. They were therefore stranded. The Consul in Montevideo arranged for them to travel to Rio on HMS "Racer", but its Commander was less than thrilled to have thirty non-seaman on his ship, and delivered them to Robert in Rio with as much alacrity as he could. Mr. Ouseley, the Chargé d'Affaires, apparently thought they ought to be repatriated at government expense as "distressed British subjects", but Robert disagreed, and, as they were capable of earning a living, had arranged for many of them to take up paid employment.[316] An even more unusual case was that of the four British lighthouse builders. They had been building a lighthouse on one of the Bermudas, but as they tried to land on the island to continue their work, they were blown out to sea in their open boat. They spent fourteen days at sea with minimal provisions, until they were sighted by the brig "Pedagro" a thousand miles north of Brazil. They were taken on board, and eventually brought to Rio, where Robert was able to find them passage north on the American ship "Wabash", which was bound for New York, and which promised to drop them off in the Bermudas, so that they could finish their work on the lighthouse.[317]

Letters frequently arrived from Britain from anxious relatives. Thomas Smith from Liverpool got himself into serious trouble in Brazil. He had been imprisoned in Rio in 1836, but was then accused of forgery while he was in prison. As a result, he had been exiled to the off-shore island of Fernando de Noronha, but his punishment had then been commuted to simple banishment from Brazil. His father, back in Liverpool, had contacted his M.P., Mr. Ewart, a close friend of Gladstone's father, and paid for his son's passage to Van Dieman's Land (Tasmania).[318] All this had to be arranged by Robert in Rio, and it is to be hoped that Thomas Smith was duly grateful to his father, and did him some credit when he finally reached Australia. More delicate was the answer to John Anstey's enquiry. In 1839, Anstey wrote to the Foreign Office in London, saying that no-one in the family had heard of his sister-in-law, Mary Ann Broughton, for four years. W.G. Ouseley, the Chargé d'Affaires, replied, doubtless after some spadework by Robert and his staff, and reported that she was living as housekeeper to a Mr. James Baxter, an engineer. A slightly later letter from Ouseley confesses that his first letter was only partly true, and that he had only called her a housekeeper, because he had not known how to describe a lady of easy virtue.[319] Mary Appleyard was another woman alone in Brazil. She had come out to Brazil to act as a servant to a family, but had proved unsuitable. Her father, "a respectable tradesman in London", had promised to pay the Government back for her passage home, and Robert arranged this.[320] A more difficult case concerned a William James Porter, who had been arrested in Brazil after absconding from the United States, where he had married bigamously, having left his first wife in England. He was dispatched back home at Government expense, in order to face trial.[321]

Also disgraced was one Mr. Vane, a British citizen in charge of the Rio

Packet Office, and therefore responsible for the safe passage of all diplomatic mail. His job was an important one, but he had a hot temper. In March, 1844, he had had an altercation with Count de Giorgi, the Austrian Chargè d'Affaires in Rio. Vane, whom Robert described as "irascible & prompt to take offence", assaulted Count de Giorgi, thereby coming very near to provoking an international incident. Robert obtained an apology, which went some way to assuaging Austrian pride, but this did not prevent Vane's being sacked from his post in July.[322]

If the problems of seamen and other distressed British subjects were not enough to keep him busy, Robert always had the local Anglican Church. The Foreign Office records contain many letters both to and from London about the church's finances, ministry, and architecture. In keeping with the ideas of the times, the Foreign Office regarded the ministrations of the Church of England in far-off places as part of its responsibility, and even Palmerston, who, it will be remembered, was not noted for his churchgoing, became involved in the many ecclesiastical disputes which enliven the pages of the archives.

The foundation stone of the British Chapel had been laid on 12 August, 1819, and it was dedicated, with at least a dash of patriotism, to St. George and St. John the Baptist, though the dedication was later changed to Christ Church. Robert presided over a series of improvements that took place in the late thirties and early forties, largely to correct the faults the Rev. Robert Walsh had described in 1828–9. In 1841, Robert wrote on behalf of the congregation to request £300 to provide an organ for the church. The request was speedily turned down by the Foreign Office. He also wrote with the congregation's plans to build a gallery, for which some subscriptions had been raised, and a French architect's services secured. Preliminary plans were included in the letter.[323] The Government again declined to help. In 1843, Robert tried again, this time for paving in front of the British Chaplaincy, but was again refused.[324] This may have had something to do with the long-standing unhappiness the Foreign Office had with the Rio community's ecclesiastical arrangements.

Trouble started well before Robert arrived. In 1816, the British community in Rio refused to accept the nominee of the Foreign Office as Chaplain, and he had to return home, at a cost of £500 to the British taxpayer. His successor was the Rev. R.C. Crane, and, according to the usual arrangement, he would have had half of his stipend paid by the Government, and half by the local community. Unfortunately, Mr. Crane became steadily less popular with his congregation for reasons that are not officially explained. Walsh's comment that numbers at divine service were quite small gives an indication of the British community's unhappiness with his ministry. In the end, the merchant community decided that they would not pay their half of his salary. This threw all the usual agreements into disarray, and, for a time, it looked as if both the Chaplaincy and the local British Hospital would have to close for want of funds. Mr. Crane also had personal difficulties – he had a quiverful of children, and was "overwhelmed with debt". In 1831, Lord Palmerston agreed to pay a surprisingly generous £500 to get Mr. Crane, his wife, and ten children home.[325] Palmerston remained sore about this, and suggested in 1833 that Mr. Crane had acted in a "surreptitious" way in obtaining the £500 before he left Rio, and presumably not returning that part which was left over after he had paid the boat fares.[326]

That was not the last the Foreign Office heard of Mr. Crane, for he wrote to the Foreign Secretary aain in 1842, asking for either a pension or church preferment, which suggests that he had failed to find a parochial incumbency in England. He was, of course, refused, and a further letter from him was answered so forcefully that even the insensitive Mr. Crane was deterred from trying again.

Apart from his evident irritation with Mr. Crane, Palmerston was unhappy that the Rio congregation had become adept at taking matters into their own hands. This had, said Palmerston, "entailed an unusually large expence upon the Publick. This has arisen from the Merchants having acted (as in the present case) independently of the Secretary of State, and occasionally at variance with his intentions." The Rio merchants were now proposing to set up a commission in England to choose a successor, thus ignoring the Secretary of State and the Bishop of London, who was in charge of all foreign ecclesiastical postings, and who advised the Secretary of State. Robert therefore received a private letter from Viscount Palmerston, ordering him, "after all the trouble we have had here with the Church Establishment at Rio", not to agree to anything until he had consulted the Foreign Office.[327]

The next Chaplain was the Rev. Arthur Maister, who was happily appointed with the agreement of the Bishop of London, the Secretary of State, and the Rio congregation, and who arrived in Rio in March, 1834. But there was again trouble over money. The committee in Liverpool who had submitted his name to the Bishop of London had apparently offered him a stipend of £500, an allowance of £86 for house rent, and the cost of his passage out to Rio and home again. This was a little presumptuous, since they had no responsibility for paying either his salary or his rent. The congregation in Rio, who were responsible for paying at least half his salary, went further and proposed to raise his stipend to £700 per annum, a giddying figure, in view of the fact that their Consul was only receiving £300 at this stage. Perhaps their delight at having rid themselves of Mr. Crane caused a rush of blood to the head, and they took no heed of the fact that the British Government was committed to providing the other half. Palmerston was not pleased at this fresh evidence of independent action on the part of the Anglicans of Rio, but agreed to raise the Foreign Office portion to £206.18s.2d., well short of the conventional 50%. He had no further objection to the £700 stipend, provided that the balance was raised locally. Robert was a little bloodied in the course of all this, partly because he had paid part of the allowance over to Maister before getting official approval, and partly for being late with the church accounts for 1835, though of course he had been seriously ill for several months at the start of 1836.

Peace then settled on the Anglican Chaplaincy for a little while, and allowed Mr. Maister to officiate at the marriage of Robert Hesketh and his bride Georgiana in 1837, and to baptise their first child later than year. But Mr. Maister decided to retire in 1839, and he was succeeded by the Rev. Thornton Champnes of the Diocese of Oxford. He too received £700 a year, paid half-yearly. Robert at this time was receiving £400, with a fairly modest amount of Fees. But until 1847, peace again reigned, only broken in that year by the Rev. Thornton Champnes taking extended leave of absence, and then resigning.

But while there were still plenty of letters about the Chaplaincy finding their way back to London, the air of conflict and vituperation had by now evaporated. The Rio residents were more accepting of their parsons, and their parsons seem to have been satisfied with their salaries, as well they might. Perhaps the new air of calm and order was due to the influence of Robert, who must have chaired a great number of tedious and confrontational meetings, particularly in his first few years in Rio. Doubtless his impartiality cooled many tempers. Robert must have often reflected on the contrasts of his job: dealing with shipwrecked and mutinous mariners, distressed British subjects, and the slave trade during the day, and sitting down in the evening to chair the sort of meeting any church group might have produced in any English village or town.

On only one occasion did Robert have to leave Rio in the course of his duties, and that was in 1837, when he was sent north to Bahia to investigate a dispute that had broken out between the Pro-Consul and the owners of the "Nimrod". Two local British merchants in Bahia had chartered the "Nimrod" to two prosperous freed slaves, Antonio da Costa and João Monteiro, who had made their money trading with Africa. Pro-Consul

Robilliard had not been in post long, and seems to have been continuing the charging regime of the previous Consul, Parkinson. Robilliard was suspicious that the "Nimrod" was involved in slave-dealing, and so he confiscated the Ship's Articles, which effectively detained her, for she could not sail without them. He also made the owners take out a Bond, with financial penalties if the terms of the Bond were broken. He charged the very considerable sum of $506 to cover his Consular Fees. The ship sailed, the Master having eventually given in to Robilliard, and accepted the Bond and paid the Fees. The ship sailed to Africa with its cargo of tobacco, delivering its passengers at various ports on the West African coast, and sold its cargo to one Francisco Felis da Souza, known as "Cha-Cha".

When the ship returned, the merchant charterers complained so greatly at Robilliard's conduct, that London sent Robert to investigate. When he arrived in Bahia – a journey taking a considerable time – Robert found tempers so hot that he was forced to interview Robilliard and the merchants separately, trying to tease out every detail of the charter and of the voyage. The involvement of "Cha-Cha" was suspicious, for he was a well-known slave-dealer in West Africa, and the charter price had also been suspiciously high.

But Robert concluded that the tobacco sale, even though it had been with a slave-dealer, had been perfectly proper, and that the ship had played no part in the slave trade. He also concluded that Robilliard had been quite wrong to impose the Bond, a device which had no legal force in Brazil, and that his action had been "unauthorised, improper, and useless." He also concluded that Robilliard had grossly overcharged for his Fees. Robert calculated that he would have been justified in charging $56 (about £8), and that he had therefore charged $450 (about £70) more than necessary. There was some suspicion that Robilliard was merely continuing the somewhat grasping policy of his predecessor, Parkinson, and there were also suspicions about the overcharging of another ship, the "Richard Watson". Robert concluded that Robilliard had "acted with undeniable Injustice and in a most culpable manner for the evident purpose of promoting his private interests". He therefore relieved him of his post, sent him packing back to his family in Rio, and appointed a successor.[328]

Robert was away from his new wife, Georgiana, for two months, returning to the news that she was pregnant with their first child. His report on the "Nimrod" was received with satisfaction in London, and Palmerston went out of his way to support him in a rebuking letter to Robilliard, and wrote to Robert giving "my entire approval of the manner in which you have conducted the difficult enquiry".[329]

Robert's expertise in the proprieties of voyages to Africa was obviously great. There is an interesting mention of him in an "Executive Document" printed by the United States Senate in 1847. In it, Henry Wise, the United States Consul in Rio de Janeiro, quotes Mr. Weetman, an American shipping broker operating out of Rio, as saying that he took great care to obtain the "counsel, opinion, and advice of Mr. Hesketh. the British Consul, who had given the opinion that the negotiation of charters of vessels for the coast of Africa was lawful, and there was no harm in it."[330] This sounds a little too simplistic, but Robert was certainly an expert on the conditions which needed to be met to avoid breaking the British laws which governed voyages to Africa. There is an implication in Wise's document that Mr. Hamilton, the British Envoy in Rio, was not possessed of the same expertise on the subject.

Robert's excursion to Bahia was not repeated, there being plenty of work to keep him busy in Rio. Two issues in particular occupied him – ships ablaze at sea, and the ongoing struggle over the Brazilian Government's inability or refusal to abolish the slave trade from Africa. The second was a continuing battle, which involved all the diplomatic and consular staff on a daily basis. The question of fire at sea, however, although it was not an everyday occurrence, put enormous stresses on the consular service when the survivors of such tragedies made their landfall in Rio.

22

FIRE DOWN BELOW

"… a melancholy catastrophe…" (Robert Hesketh)

The emigrant ship "Hibernia" left the dockside in Liverpool on 27 November, 1832, sailed down the Mersey and out into Liverpool Bay. She was a large ship by the standards of the time – 456 tons – had a crew of twenty-three officers and men, and was carrying two hundred and nine passengers: one hundred and twenty-five in steerage, seventy-four in the slightly superior second cabins, and ten in the poop cabin on deck. The "Hibernia" turned to port, with everybody on board aware that they were at the start of a very long voyage, for they were bound for Hobart Town, in what is now Tasmania, and then Sydney in New South Wales. But the "Hibernia" ran into a severe gale along the Welsh coast, sustaining some damage, and returned to Liverpool for urgent repairs. She left Liverpool again on 6 December.

The Master, William Brand, intended to follow one of the common routes of Australia-bound ships, making for the Cape of Good Hope. After re-provisioning there, he intended to sail across the Southern Ocean eastwards till he sighted the Australian coast near Augusta, and then along the Great Australian Bight past Adelaide and Melbourne to Hobart. Brand was intending to touch at St. Helena to replenish his water and food supplies, before heading further south.

In February, 1833, only a few months after Robert Hesketh had arrived in Rio to take up his new post, the convict ship "Lotus", also heading for Australia, sailed into Rio's Guanabara Bay. In addition to her convicts, she was carrying sixty-two extra passengers. They were survivors from the "Hibernia". A few days later, the British brig "Isabelle" also arrived in Rio, carrying a further seventeen survivors. There were to be no more. One hundred and fifty-three of the passengers and crew had perished.

Robert immediately arranged for the officers and crew to be distributed among the British ships in the harbour at Rio, and for the sixty-three surviving passengers to be given accommodation on shore. They were all shocked and exhausted, and had few clothes or possessions. Robert organised a collection of money and obtained clothes for them. He interviewed the survivors, including the exhausted Master and the First Mate, and was able finally to send back to the Foreign Office an account of what had happened to the "Hibernia" out in the lonely wastes of the Atlantic..

Though the voyage had not been speedy, everything had gone well until 5 February, 1833, when the "Hibernia" was almost equidistant from the northeast tip of Brazil and the West African coast, about as far from land as could be. The Second Mate, Samuel Geddes, was sent down with a boy to draw some rum from one of the barrels kept below. He had just finished pumping the rum into a bucket, when a candle was dropped into the barrel. There was an immediate flash of flames, which Geddes tried to extinguish. But he only succeeded in spreading the fire further about the storeroom, which was packed with many other barrels of rum, brandy, and pitch. Geddes was fearfully burned, but managed to stagger out to raise the alarm.

The Master, realising a major calamity was imminent, collected all the passengers and crew together, to pour as much water over the decks and into the storeroom as possible. But two hours later, soon after midday, it became obvious that the flames could not be quenched, and that the ship was doomed. The Master ordered all to the boats, but it was quickly realised that there was by no means room for all. Even after abandoning their heavy luggage, only seventy-nine people fitted into the boats: the other one hundred and fifty-three were abandoned. With its spars, yards, masts, and sails on fire, and tumbling in the swell, the ship quickly burnt down to the waterline. Robert Hesketh was later very critical of the condition of the ship's boats; he speaks of "a lamentable inefficiency of the Boats, not only to the extent of succour they were calculated to afford, but also their bad and unserviceable state". [331] He speaks sternly of "culpable negligence", though the Foreign Office records give no hint that anyone was ever punished for it. The survival figures from Robert also show that some ways of travelling on a sailing-ship were more dangerous than others: seven out of ten of the adult passengers in the poop cabin on the deck survived, but none of the seventy-four passengers who were in the below-deck cabins. These included sixty women and children. Even the steerage passengers had a better survival rate, with 45% surviving, although twenty-five women and children from steerage died.

The Captain, William Brand, and the First Mate stayed with the burning ship until the flames were coming through all the hatchways, and then threw themselves overboard. They were later picked up by one of the boats, the Master in a state "of great exhaustion". The boats were in such poor condition, and so crowded, that it was decided that trying to rescue others would only endanger those already in the boats. Some of the passengers had embarked on a raft, but it quickly disappeared and was not heard of again. It was decided that the Captain would take charge of the longboat, with fifty-three survivors; the Mate, Mr. Taylor, would take charge of the pinnace, with seventeen survivors; and the Boatswain, the gig, which was towed by the longboat. They had managed to save a few navigational instruments, and agreed to set course for Pernambuco to the west, rigging up some makeshift sails. They had limited food stocks, mostly consisting of damaged ship's biscuit, a quantity of uncooked pease soup, three live piglets, six bottles of porter, thirteen gallons of brandy, and very little water.

The next day, with the longboat leaking badly, there was some discussion between the Master and Mr. Taylor in the pinnace. The longboat, with its fifty-three survivors, was short of water, and the pinnace of food, but no agreement was reached to transfer provisions more equably between them, and the pinnace soon left the longboat far behind. Conditions on the longboat steadily deteriorated, and three days later, one of the passengers, Mr. Riley, died. Early the next day, one of the pigs was killed, and the survivors were enjoined to drink its blood and chew on the uncooked pork. Later that afternoon, a sail was sighted. As this ship shortened sail and approached them, it announced itself as the British male convict ship, "Lotus". Before long, the survivors, many of them very exhausted, were taken on board the "Lotus", which then made for Rio. The rescue came only just in time, for only half an hour later, the survivors on the "Lotus" saw the longboat sink below the waves. Not long afterwards, the pinnace was similarly rescued by the British brig "Isabelle".

With the passengers and crew on shore recovering from their ordeal, Robert arranged for the "Adelaide" to take the survivors on to their destination in Australia, and she arrived in Hobart on 20 May. Robert sent in the bill to the Foreign Office for the "Adelaide" and for the other assistance that had been necessary. It amounted to the very considerable sum of £1,463.16s.9d. He must have been gratified to hear that Palmerston immediately approved the payment and praised his conduct.

Robert would have known that there was some politics involved in this decision. The colonisation of Australia was immensely important to the British Government, and it was therefore anxious to show that it supported the large numbers of immigrants making their way to Australia, either voluntarily or as convicts. News of the sinking of the "Hibernia" soon reached Britain, and any suggestion that the survivors had not been looked after and assisted in their passage to their destination might have seriously discouraged further immigration, as well as reflecting badly on the Government. Palmerston's readiness to meet the costs of the rescue operation did,

The Burning of the Barque "India" in 1841

however, have an unfortunate consequence, for it created a precedent in Robert's mind. Next time, he would not get away so lightly with the expenditure of such a large sum.

Eight years later, history repeated itself. The barque "India", with Hugh Campbell as its Master, sailed from Greenock on the south bank of the Clyde on 5 June, 1841, bound for Port Philip in New South Wales. The ship, which had been built at McMillan's yard in Greenock, was only two years old, and had already survived one trip to Australia and back. Most of the passengers and crew were native-born Scots, part of the melancholy tide of emigration that exiled so many Scots in the eighteenth and nineteenth centuries. The "India" had a hundred and eighty-seven passengers on board, all but twelve of them "on bounty". The bounty scheme was a device to encourage immigration; under the scheme, the colonial government paid to the shipping agent a sum – which in this case averaged out at £16.3s.1d. – for every suitable immigrant landed in New South Wales. If the "India" had reached Australia, the ship's owners would have received about £2,826, which would have given them a sizeable profit from the voyage. The money, however, was never paid, for the "India" did not make it beyond the waters of the mid-Atlantic.[332]

The crew and passengers of the "India" had had a scare four weeks into the voyage. Just north of the Equator, they became aware of a fast-sailing brig with "snow-white sails" gradually overhauling them. When the stranger was level, a spokesman asked questions about the "India's" passengers and cargo. She then got ahead of the "India", returning on the other side of the ship, asking whether anyone could speak Spanish. She then sailed away without taking any further action, but the incident left many of the passengers very nervous, for there was little doubt that this ship, which was later identified as the "Gabriel", was a well-known pirate vessel. Shortly afterwards, indeed, the "Gabriel" had the bad luck to meet HMS "Acorn", a British Navy brig of 16 guns, which gave chase. Guns were fired from both vessels, but after a twelve-hour chase, the "Gabriel" was dismasted, captured, and taken to St. Helena. She had hoisted Portuguese colours as she engaged HMS "Acorn", but, as the "Gabriel's" Captain jumped overboard with all his papers, it was difficult to prove what country she came from. She did have, however, £8,000 of apparently pirated goods on board. [350]

The "India" sailed on, and a fortnight later, on 19 July, forty-four days out from the Clyde, the "India" was off the coast of Brazil, about half-way between Salvador and Rio, heading for Rio and further supplies. As with the "Hibernia", a crew-member – contemporary reports do not agree on whether it was the Second or Third Mate – went below to draw gin from a barrel in a storeroom. Again a candle was dropped, igniting some spilled rum, and the ship was soon ablaze. The fire spread so rapidly that no-one had the opportunity to gather any of their possessions. As the flames spread throughout the ship, setting fire to the rigging, the masts, the yards, and the sails, the passengers were driven forward, and began to jump off the bowsprit into the sea. Nine miles to windward, the French whaler "Roland", commanded by Olivier Lecozanet, watched with curiosity and then horror as the full scale of the disaster became apparent. The "Roland" quickly made her way towards the "India", and launched her boats. By this time, the "India" herself had launched her two boats, but there was such a rush to get into the first, that it capsized, with the result that many of the seventeen occupants were drowned. The First Mate quickly took command of the other boat, and successfully conveyed all the survivors – one hundred and seventy-seven of them – to the French boats, which then ferried them to the "Roland". Some of the survivors were wearing few if any clothes, for the fire had burned them off their backs. Indeed, several ladies arrived in Rio aboard the "Roland" wearing long shirts given to them by the French sailors. The Captain, Hugh Campbell, had been one of the first to be taken to the "Roland", for he was the only one of the crew and passengers to speak any French.

There are details in contemporary accounts of the deaths of two men – the Revd. William Mackay from Inverness, and the boatswain of the "India", Charles Clements. Mr.Mackay, who had been conducting religious services for the passengers on the voyage, spoke encouragingly to the rest of the passengers as the disaster was developing, but then, as one of the French boats approached, lost all semblance of self-control, and leapt into the water in order to reach it. Several other men did the same, but so many of them attempted to climb on board that the boat immediately capsized, with the result that Mr. Mackay and several others were drowned. Charles Clements' death was even more unfortunate. Although he had served a long apprenticeship in British warships, he could not swim, like many other British sailors of the time. Nevertheless, he jumped overboard and grabbed a line which was trailing in the water. He held the rope so tightly that every time the "India" rolled, he was pulled several feet clear of the water, and then plunged into the sea as the ship rolled back. Eventually, he was persuaded to leave go the rope, and struggled as far as the French boat, only to be drowned as it capsized.

It was, said Robert Hesketh, "a melancholy catastrophe", and he blamed the disaster on "considerable negligence of proper precautions in using candles while drawing spirits, and adding another to many lamentable instances of similar calamities from the same cause."

In spite of the "providential assistance" of the "Roland", seventeen passengers and one crew member died. All the casualties among the passengers were young men, and the disaster made four young women widows, and nine children fatherless. The survivors were crammed on the deck of the "Roland", for there was no room below, as they made their slow way towards the safety of Rio. Though the loss of life on the "India" had been much less than on the "Hibernia", a much larger number of refugees, one hundred and seventy-seven, was suddenly delivered on the doorstep of the British Consulate. Women and family survivors were landed first, on 24 July, and Robert swung into action, finding lodgings for them. The following day, the men landed from the "Roland", and further accommodation was found. Robert arranged for many of the survivors to be housed on a small island in the Bay. The crew of the "India" were placed on board HMS "Crescent", anchored in the Bay, and normally used for housing freed slaves. Robert organised a collection of garments, but found nevertheless that he had to purchase a fair quantity of clothes and bedding. One of the child survivors died in Rio, but another was born. The residents of Rio, particularly the foreign ones, rallied round to support the survivors, with £1,102.6s.10d. being collected from public subscriptions, and £292.10s.2d. from the crews of the British ships in the port. Bearing in mind that the average sailor might be earning only a few shillings a week, this was a generous sum. The French Legation and Consulate contributed £18.15s.0d., and the three United States warships in the Bay collected a splendid $700. The other foreign residents contributed the sum of £268.15s.0d., which was applied to the needs of the four women widowed by the tragedy.

It was decided that the captain and crew of the "Roland" ought to be rewarded for their humanity and courage, and the ship was presented with a brand-new gold chronometer, and 1100 francs (£40) was distributed among the French crew. A sum of money was also given to the mates and crew of the "India", but for whose efforts many more would have died. There were other expenses too – re-equipping the workmen with the tools of their trades, and providing the doctor with a new set of instruments to replace those he had lost in the disaster. The "Roland", having performed its act of mercy, continued on its whaling voyage to the South Seas.

Their immediate needs having been satisfied, Robert turned to the question of what was to happen to the survivors. Most were keen to continue to Australia, and so Robert searched for a ship capable of crossing the Atlantic and the Southern Ocean. He found one, the "Grindlay", a barque of 386 tons, owned by Walter Grindlay Junior. To check that it was properly equipped and provisioned, he sought the help of the Navy, and had the Master and the Purser of HMS "Southampton", which was stationed in Rio, survey the "Grindlay". Their report was positive, and on the 22 August, 1841, the ship sailed out of the Bay on its way to Port Philip. It now carried one hundred and sixty-six emigrants: three of the widows, with three children, had understandably decided to return home after the deaths of their husbands. Five passengers had absconded from the city. Robert appointed William Lilburne, one of the passengers who had been very active in supporting and organising his fellow-survivors, as superintendent, with powers over the distribution of provisions among the passengers. When the ship reached New South Wales, which it did on 22 October, 1841, Lilburne, together with the Master of the "Grindlay", was given authority to distribute the sum of £500 in grants to the passengers.

And so the Consulate returned to its usual activities, but, for Robert, the financial issues were only just beginning. To him, the "India" disaster was a re-run of the "Hibernia" tragedy in 1833, when his financial arrangements had been readily and rapidly approved by Palmerston, and he must have assumed that similar support from the Foreign Office would be forthcoming. Unfortunately for him, Palmerston had been recently replaced by the Earl of Aberdeen, who totted up Robert's bills, and decided that the total was quite unacceptable. Robert had been very careful to document every step and demand, and wrote a dozen letters to the Foreign Office from the beginning of August until his last letter on the subject on 9 September. He listed his actions, his purchases, and the charter of the "Grindlay", which cost £1,349, together with the food for the voyage, which cost £430. He listed the donations from the public and from fellow-seafarers, and wrote to the Governor of New South Wales, Sir George Gipps. Altogether, he spent £3,376.2s.9d., which amounted to a cost per head for relief and transport to Australia of about £20.

This total caused much consternation in London, and there was much to-ing and fro-ing of official letters between Government departments. The Foreign Office, the Lords Commissioners of the Treasury, and the Colonial Land and Emigration Board were all involved, and, for a time, it looked as if Robert Hesketh would be severely censured. Then the tide began to turn as the wider aspects of the disaster began to dawn. A Treasury Minute of 9 November, 1841 said rather cagily: "Although My Lords concur with Lord Aberdeen that Consul Hesketh's proceedings were irregular....., yet considering the very peculiar position in which Mr. Hesketh was placed by the landing of so large a number of destitute British Emigrants at Rio de Janeiro and adverting to the fact that a charge of £1,465.16s.9d. was sanctioned by the Treasury under similar circumstances in 1833, My Lords are not prepared to say that this course ... on the present occasion is deserving of official censure."[334]

Official opinion in London then turned to consider whether any of the money Robert had spent could be recovered, and two lawyers, T. Frederick Elliott and Edward E Villiers, were asked to explore whether the owners of the "India" could be approached to recompense the Government for its expenditure. In their reply of 10 January, 1842, they concluded that the answer was "No", as the ship had not been officially chartered, and as the owners did not receive the expected bounty on delivering the emigrants to Australia. They recommended that the Governor of New South Wales should be approached, and persuaded to transfer the putative bounty payment to British Government funds. They also considered, in an almost modern way, the implications for public opinion of perceived parsimony on the part of the Government. "Unless the public [coffers] had interfered, these poor people must have remained entirely destitute in a distant country, an event which could not have but acted most prejudicially on the prospects of public Emigration to Australia."[335]

And so, for reasons which had much to do with the Government's desire to be seen to support its emigration policy, Robert escaped censure. B.

Biggar, an Australian descendant of one of the emigrants on the "India", says: "Consul Hesketh, as evidenced by the despatches, was a kind and caring soul, and the immigrants owed him a huge debt of gratitude."[336] But Robert did not have long to reflect on his success in getting so many emigrants to their destination, for the battle against the Slave Trade was even then at its height.

23

RIO AND THE SLAVE TRADE

*"... a great moral evil ... from which England has at last been delivered.
But her work is not yet done." (H. Koster, 1815))*

Thomas Nelson was the Senior Assistant Surgeon on board HMS "Crescent" in the harbour at Rio de Janeiro. As well as a receiving-ship, she also acted as a prison for those awaiting trial on slaving charges, and occasionally acted as a hostel for shipwrecked crews. Anchored a few hundred yards off-shore, the top of her masts had been removed, and her deck partially covered by tarpaulins. Below the main deck, her dark recesses held cramped accommodation for slaves and prisoners. Thomas Nelson was based on the "Crescent" and it was his job to go on board the captured slavers as they arrived in the Bay, to remove the slaves, and to administer medical treatment to those who needed it.

The slaver "Dois de Fevereiro" was typical of its kind. The schooner had left Benguela on the Angolan coast with five hundred and ten slaves, but nearly 30% of them had died on the voyage across the Atlantic. When she was captured by the British Navy and brought into the harbour at Rio, only three hundred and sixty-two were still alive – two hundred and twenty-seven males, and one hundred and thirty-five females. Nelson described going on board:

> "The stench on board was nearly overwhelming. The odour of the Negroes themselves, rendered still stronger by their filthy and crowded condition, the sickening smell of the suppurative stage of small-pox, and the far more disgusting effluvia of dysenteric discharge, combined with the bilge-water, putrid jerked beef, and numerous other matters to form a stench, it required no little exertion of fortitude to withstand..... Huddled closely together on deck, and blocking up the gangways on either side, cowered, rather squatted, three hundred and sixty-two negroes, with disease, want, and misery stamped upon them with such painful intensity as utterly beggars powers of description. In one corner apart from the rest, a group of wretched beings lay stretched, many of them in the

last stage of exhaustion, an all covered with the pustules of small-pox... on every side squalid and sunken visages were rendered still more hideous by the swollen eyelids and puriform discharge of a virulent ophthalmia."[337]

At about the same time, the young Lieutenant Astley Cooper Key was in Rio on board HMS "Curaçoa". In his autobiography, written when he was an Admiral, he described a similar scene – it may even be the same scene:

"I went this morning (September 10th.) the first thing after breakfast, to see the Negroes taken off from the slaver and down to the "Crescent" (hulk), and in my life I never witnessed anything so shocking. About 400 were packed into that small vessel, as you would pack bales of goods, and disease of all sorts became rife among them. One hundred had died before she was taken, and they were, and are still (a week after) dying daily. Some were carried up the side in a state of emaciation such as I would not have imagined possible to exist with life; others with raw sores, their bones all but through them, and some some dreadful cases of small-pox, covered from head to foot. These were all sent back to the schooner, being contagious, none such being allowed in the "Crescent". Some children were in the last stage of emaciation and sores. It was dreadful; and so distressing, I could have cried. The patience, or rather the apathy, with which it was all borne, was astonishing."[338]

Nelson also describes going on board a schooner, the "Vencedora", with the Senior Medical Officer, Dr. William Gunn. The "Vencedora" was a vessel of only 70 tons, but had taken on four hundred and sixty slaves. Only three hundred and thirty-eight were left alive when she reached Rio. Some of the slaves were so sick that they had to be carried in the arms of British seamen up the ladder to the deck of HMS "Crescent".

Upon their arrival in the "Crescent", the slaves were fed immediately, and, says Cooper Key, soon recovered their spirits, those that were not ill being able to sing and dance the next day. Some of the women had infants with them, but there were also many children aged between five and nine who had no parents. "After these miserable creatures were brought on board, several women came, tolerably well-dressed, and fat and sleek – to my great astonishment, till I was told that these were the harem of the prize's crew...." The crew themselves, mostly Portuguese, and "ill-looking rascals", were taken to the prison on the "Crescent", and confined there by night, but allowed freedom on the ship by day.

As far as the slaves were concerned, there was an immediate problem: what to do with them. Illegally-landed slaves were normally taken to the Valongo slave-market in Rio, often quite openly. The American Thomas Ewbank describes an encounter with two hundred slaves: "We passed four boats laden with slaves, part of a cargo just landed east of Rio and now being smuggled – if the term can be used where next to no secresy [sic] is affected – down to Christoval, to the depot near the palace. Before morning they will be dispersed, and in a few days all [will be] at work. There were fifty in each boat, all young men."[339]

The slaves freed by the British Navy faced a different future. They could be returned to Africa, in the course of which they would have to face another long and uncomfortable voyage. This would normally only happen after the joint Brazilian-British Mixed Commission Court had met, to decide the fate of the ship that had brought them. In the meantime, they would have to spend long days in Rio harbour, either on their original transports, or in any ship the British could commandeer. It was at this time that they were at great risk of being kidnapped. In spite of the guards, and the efforts of the Brazilian police, it was not uncommon for gangs to board ships in the harbour, and make off with large numbers of slaves, who were quickly dispersed to new owners throughout the province. The task of guarding the slaves was a tiresome and dangerous one, and was largely left to the crews of British warships. The noble task of eliminating the slave trade came down, in the experience of the average British seaman or marine, to an unpleasant sentry duty, surrounded by foul smells and baked by the fierce sun.

Most of the slaves imported into Rio were quite young – with the majority aged no more than twenty-four. Two-thirds of them were children no older than fourteen or fifteen. The price of a slave in Rio varied greatly with the laws of supply and demand. In 1825, for instance, a newly-arrived and healthy slave might cost from 250–300 milreis (£30 – £40 sterling), but in 1830, when a shortage of slaves was anticipated, prices had risen to three times those figures, with a good slave costing the equivalent of £100. Slaves from some parts of Africa were prized above others – those north of the Equator were regarded as better workers than those from further south, and the Minas people in particular were highly prized for their cultural strength, their intelligence, and, sometimes, their literacy. Mozambicans from the east coast of Africa were also regarded highly.

The Brazilians would have argued that buying a slave was an uncertain investment. Disease was an ever-present threat to the well-being and even the existence of slaves. Many slaves brought diseases with them, either from their previous life in Africa or from the barracoons where they had been housed before being brought to Brazil, and other diseases could be easily contracted on the voyage itself. The result was that malaria, fever, small-pox, serious eye-diseases, and guinea-worm were very common. Nor was Rio itself free of contagion – there were quite serious outbreaks of yellow fever in the late 1840s and the early 1850s. Poor treatment of slaves often hastened their deaths, and the death rate of slaves in Rio was very high. If the sick slaves were lucky, they would be taken to the Misericordia – the hospital – but it was not uncommon to find the bodies of slaves left on waste ground in the city, or washed up on the shores of the bay. It has been suggested that in the 1840s an average of 2,800 slaves a year died in Rio.[340]

The Brazilians themselves were victims of slavery too. We have already noted the way in which having slaves freely available limited the role and the skills of the Brazilians. Thomas Nelson, for instance, talks of the "helpless" Brazilian – "at home, he is at the mercy of his slave for all his domestic comforts; abroad, his entire trust, whether for amusement of business ... depends upon the foreigner. Slavery seems to have sapped his self-dependence, emasculated his energies."

Certainly, the immediate impression of almost all contemporary witnesses who landed at Rio was of the carrying of burdens. Almost every slave had a burden of some kind to carry, often on his or her head, and the slaves provided a vast and complex distribution and transportation network, without which the port would have ground to a halt.

The Brazilians of the time liked to think of themselves as kind masters of slaves, and doubtless many were. There were many examples of slaves becoming a valuable part of the family. But there were also cases of cruelty or excessive punishment. We hear of a mistress who kept a wooden paddle to beat the palms of her erring female slaves. Thomas Ewbank described the metal contraptions for sale in Rio in 1856 The devices were made of iron, and usually involved the shackling of legs or wrists, sometimes both at once. Some slaves wore metal collars, which prevented them from bending their necks, and others, particularly those who had been caught after absconding, had logs chained to them. Ewbank suggests that his enquiries pointed to the lot of the country slave as being more severe than that of those in Rio, and tells the story of a member of the Slave Commission going to an *engenho*, a country estate, just in time to see a gathering of the neighbouring proprietors, who had come to witness the ultimate punishment – a slave being boiled alive. Exile was also used as a punishment, particularly to the northern province of Maranhão, where conditions and treatment were rumoured to be worse.

It was theoretically possible for slaves, if they had worked for fourteen years in Brazil, to be freed, and to acquire a certificate of freedom. Not all lasted as long as that, in spite of their youth. Some owners were unscrupulous, and did not bother to inform their slaves of their rights under this legislation. Successive acts of legislation supposedly made the lot of the slaves better. For instance, in 1831, a law was passed to make all slaves free who were imported after that date, but it was never implemented to any degree, and it was only in 1850 that the battle began to be won, and only in 1888 that total freedom was granted to the slaves of Brazil.

The continuing influx of slaves into Rio, from the seventeenth century onwards, meant that in 1803 the population of the city, which was about 47,000, was at least half made up of slaves or ex-slaves. Numbers of slaves grew as the century advanced, but the proportions remained much the same.

It is certainly true that the average Brazilian of this period could see no alternative to the importation of slaves, and therefore disregarded any moral argument against it. It was, says Alan Manchester, "an economic god"[341], buttressed by the belief that no white man could survive the kind of labour demanded of many slaves, particularly in the country. Some politicians openly spoke of their preference for European workers, but it was not until much later, after slavery had been finally abolished in Brazil, that sizeable numbers of Europeans settled in Brazil. There were always politicians who were uneasy about Brazil's reliance on African slaves. José Bonfacio, a major influence on Brazil in the first days of its independence, spoke of his dream of white immigration, and said: "I wanted to see no more of them [the slave-ships]". He also expressed the hope that the slave trade would be abolished "at the earliest possible period, consistent with the state of the country, and the prejudiced feelings and opinions of its inhabitants". That was the problem, and Bonfacio's political fate typical; he was forced out of office and out of the country, and his intentions never realised. The vast number of political changes in Brazil during the 1830s and 1840s meant that a consistent policy was neither agreed nor implemented. But the hope of abolition never entirely faded from some Brazilian politicians, although they did not have the influence or power to ensure a rapid cessation of slavery. The "Voz de Juventude", for instance, said "the extinction of slavery, and the colonisation of the country, are the buoys that mark out our progress in social improvement".[342]

The Brazilian Government's lack of will to take on popular belief and prejudice looked to the outsider to be morally reprehensible. Thomas Nelson, for instance, said slavery in Brazil was "the clashing of private interests with

A slave chain-gang in Rio's steep streets

public engagements [i.e. commitments]" Alan Manchester talks of "polite inertia", and the British envoy Henry Chamberlain spoke of "the system of doing nothing". Pennell, who preceded Robert Hesketh as Consul in Rio said that the Brazilians seemed "to regard the Treaties with England on the Slave Trade as the dictation of a superior authority, from which it is lawful to escape rather than as compacts, which they are bound to enforce." Some Brazilian politicians saw the abolition of slavery as an attack on all that they held dear. Barbacena, who introduced a new Bill in 1837, spoke of the damaging effects that the abolition of slavery would have: it would impoverish respectable farmers, who were "peaceful landowners, heads of respectable families, men full of industry and virtue, who promote private and public prosperity with their labour." It was easy to move from this position to another which saw the British as the enemies of all that was distinctively and proudly Brazilian. The British were regarded as self-seeking and antagonistic to the welfare of Brazilian society, and the 1840s saw them vilified and sometimes threatened or physically attacked. The Portuguese, on the other hand, from being the villains of the struggle for independence in 1822, came to be admired for their determination to continue the trade in slaves, for their creative use of the Portuguese flag, and for their boldness in taking on the British Navy. Leslie Bethell quotes the British Minister in Rio from 1846–7, James Hudson, as saying that Brazil "wants cheap labour...the African is the cheapest labourer ..... we have undertaken to prevent him getting that labour. Is it possible for two states to be beset by any question more completely by the ears?"

Certainly, the pressure on Brazil had started early. The 1810 Treaty, signed with the then Portuguese masters of Brazil, had included the requirement for the slave trade to be abolished, and Castlereagh, Secretary of State for Foreign Affairs until 1822, was consistent in his pressure for abolition: "It is high time that the Prince Regent of Portugal should seriously set about redeeming his Pledge for the abolition of this traffic in human blood."[343] His successor, George Canning, was equally determined to force abolition upon the Brazilians, and Palmerston regarded the abolition of slavery as one of the most consistent themes of his life. It was, of course, almost impossible for any British politician to espouse any other position, for the weight of public opinion was heavily in favour of abolition. By 1839, there were at least two major British societies in existence whose sole purpose was abolition – "The Society for the Extinction of the Slave Trade", and "The British and Foreign Anti-Slavery Society". Wilberforce played a large part in the British movement, of course, but suggestions that he fought a one-man campaign are wide of the mark. Almost the whole of educated society in Britain, led by the clergy as well as by politicians, and with a large women's abolition movement playing its part, was united on the issue. W. Gore Ouseley, who with Robert Hesketh had a great deal of personal experience of conditions in Rio, wrote a pamphlet on the subject after he had left Brazil, asserting of Great Britain: "The wish for it to be suppressed may be considered universal in this country."[344] The Foreign Office under Canning had not waited for public opinion to be galvanised, and had established a special department in 1824, under the leadership of James Bandinel, who wrote an important and influential pamphlet about slavery in 1842.

However, wishing something gone was not enough, and it was left to the personal pressure of men like Palmerston, and to the daily commitment of men like the consuls and the Navy to implement the policy. It depended too on the effectiveness of the Mixed Commission Court in Rio, which was supposed to bring the Brazilian and British Governments together in a common effort to abolish the Save Trade. Paulino Limpo do Abreu, the Judge of the Court, wrote a report to the Brazilian Legislative Assembly in 1837: "The Imperial Government, animated by a most sincere desire to extirpate this shameful contraband Trade (Slavery) has not only ordered inquiries to be made...., but has also continually forwarded the most precise Instructions to the Authorities of the Provinces to proceed against the delinquents, in conformity with the law of 7th. November, 1831." But he also admits that "the criminals met with sympathy and protection among a great proportion of the inhabitants, who consider the importance of Negroes to be advantageous to Agriculture."[345]

The men of the British Squadron in Brazilian waters knew this only too well, and paid for the policy with a great deal of personal danger and discomfort. Quite apart from the duty of caring for diseased and sick slaves, and of repelling attempts to kidnap them, it was not unknown for them to be set upon by thugs when they went ashore. Campaigns were conducted to make the lives of the Navy men uncomfortable, and there was scarcely anywhere on the Brazilian coast where the British were met with anything approaching civility. Their sincerity was doubted, and their motives impugned. And, apparently, the greater the British pressure, the greater the number of slaves traded. Doubtless defiance played its part. At the time of the greatest British naval activity in the 1840s, numbers of slaves landing in Brazil, and particularly in Rio, soared. Ouseley and Robert Hesketh concluded that the total abolition of slavery could not be achieved by force alone, although force was an essential element: "If we cannot entirely prevent the Slave Trade by means of the Squadron, we can, at least, check and diminish it." The institution of slavery itself needed to be removed, and only the Brazilians could do that through their legislative processes. Until they did, with the 1850 Law of Eusebio Queiroz, the matter would be "a festering sore" (Alan Manchester). Brazilian gratitude for British support against the French in Portugal in 1807 and then for Brazilian independence ebbed away the more the British conscience about slavery pricked, and the more its government demanded of its Navy.

Theoretically at least, Britain had allies in the matter. All the European nations, even Portugal, had agreed to the abolition of the slave trade after the Napoleonic Wars. The Pope was not backward in supporting the abolitionist cause, publishing a Bull on the matter in 1840. But not all, in the opinion of the British, were equally active in pursuing the logic of their beliefs. Thomas Nelson, fresh from his personal involvement with the freed African slaves on HMS "Crescent", boldly stated his belief: "While Great Britain has been thus laudably employed, and at an expence and temporary self-sacrifice which shows the sincerity of her repentance, other nations have been either sluggishly indifferent or obstinately purblind". There were even suggestions that some Portuguese representatives were assisting the slave trade – the Portuguese Consul in Pará was accused in 1840 of supporting some of his countrymen accused of slave-trading.

The French competed with the British for unpopularity in Brazil in the 1830s and 1840s. The causes were, however, largely political – because of French political activities in the River Plate, and because of their claims for Brazilian territory in the far north. They did not achieve their unpopularity as a result of chasing slavers, for that was not an activity the French Navy assisted with. The Americans sent a few ships to West African waters to join the blockade, but refused to allow the British Navy to stop and search any ship which raised the Amerocam Flag. The temptation for slavers to do so was therefore overwhelming. And in the years before the United States fought its own internal battle for the abolition of slavery, no conscientious objection prevented American ship-builders from using their very consider-able expertise to supply very fast ships for the slaver-dealers to buy. This gave the slave-captains a tremendous advantage over some of the rather less streamlined British ships the Lords of the Admiralty felt they could spare for the Brazilian and West African squadrons. Viscount Palmerston complained that "the number of vessels bearing the American flag ... has of late been so great, as to make it evident, that the slave traders now believe that to hoist American colours gives them the finest chance of escaping."[346] The gradual introduction of steam changed the nature of the struggle, though some of the early wooden-hulled paddle-steamers were not neces-sarily very efficient vessels. As the technology of screw vessels improved, the slavers were not slow to see the advantages, and the Brazilian steam vessel "Cacique" was able to convey nine hundred slaves across the Atlantic in one voyage.

There was sometimes a degree of tension between the Secretaries of State or Foreign Affairs and the Lords of the Admiralty over the importance the Navy attached to its duties in the suppression of slavery. Palmerston rather bitterly commented: "As to the description of vessels employed in the suppression of the Slave Trade; till lately they have been very bad. The Naval Lords of each successive Board of Admiralty have never cared a farthing about the suppression of the Slave Trade, & have considered the Slave Trade suppression service as a sort of penal duty & have sent to it all the old tubs that were fit in their opinion for nothing else."[347] Two of the "old tubs" were captured slavers that had been recycled for use in anti-slaving duties. The "Fawn", as it was renamed, was particularly useful, because of her shallow draught, which allowed her to sail into harbours and rivers denied to larger ships.

Nevertheless, the British Navy was very active, with ships continually coming into and out of the harbour at Rio. The perception of the Brazilians was certainly that the British were determined to interfere with the transport of slaves to Brazil, even though the reality was that the slaver-dealers still found many ways and means of landing slaves along the very extensive Brazilian coast. They had, of course, the advantage of local knowledge and of local support. Many of them became very rich as a result of their slave-dealing. They were, according to Nelson, "the nabobs of the Brazilians". Two of the most prominent were José Bernardino da Sá and Manoel Pinto da Fonseca. Both were very rich, and both were ennobled by the Brazilian state. Fonseca, who had a fleet of ships and a number of depots, appears in Thomas Ewbank's description of the architecture of Rio; "Fonseca, the great slave-trader, one of whose vessels got in a few days ago with a full cargo, by which he is said to have cleared nearly two hundred thousand dollars, has a splendid dwelling nearly finished in Rua Quitanda. The front is panelled, and colored light-blue, pink, and white. The spouts which shoot the water from the roof are gilt and burnished."[348]

There were other dealers too, most of them of Portuguese birth, who also flourished on the supposedly illegal trade. Robert Hesketh called them "pariahs", but they were regarded as heroes in Brazil for taking on the might of the British Navy. Until 1850, there seemed no will in Brazil to deal with their activities. Robert Conrad quotes Robert Hesketh writing in 1849 of the "travelling parties of newly arrived Africans [who] may be met every day in every road leading to the interior." Sailing-ships and steamships were also employed in ferrying the new slaves around the area. "In short, Rio de Janeiro and its vicinity is now one large slave market."[349]

Slave-dealing on such a vast scale involved many of Rio's citizens. More awkwardly for Britain's diplomats and consuls, it almost certainly involved some of the city's British merchants. Henry Wise, American Minister from 1844–1847, is quoted by Robert Conrad asserting perhaps a little too self-righteously, that "the largest interest in the world, next to those of Brazilian subjects, now favoring the Slave Trade, are those of a certain class of British manufacturers, merchants, and capitalists."[350] The vast range of supplies needed by any sea-going ship, whether food, drink, chandlery, ironmongery, cabling, clothing, sailcloth, anchors, or whatever, had to be supplied by someone in the port of Rio. Even as early as 1808, there were between one hundred and fifty and two hundred British merchants in Rio, and the number continued to grow steadily over the next fifty years. A majority of the goods imported into Rio came from Britain, and so it was hardly surprising that some of these supplies found their way into the hands of slave-dealers. Presumably the merchants knew very well which ship-owners and which ships were likely to be used for slave-trading, but there must have been a very considerable grey area, especially where men like Fonseca were concerned, who had interests in legitimate imports and exports, as well as in slave-trading. Doubtless some British merchants took their Government's position on slave-trading very seriously, and designed their trading activities to avoid any imputation that they were supporting it, but it is not hard to imagine that others were less fastidious, believing money was money, whatever its source.

We have already met the problem in Bahia, in Robert Hesketh's investigation into Consul Robilliard's conduct in relation to the "Nimrod". That enquiry involved a very detailed study of the terms of charter, the purpose of the voyage, and the nature and final destination of the cargo. It was possible to take action against British merchants if the evidence of involvement in the Slave Trade was clear and obvious, but most transactions would have been more opaque. The ease with which mercantile business could become involved with illegal activity was surely further reason for the Consul to hold himself aloof from trading activities of his own. William Hesketh, Robert's brother, who had often undertaken consular responsibilities in Maranhão, wrote in 1832 in defence of his assertion that he had been underpaid: "The superintendance [sic] of the Slave Trade is itself a duty peculiarly obnoxious to the Merchants whose interests are so intensely connected with it, and subjects also the Consul to the ill-will and to the violent passions of the Brazilians engaged in it."[351]

Thomas Nelson suggested that "scarcely an individual exists, who, either directly or indirectly, is not personally interested in the support of the slave system, and who would not look with the utmost distrust upon any change in it which may be proposed.". A particular case concerned a Dr. William Cullen, a Scotsman, who complained in 1835 to the Foreign Office about the behaviour of Robert Hesketh and the Envoy, H.S. Fox. Cullen's two slaves had been kidnapped, and he himself had been attacked by two "catchpoles" [bailiffs]. Robert refused to take any action to recover the two slaves, who had, of course, been illegally purchased by Cullen. Robert told Cullen that he should obey the laws of the country, and not acquire slaves.[352] Palmerston was strong in his support of his officials, but there were doubtless many British residents who continued to purchase African slaves.

The British Mission in Rio, however, could not be accused of a lack of commitment to the cause of the abolition of slavery. Led by Palmerston at home, every British Envoy in Rio during the 1830s and 1840s espoused the cause of abolition. But it was the consuls, with their daily contacts with the British Navy and with the slaves the Navy had liberated, who bore the brunt of the daily struggle. Again, they were "Martha" to the "Mary" of the diplomatic service, providing the practical implementation of the high-minded aims of the diplomats. Nevertheless, there seems never to have been any disagreement between representatives of the two parts of the Foreign Service based in Rio about either aims or tactics. The Navy grumbled, but its officers and seamen were not found wanting in the long campaign to deter the transport of slaves across the Atlantic. It was perhaps one of the nobler if not the happier moments in the history of Great Britain.

24

CONSULS, SEAMEN,
AND SLAVES

"...anxious that slavery may be abolished universally ... all parties will agree that great difficulties attach to its accomplishment" (Smithers, 1825)[353]

In 1835 down on the River Plate, a slave-ship was captured and brought into port with five hundred Africans on board. The ship was flying the Buenos Ayres flag. The Admiral in charge of the British squadron in the area was anxious to be off to the Falkland Islands, and sailed from the River Plate without leaving even a small company of marines to guard the prize. Sickness broke out on the captured slaver, which was in any case in poor condition, and so the Brazilian Government, then in charge of the north bank of the River Plate, allowed the slaves to be landed. Only eight men from a small Brazilian Brig of War, and provided with only two or three muskets between them, were available to guard the slaves. It was not long before a gang of thirty or forty men attacked the small guard-party, overpowered them, and spirited away two hundred of the strongest black slaves.[354] This event set the pattern for many attempts to do the same in Rio.

The issues in the port of Rio could often be very complex. In 1837, the Portuguese "Especulador" , whose Master was José Alves de Abri Guima-rães − arrived from Liverpool with a cargo which its manifest declared was bound for Brazil. According to Robert Hesketh, the cargo was actually intended for Africa, where, in accordance with long-held practice, its cargo would be sold to pay for slaves, who would then be brought across the Atlantic, on the "middle passage" to Brazil. The owner of the ship seems to have made a tactical error out of greed, for he maintained to the Brazilian authorities that the ship was only touching at Rio, and was actually bound for Africa, and should not therefore pay any duty. The Brazilian Custom-House authority was at first adamant that the cargo was to be sold in Rio, and full duty would therefore need to be paid. If the cargo had indeed been unloaded in Rio and full duty paid, there would, of course, have been no capital to finance the return trip with slaves. The "Especulador" was detained for some time, and only allowed to sail provided that she went south to Montevideo, and took out a bond to guarantee that the cargo would only be unloaded there. So, on this occasion, Brazilian bureaucracy frustrated a slave-trading expedition.

By 1838, public opinion cared little about the legal niceties of the Custom-House, and was mobilizing itself to resist the pressure which British diplomats, consuls, and naval personnel were exerting on Brazil. 1838 saw an increase in diplomatic activity in Rio, largely as the result of the personal involvement of W.G. Ouseley, the Chargé d'Affaires who had been left in charge during the extended furlough of Hamilton Hamilton. Ouseley's pamphlet on the Slave Trade, published later in London, was well-informed and sensible. Early in the year, the media attacks on the British began: the "Jornal dos Debatos" referred to the British as "Mylords", and accused them of acting high-handedly towards Brazil.[355] There were, however, at the same time international moves against the slave trade: arrangements with the Dutch were now in place, affecting their possessions in South America, and an Anglo-Brazilian Mixed Commission was sitting in Sierra Leone. The British were, however, not convinced that all Brazilians were as committed to abolish the slave trade as they were. Joaquim Feliciano Gomes arrived in Sierra Leone in February, 1838, having been appointed to act as a Brazilian judge in the Mixed Commission Court. He very soon aroused the suspicions of the British officers of the court by mixing with known slave-dealers and slave-shippers. He did not last long in Sierra Leone, and left on the "Lord Wellington", to go, curiously enough, to England.

The second part of 1838 saw a great deal of naval activity. The schooner "Brilhante", under Portuguese colours, was captured. When she was boarded, it was discovered that the crew had confined the slaves so closely in a small space that a considerable number had to be sent immediately to the hospital, where six died. Those slaves left on board the "Brilhante" were the target of nightly attempts to steal them, and the British Commander, Commodore Sulivan, wrote to complain of the time the Rio Mixed Commission was taking to consider the case. The Brazilians had said they were unable to provide a ship which might be used for the purpose of housing the Africans while their fate was decided, and so Sulivan suggested that Great Britain ought to provide one. The Foreign Office quickly agreed, but it took time to identify HMS "Crescent" and have her sent to South America. Her eventual arrival certainly eased the situation, but did not resolve it.

Other ships, all under the Portuguese flag, were known to have landed large numbers of slaves on the nearby coast – over seven hundred from Angola, and another ship, the "Jupiter", had lost fifty of its slaves when two canoes which were landing them had capsized. Certain ships became notorious for their slaving activities: the "Flor de Loanda", whose name appears frequently in the records, was reported to the Mixed Commission in Sierra Leone, but escaped capture because of the time it took to send evidence back to England, and then back again to West Africa.[356] On another occasion, the "Flor de Loanda" was reported as lost between Rio and Cape Frio, with the loss of its crew and its cargo of slaves. However, reports of her sinking seemed to have been premature, and she was later captured by HMS "Rover", and brought into Rio. Consul Moon in Maranhão reported considerable slaving activity there, too: the schooner "Tres Amigos" had been re-rigged as a brig, and had been fitted out to carry slaves. The schooner "Amalia", often mentioned in reports from the consuls in the northern ports of Brazil, had left for the Cape Verde Islands off the coast of Africa on 12 May, undoubtedly to carry out a slaving voyage.[357]

1839 saw a redoubling of effort – by the British Navy to capture slave-ships, and by the Brazilian pro-slaving party to cause as much difficulty for the British as possible. The Foreign Office was aware of this, and issued instructions to its consuls in March, 1830, that a list of suspicious vessels should be collected, and returned to London. On the same day, consuls were reminded that African slaves found on board detained vessels should be sent to the nearest British port, and put under the care of the Governor.[358] This policy, meant to ensure the safety and freedom of the slaves, was, of course, fraught with difficulty. When ships were captured near the Brazilian coast, and brought into Brazilian ports for judgement, it meant a long wait for the slaves in extremely unpleasant conditions, the risk of kidnap, and a long and equally unpleasant voyage back to West Africa, or at least to the West Indies.

In Rio, enmity was growing in proportion to the success of British policy and of the British Navy. In April, 1839, there were six captured slavers in the harbour: "Diligente", "Feliz", Especulador", "Carolina", "Ganges", and "Leal". This meant a great number of Africans were also in the port on board these ships, and the Mixed Commission Court was at its busiest. After Robert Hesketh had taken over as Proctor to the Mixed Commission, following the resignation of Mr. Shearman, he wrote to James Bandinell, who led the special Slave Trade Department at the Foreign Office, listing the problems the British Navy and the British Consulate had in Rio. Some of the problems, he said, were caused by Brazilian attitudes: Brazilian hearts were not always in the cause of abolition, and the Brazilian authorities were loath to provide a proper guard for prisoners going to the Court. Consequently, the general duty of looking after the crews taken into custody was left, "very unjustly and inconveniently", to the British seamen. When the prisoners eventually reached the Court, they found its Brazilian members in a "sour temper". The sick, said Robert, were not being properly cared for on the hulks anchored in the harbour, and there was a lack of regular provisions. The slave-dealers themselves were, said Robert, "unprincipled villains", and the duties of the consulate and the Navy personnel were "uphill and disgusting work".[359]

Robert described one incident which happened towards the end of April, 1839. A prisoner from "Ganges" had escaped by jumping overboard from a boat belonging to HMS "Stag", one of the British men-of-war in the harbour. He was recaptured, but again jumped overboard, this time swimming to the shore, where he jumped into a waiting carriage, and made his escape. Later, when a large group tried to free some of the prisoners, even the Brazilians were forced to take action, deploying a troop of cavalry. This, at least, said Robert, was a "gleam of hope".

At the end of May, Robert wrote to Palmerston, again listing the difficulties that were having to be faced every day on the waterfront.[360] There were still problems in feeding the Africans, but even when sufficient food – beef, flour, vegetables – was available, it was different in nature from what the Africans were used to. The consequence was that many became ill. However, the treatment of those Africans who were sick had improved with the deployment of HMS "Crescent" after 1840, and with the use of use of more medical personnel; as a result, "many evils have been remedied". The two largest problems were, however, the time taken to deal with the ships in the Mixed Commission Court, and the consequent difficulties for the Africans and for the Navy. He says that the average time before judgement was made was fifty-eight days. This was caused by numerous difficulties within the Court itself – lack of a permanent interpreter, and a shortage of Court Messengers and of Constables. The Registrar, whose job was very demanding, was so poorly paid that he had to work for the Court part-time, supplementing his income with another post in the Brazilian Board of Trade. Once the ships had been condemned and seized, the process was inefficient, and Robert suggested a professional auctioneer ought to be employed to dispose of them. Even after the Court had adjudicated, there were long delays before the Africans were freed, with the slaves on the "Brilhante" having to endure a total of a hundred and nine days before they were freed from their small and foul-smelling ship. Robert wrote:

> "Under any circumstances, to retain on board a vessel a number of human Beings, in a crowded state, afflicted with various deseases [sic] and many of an infectious nature is an inhuman proceeding …..Men,

women, children, some sinking under desease, and others disgusting from their savage apathy, and their brutal ferocity when fed, and all unconsciously inflicting pain, trouble, and anxiety." The death-rate of Africans on four captured slave-ships during the period in which the Court was deciding on their fate was 16%.

There were complex problems too with the crews of the slave-ships. It was necessary to keep those crew members who had already given evidence away from those yet to give evidence, and so two sets of prison accommodation had to be provided and staffed. Robert pays tribute to the efficiency and behaviour of the Brazilian Police guards, who were constantly being offered bribes, but who steadfastly refused to waver from the path of duty. But even they could not prevent prisoners who were taken to hospital from escaping. But the main burden fell upon the members of Her Britannic Majesty's Navy: "... the great inconvenience of living under an awning, exposed to a tropical Atmosphere day and night, and under the constant responsibility of keeping a proper watch to guard against increasing attempts to abstract the negroes – when all this annoyance, privation, and anxiety is understood, then the extent of suffering to which any of Her Majesty's Naval Officers in charge of a Slave Vessel is exposed will be acknowledged." Nor was their suffering appreciated on shore, where they were regarded as "hostile strangers and intruders".

One of the regular irritants to the British in Rio was the behaviour of the steamship "Especuladora". First of all she had run down a boat belonging to HMS "Arrow", and, instead of going to the assistance of the sailors, the crew had shouted insults at them. One sailor was seriously hurt in the incident. The same month, she had carried away the jib boom of HM Packet "Spider". Now, six months later, as she came into the harbour, she ran, deliberately it would seem, stem-on into one of the captured slavers, the "Ganges". The incident would have been annoying rather than serious, had not a British marine on sentry duty on the "Ganges" discharged his musket during the confusion, and killed Senhor Bulhões, a passenger on the "Especuladora". The incident, though no evidence was ever produced to suggest it was anything other than accidental, produced many months of ill-feeling between the Brazilians and the British, the Brazilian Government demanding the punishment of the marine concerned. The death of Senhor Bulhôes gave the local pro-slaving party an excellent cause to pursue, and it was 1841 before the Brazilian Government finally decided to drop the case.

Commodore Sulivan's squadron in Brazilian waters was, indeed, under pressure. There were, at this time, rebellions breaking out in various parts of

Brazil – in Rio Grande and St. Catherine to the south of Rio, and in Maranhão in the north. British merchants in those places were asking for the protection of the British Navy, but Sulivan had very few spare ships available. His flagship, HMS "Stag", was in Rio, but HMS "Grecian" was in Montevideo, and HMS "Wizard" was on her way back to Great Britain. HMS "Orestes" and HMS "Fawn", the converted slaver, were "cruizing" against slave-ships. Only HMS "Chameleon" was available. Unfortunately, she was only small and "a remarkably bad sailer", and next to useless for chasing slavers..[361] When William Wilson, the Heskeths' old partner in Maranhão, and now Acting British Consul there, asked for help, he was advised to charter a fast-sailing American schooner, and send for help to the British Squadron in the West Indies.

British ships were not, therefore, readily available, but in other ways the British Foreign Office was supportive. Palmerston sent parliamentary papers to his consuls in Brazil – "These Papers afford an additional Proof of the increasing and earnest Desire of the Parliament & Government of this Country for the total Extinction of the Traffic in Slaves."[362] Robert Hesketh was praised for his readiness to take on the duties of the Proctor of the Mixed Commission Court. In the north, the new Consul in Pará, who had suggested a Mixed Commission Court in either Pará or Maranhão to deal with slave-dealing there, received a thoughtful response from Palmerston.[363] The British Government, aware that many of the captured slave-ships flew the Portuguese flag, and were often owned by Portuguese-born Brazilian citizens, had recently approved the stopping and searching of any vessel flying Portuguese colours. The Portuguese Minster of Foreign Affairs protested against this as "unprovoked, oppressive, and unjust ….. a flagrant violation of the Law of Nations, and a direct attack upon the rights of an independent state", but it would have taken more than this for Palmerston to have lessened his support for the abolition of the transatlantic trade in slaves.[364] His determination to deal with the Portuguese was strengthened by the case of the "Recuperade", a slave-ship which had made illegal use of the Portuguese flag in its attempt to escape the attentions of the British Squadron.[365]

1839 ended with another letter from Palmerston voicing his support for the stand which the British Mission in Rio had taken against the slave trade.

There were fewer incidents reported in 1840, but Ouseley complained again in February of the slender representation of British ships at Rio; the more successful the naval "cruizers" were, the more slaves there were to look after, and the more prisoners there were to bring before the Court. British manpower was not up to the task. Ouseley's other complaint at this time, that he did not have enough money to entertain official guests, was found easier to deal with, and Palmerston gave him a further £150 to cover his house rent.

In October, 1840, a gang attacked the headquarters of the Brazil Steam Packet Company at Praia Saude to the north of the city centre. The gang, claiming to be fishermen, was armed with "bludgeons and daggers", and stabbed a British citizen, one John Williams, to death. The Foreign Office records show that eleven years earlier, in 1829, a John Williams, a native of Plymstock near Plymouth, and formerly of HMS "Isobel", was reported as claiming wages due to him for two years' service in the Brazilian Navy. Presumably his claim was successful, and it may be the same man who met his end so violently.[366] Robert Hesketh reported to Ouseley that the man who stabbed Williams was a mulatto, one Chiquino dos Copes, though he does not mention whether legal action was taken against the alleged assassin.

The year ended with an update from Cowper in Pará.[367] Cowper had written several letters about slave-landings on the north coast, and in the tributaries of the Amazon. In particular, the "Amalia" was again accused of landing large numbers of slaves from Africa. A letter from Cowper in January, 1840, mentions a voyage of the "Amalia", in which two hundred and fifty slaves had been landed, with a further hundred dying on the passage. He had also protested to the Governor of Pará about the "Emulação", which had brought some slaves from Maranhão, claiming them to have been long-established in Brazil. Cowper pointed out to the Governor that they were in all likelihood new, for they could not speak a word of Portuguese. But in November, 1840, Cowper was able to point to a success – the pressure brought to bear on the slave trade had caused a change of heart in one of the Pará merchants. Senhor Machado,who had been heavily involved in the importation of slaves to Pará, had ordered his ship, the "Augusto", to abort a trip to Africa, and to return to Liverpool instead, from which it had recently arrived with a full cargo of goods to be sold in Brazil. Cowper was optimistic that this betokened a change in Brazilian practice and ethics.

The slave trade looked no nearer to its abolition in 1841, however. When the British Navy was accused of ignoring Rio's Port Regulations in early August, a vituperative article entitled "The English again" in the local periodical "O Brasil" showed the depth of ill-feeling towards "these Islanders ...these poisoning pirates, who cover the world with their Depre-dations and Infamies". "Let us determine for once to show the English Government that we confide in our resources and that it is in more need of us, to consume its products and to give work and bread to its famished poor, than we are of it and its industry." It then goes on, rather surprisingly: "Belgium, Germany are our natural allies, are the consumers of our produce. England is, under the Title of our Friend and Ally, our Insolent Oppressor... Hatred therefore to Insolence & Oppression, whatever may be its consequences!"[368] The Belgian Charge d'Affaires, M. de Jaegher, did not share the hostility to the British, for at about the same time, he asked for a passage to Cayenne in the British Navy steamer HMS "Ardent".

At almost exactly the same time, the "India" was destroyed by fire, and Robert Hesketh and his staff had to concern themselves with the survivors, and with the other distressed British subjects who always seemed to be appearing in Rio. He was busy too with plans for a new organ and gallery in the British Chapel, as well as continuing the processing of slave-ships brought in by the British anti-slave trade squadron operating out of Rio. At home, his family was growing rapidly. We hear nothing of personal antipathy to Robert Hesketh in Rio, but the tensions caused by Britain's stance on the slave trade, and by Brazilian intransigence over the matter, must have made life tense and even dangerous at times. The Brazilian Government's refusal to countenance a new Treaty in 1842 put the enmity on an official footing, and it was not long before there was an outbreak of hostility to the crews of British Navy ships at various points along the coast.

In 1843, some of the crew of the paddle-steamer HMS "Growler" were returning to their ship after a night out in Pernambuco, when they were confronted by a drunken soldier. Under the instruction of the most senior officer present, Lieutenant Blakey, Sergeant Burns of the Marines disarmed him, but they were then all attacked by a gang of about twenty men. The Lieutenant was assaulted, Sergeant Burns cut about the face, three of the sailors received bayonet wounds, and another had his collar-bone broken. They were thrown into prison, and only released after a fortnight. HMS "Growler"'s Captain received death threats, and even the Consul (Cowper had moved from Pará to Pernambuco by this time) was pelted with stones. This was apparently because HMS "Growler" was rumoured to have captured a slaver. The following year, at Santos, on the coast below São Paulo, where various boats were fitting out for the slave-trade, the Commander, Acting Captain, and Steward of HMS "Frolic" went ashore to see the British Vice-Consul and the American Consul. On their way back to their ship, they were set upon, severely beaten, and left for dead. Commander Willis was particularly badly injured, sustaining a broken arm and a cracked skull.[369] Elsewhere, HMS "Dolphin's" gig went ashore to collect provisions, only to have the crew arrested, and the boat confiscated by the local police, on the

grounds that the men might be deserters. They were released at the insistence of "Dolphin's" Captain, Captain Hoare, but he was quite convinced
that this was a result of anti-British feeling about the slave trade.[370]

By 1845, Brazilian slave-ships were still being arrested, and most of them
brought into Rio. By the end of the decade, the number of captures was
beginning to decline – there were, for instance, only nine ships seized
between October 1849 and May, 1852 – and the "Queiroz Law" of 1850
finally convinced the Brazilian people as a whole that the Brazilian Government meant business. Between 1852 and 1856, there were only two recorded
landings of slaves in Brazil. Slavery continued to exist in Brazil for another
forty years, but the transporting of slaves across the Atlantic had finally
come to an end. Historians argue about whether the British pressure against
the slave trade was effective, or whether it encouraged the Brazilians obstinately to prolong the transatlantic trade. Certainly, the slave-merchants
acquired heroic status in Brazil, particularly along the coast, and this
encouraged them to redouble their efforts and their profits. Not all Brazilians were in favour of the slave trade, however, and it was only a matter of
time before the combined forces of the economy and the law brought the
slave-trade to an end. The large numbers of African slaves brought into
Brazil during the thirties and forties did much to lower their price, and
make it less profitable, and, although the British pressure and British presence was highly unpopular in Brazil, the nation could not hold out against
the force of international opinion for ever.

It is possible now to see the slave-trading activity of the 1830s and 1840s
as the last frenzied flush of a dying trade, taking advantage of the economic
benefits while they lasted, and stimulated by defiance of the old ally, Great
Britain. Thomas Nelson expressed the frustration of the British Navy and of
the British Mission in Rio: "It is a matter of deep annoyance to think that ,
from the first moment humanity raised her voice against the revolting
traffic, it has continued steadily on the increase."[371]

Smithers' perception that the abolition of slavery would not be easy of
accomplishment, and would therefore take some considerable time and
effort to achieve, was very accurate. The apparent burgeoning of the traffic
before it came to an end must have been depressing to the British Mission in
Rio, but Robert must have gone into his retirement more cheerfully knowing
that the long and difficult battle was at an end.

Robert Hesketh's residence in Rio de Janeiro, from 1832 to 1852, neatly
covered the period of greatest conflict with the Brazilians over the abolition
of slavery. The strong stance taken by the British Government meant that
there was no room for doubt or ambiguity in British official responses, and

Rio's position as the home harbor of the British anti-slaving squadron in Brazilian waters meant that a very great deal of the time of Robert Hesketh and his staff must have been spent down on the waterfront. Though he never complains about it, his daily life must have been largely taken over by the problems created either directly or indirectly by slaving. It was true that the various Envoys, with their political roles, were supportive, making strong representations to the Brazilian Government about the trade. Judging from the official records, there were isolated incidents in the 1830s after the 1831 Law had been enacted, but the tension only began to rise as the decade ended, and the antagonism of the average Brazilian towards the British cannot have made his daily life comfortable. Alan Manchester speaks of Great Britain taking "zeal to reprehensible lengths", but it is difficult to imagine how half-measures may have helped. Both British consuls and diplomats remained utterly steadfast in the face of both official ambiguity and popular enmity, and Robert and his young family will have known the daily cost of opposing the slave trade. Back in Great Britain, the abolition of slavery seemed an obvious course for all decent men and women to embrace; in Brazil, the representatives of the British Government had to defend this most unpopular of causes in a very hostile environment.

Amidst all the contemporary discussion of the evils of transatlantic slave trade, and the responsibility of Britain and other European nations for its development, it is worth remembering that its consuls and its naval personnel were the men who put their own lives and comfort on the line in abolishing it. Their commitment to the cause of abolition was unquestioning. It is one thing to discuss the ethics of the slave-trade from the safe distance of a century and a half; it was another to have to deal in Rio from day to day with the sick slaves, the disease, the foul smells, the corrupt crews, and the local thugs. They, as well as the speechmakers and the politicians back home, were the heroes of the abolition of slavery.

SECTION V

AFTERWARDS

The Hesketh Family Bible

25

AFTERWARDS

Robert Hesketh finally returned to England in 1852, to rejoin Georgiana, his wife, in Hampshire. Soon after his return, they moved, with their family, into Pear Tree House across the River Itchen from Southampton, on the high land overlooking the city. Pear Tree House, which is now a rehabilitation centre, is an old and rather fanciful structure, with castellated walls and an elaborate verandah. It is close to Jesus Green, which is an open common with the Jesus Chapel of St. Mary Extra at its centre. Robert became friends with the incumbent of St. Mary Extra, the Rev. Thomas Lewis Owen Davies. In 1857, they named their new son Harold Owen, and in 1861 Robert made him an executor in a codicil to his Will. Robert and Georgiana lived at Pear Tree House for several years, accompanied by an increasing number of children.

In spite of settling in his retirement on the south coast, Robert kept up his links with Liverpool. His Will was drafted and signed there in 1860, and was witnessed by two Liverpool solicitors. A few years earlier, his sister, Mary Ann, who had cared for Henry, Thomas, and James, three of the orphaned sons of John Hesketh, was in her early sixties and suffering from failing health. She had lived in Mount Pleasant in Liverpool for several years after her elder sister Louisa's death in 1845, but then moved to a house in Grove Street nearby before 1851. James, her youngest nephew, had died in 1848 at the age of eleven, and Henry, the oldest of the three boys, married and emigrated to California in 1854. The remaining nephew, Thomas, was unmarried, but was now largely independent, though in poor health. Mary Ann judged the time ripe to give up her own independence, and moved down to Southampton to join her brother, Robert and his family at Pear Tree House. She did not last long, however, and died in 1856. She is buried in the churchyard at St. Mary Extra, under a simple gravestone which has survived the years well.

Robert and Georgiana were still living at Pear Tree House at the time of the 1861 Census, but some time shortly after that, they moved into South-ampton itself, and lived in Carlton Crescent until Robert's death in 1868. The house, which still exists, was a large and substantial city house in a most respectable part of the city.

After 1856, Robert was the only survivor of the children of John Hesketh of Oporto and his wife, Louisa Ann Beete. Harriet, born in 1797, had been the first to die, at the age of thirty-five. She was buried on 15 August, 1833, at Our Lady and St. Nicholas Church, on the Liverpool waterfront, only yards from where her grandfather had had his wine vaults, and where her brother John had had his "counting-house". Thomas, the youngest brother, who had run the Liverpool end of the Brazilian business, had retired from business by 1839, even though he was still only forty years old, and died of consumption [tuberculosis] in August the following year. He too was buried at St. Nicholas. At the start of 1845, Robert's twin sister, Louisa, who had been head of the household in the two Mount Pleasant houses, became ill with the same disease and died nine months later. Her burial service at St. Nicholas was taken by the Rector rather than by the curate, like her father's thirty years before. She and her sisters had never married.

Robert's two other brothers, William and Henry, died, like Mary Ann, in 1856, both of them far from home. William died, as we have noted, in Sâo Luis, Maranhâo, to whose commerce he had devoted his working life. Henry died in Sacramento, California, where he had set up a business. We know no more of the circumstances, for registration records in the newly-acquired state of California no longer exist, probably destroyed in the disastrous earthquake and fire in San Francisco in 1905.

Robert's involvement in his nephews' dispute with Archibald Campbell in Pará occupied some of his time in the mid-1850s. He seems to have been successful in restoring their father's assets to them. Otherwise, Robert seems to have given himself up to his wife and still-growing family. By 1852, when he retired from Brazil, his eldest son, Robert Raynsford Hesketh, was fifteen years old, and his other children ranged from thirteen down to four. Sadly, the youngest, Hanbury Bold, died in May, 1852, two months before his fourth birthday. Once Robert was home, he and Georgiana continued to have children. There were twins in 1853: Spenser Bold and his sister Mary Sophie, born an hour and three-quarters after her brother. Harriett Lucy was born the following year, Ernest Johnston (Robert called him "Earnest" in the family Bible) in 1856, and Harold Owen in 1857. He and Georgiana had had thirteen children in all.

Robert himself died on 24 May, 1868. His address at his death was given as 30 Weymouth Street, in London. The house is just round the corner from Harley Street, and it may be that Robert was in London undergoing treatment for his old kidney problems. His Death Certificate records the cause of death as "Calculus Vesicae" [stones on the bladder], a condition he had suffered from for seven years. It sounds as if it was a continuation of the old

Robert Hesketh's grave (with the broken cross) at St. Marty Extra, Southampton. His sister Mary Ann's grave lies in front of the railings to the left

bladder problems he had suffered in Brazil. His body was taken back to Southampton, where he was buried a few days later, near his sister Mary Ann, in the graveyard of St. Mary Extra. A notice appeared in "The Times": "On the 24th. inst. at 30 Weymouth Street, Portland Place, Robert Hesketh Esq., of 22 Carlton Crescent, Southampton, and late H.B.M. Consul at Rio de Janeiro, aged 78."

Before his death, however, Robert and Georgiana had suffered two family tragedies. Their eldest son, Robert Raynsford Hesketh, went out to India to join the 22nd Regiment of the Madras Native Infantry. In November, 1854, he died in India at the age of only seventeen. Two and a half years later, the Indian Mutiny broke out in Meerut.

The other tragedy was of a different kind. Their second son, William Crosbie Hesketh, had joined the Royal Marines at the age of sixteen, and by the age of twenty-three was doing well. He was in charge of artillery on HMS "Curaçoa", a screw-driven steam frigate, and was fourth in line of command of the ship. HMS "Curaçoa" had been based in Portsmouth, but in 1861 she was ordered to the Far East. Before she left, William "ran from" the ship in July of that year. As a Marine, William was in both Army and Navy, and he was immediately removed from the Navy List, and then from the Army. According to the family Bible, he "enlisted" [again] on 23 August, 1861, but bought his discharge in October, 1862. By that time. he had sailed for Calcutta, and that is the last we hear of him in the family records. Certainly, his father Robert was very angry with him, and immediately removed him from the list of his executors. The official Army and Navy records give no clue as to William's reasons for throwing over such a promising career. His behaviour was to have an echo twenty-odd years later. His much younger brother, Spenser Bold Hesketh, who was born in the years after Robert retired from Brazil, was dismissed from the Australian Navy in the 1870s for "conduct unbecoming an officer"; he later went on to become a Government Surveyor in Queensland.

Robert and Georgiana must have been much happier with the progress of two of their younger sons – George and Henry John, both of whom also joined the Navy. By 1860, when he was twenty years old, George was serving as Acting Mate on HMS "Chesapeake", another screw steam frigate, and the flagship of the East Indies and China Squadron. In 1861, he was made a Lieutenant, and joined HMS "Eden", a more powerful frigate. Four years later, in 1865, he was serving in home waters, on HMS "Indus" and HMS "Cumberland", both guardships of the Reserve at Sheerness. He does not seem to have served abroad after that date. He died at his home in London in 1878, ten years after his father, leaving a widow, Alice.

His brother, Henry John Hesketh, was also doing well in the Navy. He had been made Sub-Lieutenant at the age of nineteen in 1862, and then Lieutenant in 1866. He served in a variety of vessels mostly in North American waters and in the West Indies. In 1867, he was serving on HMS "Vestal", on "Particular Service". The ship was off West Africa in 1867, and in the West Indies the following year. In 1871, HMS "Vestal" was at Port Royal in Jamaica. Henry, by now twenty-seven years old, died there on 3 February. His Will was proved by his brother-in-law, Captain G.E.L.S. Sanford of the Royal Engineers, who was one of his executors. Captain Sanford had married Henry John's sister, Hamilton Maria, and they had four children, one of whom, Harriett Maria, died in Portsea in September, 1884, and is buried with her grandfather, Robert Hesketh, at St. Mary Extra in Southampton. Hamilton Maria, her mother, died in 1895. By that time, her husband was a very senior soldier. He reached the rank of Lieutenant-General, and was a Companion of the Bath, and Companion of the Star of India. He appears in the 1901 Army List next to Kitchener of Khartoum.

Robert and Georgiana's eldest daughter, Eliza Jane Hesketh, married Colonel Henry Helsham Jones in 1867 when she was twenty-five years of age. She had two children, Constance and Arthur, but died only two years later in 1869. Colonel Helsham Jones later remarried. His family's descendants still possess a portrait of Eliza Jane's father, Robert Hesketh, his Will, his original 1812 Commission, and two Family Bibles, amongst other memorabilia.

Georgiana lived on long past her husband's death, and moved from Southampton to Bedford only a few years afterwards. She had certainly moved from Southampton by 1876, for her youngest son, Harold Owen Hesketh, died in Ashburnham Road, Bedford, in 1876. Georgiana does not appear in the 1871 Census, and may have been out of the country – perhaps visiting her family in Rio de Janeiro for the last time. By 1881, she was living in Castle Road, Bedford, in a new house built that year. She occupied the house for the next thirty years. She died in 1910 at the age of ninety-one. Her Death Certificate records that her youngest daughter, Harriet Lucy, was present at her death. Georgiana is buried in Bedford Cemetery, but her grave is one of the few in the cemetery to have no cross or gravestone.

Harriet Lucy was one of the three daughters who did not marry, and all worked for a living at one time or another. The 1901 Census records Harriet Lucy living as a governess with the Pelham family at Bisbrooke Hall, near Uppingham in Rutland. After her mother's death, in 1910, she continued to live in Bedford, and died there in March, 1940. Her sister Georgiana Sarah is recorded in the 1881 Census as boarding in Horton near Aylesbury in Buckinghamshire, and working as a teacher. She then changed direction, and in the 1891 Census she appears as a "Lady's Help" and living as a boarder at the Mansion House in the City of London. Her entry appears immediately after that of Helen P. Savory, the Lady Mayoress, so presumably Georgiana Sarah was acting as her personal assistant. When she died in June 1921, she was living in Portsmouth. The third unmarried sister, Mary Sophie, was living in Marylebone, West London, and listed as a "servant" in the 1881 Census, though her position at the head of a long list of servants suggests that she too may have been a governess. By 1891, Mary Sophie in Bedford, and appears in the 1901 Census as living with her mother in Castle Road and earning her living as a teacher. Mary Sophie had the longest life of anybody in our narrative: she died in September, 1954 at the age of one hundred and one.

Georgiana's long life had been eventful: she had been born in 1819 in Rio de Janeiro, had married the British Consul there, a man thirty years her senior, had thirteen children, and outlived her husband by over forty years. When Robert died in 1868, he had left property and shares worth £4,000, and she must have lived on this for the rest of her life. When she died, she left £295 to each of her three surviving daughters. Her house in Bedford still survives, a stone's-throw from the River Ouse, and close to the Castle Mound. It must have been a pleasant place to retire to, though as different as can be imagined from her birthplace in Rio. The volcanic mountains and wide bay of Rio were replaced by the flat English landscape, the brick and timber buildings, and the sometimes fast-flowing river squeezing its way under the bridges of Bedford.

* * *

The children of John Hesketh, British Consul in Pará, were to receive a less privileged upbringing. The sudden deaths of their parents in 1838 had left eight of them orphaned, and being looked after by their maternal grandmother in Belém. The efforts of successive British Consuls in Pará to help them had some success, but at the cost of splitting up the family. The majority of the children stayed in South America, and were quickly dispersed across the continent. In 1856, Mariano, Robert, and William were still living in Pará, but John, one of the eldest of John and Margarida's children, was living in the capital of Peru, Lima. We know that John's wife Margarida spoke mostly Portuguese at home, so it is likely that all the children were fluent in that language. Today, there are quite a few citizens of Pará with "Hesketh" as either a middle or a final name. Some are prominent in the arts, in business, or in politics.

The lives of those of John and Margarida's children who were sent to England – Henry, Thomas, and James – can be followed in more detail. The three boys, aged between nine and three, came back to England at the Foreign Office's expense, and were brought up by their father's sisters, Louisa and Mary Ann. After their rapid baptism at St. George's Church in Derby Square in Liverpool almost as soon as they arrived, they lived with their aunts in their large house in Mount Pleasant. Louisa's death in 1845 left Mary Ann to bring up the orphans on her own, though she had several servants. One of them was Mary Hill, who was present at Louisa's death and also at the next death, that of the youngest child, James, in 1848. James was eleven when he became ill with dysentery and diarrhoea, and was sent to convalesce at one of the newly-built villas on the sea-front at Waterloo, Great Crosby, north of Liverpool. Unfortunately, James did not recover, in spite of Mary Hill's care.

Thomas's health was also far from robust, but in December, 1856, he sailed from Liverpool on the Barque "Emily", bound for South America, doubtless looking forward to a reunion with the rest of his family. On 16 April, 1857, as the "Emily" arrived in Pará, Thomas died. His Death Certificate records no further information, other than that he was a "Gentleman", that he was male, and that he was twenty-three years of age.

It is significant that of the orphans who stayed in South America, most if not all seem to have survived, in spite of the range of tropical diseases rampant there, whereas of the three who went to England, only one survived. Henry had been born in 1831, and by the early 1850s was working in the impressive Custom-House in Liverpool as a Customs Officer. His name appears regularly in the list of Customs Officers in Gore's "Directory of Liverpool" as one of the Clerks in the "Long Room". By 1851, he was living in Grove Street, Liverpool, with his aunt. On 27 October, 1854, he married Sophia Tamberlane at the Great George Street Chapel in Liverpool. Sophia was a local girl who was only just eighteen on the day of the wedding. Henry and Sophia lost no time in sailing for the United States to join Henry's Uncle Henry in California, which must have seemed an exciting prospect to the young couple. Perhaps Uncle Henry had offered his nephew a role in his business. Uncle Henry's death, however, meant that they had nowhere to go but home, and they returned to Liverpool, this time accompanied by a baby son, also called Henry, who had been born in California.

Henry seems to have returned to his job as a Customs Officer, at least for a time. But by 1862 and 1865, he is describing himself on some of his children's Birth Certificates as a "Gentleman", and in 1881 as a "landed proprietor". At other times, he describes himself either as a "weight-taker", perhaps working again in the Customs-House, or as a "Commercial Clerk", a "Corporate Clerk", or a "Bookkeeper". As well as receiving his share of his father's estate, he had received some money through the Will of his aunt Mary Ann, and his brother Thomas's early death meant that he had received Thomas's share too. He seems to have lived off that and his father's inheritance for some of the time, but earned his living at other times. Over the years, and as their family grew, he and Sophia moved house a considerable number of times. In 1862, for example, they were living in Fletcher Grove, Edge Lane, in 1865 in Liffey Street, Toxteth Park, in Edgeware Street, West Derby, in 1871, and in Cecil Street, Wavertree, in 1875. In 1881, they had moved to Lancaster Street, Walton-on-the-Hill. Most of their houses were solid and respectable, many newly-built as the city rapidly expanded.

Henry and Sophia had eleven children – Henry (born in California in 1855), James (born in October 1856), John (born in 1858), Thomas (born in

1860), Robert (born in 1861), Alfred Mariano (who was born and died within a month in 1865), Sophia Alice Maud (1866), and then Reginald (1869), Peter (1870), Edwin (1873), and Gertrude (1875). Unusually, the five younger children were only baptised in 1879, all at once in an echo of Henry's own belated baptism. The eldest child, Henry, became a shipping clerk, John and his younger brother Reginald bakers in Birkenhead, Peter a plumber, and Edwin a grocery manager in Burscough near Ormskirk. James seems to have been the most successful commercially. He joined one of his mother's relatives in a haberdashery business in the then fashionable area of Great George Place in Liverpool, near the chapel where his parents had married. In the next twenty years, his business flourished, and he gradually increased the number of his shops to three by 1892, calling himself a Haberdasher, Hosier, and Laceman, adding later the title of Outfitter. Of the girls, Sophia Alice Maud married Alfred Hazelby, had several children, and settled in Toxteth Park, Liverpool; and Gertrude seems to have lived with her parents certainly until her father's death in 1901. Most of the boys married, most had children, and all lived in the Merseyside area.

By the 1890s, Henry and Sophia were living in Formby along the railway line between Liverpool and Southport near their eldest son, Henry. In 1901, Henry senior fell in the street, fracturing his thigh, and died soon afterwards on 23 September. The Lancashire Coroner held an inquest on 28 September, which was reported in "The Formby Times" under the headline: "Sad Fatality to a Formby Gerntleman". His doctor, Dr. Rougham, is quoted as identifying the causes of death as "fracture of the thigh bone, alcoholism, and collapse". On his Death Certificate, he is described as a "Retired Brazilian Merchant". It is a description that would have fitted his father or some of his uncles much better than he, but it shows how important his birthplace and his background were to Henry. One suspects that his childhood in Brazil and his memories of that far-distant land will have occupied a part of Henry's mind for the rest of his adult life. He was, after all, separated from the rest of his family, and the only one of John and Margarida's children to make it back to England and survive.

Henry's wife. Sophia, lived on till 1912, when she died in Alwyn Street, Toxteth Park, Liverpool, at the age of seventy-five. She was described as "Widow of Henry Hesketh, a Brazilian Merchant".

His eldest son, Henry, after his time in Formby, returned to live in Liverpool, marrying Barbara Salisbury, a girl slightly older than he from the village of Llanelidan near Ruthin in North Wales. She had been brought up in the country, where her father, Shem Salisbury, was a farmer, but Barbara had been part of the influx of country-dwellers to the city. Henry's brother,

James, was a witness at the wedding. Henry and Barbara had three sons: Douglas Tavares Salisbury Hesketh (who died in childhood, and who is buried in Formby); Lancelot Lygon Salisbury Hesketh, and Raynsford Bold Salisbury Hesketh, both of whom lived on until well into the twentieth century. Douglas and Raynsford bore names which linked them not only to their mother, but also to the past, whether to eighteenth century Liverpool or to Brazil.

* * *

The forty years in which the Hesketh brothers worked in Brazil – 1812–1852 – coincided with the birth of one of the largest nations on earth. Brazil has still, one feels, to fulfil its potential among the nations, but the Hesketh brothers were there at its beginning, and made a contribution to its growth and prosperity.

The forty years also coincided with the time of Brazil's great ethical tug-of-war, between those who could not envisage the country managing without slave labour, and those who wanted to put it behind them. John died too early to influence this battle, although his attitude to it can be inferred from his furious defence of the "mulatto" ship's Master in Pará shortly before his death. Robert, however, in his daily work on the Rio waterfront, was very much a part of the struggle against slavery, though he never complained about its ill-effects on him or his family, and only concerned himself with the quality of the care afforded to the unfortunate Africans caught up in the trade, and with the need to support the Navy in its work.

We have seen that the great British politicians of the time – Castlereagh, Canning, Wellington, Palmerston, and Aberdeen – based their policies not only on the great moral issues, like the abolition of slavery, but also upon the growth of British trade, which they saw as their nation's destiny. The existence of British consuls abroad had as its *raison d'être* the encouragement, management, and regulation of British commerce throughout the world. The brothers' involvement in trade not only fed the growing textile trade of Great Britain, but supplied Brazil with many of the manufactured products which Britain was so anxious to export throughout the world, and which Brazil and its fellow developing countries were so anxious to acquire.

The overriding impression one receives from the records, however, is not of the Heskeths' involvement in great philosophical debates about politics or ideas, but of the practical contribution they made to the daily lives of their contemporaries. There were hundreds of sailors and travellers who benefited from their presence in Brazil, and thousands of Africans, both slave and free, whose sufferings were a daily concern. Robert was able to complete his forty years in Brazil, and retire to Great Britain, but John died in harness at the age of forty-seven, leaving his orphan family to be brought up by his own and his wife's relatives. The Heskeths are still remembered in Brazil, where their descendants have gone on to contribute to its life and development.

This book has been about the daily lives and concerns of three brothers from a Liverpool family representing their country far from home, often dealing with difficult personal and social problems with minimal support from the Foreign Office. Sometimes their fellow-exiles did not make their lives any easier, and, even though they were only of consular rank, they were often charged with responsibilities of a diplomatic kind, simply because their diplomatic superiors were many hundreds of sailing-hours away. Far from being "a miscellaneous and often undesirable set" as Harold Temperley called British consuls, their loyalty to the Crown and their daily efforts seem at this distance little short of heroic.

NOTES

Numbers in the text correspond to the notes below, which indicate the source of the references.

"TNA" is the National Archives of the United Kingdom, and "PRO" the Public Record Office. "FO" references indicate that the source is the Foreign Office series of documents in the National Archives.

Chapter 1: Origins
1 Peter Ackroyd makes out a good case in his *Shakespeare. The Biography*.
2 Lancashire Record Office (Ref.: DX 1815).
3 Parish Register of the Church of Our Lady and St. Nicholas, Liverpool. (Liverpool Record Office).
4 On the left near the main entrance to the cemetery at St. Elphin's Church, Warrington, Cheshire. (Warrington was formerly in Lancashire).
5 The Offley archives are held in the Ferreira Archives in Vila Nova da Gaia, across the River Douro from Porto.
6 At the time when Louisa Anne was buried in the British Cemetery in 1799, no monuments or inscriptions were allowed by the Portuguese authorities, and no plans exist for early burials. So her burial-plot is unmarked and unknown.
7 The Liverpool Record Office copy of Gore's "Directory" for 1815 has the word "Dead" written in ink opposite John Hesketh's name.
8 The document exists in the Arquivo Distrital de Porto.
9 Reproduced in *Anglicans Abroad – the History of the Church and Chaplaincy at Oporto* by John Delaforce, 1982.
10 From *Sketches of Society and Manners in Portugal* by Arthur William Costigan, Letter XV, 1779.
11 Lancashire Record Office: WOW/John Hesketh/1815

Chapter 2: From Mersey to Maranham
12 Russell Street has lost its splendid old brick terrace houses, which have been replaced by more modest modern dwellings. Nearby Seymour Street retains its old Georgian-style houses.

Chapter 3: Joining the Consular Service
13 *The Cinderella Service: British Consuls since 1825* by D.C.M. Platt, 1971.
14 Foreign Office Memorandum of 1809 – TNA: PRO FO95/592.

15   Joseph Chitty, 1820.

16   Quoted in Platt; see 13 above.

17   *The American Consul, 1786–1914* by Charles S. Kennedy.

18   Quoted in *The Administration of British Foreign Policy, 1782–1846* by C.R. Middleton, 1977.

19   *The Origin, Nature, Progress, and Influence of Consular Establishments* by D.B. Warden, 1813.

20   *The Times*, 23 April,1820, quoted by D.C.M. Platt; see 13 above.

21   *The Unreformed Diplomatic Service, 1812–1860* by S.T. Bindoff, in "Transactions of the Royal Historical Society", Vol. 18, 1935.

22   *The Foreign Policy of Canning, 1822–1827* by H.W.V. Temperley, new edition, 1966.

23   Middleton; see 18 above..

24   Platt; see 13 above.

25   *The Diplomats: The Foreign Office Today* by G. Moorhouse, 1977.

Chapter 4: The Spider of Downing Street

26   TNA: PRO FO13/122.104

27   TNA: PRO FO13/122.159

28   TNA: PRO FO13/187.256

29   TNA: PRO FO13/168.28.

30   Quoted in *Lord Palmerston at Work, 1830–41* by C.K. Webster, 1934.

31   Quoted in *The British Diplomatic Service, 1815–1914* by Raymond A. Jones.

32   TNA: PRO FO63/30, letter of 19 March, 1799.

Chapter 5: The Appointment

33   Roger Casement testifying to a British Parliamentary Select Committee investigating "Diplomatic and Consular Services", quoted by D.C.M. Platt in *The Cinderella Service.*

34   TNA: PRO FO13/12.161

35   TNA: PRO FO13/12.158.

36   TNA: PRO FO63/149.68

37   Quoted in *The Cinderella Service*, by D.M. Platt.

38   *Os Inglezes no Brasil* – by Gilberto Freyre.

39   D.C.M. Platt in *The Cinderella Service;* see also FO13/128.22, and FO1357.91.

40   TNA: PRO FO13/87,1

41   TNA: PRO FO87/11.

42   D.B. Warden: see 19 above.

43   Huskisson, now largely known only for the melancholy fact that he was the first man to be killed by a railway train, had been a hard-working and influential colleague of Canning.

44   TNA: PRO FO13/12.150.

45   TNA: PRO FO13/30.188.

46   TNA: PRO FO13/103.219.

47   TNA: PRO FO13/240.355, 363.

48   TNA: PRO FO13/240.347.

49   TNA: PRO FO63/280.308.

50   TNA: PRO FO13/176.35.

Chapter 6: The Empire of the Brazils

51   The estimate is Leslie Bethell's.

52   Quoted in *British Preëminence in Brazil: its Rise and Decline* by A.K. Manchester, 1933.

53   *Notes on Rio de Janeiro, and the Southern Parts of Brazil* by J. Luccock, 1820.

54   TNA: PRO FO63/206.212

55   *Brazil, Empire and Republic, 1822–1950,* edited by Leslie Bethell, date.

56   *History of Brazil* by Robert Southey, 1819.

57   *British Preëminence in Brazil: Its Rise and Decline* by A.K. Manchester, 1933.

58   A remark allegedly made in the Cortes, and quoted in A *Concise History* of *Brazil* by Boris Fausto. 59 TNA: PRO FO13/12.108

60   Quoted in Vol. III of the Cambridge *History of Latin America ("Brazil: Empire and Republic, 1822–1930"),* ed. Leslie Bethell, 1989.

61   *The Foundations of Brazil's Foreign Policy* by J.H. Rodrigues, "International Affairs", Vol. 38, 1962.

62   Quoted in *British Preëminence in Brazil: its Rise and Decline* by A.K. Manchester, 1933.

63   TNA: PRO FO172.161

64   Rodrigues; see 61 above.

Chapter 7: The Consul's Daily Life

65   Middleton; see 23 above.

66   TNA: PRO FO13/173.26.

67   TNA: PRO FO63/9.Letter of 2 January, 1787.

68   TNA: PRO FO63/29. Letter of 13 October, 1798.

69   TNA: PRO FO13/187.341

70   TNA: PRO FO63.223.38

71   TNA: PRO FO13/31.173

72   TNA: PRO FO13/77.76

73   TNA: PRO FO13/187.288

74   *Voyage d'un Poitevin á Rio de Janeiro en 1830–1* by J.N. Metayer, ed. M.R. de Lima, 1976.

75   *Travels in Brazil, 1809–1815* by H. Koster, 1815,

76   TNA: PRO FO13/343.83 [?]

77   TNA: PRO FO/30.1185

78   TNA: PRO FO13/16.19

79   TNA: PRO FO63/230.127

Chapter 8: São Luis de Maranhão

80   TNA: PRO FO63/149.68

81   Koster; see 75 above.

82   For a study of the early history of the cotton import trade in Liverpool, see *The Commerce, Statistics, and Institutions of Liverpool with a History of the Cotton Trade*, by Smithers, 1825.

83   *The Commercial Relations of England and Portugal* by V.M. Shillington and A.B. WallisChapman, 1907.

84   *Travels in the Interior of Brazil, 1836–1841* by G. Gardner, 1846.

Chapter 9: Robert at Maranham

85   *Estatistica Historico-Geografica da Provincia do Maranhão* by Antonio Bernardino Pereira do Lago, 1821, reprinted 2001.

86   TNA: PRO FO13.31

87   TNA: PRO FO63/206.208

88   TNA: PRO FO63/206.212

89   TNA: PRO FO63/206.218

90   TNA: PRO FO62/215.55, 66

91   TNA: PRO FO63/215.68

92   TNA: PRO FO63/215.94

93   TNA: PRO FO63/215.95

94   TNA: PRO FO63.215.68

95   TNA: PRO FO63/223.14

96   TNA: PRO FO63/223.44

97   TNA: PRO FO63/223.15

98   TNA: PRO FO63/240.162

99   TNA: PRO FO63/240.195

100 TNA: PRO FO63/249.120

101 *British Exploits in South America; A History of British Activities in Exploration, Military Adventure, Diplomacy, Science, and Trade, in Latin America* by W.H. Koebel, 1917.

102 *Narrative of Service in the Liberation of Chili, Peru, and Brazil from Spanish and Portuguese Domination* by Thomas, Lord Cochrane, 1859.

103 TNA: PRO FO63/280.296

104 TNA: PRO FO63/280.296

105 Cochrane, see 102 above.

106 Koebel; see 101 above.

107 TNA: PRO FO13/12.166

108 TNA: PRO FO13/12.176,193

109 Cochrane; see 102 above.

110 TNA: PRO FO13/12.184

111 TNA: PRO FO30.153, 169

112 TNA: PRO FO13/30.229
113 TNA: PRO FO13/30.224
114 TNA: PRO FO13/30.158
115 TNA: PRO FO13/40.220,233
116 TNA: PRO FO13/40.205
117 TNA: PRO FO13/53.47
118 TNA: PRO FO13/65.228

Chapter 10: William Hesketh – H.M. Deputy Consul

119 TNA: PRO PROB 11/2843.
120 TNA: PRO FO13/65.275
121 TNA: PRO FO13/77.56
122 TNA: PRO FO13/87.62
123 TNA: PRO FO13/87.72
124 TNA: PRO FO13/87.78
125 TNA: PRO FO13/87.82
126 TNA: PRO FO13/95.3
127 TNA: PRO FO13/95.7
128 TNA: PRO FO13/95.3
129 TNA: PRO FO13/95.7
130 TNA: PRO FO13/95.15
131 TNA: PRO FO13/138.38
132 TNA: PRO FO13/148.62

Chapter 11: Santa Maria de Belém

133 TNA: PRO FO13/164.23
134 *A Voyage up the River Amazon, including a Residence at Para* by W.H. Edwards, 1847.
135 *The Naturalist on the Amazon* by H.W. Bates, 1853.
136 *Journal of a Passage from the Pacific to the Atlantic, crossing the Andes in the Northern Provinces of Peru and descending the River Marañon or Amazon*, by Henry Lister Maw, 1829.
137 *Narrative of a Journey from Lima to Para, across the Andees and down the Amazon, undertaken with a view of ascertaining the Practicalities of a Navigable Communication with the Atlantic by the Rivers Pachitea, Ucayali, and Amazon*, by W. Smyth and F. Lowe, 1836.
138 *Brazil: the Amazon and the Coast* by H.H. Smith, 1880.
139 TNA: PRO FO13/187.319
140 *Brazil: Its Provinces and Chief Cities* by W. Scully, 1868.
141 *Travels on the Amazon and the Rio Negro* by A. R. Wallace, 1853.
142 TNA: PRO FO13/187.288

Chapter 12: John Hesketh – Counting-House to Cabanagem

143 Maw; see 136 above.
144 TNA: PRO FO63/281.151
145 See 144 above.
146 TNA: PRO FO13/280.210
147 TNA: PRO FO13/280.248
148 See 147 above.
149 TNA: PRO FO13/280.310
150 TNA: PRO FO13/280.311
151 TNA: PRO FO63/280.238
152 TNA: PRO FO13/187.290

Chapter 13: John Hesketh at Work

153 TNA: PRO FO13/1.9
154 TNA: PRO FO13/12.200
155 TNA: PRO FO13/12.198
156 TNA: PRO FO13/30.146
157 TNA: PRO FO13/65.287
158 TNA: PRO FO13/66.61, 63
159 TNA: PRO FO13/77.16
160 TNA: PRO FO13/77.190
161 TNA: PRO FO13/87.7
162 TNA: PRO FO13/96.277
163 TNA: PRO FO13/97.145
164 TNA: PRO FO13.97.143
165 TNA: PRO FO13/97.173
166 TNA: PRO FO13/114.156
167 TNA: PRO FO13/105.262
168 TNA: PRO FO13/114.145
169 Wallace; see 141 above.
170 TNA: PRO FO13/129.71
171 TNA: PRO FO13/129.78
172 TNA: PRO FO13/129.75
173 TNA: PRO FO13/129.131
174 Southey; see 56 above.
175 TNA: PRO FO13/142,54
176 TNA: PRO FO13/148.110
177 TNA: PRO FO13/148.137
178 TNA: PRO FO13/150.268
179 Correspondence between John Hesketh and President d'Andrea of Pará, February, 1838, in possession of the British Consulate, Belém.

Chapter 14: The Campbells of Bute

180 TNA: PRO FO13/348.7
181 Maw; see 136 above.
182 TNA: PRO FO13/187.288
183 TNA: PRO FO13/240.333
184 TNA: PRO FO13/240.339
185 TNA: PRO FO13/187.262
186 TNA: PRO FO743/12
187 TNA: PRO FO13/348.3
188 TNA: PRO FO13/348.7
189 TNA: PRO FO348.36
190 TNA: PRO FO13/348.89

Chapter 15: The Cabanagem Rebellion

191 TNA: PRO FO13/87.122
192 John Hesketh's writing of the surname of the dissident is unclear.
193 TNA: PRO FO13/122.121
194 TNA: PRO FO13/122.117
195 TNA: PRO FO13/122.133
196 TNA: PRO FO128, Box 21, F298–301.
197 Neither the Royal Naval Museum in Portsmouth nor the National Maritime
     Museum in Greenwich could explain what the "blue lights" were, apart from
     opining that they were some sort of signaling device. However, a friend,
     formerly a Royal Navy Leading Signalman, has drawn my attention to
     "Trafalgar – the Men, the Battle, the Storm" by Tim Clayton and Phil Craig
     (Hodder and Stoughton, 2004), where Chapter 8 is entitled "Blue Lights", and
     where the lights were shown by one of the British frigates every hour to reas-
     sure Nelson that the French and the Spanish fleets were still under
     observation.
198 Smyth and Lowe; see 137 above.
199 TNA: PRO FO13/123.275
200 TNA: PRO FO13/122.134
201 From an article entitled "Massacre at Pará" in "a NewYork Newspaper" of 20
     September, 1835 – a copy exists in the National Archives, Kew.
202 TNA: PRO FO13/122.134
203 TNA: PRO FO13/122.146
204 TNA: PRO FO13/123.302
205 TNA: PRO FO13/136.103
206 For example, in an article on the Cabanagem in the Lonely Planet Guide to
     Brazil (6th. Edition, 2005).
207 TNA: PRO ADM1, Box 295, P42, 2nd. Enclosure.
208 TNA: PRO FO13/132.193

209 TNA: PRO FO13/131.63
210 TNA: PRO FO13/122.104
211 TNA: PRO FO122/161
212 TNA: PRO FO13/129.69
213 TNA: PRO FO13/129.71
214 TNA: PRO FO13/129.73
215 TNA: PRO FO13./129.78
216 TNA: PRO FO13/135.252
217 *O Negro no Pará* by V. Salles, 1971.
218 *Amazon Frontier* by John Hemming, 1995

Chapter 16: Henry Dickenson
219 TNA: PRO FO13/343.125
220 TNA: PRO FO13/240.256
221 In the possession of the British Consulate in Belém.
222 TNA: PRO FO63/233.44
223 TNA: PRO FO63/233.29
224 TNA: PRO FO63/249.106
225 TNA: PRO FO13/280.232
226 TNA: PRO FO63/280.248
227 TNA: PRO FO63/280.201.
228 TNA: PRO FO63/280.310
229 Maw; see 136 above.
230 Letter of 17 October, 1825 – in the possession of the British Consulate in Belém.
231 TNA: PRO FO13/123.298
232 TNA: PRO FO13/129/84
233 TNA: PRO FO13.131.94
234 TNA: PRO FO13/131.112
235 TNA: PRO FO13/130.244
236 TNA: PRO FO13/138.97
237 TNA: PRO FO13/138.91ff.
238 TNA: PRO FO13/138.114
239 TNA: PRO FO13/138.115
240 TNA: PRO FO13/138.116
241 TNA: PRO FO13/138.119
242 TNA: PRO FO13/138.121
243 TNA: PRO FO13/136.81
244 TNA; PRO FO13/138.68
245 TNA; PRO FO13/123.3; FO13/157.120
246 TNA; PRO FO13/165.96
247 TNA: PRO FO13/174.7

248 TNA: PRO FO13/173.273
249 TNA: PRO FO13/174.76
250 Letter in possession of the British Consulate in Belém.
251 TNA: PRO FO13/187.341
252 TNA: PRO FO13/240.256

Chapter 17: Death and the Orphans
253 TNA: PRO FO13/187.272
254 TNA: PRO FO13/156.79
255 TNA: PRO FO13/156.4
256 TNA: PRO FO13/157.127
257 TNA: PRO FO13/150.268
258 TNA: PRO FO743/12
259 See 254 above,
260 Copy in the possession of the Consulate in Belém.
261 TNA: PRO FO13/156.79
262 TNA: PRO FO13/156.82
263 TNA: PRO FO13/165.81
264 TNA: PRO FO13/218.7
265 TNA: PRO FO13/218.41
266 TNA: PRO FO13/343.101
267 TNA: PRO FO13/343.198
268 TNA: PRO FO13/355.7
269 TNA: PRO FO13/367.375, 379.
270 TNA: PRO FO13/367.400

Chapter 18: The City of São Sebastian de Rio de Janeiro
271 *A Voyage to South America by order of the American Government in the years 1817 and 1818 in the Frigate 'Congress'* by H.M. Brackenridge, 1820.
272 See Luccock 53 above.
273 *Life in Brazil, or a Journal of a Visit to the Land of the Coco and the Palm*, by T. Ewbank, 1856.
274 *Narrative of a Voyage to Patagonia and Tierra del Fuego* by John Macdouall, 1833.
275 Ewbank's book (see 273) has illustrations of some of them. There is a small but chilling museum, "O Museo do Negro" in São Luis.
276 Gardner: see 84 above.
277 *The Abolition of Slavery in Brazil*, by R.B. Toplin, 1972.
278 *Viagem Pitoresca e Historica no Brasil*, by J.-B. Debret, 1834.
279 *Slave Life in Rio de Janeiro, 1808–1850"* by Mary L. Karasch, 1987.
280 *Notices of Brazil in 1828 and 1829*, by Rev. R. Walsh, 1831.
281 Koebel; see 101 above.

Chapter 19: Rio – City of Commerce and Politics

282 Karasch; see 279 above.
283 Manchester; see 57 above.
284 TNA: PRO FO13/134.28
285 TNA: PRO FO13/155.131
286 TNA: PRO FO13/173.92

Chapter 20: Robert's Life in Rio

287 TNA: PRO FO13/94.238
288 TNA: PRO FO13/95.75
289 TNA: PRO FO13/16.121
290 TNA: PRO FO13/94.240
291 TNA: PRO FO13/103.207
292 *A Narrative of the Briton's Voyage to Pitcairn Island including an Interesting Sketch of the Present State of the Brazils and of Spanish South America*, by J. Shillibeer, R.M., 1818.
293 In the Guildhall Library in London.
294 Robert's aunt Margaret, who was his father's elder sister, married William Crosbie on 3 June, 1776, at St. George's Church in Liverpool. William Crosbie's father had been prominent in Liverpool life from the 1740s onwards.
295 TNA: PRO FO13/173.26
296 TNA: PRO FO13/128.104
297 TNA: PRO FO13/176.198
298 Ewbank; see 273 above.
299 *Memoirs of Admiral the Rt. Hble. Sir Astley Cooper Key*, by P.H. Colomb, 1898.
300 TNA: PRO FO13/154.249
301 *Description* of *Views in South America*, by Sir W.M. Gore Ouseley, 1852.
302 *Notes on the Slave Trade*, by Sir W.M. Gore Ouseley, 1850.
303 TNA: PRO FO13/119.9
304 TNA: PRO FO13/128.88
305 TNA: PRO FO13/286.115

Chapter 21: Rio – Ships and the British in Distress

306 TNA: PRO FO13/146.7
307 TNA: PRO FO13/119.41
308 TNA: PRO FO13/203.143
309 TNA: PRO FO13/216.68
310 TNA: PRO FO13/239.89
311 TNA: PRO FO13/146.124
312 TNA: PRO FO13/163.138
313 TNA: PRO FO13/186.152
314 TNA: PRO FO13/239.87
315 TNA: PRO FO13/239.119

316 TNA: PRO FO13/228.125

317 TNA: PRO FO13/228.178

318 TNA: PRO FO13124.42; FO13/126.215

319 TNA: PRO FO13/ 152.83, 192

320 TNA: PRO FO13/260.164

321 TNA: PRO FO13/147.266

322 TNA: PRO FO13/211.165, and FO13/213.33

323 TNA: PRO FO13/173.29

324 TNA: PRO FO13/203.5

325 TNA: PRO FO13/97.94.

326 TNA: PRO FO13/103.45

327 TNA: PRO FO13/103.25

328 TNA: PRO FO13/131

329 TNA: PRO FO13/141.504

330 US Senate Records, Vol. IV, 1847, Ex. Doc. 28,66.

Chapter 22: Fire Down Below

331 TNA: PRO FO13/106.103

332 Robert Hesketh (FO13/173 *passim*) gives a good deal of information about the destruction of the "India", but I am also indebted to the research of the late Bruce Biggar, an Australian, one of whose ancestors survived the shipwreck.

333 TNA: PRO FO13/173.123

334 TNA: PRO FO13/186.77

335 TNA: PRO FO13 – letter of 10 January, 1842

336 On his website – bbiggar@gil.com.au

Chapter 23: Rio and the Slave Trade

337 *Remarks on Slavery and the Slave Trade of the Brazils*, by Thomas Nelson, Surgeon (late Senior Assistant Surgeon) of HMS "Crescent" in Rio de Janeiro, 1846.

338 Cooper Key: see 299 above.

339 Ewbank, see 273 above.

340 Suggested by Mary C. Karasch – see 279 above

341 Manchester; see 57 above.

342 Quoted in *Notes on the Slave Trade* by W.M. Gore Ouseley, 1853.

343 Quoted in *British Preëminence in Brazil: its Rise and Decline* by A.K. Manchester, 1933.

344 Gore Ouseley; see 302 above.

345 TNA: PRO FO13/134.344

346 Quoted in *The Navy and the Slave Trade* by C. Lloyd, 1968.

347 Lloyd: see 346 above.

348 Ewbank; see 273 above.

350 *World of Sorrow – the African Slave Trade to Brazil*, by Robert E. Conrad,

1986.

351 TNA: PRO FO13/95.8

352 TNA: PRO FO13/119.43; FO13/123.241, 314; FO13/128.98

Chapter 24: Consuls, Seamen and Slaves

353 Smithers; see 82 above.

354 Quoted in *The Abolition of the Brazilian Slave Trade*, by Leslie Bethell, 1970.

355 TNA: PRO FO13/147.217

356 TNA: PRO FO84/254.94

357 TNA: PRO FO84/255.91

358 TNA: PRO FO84/89.4

359 TNA: PRO FO84/89.28, 30.

360 TNA: PRO FO84/89.40

361 TNA: PRO FO/13.154.14

362 TNA: PRO FO84/89.26

363 TNA: PRO FO84/259.280

364 TNA: PRO FO84/89.16

365 TNA: PRO FO FO84/259.84

366 TNA: PRO FO13/171. 19, 41

367 TNA: PRO FO84/326.341

368 TNA: PRO FO13/172.161

369 TNA: PRO FO13/2115, 46

370 TNA: PRO FO13/211.112

371 Nelson; see 337 above.

APPENDICES

APPENDIX I

The British community in Belém in 1824. (FO63/281.160)

The following list of the British community was submitted to the Governor of Pará by Henry Dickenson, then Vice-Consul in Belém, in early 1824. "Da." is the short form of "Dona", the Portuguese equivalent of "Mrs." There are 45 people in this list, with Da. Poole and her son counted as only one.

1.   Henry Dickenson
2.   Da. Ignes Fausta Dickenson
3.   Robert Corbett
4.   David Henry Weetman
5.   Josepha, black slave of Senhora Dona Ignes
6.   Da. Victorina Sabina Poole and her son Thomas
7.   Luzia, her black slave
8.   Henry Haughton
9.   John Gay
10.   Da. Cordelia Gay
11,12. Their two sons
13.   Edward Jeffreys
14.   Benjamin Briston
15.   Maria, a mulatta   } the Gays'
16.   Maria, a black   } slaves
17.   Maria Southby
18.   Eaton Hall
19.   Joâo Tapuia, his servant
20.   James Campbell
21.   John Campbell
22.   Archibald Campbell
23.   George Henderson
24.   George Bird
25.   Stephen Powell
26.   Edward Holland
27.   John Carter
28   John Salter
29.   Ralph Gibson
30.   Joseph Gibson

31.   John Wilson
32.   Thomas, black slave of the Campbells
33.   Syringa, servant of ditto
34.   Tippou slave of ditto
35.   Româo servant of the Gibsons
36.   William Pendleton
37.   Henry Patterson
38.   John Campion
39.   Francisco, slave of Mrs. Southby
40.   John Hesketh
41.   Da. Margarida Hesketh
42. }   Their son and
43. }   their daughter
44.   Maria black slave of the Heskeths

APPENDIX II

List of Effects belonging to John Hesketh. (FO13/343.148).

1. Country house with gardens planted in the street of St. Joseph
2. The slaves of both sexes: Francisco, Serafina, Anna, Henriqueta, Gregorio, Hermenegildo, Catharina, Macaria, Bernardina, and Amalia.
3. Effects.
   2 soup ladles
   2 spoons for rice
   2 spoons for sauce
   1 fish spoon
   6 salt spoons
   20 soup spoons
   17 spoons for table use
   14 spoons for tea
   1 sugar spoon
   1 wine funnel
   4 salvers of salt cellars (plated)
   1 dinner service of blue china ware
   1 service of green china ware for fruit – incomplete
   2 ditto for tea (gilt)
   4 glass plates for sweetmeats
   1 glass cruet
   25 wine glasses
   17 glasses for water
   1 preserve glass
   4 dozen black-handled knives and forks and 2 carving ditto
   11 plain knives of different sizes
   2 pairs plated candlesticks
   1 lot of plates crossed with blue
   1 flask-stand with six flasks
   11 glazed pots (earthenware)
   3 decanters
   4 scales and weights
   1 dinner table
   1 sideboard

9 tables of different sizes
1 office press with books and commercial papers
1 map of Brazil, in two parts
2 iron safes
2 sofas
1 box with uniforms, and other consular uniforms
30 straw chairs
3 chairs with arms
9 wooden chairs
2 saloon tables
2 pairs of cut-glass shades
5 candlesticks with pendent globes
1 large looking-glass (without glass)
1 toilet
2 mortars
2 mills for coffee
1 copper saucepan
2 brass basins
2 bronze locks
1 corkscrew

Signed: Francisca de Mattos and Archibald Campbell
9 September, 1845.

THE HESKETH FAMILY TREE

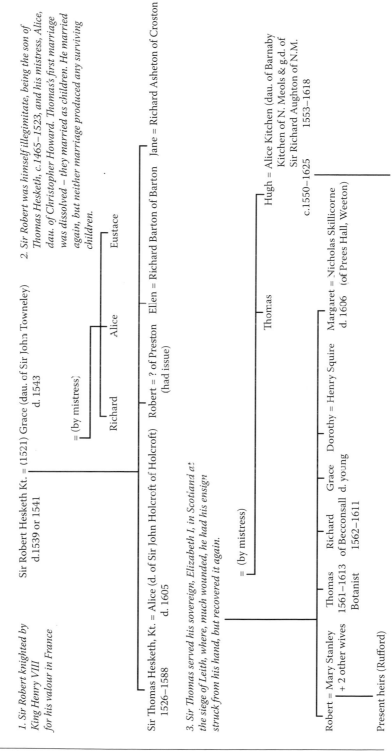

1. *Sir Robert knighted by King Henry VIII for his valour in France*

Sir Robert Hesketh Kt. = (1521) Grace (dau. of Sir John Towneley)
d.1539 or 1541   d. 1543

2. *Sir Robert was himself illegitimate, being the son of Thomas Hesketh, c.1465–1523, and his mistress, Alice, dau. of Christopher Howard. Thomas's first marriage was dissolved – they married as children. He married again, but neither marriage produced any surviving children.*

= (by mistress),

Richard   Alice   Eustace

Robert = ? of Preston   Ellen = Richard Barton of Barton   Jane = Richard Asheton of Croston
(had issue)

Sir Thomas Hesketh, Kt. = Alice (d. of Sir John Holcroft of Holcroft)
1526–1588   d. 1605

3. *Sir Thomas served his sovereign, Elizabeth I, in Scotland at the siege of Leith, where, much wounded, he had his ensign struck from his hand, but recovered it again.*

= (by mistress)

Hugh = Alice Kitchen (dau. of Barnaby Kitchen of N. Meols & g.d. of Sir Richard Aughton of N.M.
c.1550–1625   1553–1618

Thomas

Margaret = Nicholas Skillicorne
d. 1606   (of Prees Hall, Weeton)

Thomas   Richard   Grace   Dorothy = Henry Squire
1561–1613   of Becconsall   d. young
Botanist   1562–1611

Robert = Mary Stanley
+ 2 other wives

Present heirs (Rufford)

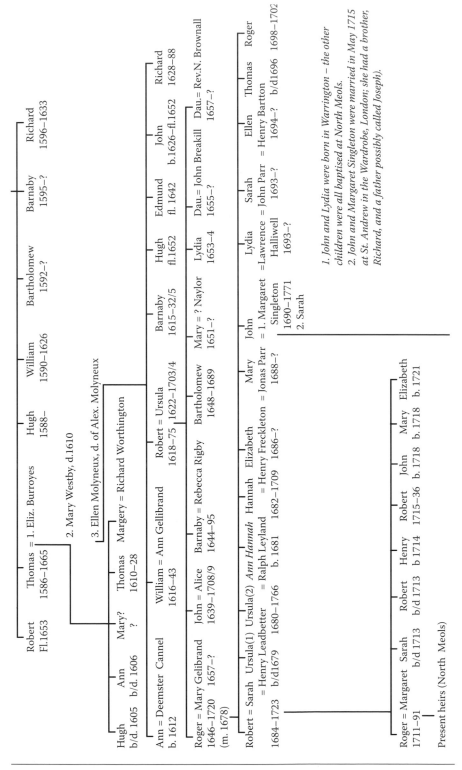

Robert
Fl.1653

Thomas = 1. Eliz. Burroyes
1586–1665

    2. Mary Westby, d.1610

    3. Ellen Molyneux, d. of Alex. Molyneux

Hugh
1588–

William
1590–1626

Bartholomew
1592–?

Barnaby
1595–?

Richard
1596–1633

Hugh
b/d. 1605

Ann
b/d. 1606

Mary?
?

Thomas
1610–28

Margery = Richard Worthington

Ann = Deemster Cannel
b. 1612

William = Ann Gellibrand
1616–43

Robert = Ursula
1618–75   1622–1703/4

Barnaby
1615–32/5

Edmund
fl. 1642

John
b.1626–fl.1652

Richard
1628–88

Roger = Mary Gelibrand
1646–1720   1657–?
(m. 1678)

John = Alice
1639–1708/9 1657–?

Barnaby = Rebecca Rigby
1644–95

Bartholomew
1648–1689

Mary = ? Naylor
1651–?

Hugh
fl.1652

Lydia
1653–4

Dau.= John Breakill
1655–?

Dau.= Rev.N. Brownall
1657–?

Robert = Sarah   Ursula(1) Ursula(2) *Ann Hannah* Hannah Elizabeth
1684–1723 b/d1679 1680–1766 b. 1681 1682–1709 1686–?
= Henry Leadbetter = Ralph Leyland = Henry Freckleton = Jonas Parr

Mary
= Henry Freckleton = Jonas Parr
1688–?

John = 1. Margaret
1690–1771   Singleton
    2. Sarah

Lydia
=Lawrence
Halliwell
1693–?

Sarah
= John Parr
1693–?

Ellen

Thomas

Roger
1694–? b/d1696 1698–1702

Henry Bartton

Roger = Margaret Sarah   Henry   Robert   John   Mary   Elizabeth
1711–91 b/d 1713   b/d 1713 b 1714 1715–36 b. 1718 b. 1718 b. 1721

Present heirs (North Meols)

*1. John and Lydia were born in Warrington – the other
children were all baptised at North Meols.*
*2. John and Margaret Singleton were married in May 1715
at St. Andrew in the Wardrobe, London; she had a brother,
Richard, and a father possibly called Joseph).*

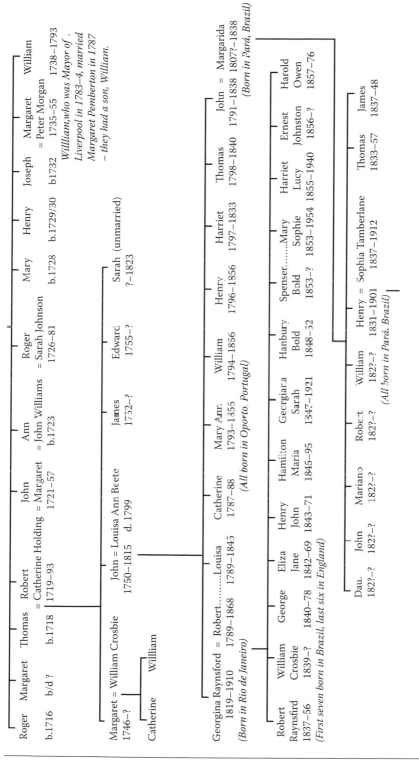

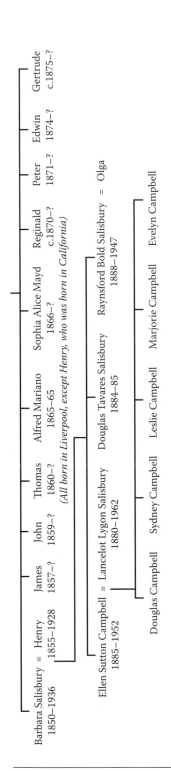

Barbara Salisbury = Henry
1850–1936   1855–1928

James
1857–?

John
1859–?

Thomas
1860–?

Alfred Mariano
1865–65

Sophia Alice Mayd
1866–?

Reginald
c.1870–?

Peter
1871–?

Edwin
1874–?

Gertrude
c.1875–?

(All born in Liverpool, except Henry, who was born in California)

Ellen Sutton Campbell = Lancelot Lygon Salisbury   Douglas Tavares Salisbury   Raynsford Bold Salisbury = Olga
1885–1952   1880–1962   1884–85   1888–1947

Douglas Campbell   Sydney Campbell   Leslie Campbell   Marjorie Campbell   Evelyn Campbell

A SELECT BIBLIOGRAPHY

I have listed below books in English that I have found particularly useful. A very full list of books about Brazil and the Slave Trade can be found in Leslie Bethell's "The Abolition of the Brazilian Slave Trade", 1970.

A. Nineteenth Century Books about Brazil. (Some of these will need to be sought out at a university or national library).

1. "The History of Brazil" by John Armitage, 1836.
2. "Some Account of the Trade in Slaves from Africa" by James Bandinell, 1842
3. "The Naturalist on the Amazon" by H.W. Bates, 1863.
4. "A Voyage to South America by order of the American Government ....." by H.M. Brackenridge, 1820.
5. "A Voyage up the River Amazon....." by W.H. Edwards, 1847.
6. "Life in Brazil, or a Journal of a Visit to the Land of the Cocoa and the Palm" by Thomas Ewbank, 1856.
7. "Travels in the interior of Brazil" by George Gardner, 1846
8. "Travels in Brazil, 1809–1815" by Henry Koster, 1816.
9. "Notes on Rio de Janeiro" by John Luccock, 1820.
10. "Narrative of a Voyage to Patagonia and Tierra del Fuego" by John Macdouall, 1833.
11. "Journal of a Passage from the Pacific to the Atlantic....." by Henry Lister Maw, 1829.
12. "Remarks on the Slave Trade....." by Thomas Nelson, 1846.
13. "Brazil – the Amazon and the Coast" by Herbert H. Smith, 1879.
14. "Narrative of a Journey from Lima to Para....." by W. Smyth and F. Lowe, 1836.
15. "A History of Brazil" by Robert Southey, 1819.
16. "Travels to the Amazon and the Rio Negro" by Alfred Russel Wallace, 1853
17. "Notices of Brazil 1828 and 1829" by the Rev. Robert Walsh, 1831.

B. Modern Books about Brazil.

1. "Brazil: The Forging of a Nation, 1798–1852" by Roderick J. Barman, 1988.
2. "Brazil: Empire and Republic"1822–1880" by Leslie Bethell, 1989.
3. "Cambridge History of Latin America" by Leslie Bethell, 1970.
4. "The Abolition of the Brazilian Slave Trade" by Leslie Bethell, 1970.
5. "A History of Brazil" by E. Bradford Burns, 1993.

6. "World of Sorrow – The African Slave Trade to Brazil" by Robert E. Conrad, 1986.
7. "A Concise History of Brazil" by Boris Fausto, 1999.
8. "Britain and the Onset of Modernisation in Brazil, 1650–1914)" by Richard Graham, 1968.
9. "Amazon Frontier" by John Hemming, 1987.
10. "Slave Life in Rio de Janeiro, 1808–1858" by Mary C. Karasch, 1987.
11. "The Navy and the Slave Trade" by Christopher Lloyd, 1968.
12. "British Preëminence in Brazil" by Alan K. Manchester, 1933.
13. "A History of Brazil" by Joseph Smith, 2002.
14. "The Abolition of Slavery in Brazil" by R.B. Toplin, 1972.

C. Books on the British Foreign Office and the Consular and Diplomatic Services.

1. "The Unreformed Diplomatic Service 1812–1860" by S.T. Bindoff (Transactions of the Royal Historical Society, 1935).
2. "Palmerston: The Early Years" by Kenneth Bourne, 1982.
3. "Palmnerston" by Philip Guedella, 1926 and 1937.
4. "The British Diplomatic Service, 1815–1914" by Raymond A. Jones, 1983.
5. "The Administration of British Foreign Policy, 1782–1846" by Charles R. Middleton, 1977.
6. "The Cinderella Service...." by D.C.M. Platt, 1971.
7. "Lord Palmerston" by Jasper Ridley, 1972.
8. "Life of Canning" by H.W.V. Temperley, 1905.
9. "The Foreign Policy of Canning" by H.W.V. Temperley, 1925, new ed. 1966.
10. "Lord Palnerston at Work, 1830–1841" by C.K. Webster, 1934.
11. "The Foreign Policy of Castlereagh, 1815–1822" by C.K. Webster, 1934.

D. Original Sources.

Most of the original documents quoted are to be found at the National Archives in Kew, London, although some have to be ordered specially. The Provincial Government of Pará has produced a transcription of some of the documents from Kew in "Cabanagem: Documentos Ingleses", edited by David Cleary. Other original sources were found in various archive and record collections as indicated in the Notes.

INDEX

ABOUT THE AUTHOR

Ian Sargen wrote this book after he and his wife uncovered a wealth of material in British Government Archives about three of his wife's ancestors two hundred years ago. He took up history after a career spent in secondary education, and following his retirement as the Head of Sir John Leman High School in Suffolk. This is his first full-length book, and follows a shorter article entitled "Wool, War, and the Indies", a study of a Yorkshire family in the early nineteenth century, published in 2002. He and his wife have four grown-up children, and live in North Suffolk.